THE FRANKLIN D. MURPHY SCULPTURE GARDEN AT UCLA

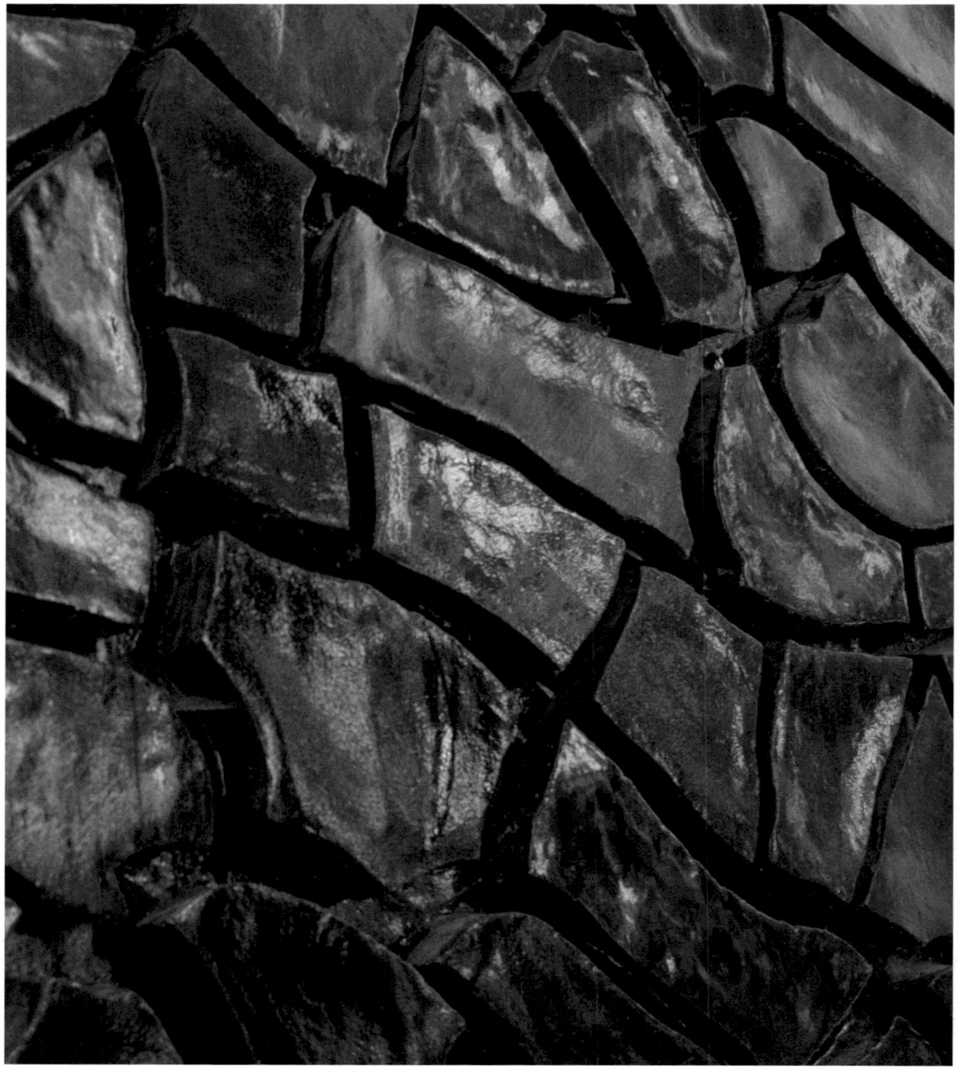

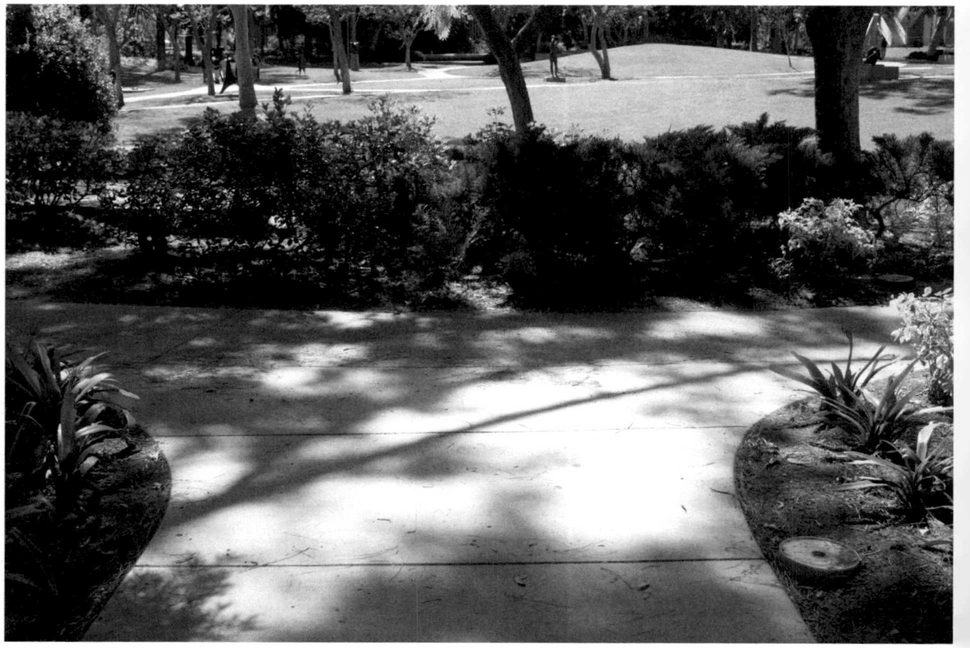

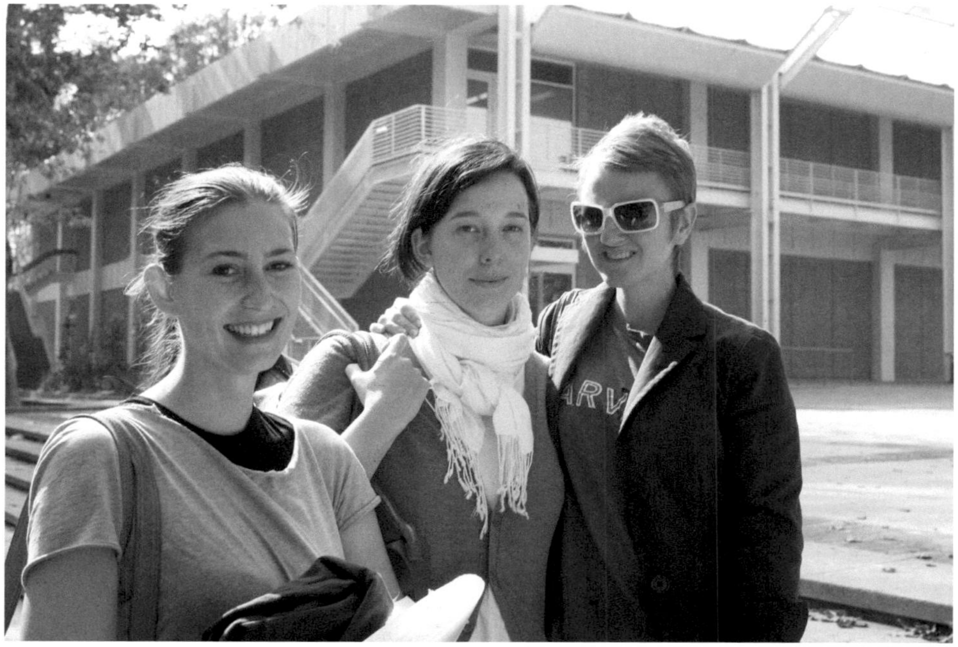

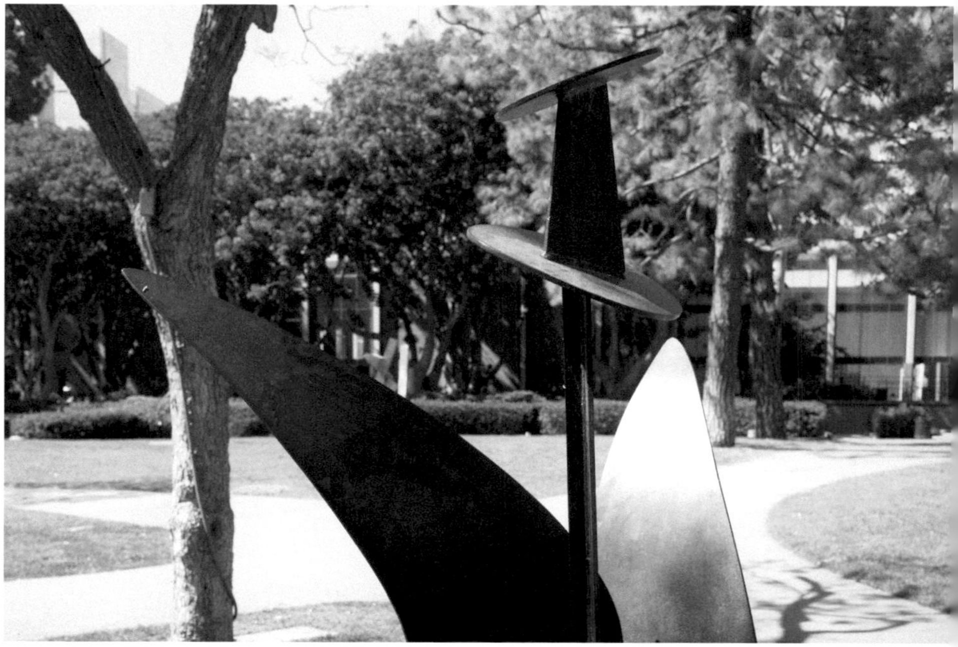

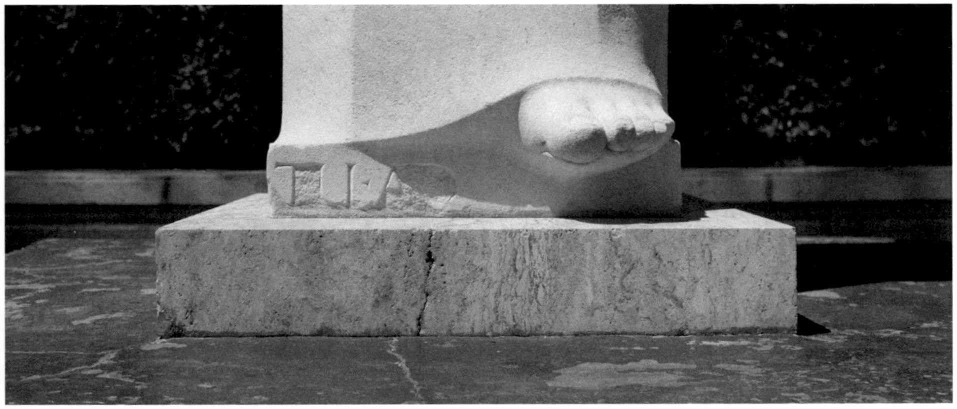

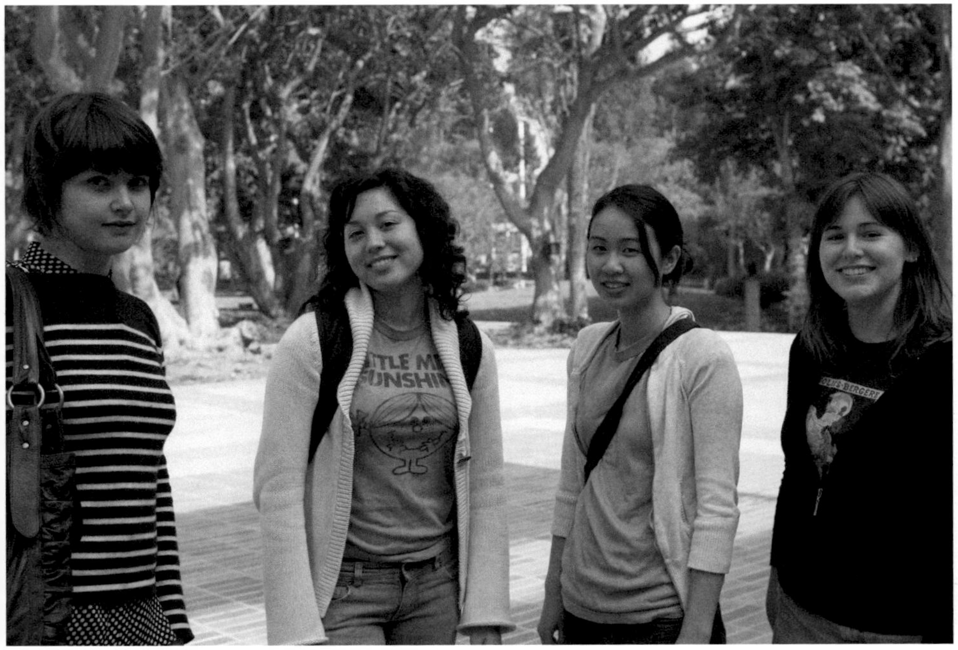

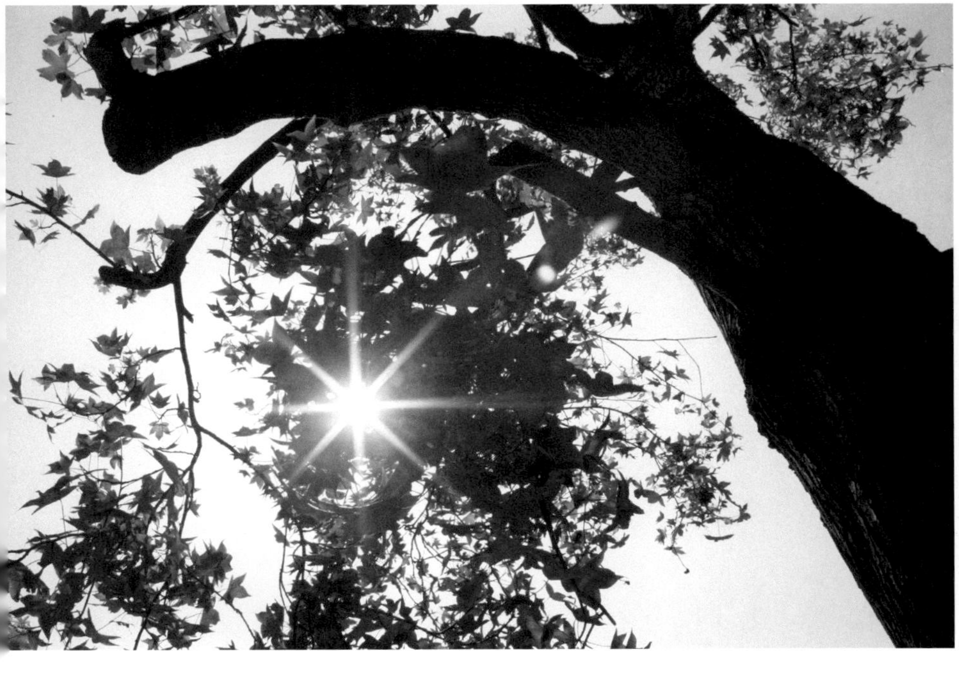

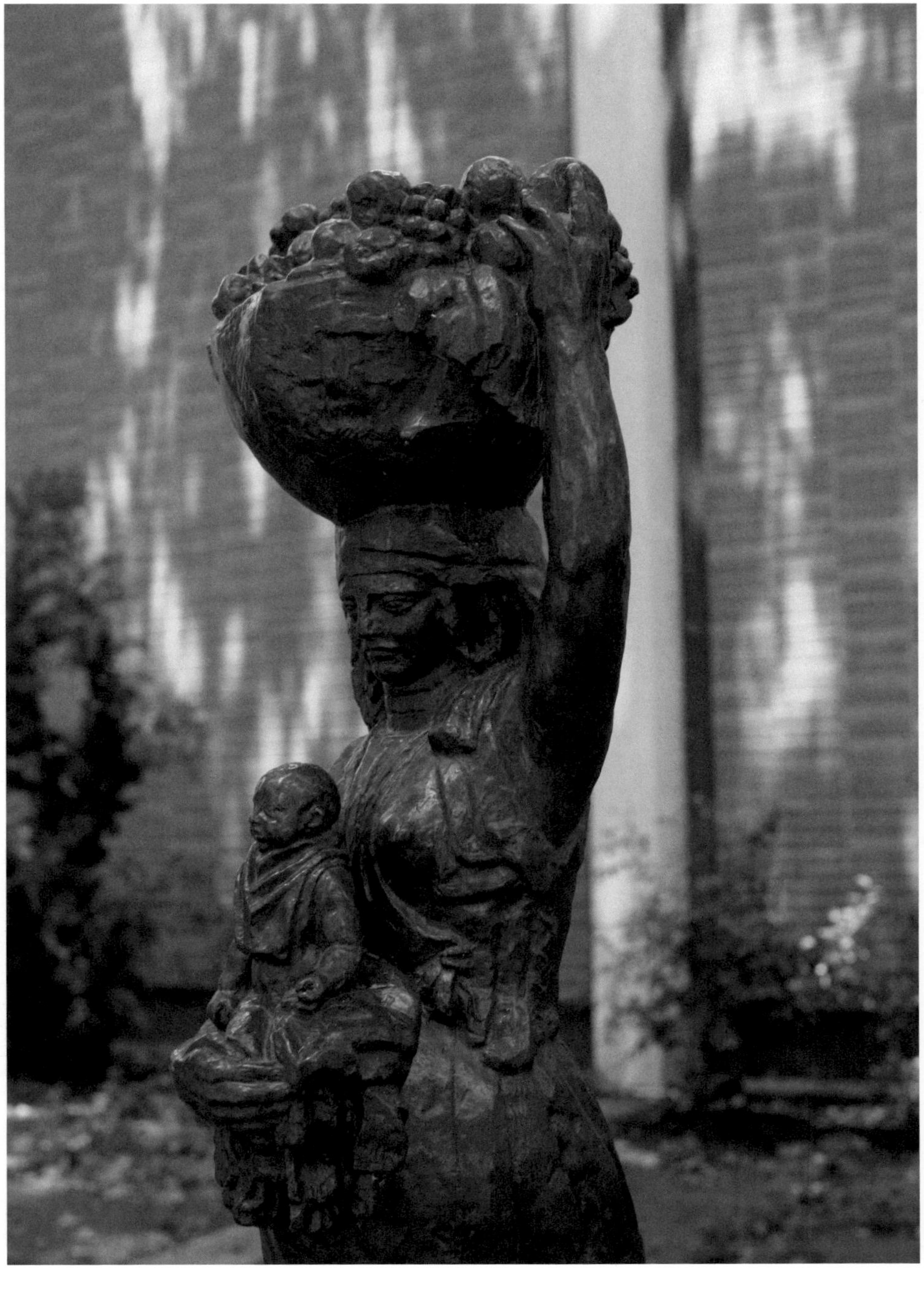

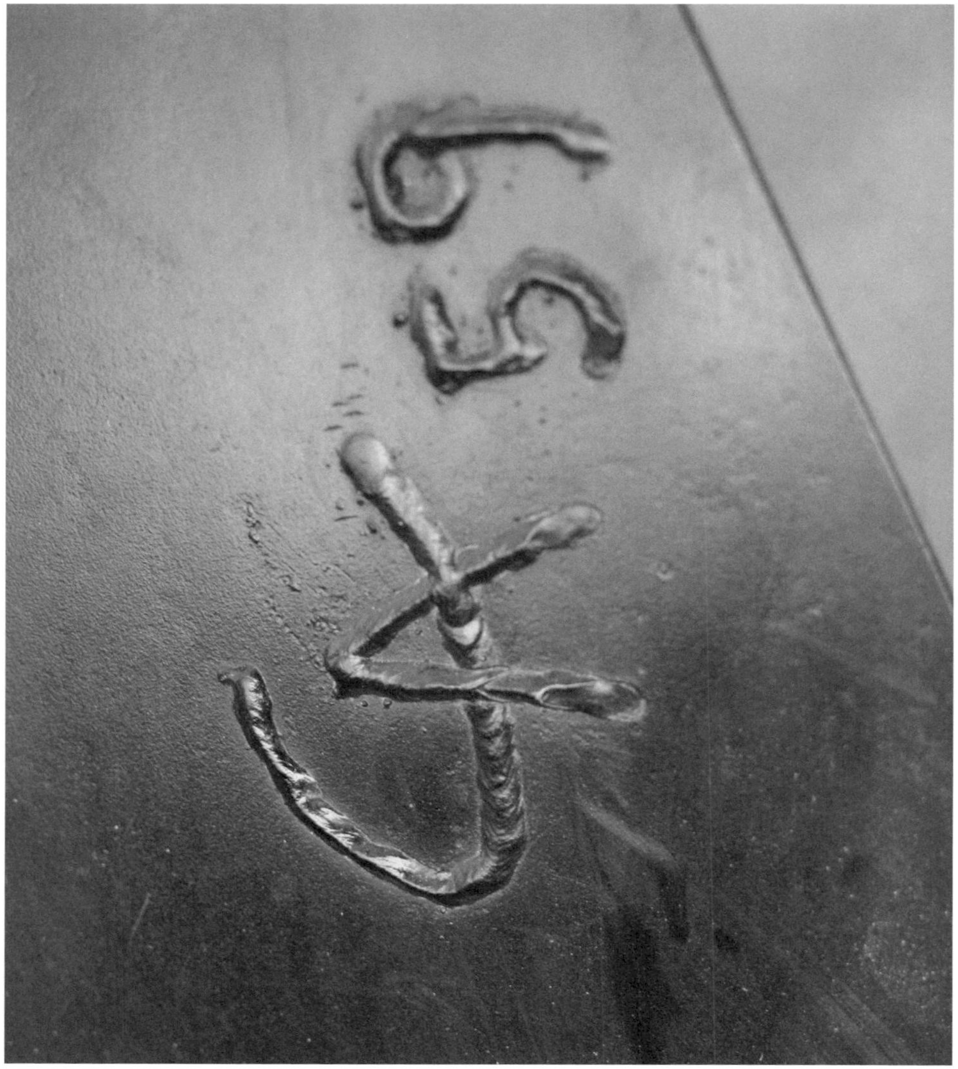

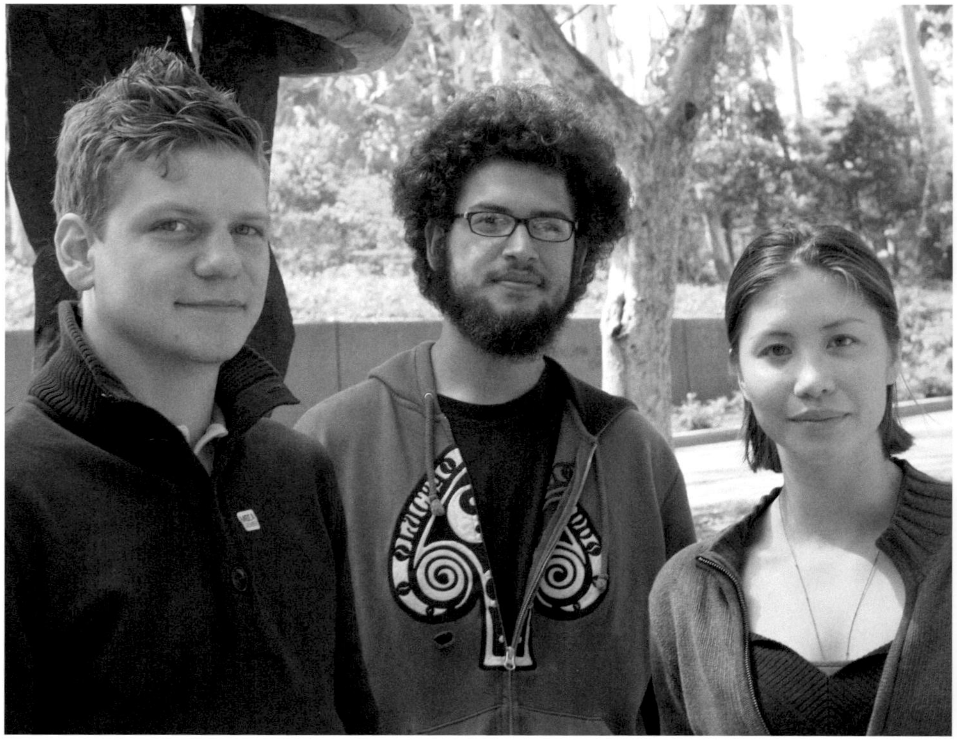

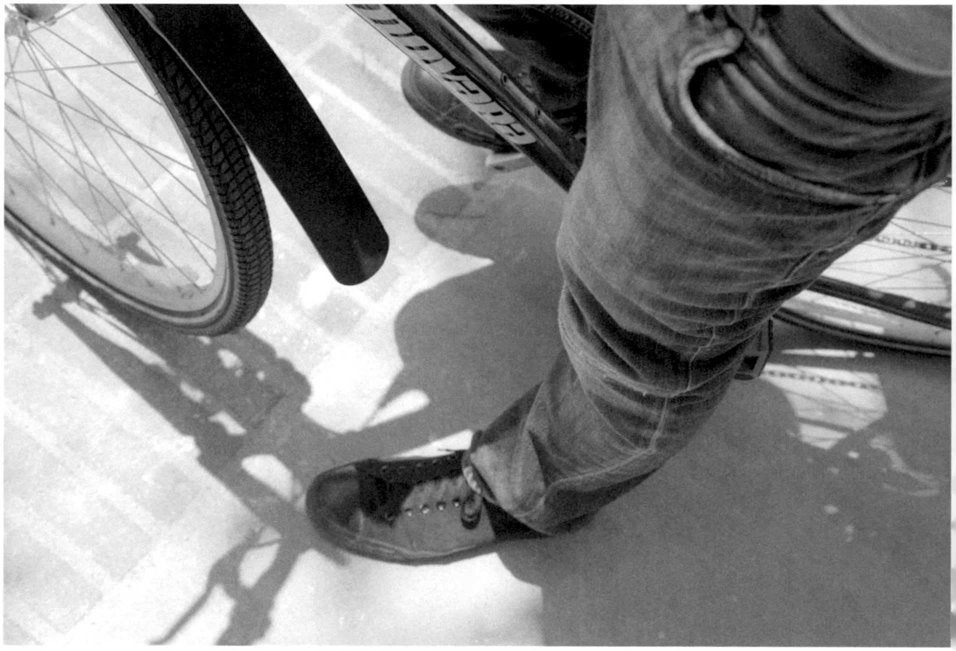

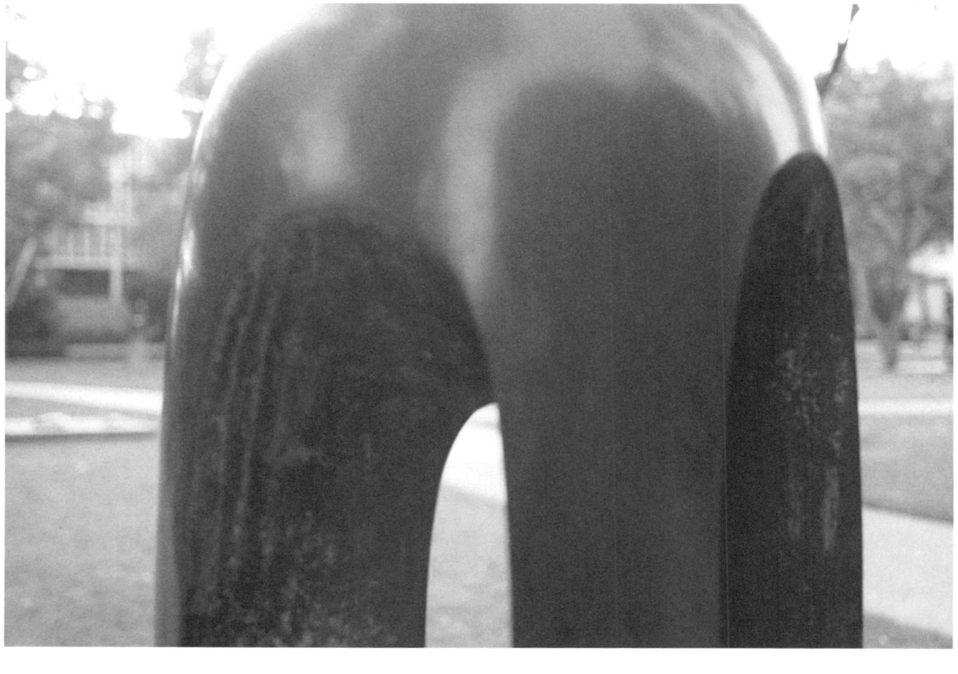

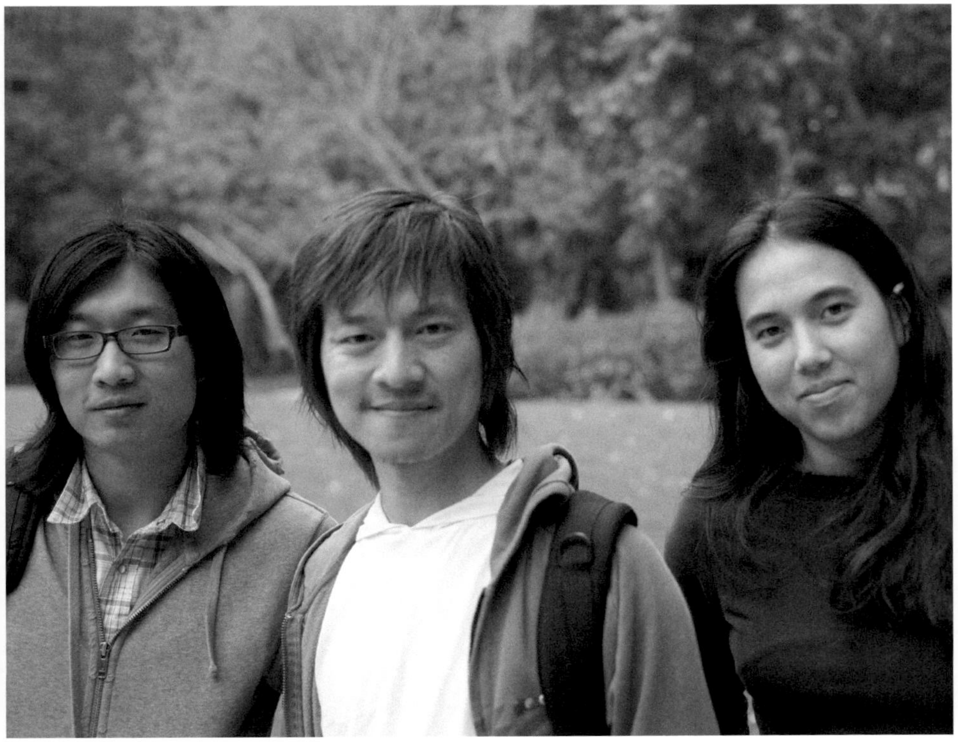
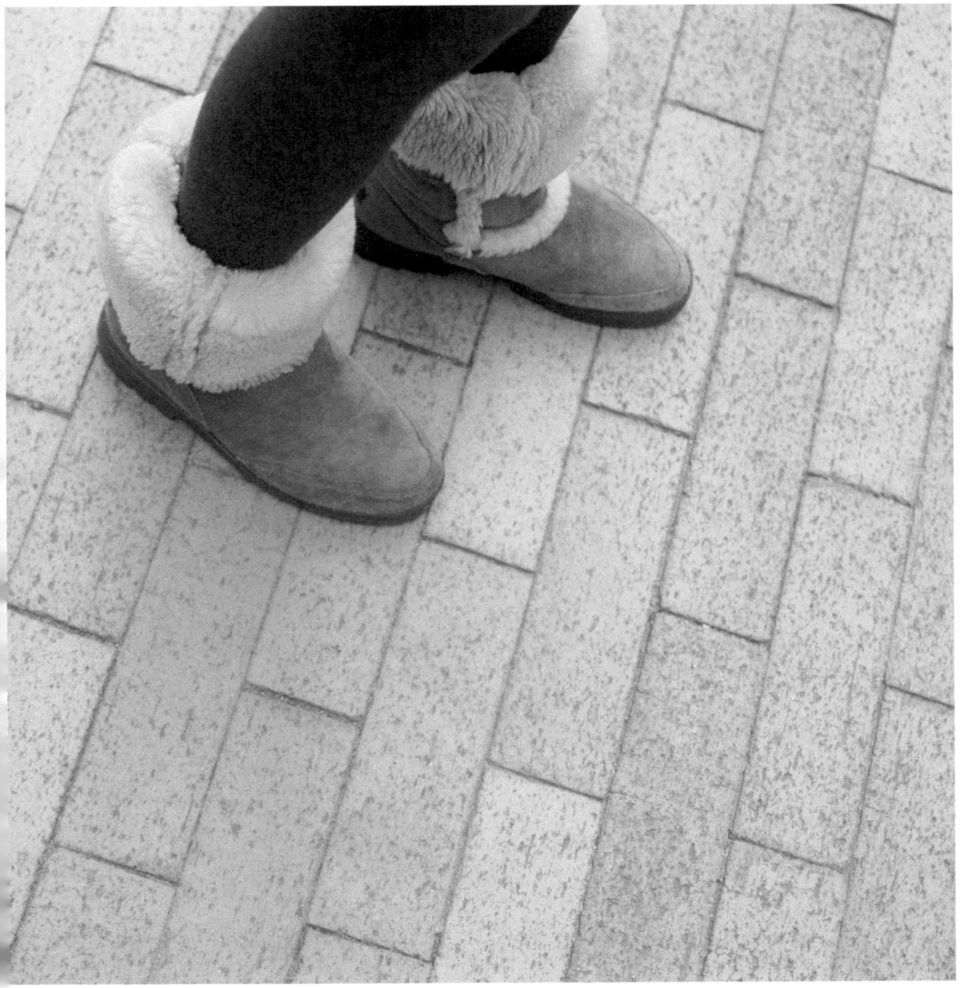
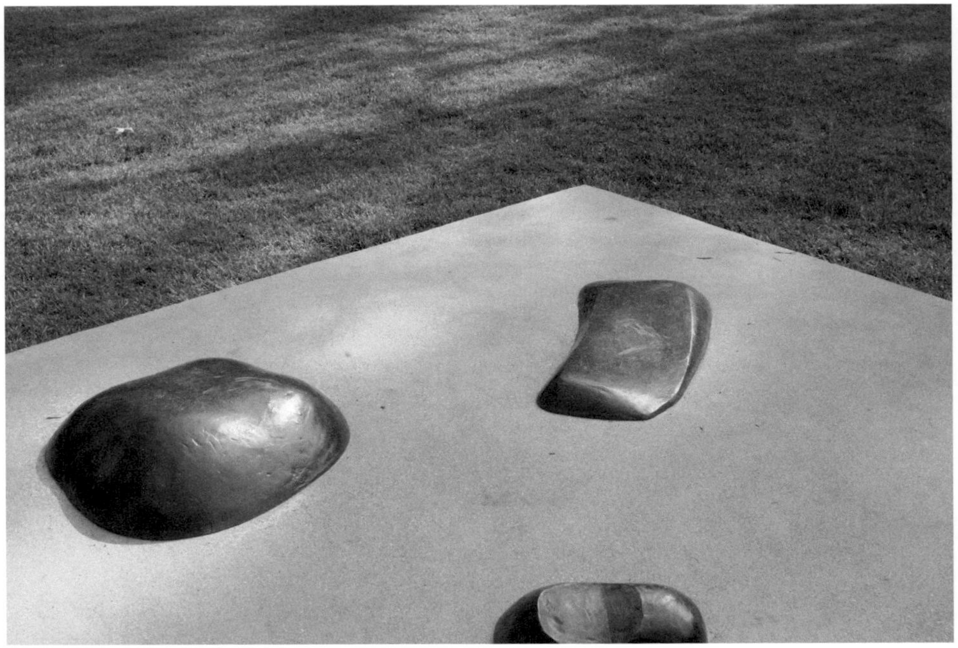
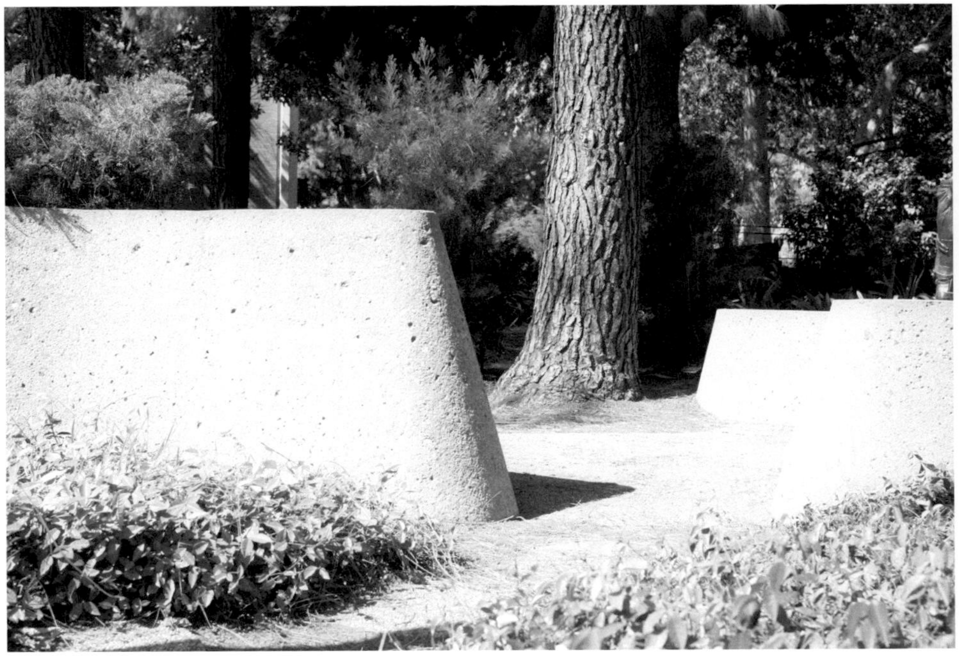

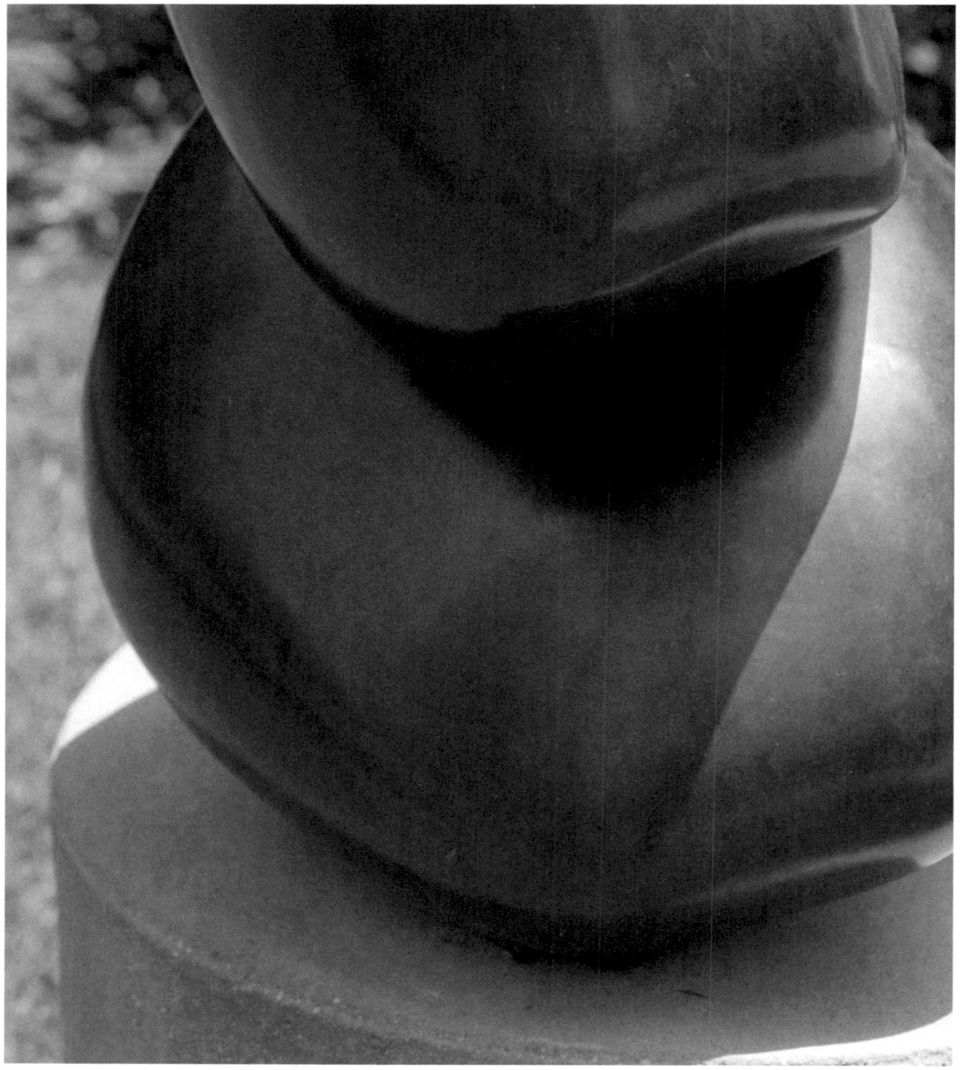
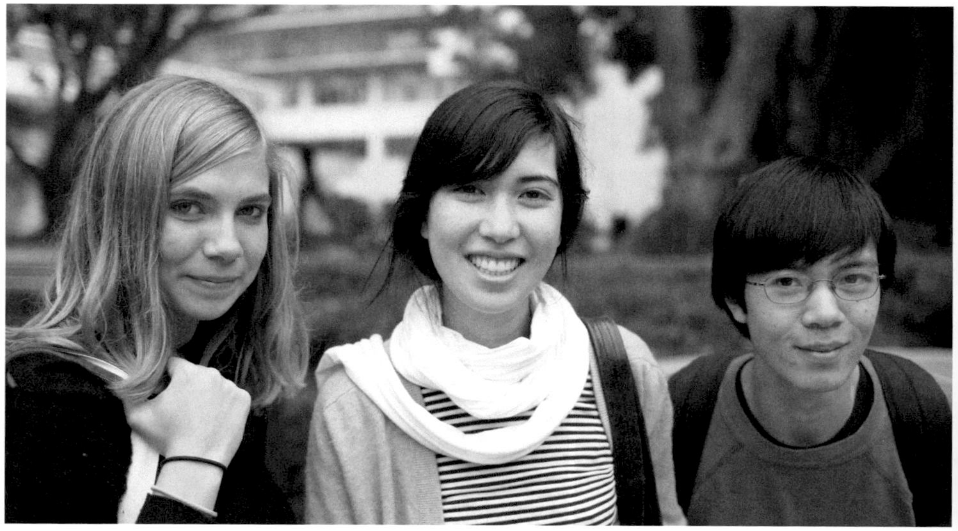
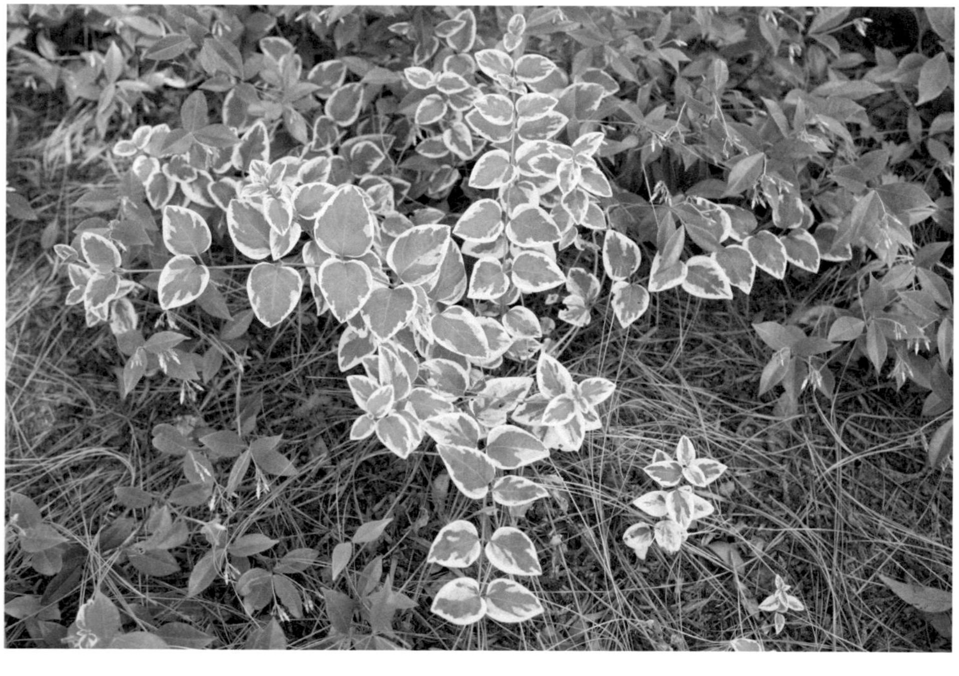
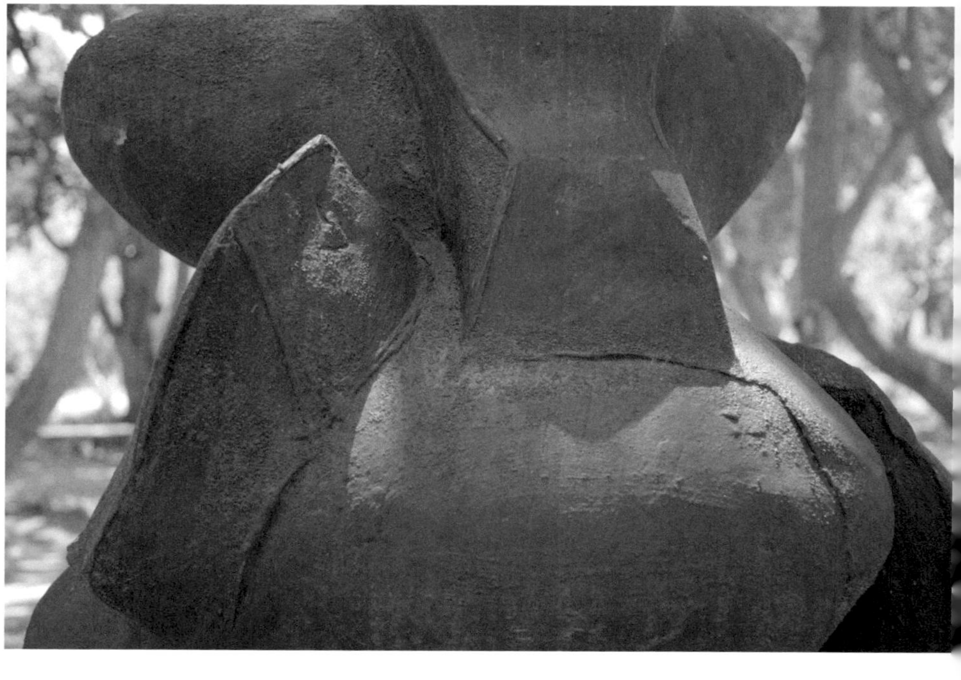

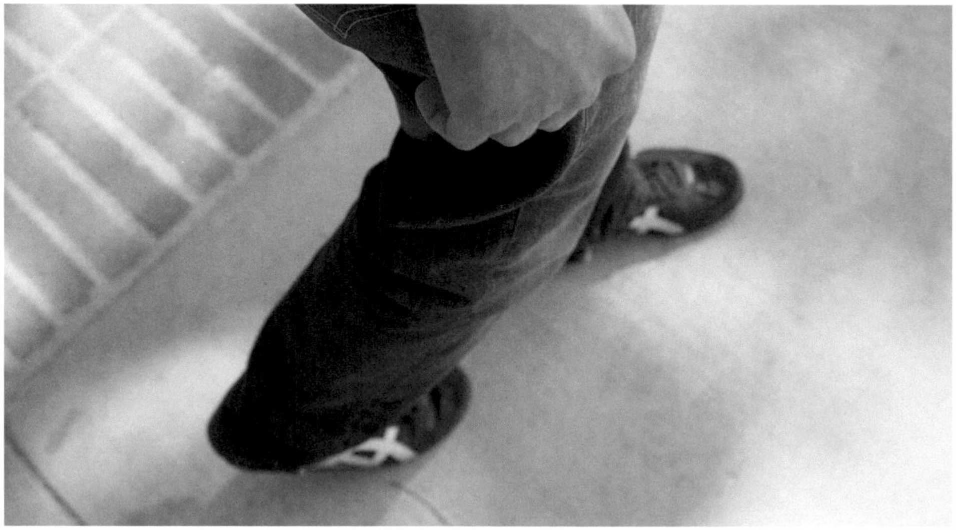
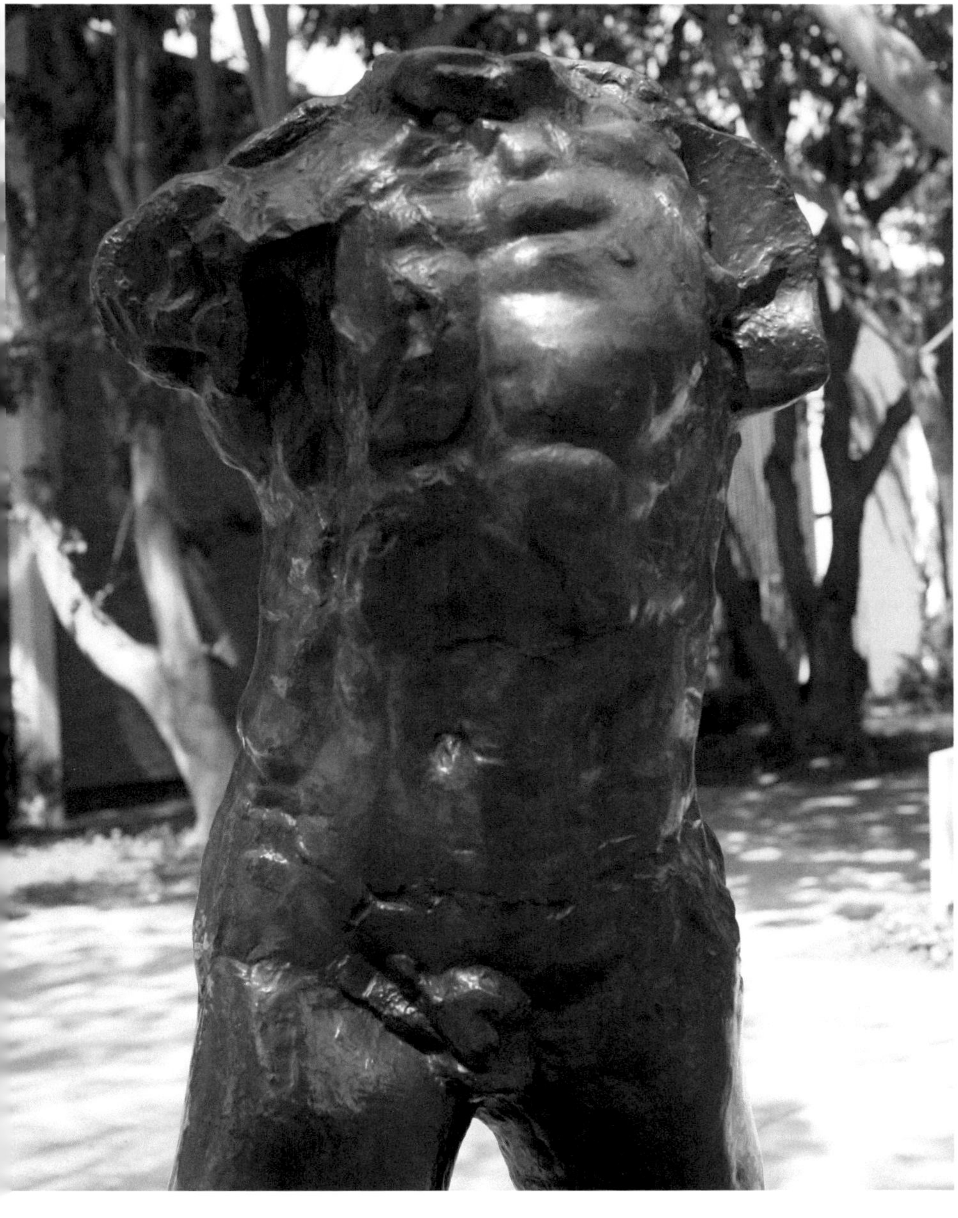
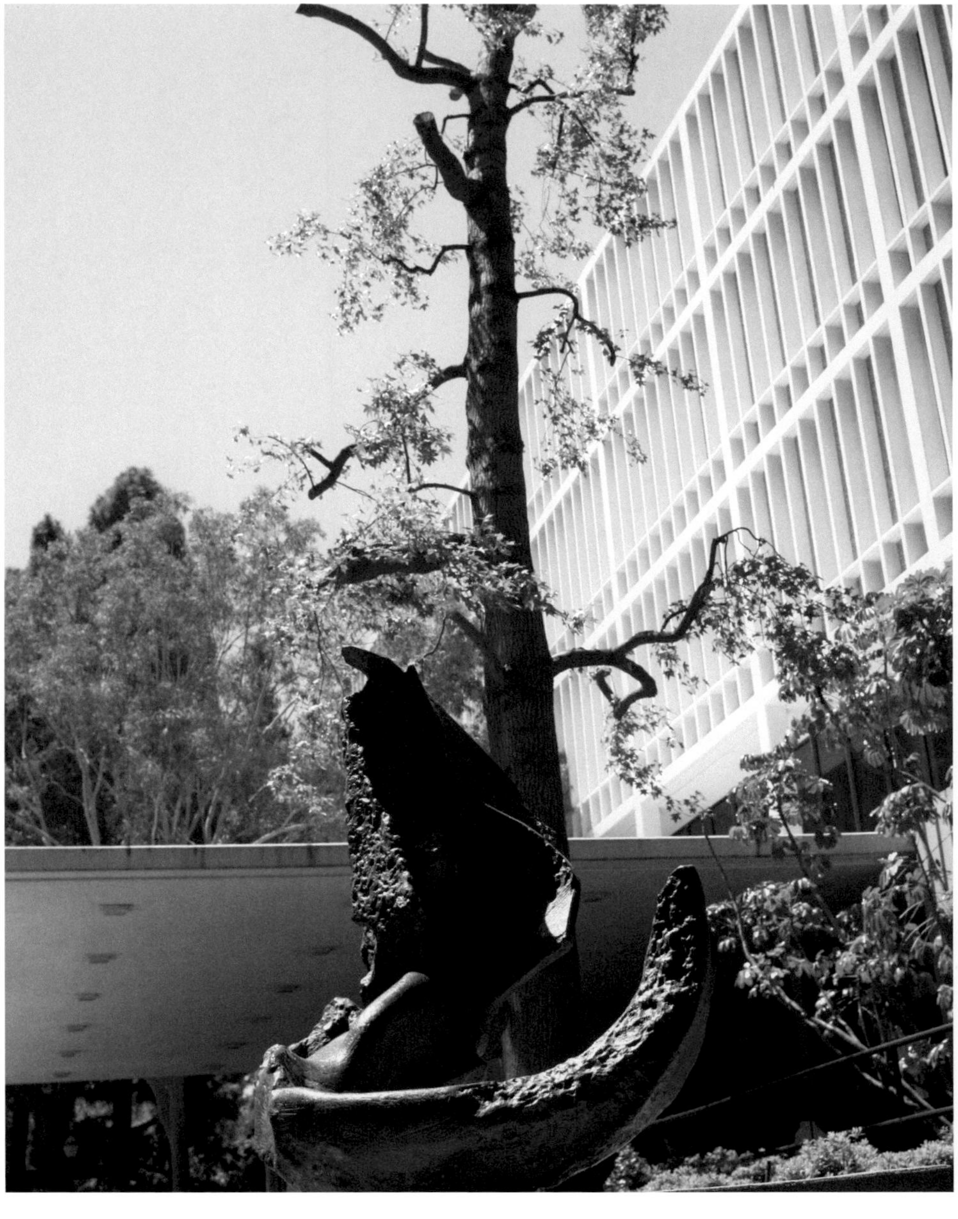

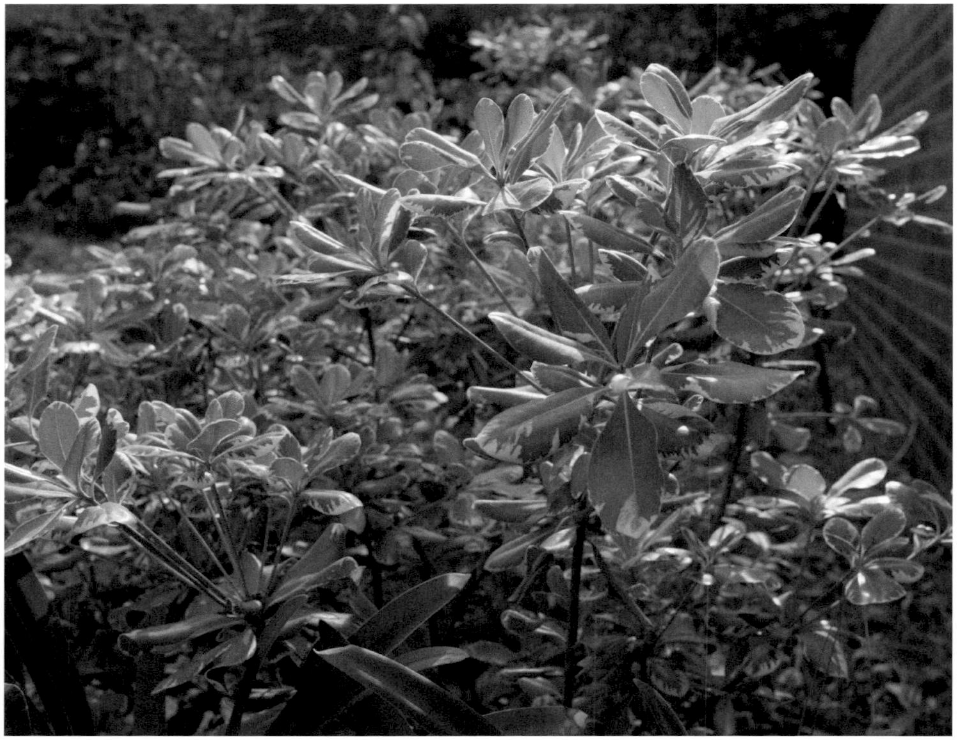
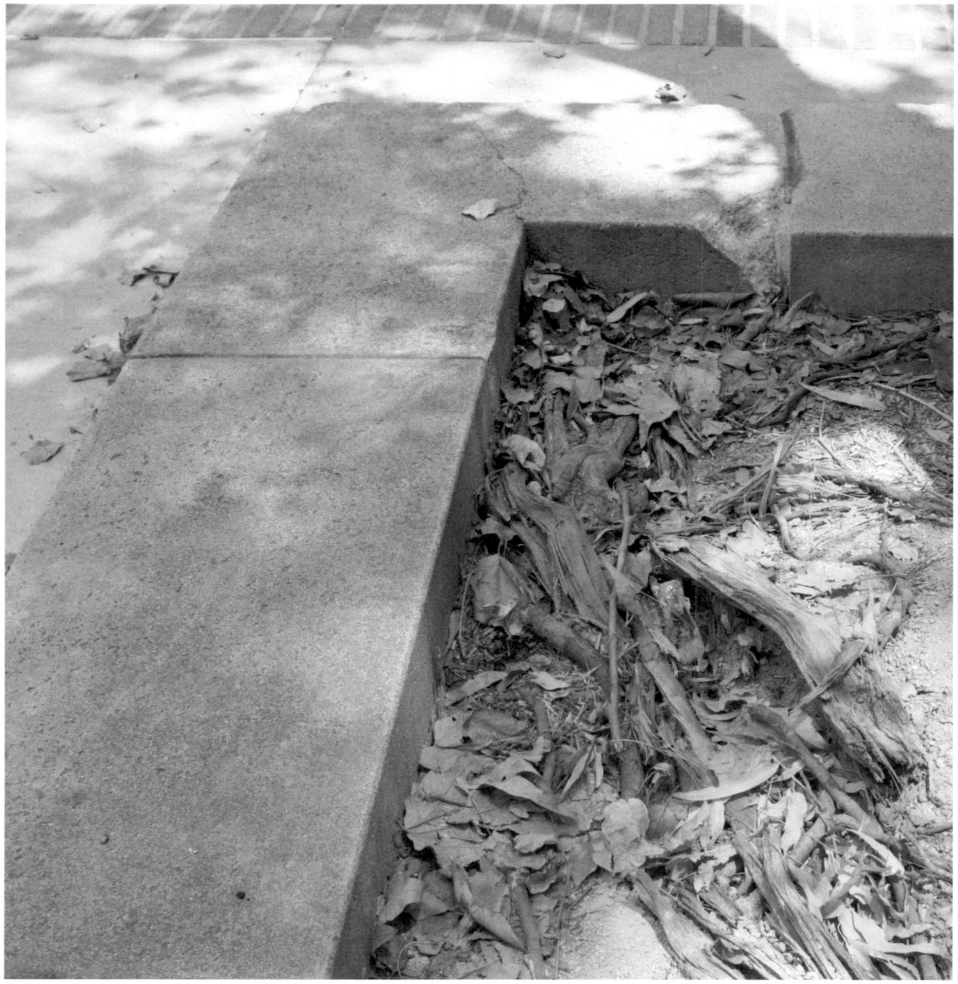
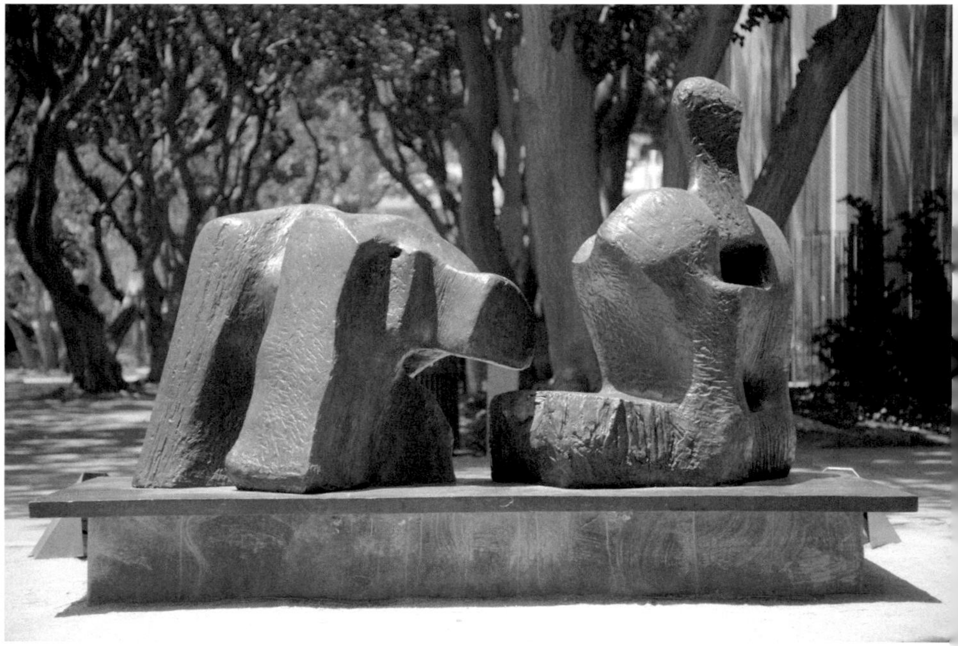
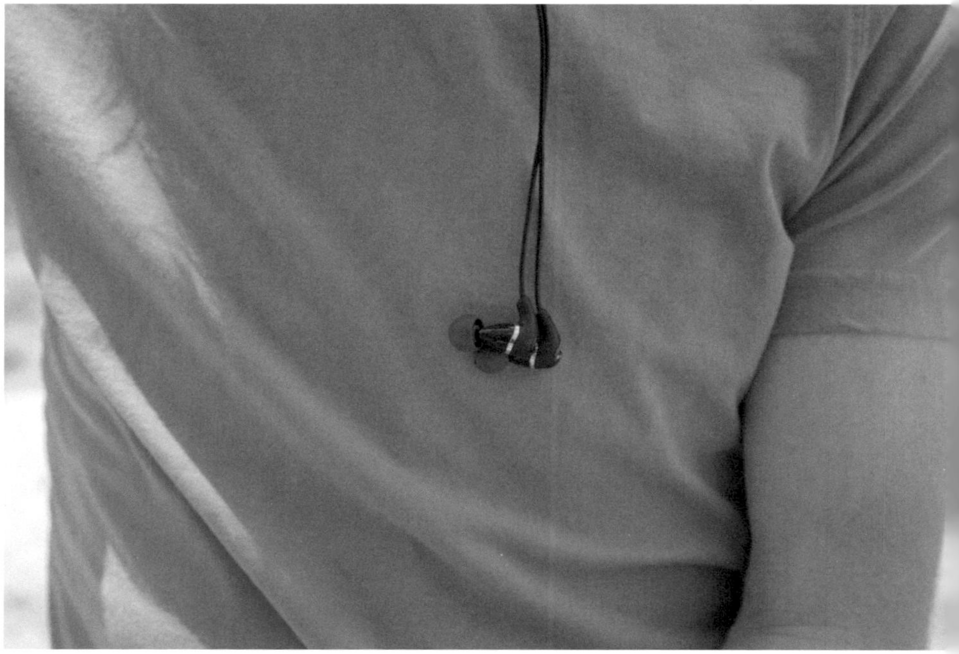

CYNTHIA BURLINGHAM

with essays by
VICTORIA STEELE
MARC TREIB

and contributions by
CLAUDINE DIXON
ALLEGRA PESENTI

HAMMER MUSEUM
University of California, Los Angeles

THE FRANKLIN D. MURPHY SCULPTURE GARDEN AT UCLA

Publication of this catalogue was made possible
by a generous grant from the Ahmanson Foundation.

Published in 2007 by the Hammer Museum,
10899 Wilshire Boulevard, Los Angeles, California
90024-4201, 310-443-7000
http://www.hammer.ucla.edu

Distributed by University of California Press
Berkeley and Los Angeles, California
www.ucpress.edu

Editor: Karen Jacobson
Designers: Lorraine Wild and N. Silas Munro,
Green Dragon Office, Los Angeles
Principal photographer: Joshua White
Proofreader: Dianne Woo
Indexer: Kathleen Preciado
Printed in Canada by Hemlock Printers Ltd., Burnaby, BC

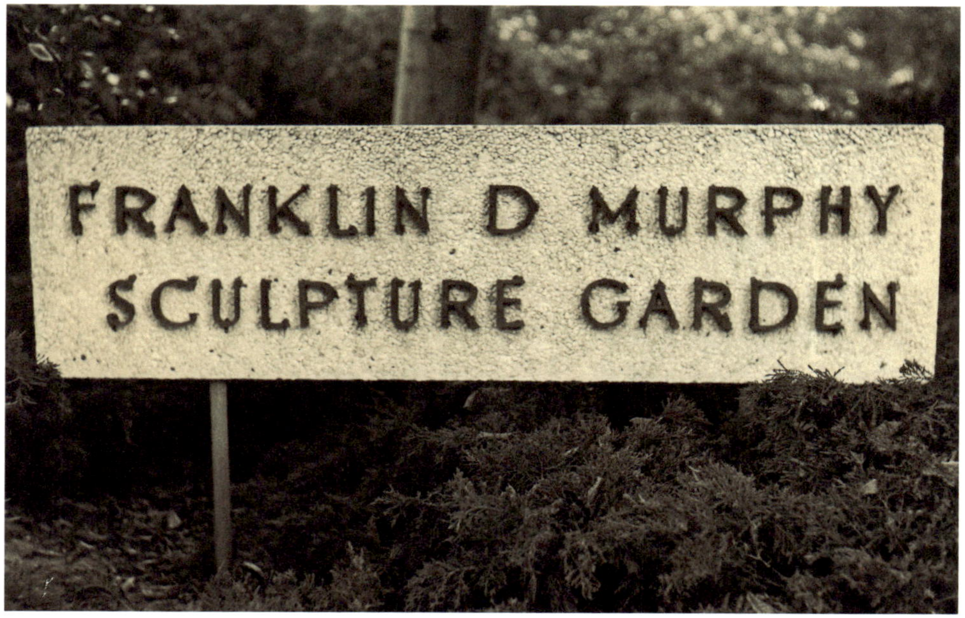

Library of Congress Cataloging-in-Publication Data

Burlingham, Cynthia, 1955–.
The Franklin D. Murphy Sculpture Garden at UCLA / Cynthia Burlingham ; with essays by Victoria Steele, Marc Treib; and contributions by Claudine Dixon, Allegra Pesenti.
p. cm.
Includes bibliographical references and index.
ISBN: 978-0-943739-33-5 (cloth : alk. paper)
1. Sculpture, Modern—19th century—Catalogs. 2. Sculpture, Modern—20th century—Catalogs. 3. Sculpture—California—Los Angeles—Catalogs. 4. Franklin D. Murphy Sculpture Garden—Catalogs. I. Title.
NB197.B87 2007
735.29'074019494—DC22 2007037700

Front cover: View of the Franklin D. Murphy Sculpture Garden with (from left to right) Deborah Butterfield's Pensive *(ca. 1997), Gerhard Marcks's* Maja *(1941), and David Smith's* Cubi XX *(1964)*

Back cover: View of the Franklin D. Murphy Sculpture Garden with Jean Arp's Ptolemy III *(1961) and* Hybrid Fruit Called Pagoda *(1934)*

CONTENTS

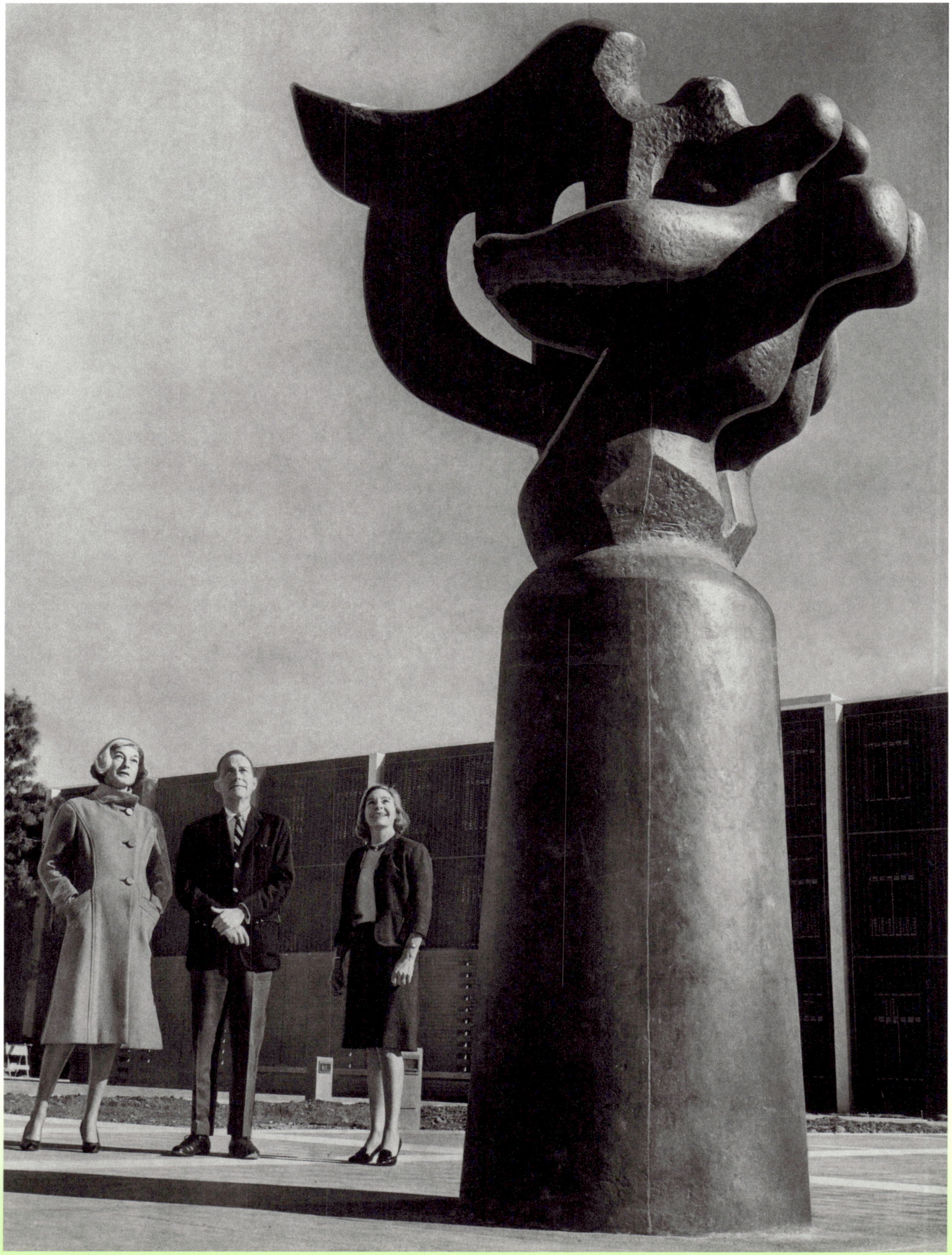

Frances Brody, Franklin D. Murphy, and Lillian Weiner with Jacques Lipchitz's Song of the Vowels *(1931–32), 1965*

For the last forty years UCLA chancellors have enjoyed the great pleasure of walking through the Franklin D. Murphy Sculpture Garden en route to Murphy Hall from the Chancellor's Residence. The garden is a spectacular vantage point from which to observe daily activities on the north campus through changing times and seasons.

UCLA's academic and cultural missions have developed significantly over the last four decades, with burgeoning enrollment and new programs, departments, and buildings. During this period the sculpture garden's collection has more than doubled. Yet this five-acre melding of art and nature has remained true to its original purpose and design. As a center of campus life, the garden brings students into close contact with great works of art, just as Franklin Murphy, one of my esteemed predecessors, so brilliantly envisioned.

Today, complemented by the new Eli and Edythe Broad Art Center and its Richard Serra sculpture, the Murphy Sculpture Garden is more than ever at the intersection of arts activity on campus. Its openness to the campus community and to our visitors embodies UCLA's promise, as a great public university, to provide broad access to excellence.

I am honored to join the distinguished group of UCLA chancellors, and I look forward to many walks through the Murphy Sculpture Garden, observing the changing life of this great campus community and admiring the remarkable realization of Franklin Murphy's dream.

GENE BLOCK
Chancellor
University of California, Los Angeles

CHANCELLOR'S FOREWORD

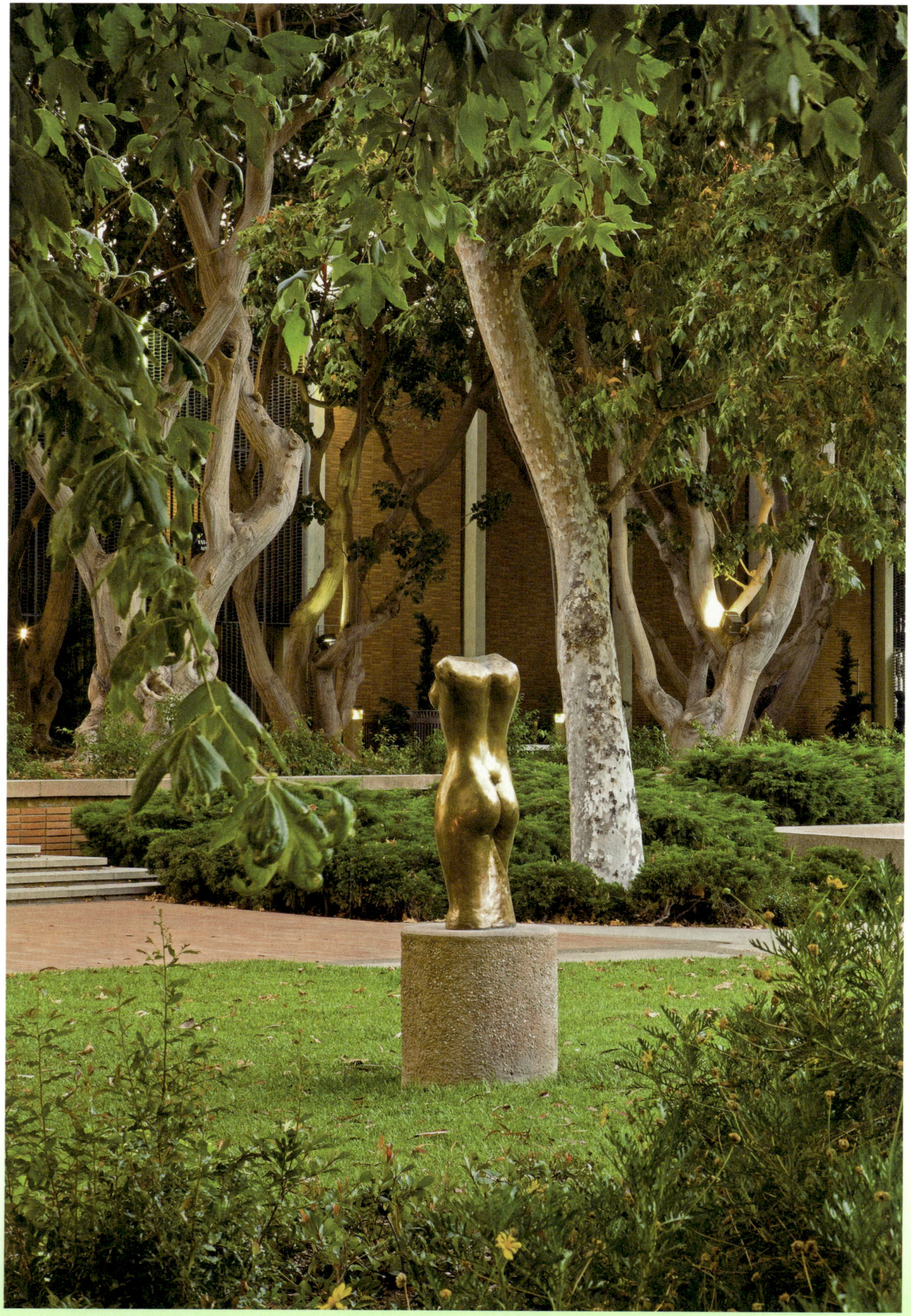

DIRECTORS' FOREWORD

Forty years ago the Franklin D. Murphy Sculpture Garden was dedicated, with its newly landscaped five acres and the core of what would soon become a world-renowned collection of modern and contemporary sculpture. Franklin Murphy had become chancellor of UCLA seven years prior, when the site was merely a dusty parking lot in the still undeveloped area of north campus. Today the Murphy Sculpture Garden remains both the former chancellor's most visible legacy and a testament to UCLA's ongoing commitment to the arts. A true outdoor museum without walls, its green lawns, jacarandas, and seventy-two sculptures are an integral part of daily life for the entire campus community and its visitors. Murphy's conception of the garden was farsighted when seen within the context of public art and institutional collections during the 1960s. There were few outdoor art collections at either museums or universities, and even fewer of the caliber envisioned by Murphy. Inspiration from the magnificent civic plazas that had captivated him on his European travels combined with his practical understanding that a campus garden also should provide a more intimate environment conducive to study and contemplation. This unique approach to the site and the high quality of its collection make the Murphy Garden a monument of twentieth-century art, as vital today as at its founding.

This book is the most comprehensive publication on the garden in its history. Such an endeavor would not have been possible without the extraordinary support of the Ahmanson Foundation. The foundation's continued generosity toward the garden, including a previous major conservation endowment, has ensured its legacy for generations to come.

We owe a debt of gratitude to Franklin D. Murphy for understanding that an outstanding art collection is fundamental to a university's teaching and research mission. We also acknowledge the generous donors who so enthusiastically shared his vision. Finally, we are grateful to chancellor emeritus Charles E. Young for his ongoing dedication to the Murphy Garden, and we thank our new chancellor, Gene Block, for contributing a foreword to this volume. We hope that he enjoys this cherished part of campus life.

CYNTHIA BURLINGHAM
Director
Grunwald Center for the Graphic Arts
Deputy Director of Collections
Hammer Museum

ANN PHILBIN
Director
Hammer Museum

ACKNOWLEDGMENTS

The publication of this book presents the opportunity to thank not only the many individuals who helped bring it to fruition but also those who have contributed to the care and preservation of the Murphy Sculpture Garden itself. First, I would like to acknowledge the Ahmanson Foundation, which has provided a generous grant to support this publication as well as establishing an endowment in 1993 for conservation of the sculpture collection. We also thank all the donors to the Murphy Sculpture Garden collection, whose names are listed on page 187. Together they helped realize Franklin Murphy's promise that no university funds would be spent on acquiring works of art, setting a new standard for the enrichment of public space through private donations. We are grateful to the artists represented in the garden, for many of them contributed their time and talents to make it a success. In addition, nothing would have been possible without the ongoing support of the UCLA administration. During and following his twenty-nine-year tenure as chancellor, chancellor emeritus Charles E. Young supported the garden in ways too numerous to count, from his vigilant monitoring of the garden's maintenance during his morning walks to his encouragement to publish this catalogue. I am also grateful to administrative vice chancellor emeritus Peter W. Blackman for his commitment to the recent revitalization of the garden through much-needed landscape improvements that have returned the garden to its original splendor.

Publication of this volume required the time and talents of numerous individuals. Artist James Welling has contributed a splendid series of photographs that consider the role of the garden in contemporary campus life. Victoria Steele, head of the Department of Special Collections at UCLA's Charles E. Young Research Library, contributed an insightful memoir of Franklin Murphy. I am grateful to Marc Treib, professor emeritus of architecture at the University of California, Berkeley, for his intelligent essay contextualizing the garden within the history of sculpture garden design. My sincere thanks go to Lorraine Wild and N. Silas Munro of Green Dragon Office for designing a book that so perfectly conveys the spirit of its subject. Joshua White photographed the entire collection, and several of his striking photographs are the first to document the new installation of some of the sculptures. Karen Jacobson edited the text to her usual high standards, and Claudine Dixon, curatorial associate at the Hammer Museum, ably coordinated the publication and has helped bring the project forward on every level. Claudine and associate curator Allegra Pesenti researched and wrote most of the expanded entries for individual sculptures. We thank Mark Swope for providing access to the historical photographs taken by his father, John Swope, and express our gratitude to photographers Grey Crawford, Elon Schoenholz, and Robert Wedemeyer for their contributions. We are also indebted to Deborah Kirshman and Ren Thompson at the University of California Press and Lee Wolcott at the Ahmanson Foundation for understanding the importance of the garden's legacy.

The ongoing care of the garden is carried out with the superior professionalism of the staff of the Hammer Museum. I particularly wish to acknowledge the skill and dedication of senior registrar Portland McCormick, associate registrar Julie Dickover, and assistant registrar Kate Bergeron. An extensive outdoor sculpture collection presents a major challenge, and their high standards and vigilant care enable us to maintain the accessibility so integral to the garden. I also wish to acknowledge my other colleagues at the Hammer, beginning with director Ann Philbin, who offered inspired ideas and insight. I am also grateful to my fellow deputy directors, Gary Garrels and Deborah Snyder, for their constant collegial support; security chief Paul Butler and chief preparator and exhibition designer Peter Gould and their staffs for their willingness to respond to the needs of the garden at the least convenient times. Other past and present Hammer staff members who have lent their expertise include Cole Akers, James Bewley, Lynne Blaikie, Mitch Browning, Miranda Carroll, Laura Cogburn, Jennifer Cox, Sean Deyoe, Amy Dove, Russell Ferguson, Tammy Fink, Jennifer Fletcher, Gloria Gerace, Jennifer Green, Henry Hopkins, Jenni Kim,

Darin Klein, Morgan Kroll, Susan Lockhart, Mo McGee, Jenée Misraje, Catherine O'Brien, Dave Paley, Alison Perchuk, Carolyn Peter, Steven Putz, Vickie Reese, Claire Rifelj, David Rodes, Maggie Sarkissian, Elizabeth Shepherd, Sarah Stifler, Sally Suchil, and Farida Sunada. Our staff is also enriched by several students who work at the museum, and we thank Olivia Blakely Caswell, Amy Croft, Hillary Ellenshaw, Lily Kasiske, and Kanchan Wali-Richardson for their assistance with this catalogue.

The enthusiasm and prudence of the Campus Sculpture Committee, chaired by Pete Blackman, have contributed substantially to the awareness of the importance of the garden. We acknowledge campus architect Jeff Averill, associate dean Pat Baxter, principal architectural associate Lyndsey Cameron, professor Barbara Drucker, assistant chancellor Antoinette Mongelli, Hammer Museum director Ann Philbin, and assistant vice chancellor Jack Powazek. Jeff and Lyndsey skillfully managed the recent reinstallation and resiting of a number of sculptures. Also key to the relandscaping of the garden and its ongoing maintenance is the UCLA Facilities staff, headed by Jack Powazek. In particular we would like to acknowledge the commitment of Miles Kitasato, Ronald Lai, Rich Ohara, and E. J. Kirby. Dean Chris Waterman and the staff of the School of the Arts and Architecture—particularly Pat Baxter, Carolyn Campbell, Guy Custis, Etsu Garfias, and Terry Morello—have been the watchful eyes of north campus. Over the years Andrea Morse and her staff at Sculpture Conservation Studio have lent their considerable skills to protecting and preserving the sculptures.

Various staff, faculty, and students at UCLA have contributed to the care, interpretation, and success of the garden over many years. Our appreciation goes out to all, and in particular, for their assistance on past and present projects, we extend thanks to Claire Bellanti, Marla Berns, Charlotte Brown, Truc Bui, Todd Cheney, Laura Danielson, Debra Dorris, Tanya Echols, Simon Elliott, Heather Hanunian, Monique Leahey-Sugimoto, Betsy Metzgar, Christina Morache, Octavio Olvera, Susan Parker, Jack Raab, John Sandbrook, and Linda Takemoto. Other individuals and institutions, including artists and their representatives, have been supportive of this book in many ways, including Paule Anglim; Sarah Arnett and Paula Hornbostel of Salander O'Reilly Galleries; Annie Barbera of the Musée Bourdelle; Lucinda Barnes; Mary Beebe and Jane Peterson of the Stuart Collection; Karyn Behnke of the McKee Gallery; Sophie Bowness; Aldo Casanova; Julie Casemore and Stephen Wirtz of the Stephen Wirtz Gallery; Francesca Consagra; Mark Davidson, Nancy Harm, and George Helfand at Luna Imaging; Alexis Dean of the Zabriskie Gallery; Gabriella Di Milia of the Archivio Pietro Consagra; Carol Eliel; Noriko Fujinami; Christian Gansicke and Katharina Lepper of the Lehmbruck Museum; Lucinda Gedeon; Robert Graham; Cynthia Hadzi; Katherine Hart; Sam Jornlin; Karen S. Kadlecsik of the Marlborough Gallery; Amalyah Keshet of the Israel Museum; Marina Mahler; Christian Marcks; Kate McLeod of Barford Sculptures; Mary McNaughton; Tam McPartland; Maria Fernanda Meza of Artists Rights Society (ARS); Andrea Mihalovic-Lee of Visual Artists and Galleries Association (VAGA); Paul Nakian; Sophie Petit; Phillip Rickey; Jennifer Ritchie of the Nasher Sculpture Center; Jack Rutberg; Nemo Sarteanesi of the Fondazione Palazzo Albizzini Collezione Burri; Louis Stern; Emma Stower of the Henry Moore Foundation; Gerard Tsutakawa; Edward Whitley of the Bridgeman Art Library; Jack Zajac; and Ariel Zúñiga.

The exhibition of art in public places requires commitment and resolve from those who support it. We thank all past, present, and future supporters who understand the importance of Franklin Murphy's visionary optimism.

CYNTHIA BURLINGHAM

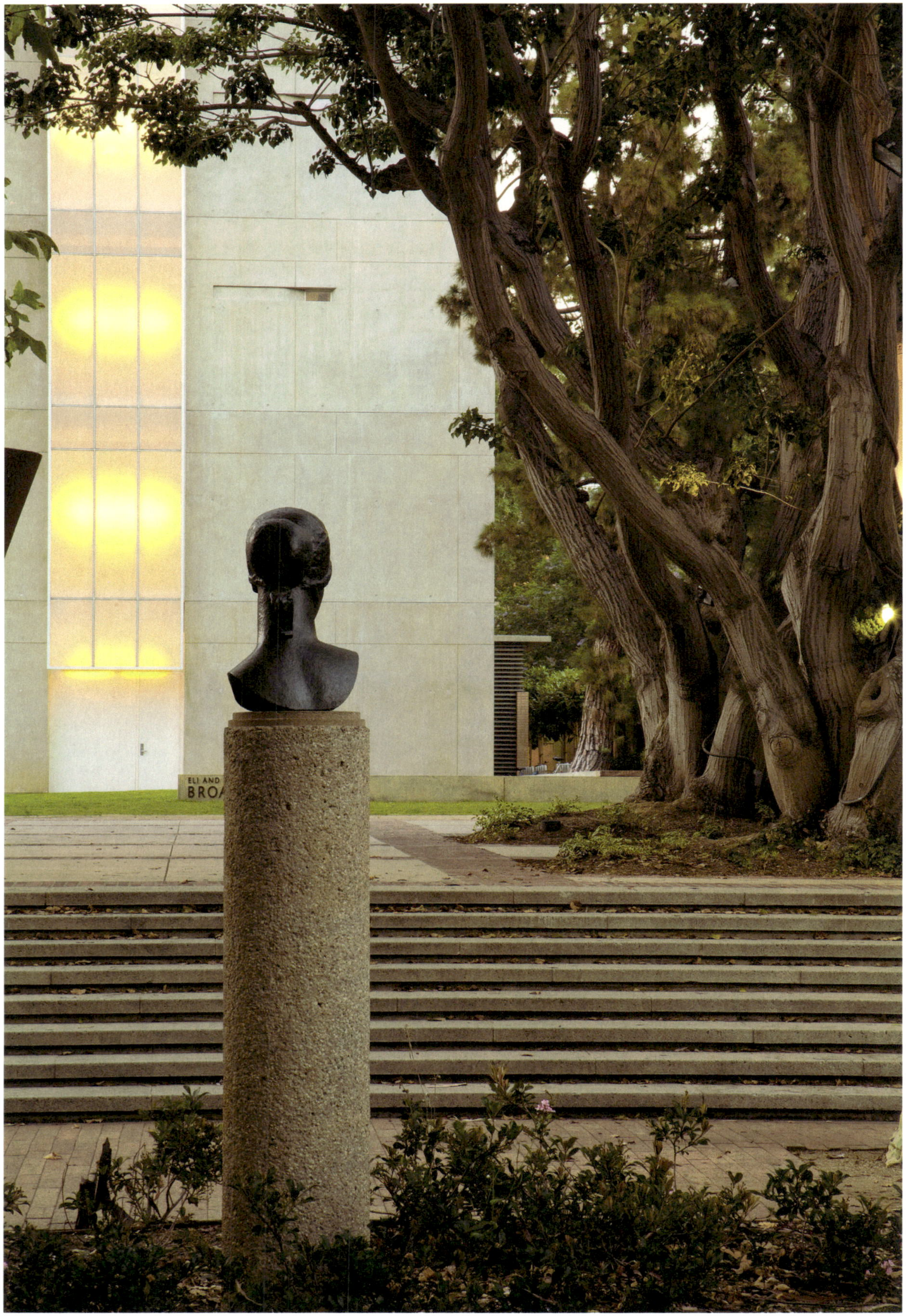

AN EDUCATION IN BEAUTY

FRANKLIN D. MURPHY AND THE UCLA SCULPTURE GARDEN

Victoria Steele

Franklin D. Murphy shared Benjamin Disraeli's belief that "a university should be a place of Learning, Light, and Liberty,"[1] but to this alliterative trio he would have added a fourth requisite: Beauty. "All my life in academia," Dr. Murphy recalls in his oral history, "I've believed that a university campus ought to be a good deal more than just efficient and functional, that it ought to have beauty in it; because I think that young people should be encouraged to grow up in the presence of beauty."[2] The creation and successful development of UCLA's sculpture garden would not have occurred without Dr. Murphy's visionary leadership, gift for negotiation, and pragmatic skill at coordinating ideas with opportunities. Ultimately, however, the sculpture garden reflects most his love of art and beauty and his conviction that a great university should possess and foster aesthetic virtues as well as intellectual excellence.

A few months after arriving at UCLA in 1960 to assume the chancellorship of the university, Dr. Murphy put this conviction into action. At the time, the northern sector of the campus was developing into the center for the arts and humanities we know today, but this area was not notably attractive. Indeed, much of the roughly five acres between the Research Library, Dickson Art Center, the Social Sciences Building, Macgowan Hall, and the Graduate School of Business Administration (as these buildings were then known) was occupied by an open-air parking lot. Loosely graveled, grimly flat, and potholed, it was dusty in dry seasons and muddy in wet ones. When Dr. Murphy came to this unsightly spot on a walking tour of the campus with Ralph Cornell, supervising landscape architect at UCLA, he immediately recognized an opportunity. In his previous post as chancellor at the University of Kansas, he had tried to improve the school's visual appeal by setting fountains and pieces of sculpture at different points on the campus. Here, however, was a prospect for a much more focused enterprise in aesthetic enhancement. Here he would create a garden with outstanding examples of sculpture of various sizes and styles disposed about a pleasing grassy landscape with gentle mounds and winding paths and recessed niches where people could wander, contemplate, talk, and observe art. Here he would establish a space in which art and nature would unite to relax and stimulate the mind and spirit.

Although the regents initially expressed reservations and skepticism about this grand vision—"it would have been cheaper and easier," Dr. Murphy later commented, "to have a flat piece of land with nothing on it"[3]—he persuaded them to let Cornell undertake the transformation of the area into a garden. When Dr. Murphy was asked with what specific sculptural works he intended to ornament the garden, he replied: "I have none, but forget about that. My responsibility is to find the sculptures."[4]

Anyone who knew Dr. Murphy will recognize in this last remark the confidence that was so central to his genius. He understood that good ideas create their own energy and generate their own realizations. Whatever endeavor he launched, he communicated his ambitions and faith in such a way that an almost magical momentum ensued. In the eight years that he led the university, it enjoyed unprecedented physical development—his chancellorship witnessed the construction of some forty new buildings—and an even more impressive upgrading of its academic departments and programs. The UCLA library system grew, with his support, into one of the very top institutions of its kind in the nation and the world. And in the realm of the arts, his seasoned and imaginative leadership nurtured the growth of the distinguished Grunwald Center for the Graphic Arts and Fowler Museum—and produced the Franklin D. Murphy Sculpture Garden.

In the case of the sculpture garden, the magical momentum began even as the garden was merely under discussion. UCLA Art Galleries director Frederick S. Wight and the UCLA Art Council had mounted an exhibition of the sculpture of Jacques Lipchitz, and Lillian Weiner, an active member of the art council, overheard Dr. Murphy discussing his proposed garden and suggested to him that he purchase for his project Lipchitz's *Song of the Vowels*, the major piece in the exhibition. Dr. Murphy responded enthusiastically but added that it might be difficult to find the ninety thousand dollars needed to purchase the work. Fortunately Weiner happened to be a close friend of Lucille and Norton Simon, and she persuaded them to put up half of the purchase price—the remainder being supplied by the art council.

The sculpture garden was on its way to becoming a reality.

A second key acquisition occurred as a result of sadder happenstance, but once again Dr. Murphy's resourcefulness—

here expressing itself with consideration, sympathy, and tact—was critical. Another member of the UCLA Art Council was David E. Bright, an art collector who had amassed a considerable fortune in the early days of the cable television business and who had a large estate in Holmby Hills with a sculpture garden featuring works by Lipchitz, Barbara Hepworth, Henry Moore, Alexander Calder, and others. Bright had already bequeathed a number of paintings to UCLA when in 1965 he died unexpectedly while still in his fifties. Knowing the Brights and knowing that Dolly Bright did not wish to stay on the estate after her husband's death, Dr. Murphy conceived of an arrangement whereby both she and UCLA might benefit from her husband's legacy. As Dr. Murphy tells it in his oral history:

> *So here we were, needing lots of sculpture, having been willed an important collection of paintings, and with his widow not wishing to live in this great big estate. So logic prevailed. I sat down with her, and I said, "Look, Dolly, we have paintings, you have the sculpture. Let's trade them, because you can put [up] the paintings no matter where you live, an apartment or what[ever]." Great idea, as far as she was concerned. We got appraisals so everything was very legal, and I got the Regents to agree to this trade. Overnight we had ten very important pieces of sculpture.*[5]

With this arrangement, the collection for, and the project of, the sculpture garden had acquired sufficient gravitational force to attract additional donations and purchases.

The general layout and particular features of the garden testify to the wonderful talents of Ralph Cornell, whose achievements are discussed elsewhere in this catalogue, but Dr. Murphy contributed crucially to the most distinctive characteristic of the garden—its accessibility and integration into the landscape and community of UCLA. When he was a twenty-year-old student traveling in Europe, Dr. Murphy had been struck by the public nature of the sculpture there. "The thing that fascinated me the most in Europe," Dr. Murphy once remarked in a newspaper interview, "was the outdoor sculpture—the great fountains and piazzas of Rome, the magnificent public squares in France."[6] He particularly remembered children playing about the Barcaccia Fountain in the Piazza di Spagna in Rome. These experiences led to his feeling that people should be encouraged, to cite his oral history once more, "to think of art as something you live with rather than something you look at."[7] This also accounts for the pride he felt when, some time after retiring as chancellor, he toured the garden with guests from the East Coast and heard them commenting on the fact that "students were . . . studying and leaning against [the sculptures] and all the rest of it, and the point was that this was unlike the sculpture garden in the Museum of Modern Art where people have to go into a building and go by guards and then go out in a cluttered area. But [the Murphy Sculpture Garden] was a place where people lived."[8]

Although we take for granted today that the sculpture garden is part and parcel of everyday life at UCLA, Dr. Murphy had to argue forcibly in favor of its accessibility. Especially during the unrest of the late 1960s, when the garden was nearing completion, many people were afraid the art would be vandalized, and they urged that the garden be fenced off. But Dr. Murphy objected that the place belonged, first and foremost, to the students: "I said, 'Absolutely not. If we put up a fence, it will imply that the garden belongs to the Establishment....If we leave it open, it'll demonstrate that it does indeed belong to them and they can continue to use it.'"[9] Dr. Murphy's faith was vindicated. While other buildings and landmarks at UCLA were graffitied during the turmoil of the Vietnam War era, the sculpture garden was untouched.

If the garden reflects Dr. Murphy's long-standing love of public art, it is also informed by his own instincts as a collector. He had caught the collecting bug early in life from his father, a practicing physician who avidly collected rare books. And though Dr. Murphy never seemed to have been greatly interested in collecting as a private individual, he was unabashedly energetic in building collections for the university, whether these involved Aldines (rare books printed by the early Venetian printer Aldus Manutius), prints, medical history, or the art of nonindustrial societies. Further, he had a keen sense of the way different works of a particular type might work together, visually or intellectually. This collector's sense is subtly evident in the sculpture garden, in which large pieces by Henry Moore, Jacques Lipchitz, and Gaston Lachaise blend with medium-size or small works by Aristide Maillol, Jean Arp, and Émile-Antoine Bourdelle.

Given Dr. Murphy's contributions to the creation of the sculpture garden, it is appropriate that his spirit continues to preside over it today. It is the garden of his happy imagining—a place where young couples can rendezvous and court, where students throw Frisbees or nap, where classes gather on fair days, where staff lunch, where art students create new work, where theater students practice and perform, where art lovers come to view the sculptures, and where on weekends and holidays members of the community come to picnic. One of the loveliest spots in Los Angeles, it seems mysteriously attuned to the city's changing moods and seasons—to rainy winter mornings, when pedestrians hurry past Rodin's darkly slicked *Walking Man;* to spring days, when the jacarandas bloom up high and the agapanthus flower down low, and earth and air are washed with lavender; to summer evenings, when warm breezes stir past the sensuous forms of Maillol's *Torso* and Lachaise's imposing *Standing Woman*; to autumn, when the sycamores drop their huge dry leaves and send them rustling about the bases of the statuary.

Finally the garden is an education in beauty, natural and artistic. Here students learn the names of plants and familiarize themselves with art by masters of the sculptural medium. Some simply pass through the garden; some take away a deeper impression of it. As Dr. Murphy said: "I think that a lot of students find this a palatable introduction to art. Not all, but some, have their interest sparked by being in this garden. They might go out and buy a book on art, maybe take a class or visit a museum for the first time. And if it affects just one person that way . . . then it has served its purpose."[10]

Notes

1 *Speech to the House of Commons, March 11, 1863.*

2 *Franklin D. Murphy, "My UCLA Chancellorship: An Utterly Candid View," oral history transcript, interviewed by James V. Mink (Los Angeles: Oral History Program, University of California, 1976), 222.*

3 *Diana Rico, "Garden Sprouts Sculptural Delights,"* Los Angeles Daily News, *L.A. Life section, August 26, 1984.*

4 *Murphy, "My UCLA Chancellorship," 222–23.*

5 *Ibid., 224–25.*

6 *Rico, "Garden Sprouts Sculptural Delights."*

7 *Murphy, "My UCLA Chancellorship," 222.*

8 *Ibid., 225.*

9 *Rico, "Garden Sprouts Sculptural Delights."*

10 *Ibid.*

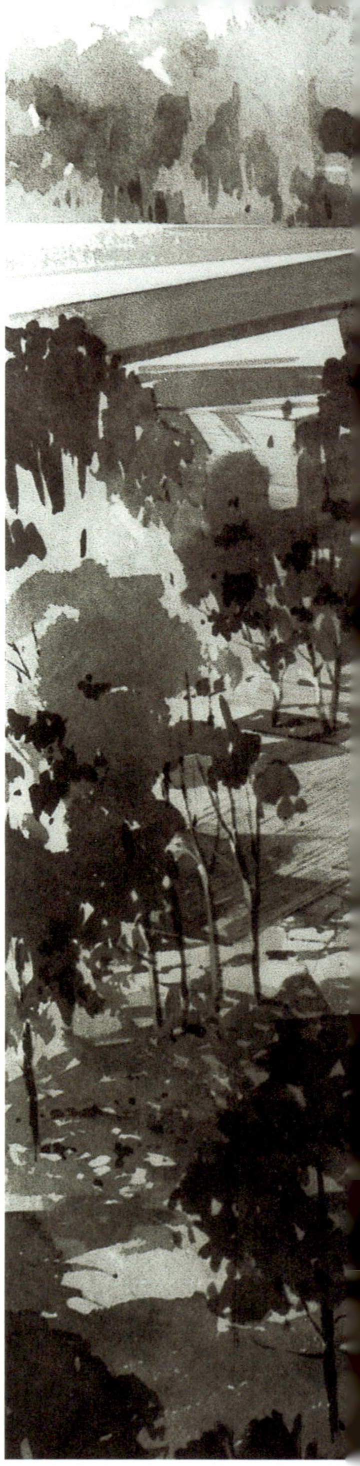

THE FRANKLIN D. MURPHY SCULPTURE GARDEN

A HISTORY IN PICTURES, 1964–2007

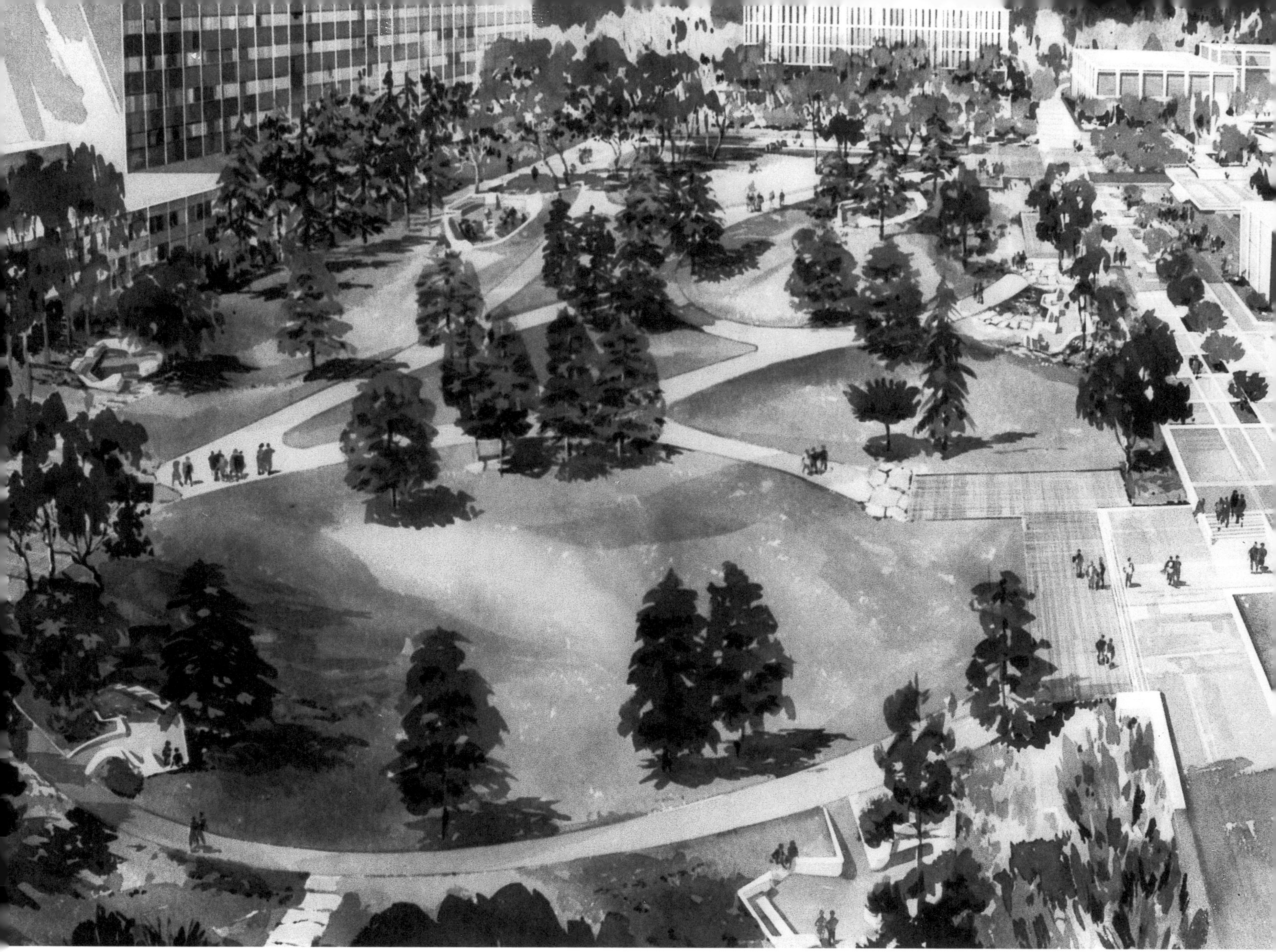

Designer's rendering of the North Campus Court (Cornell, Bridges and Troller)

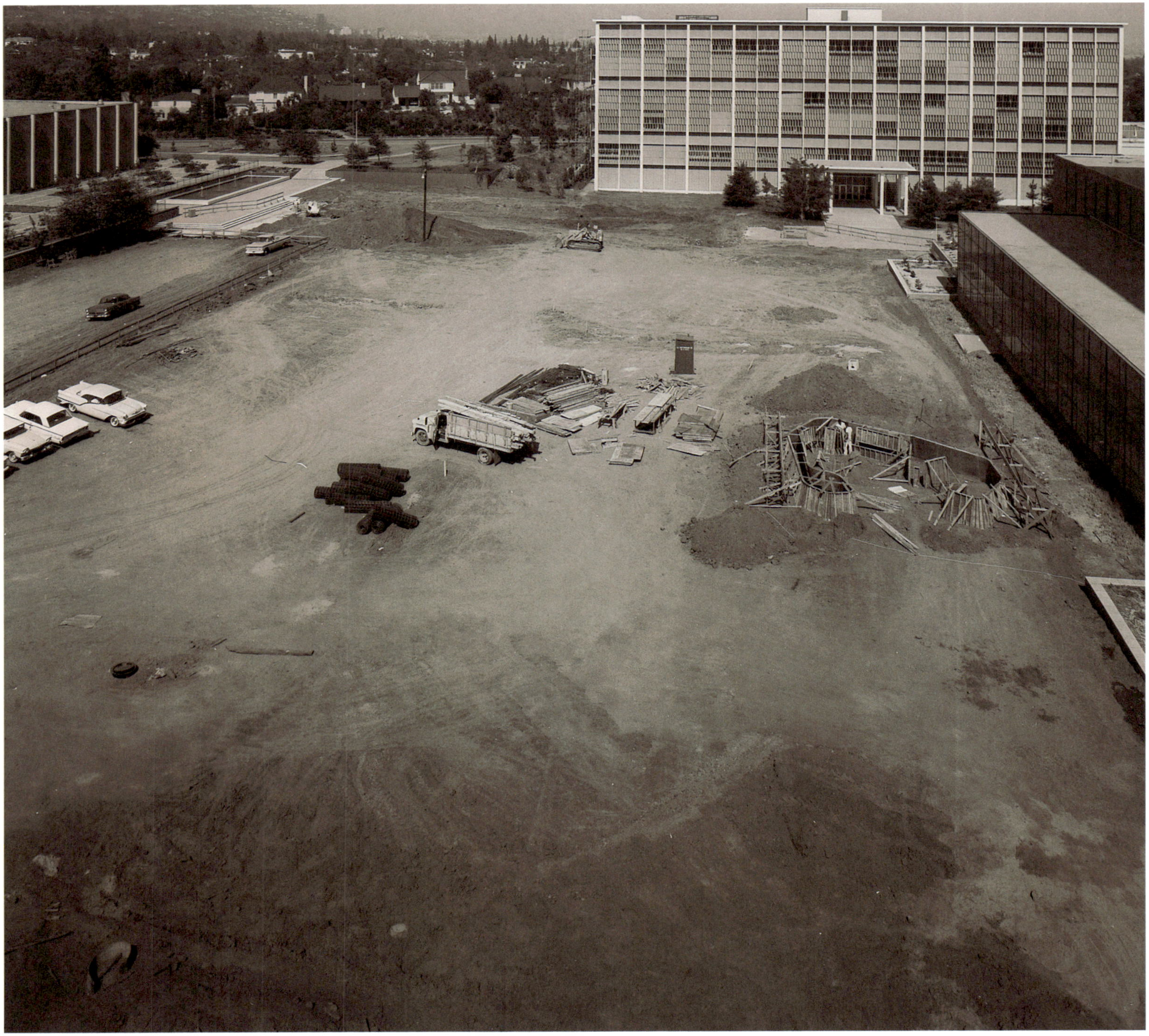

North Campus Court, July 22, 1964

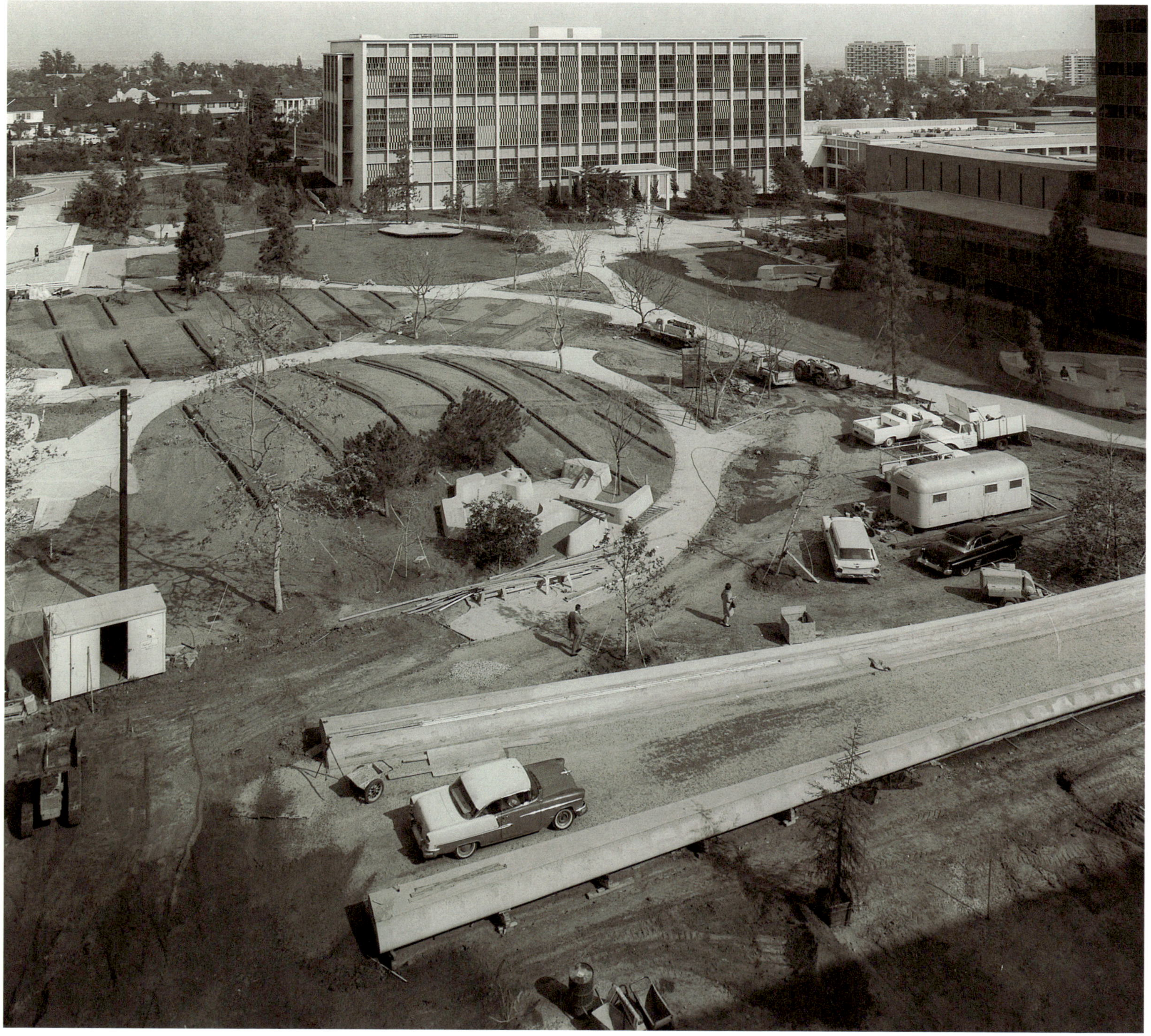

North Campus Court, March 25, 1965

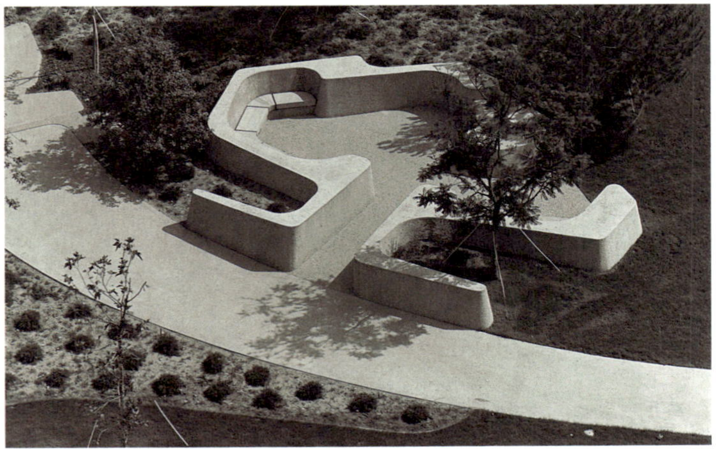

Seating area, North Campus Court

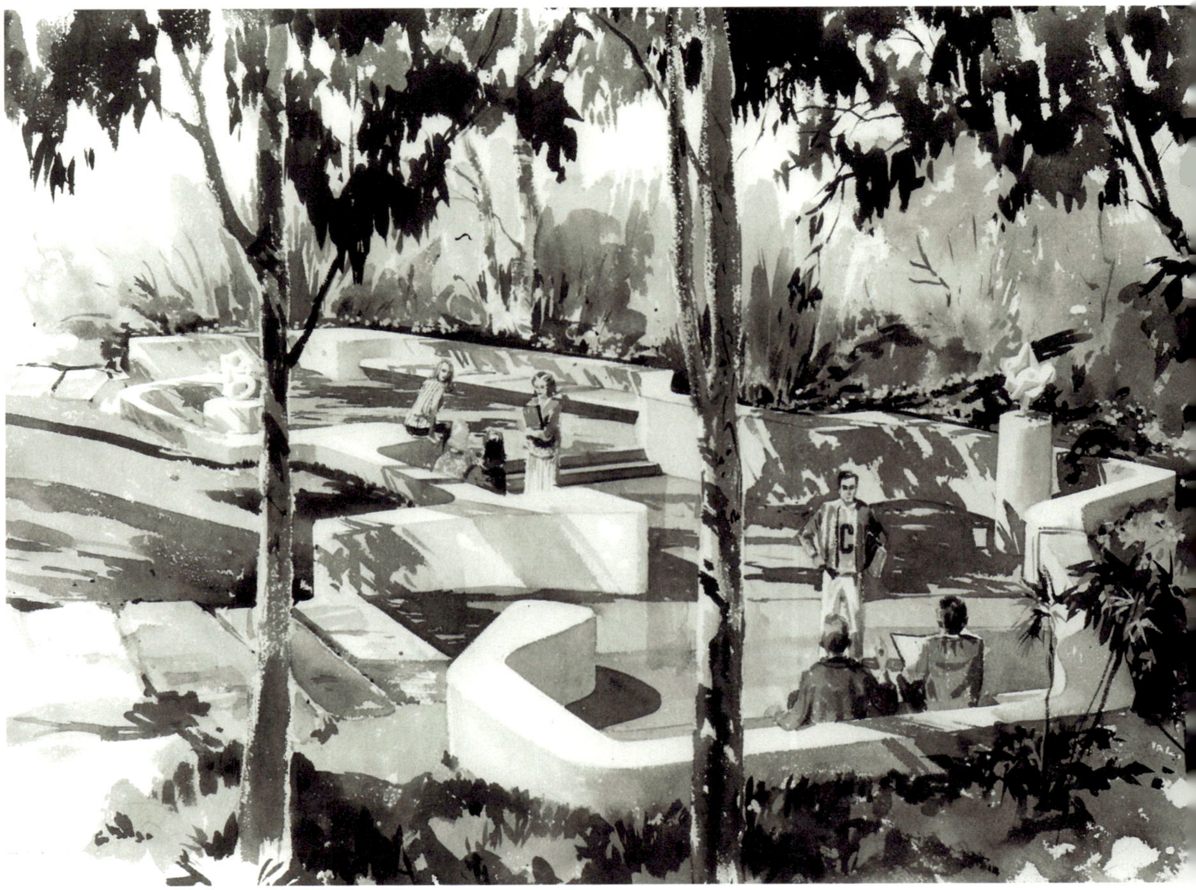

Design for seating areas, North Campus Court (Cornell, Bridges and Troller)

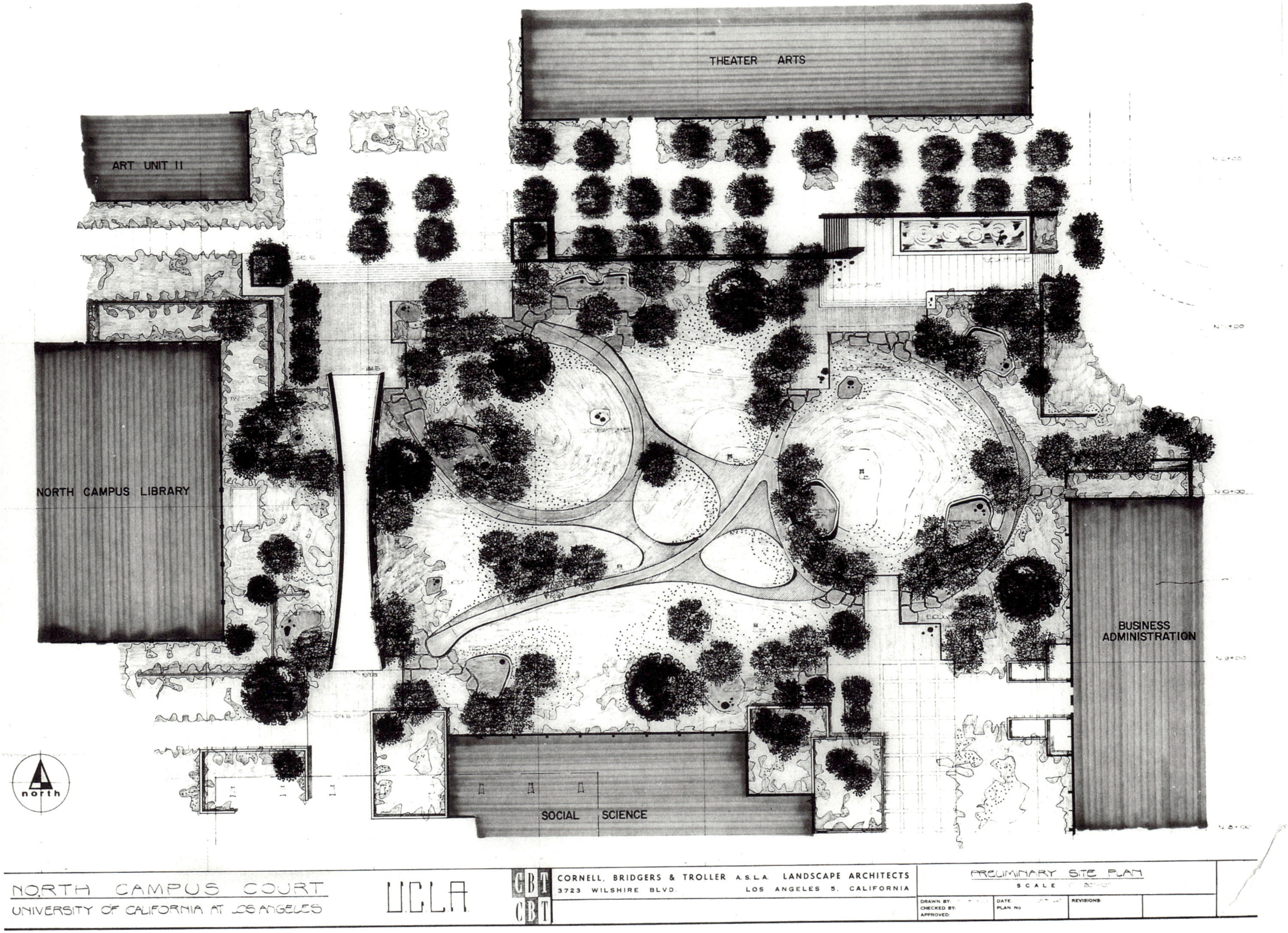

Preliminary site plan, North Campus Court (Cornell, Bridges and Troller)

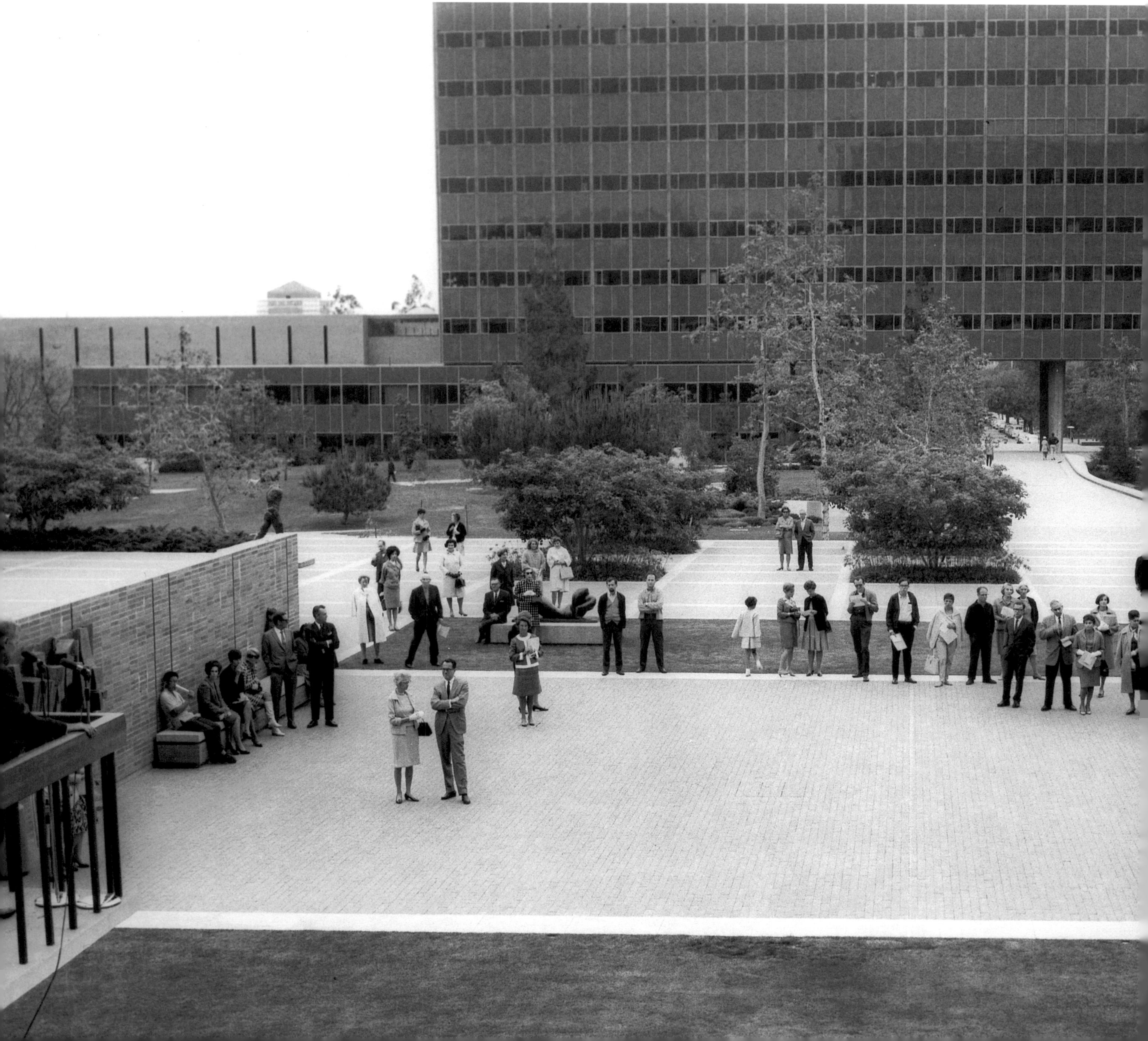

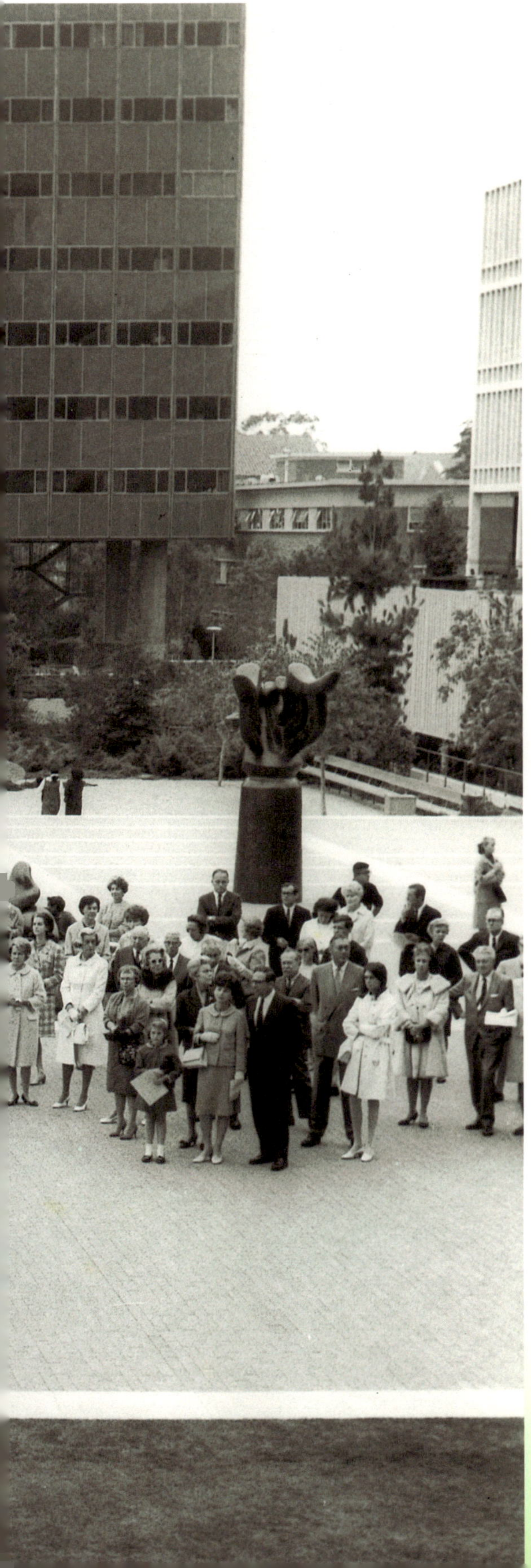

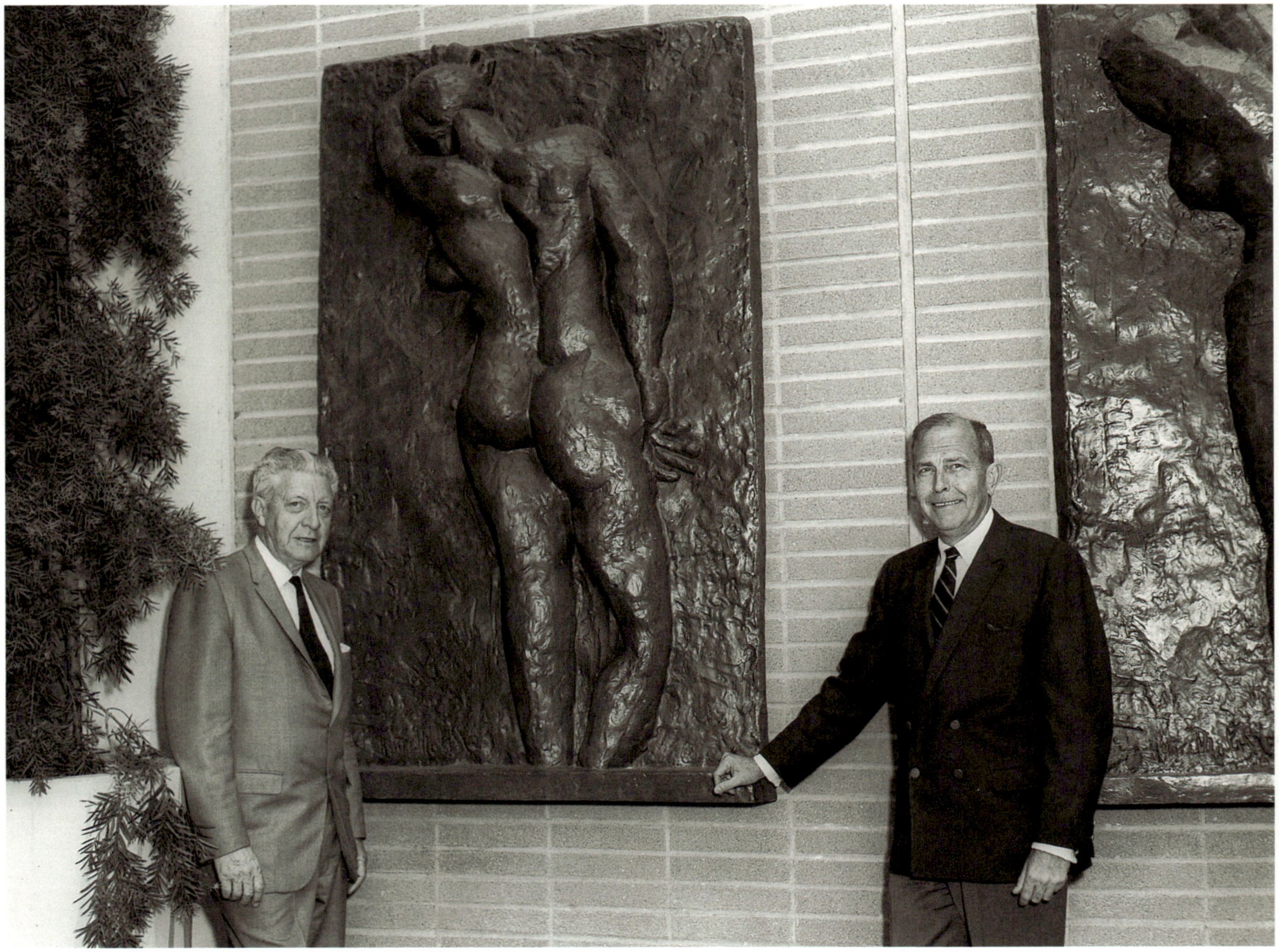

Dedication ceremony, Franklin D. Murphy Sculpture Garden, June 11, 1967

Frederick S. Wight and Franklin D. Murphy with Matisse's Bas-Relief I *(1909), June 11, 1967*

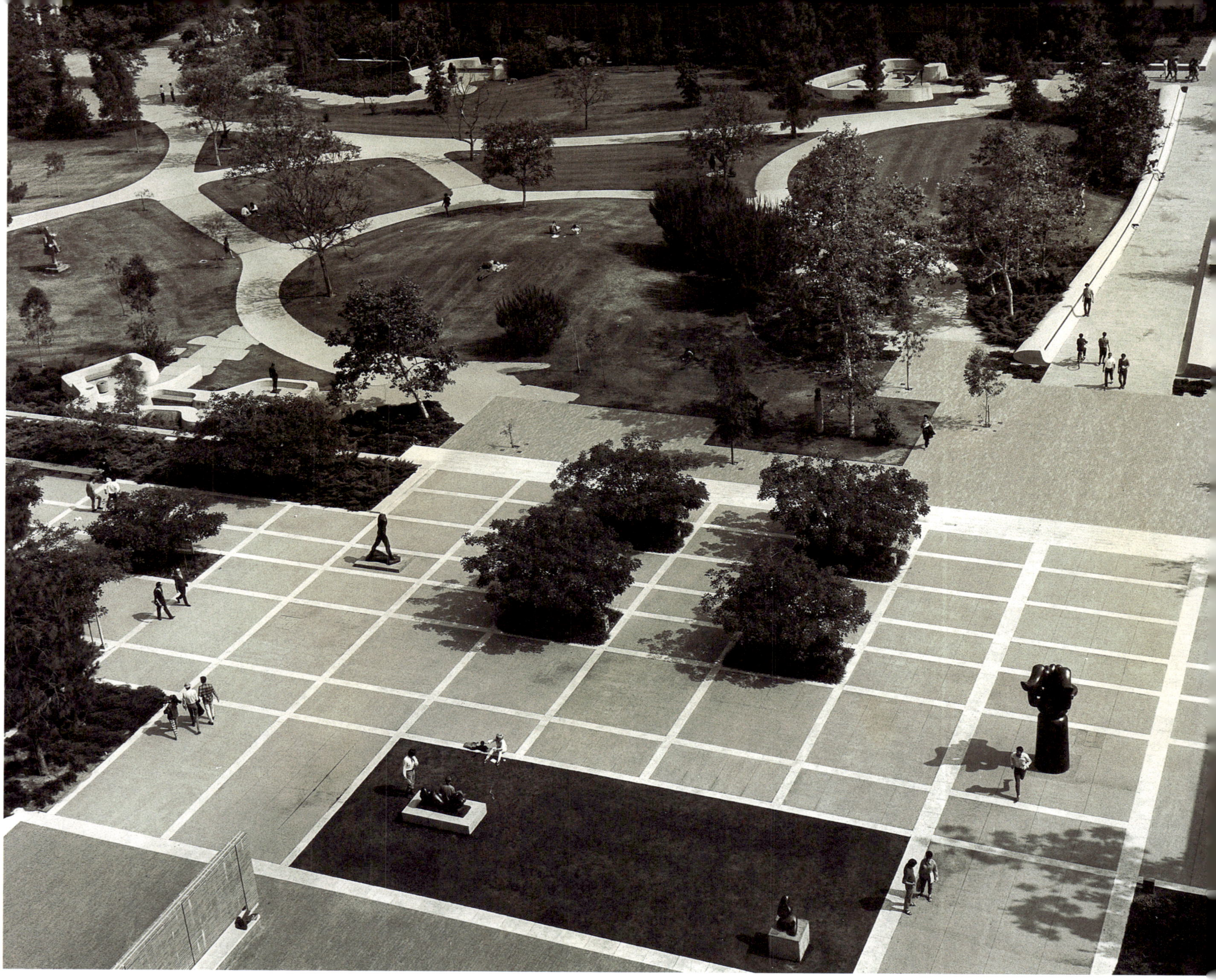

Aerial view of the Franklin D. Murphy Sculpture Garden, ca. 1967

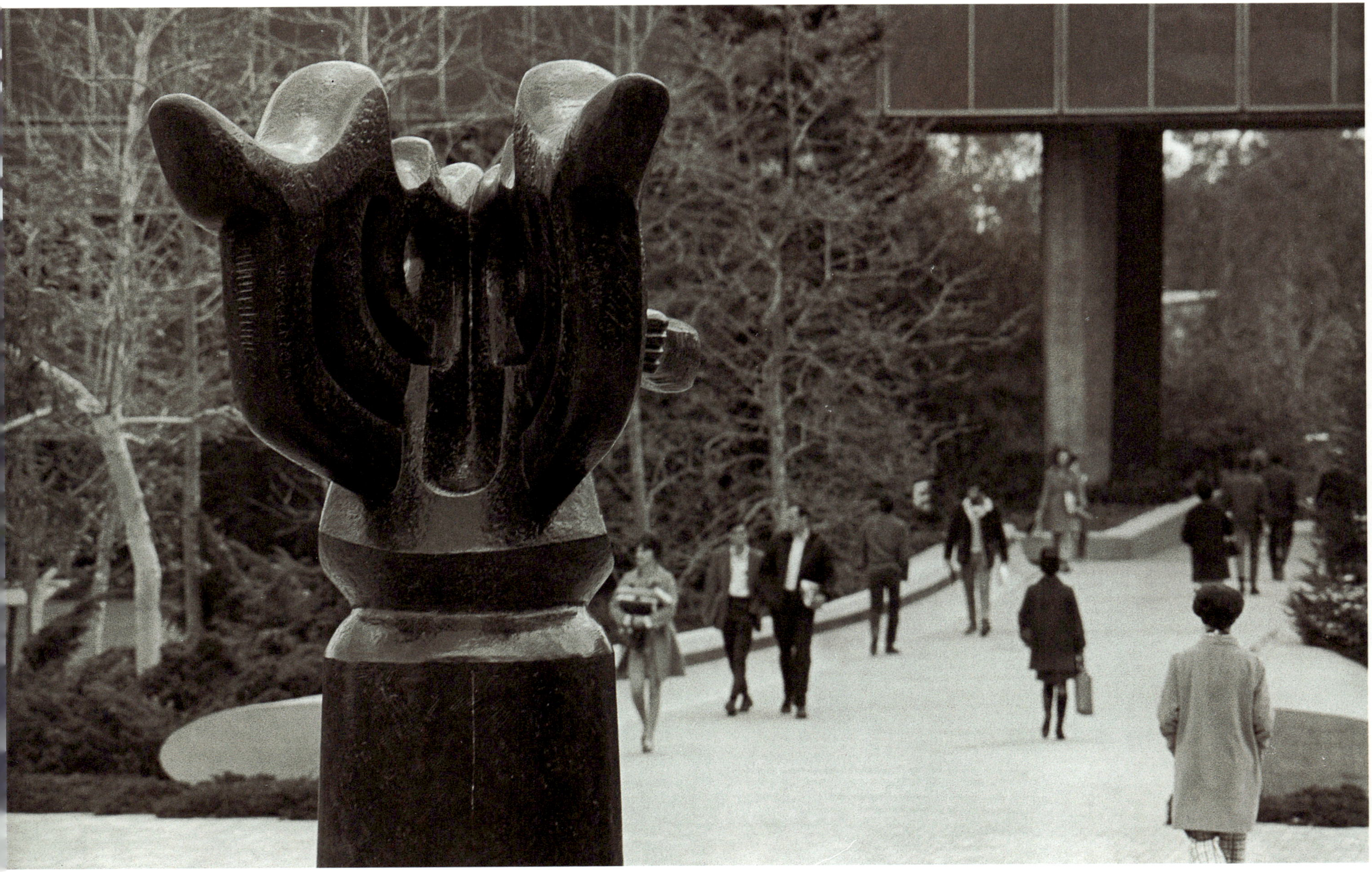

View of walkway with Jacques Lipchitz's Song of the Vowels *(1931–32)*

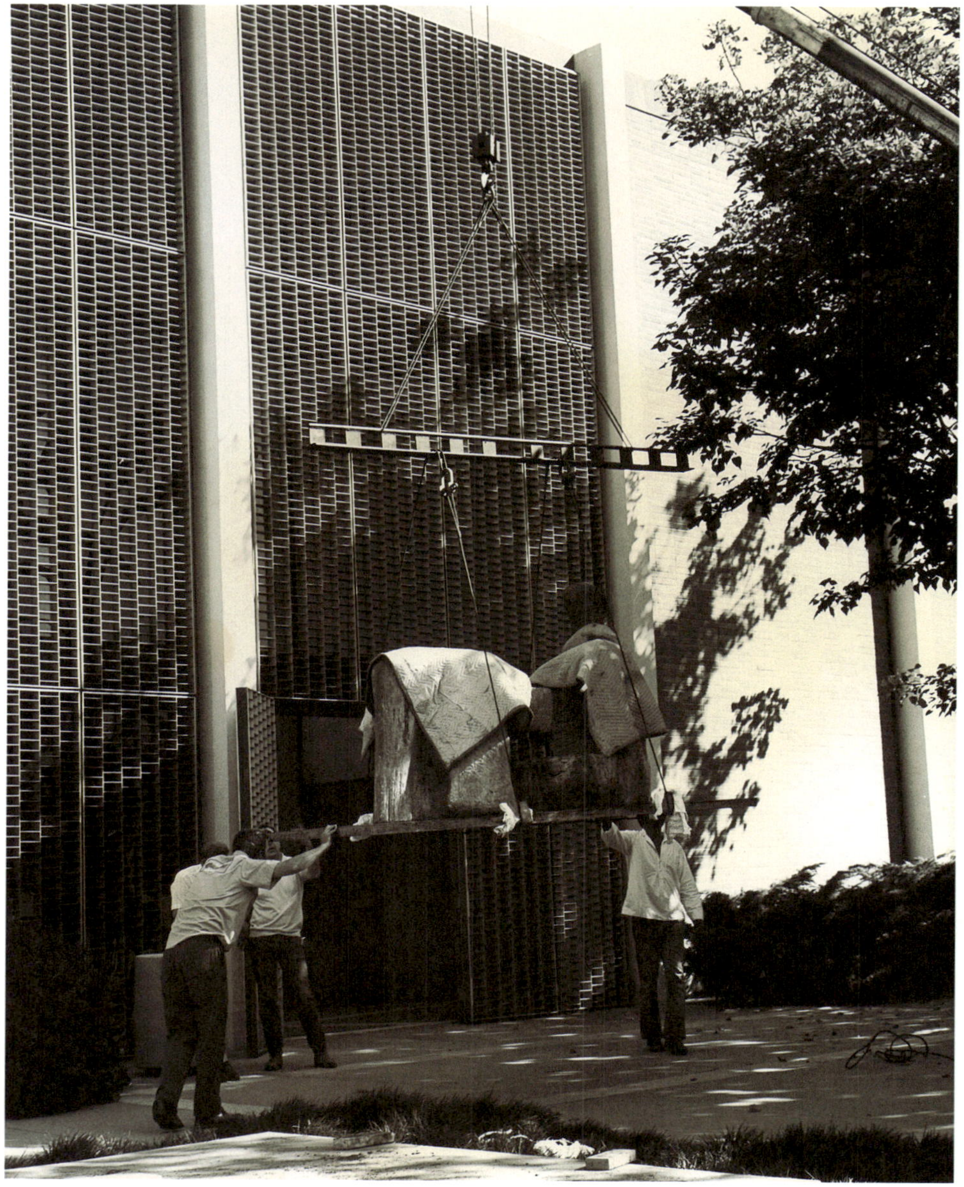

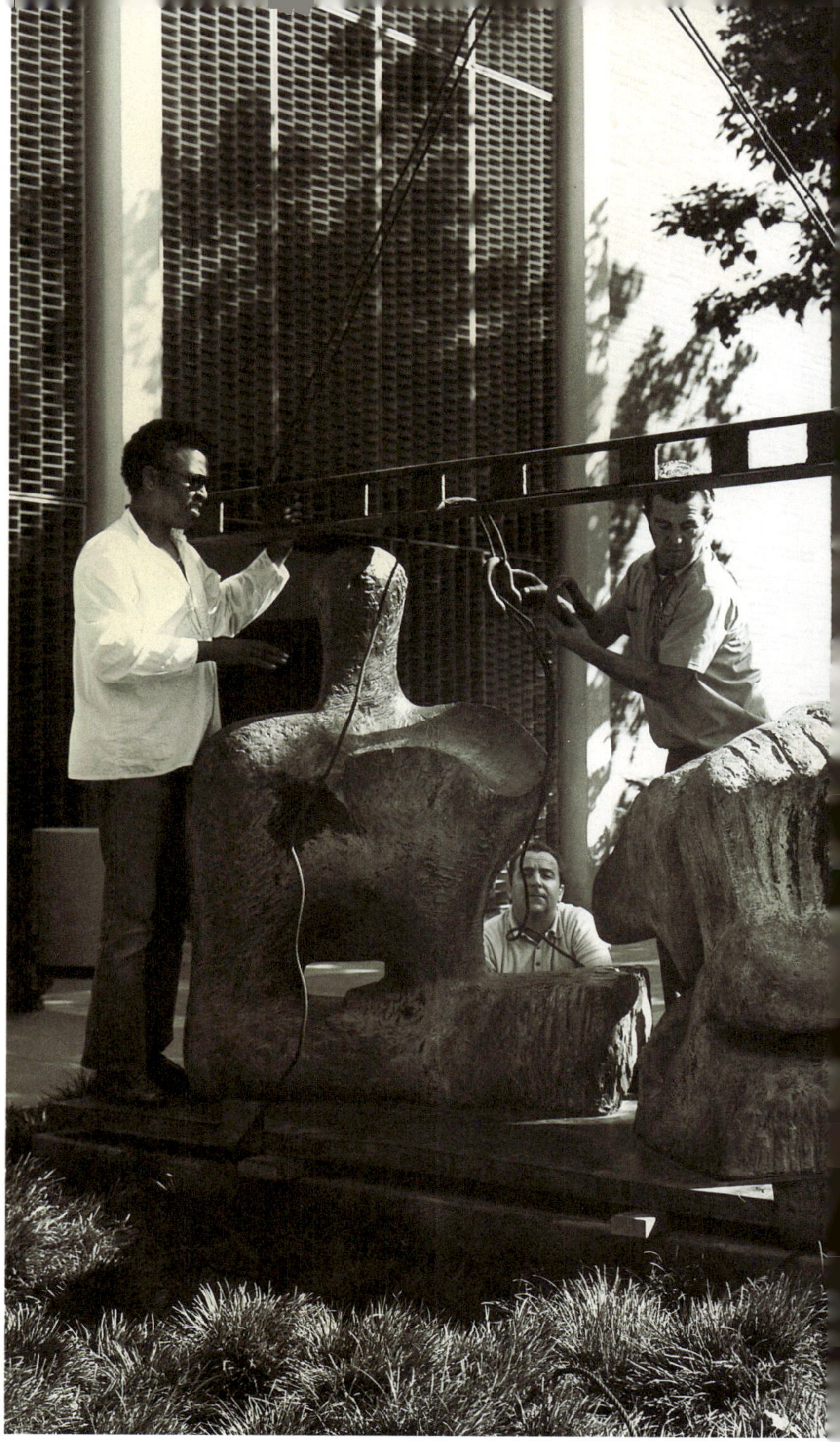

Installation of Henry Moore's Two-Piece Reclining Figure, No. 3 *(1961), Franklin D. Murphy Sculpture Garden, 1967*

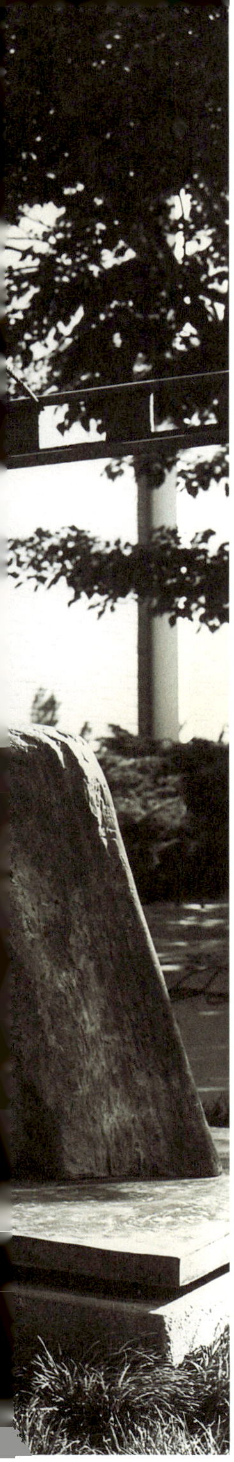

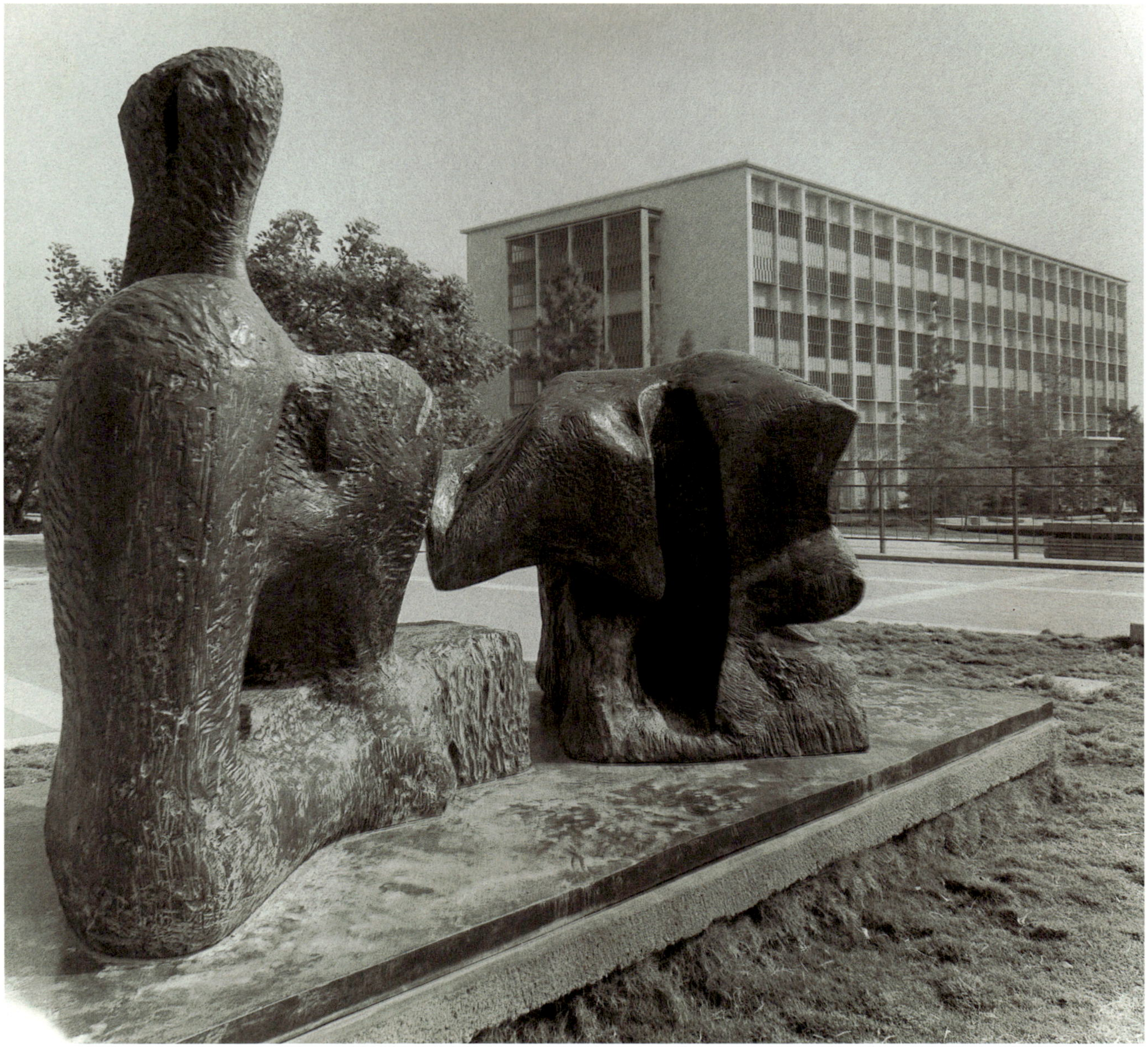

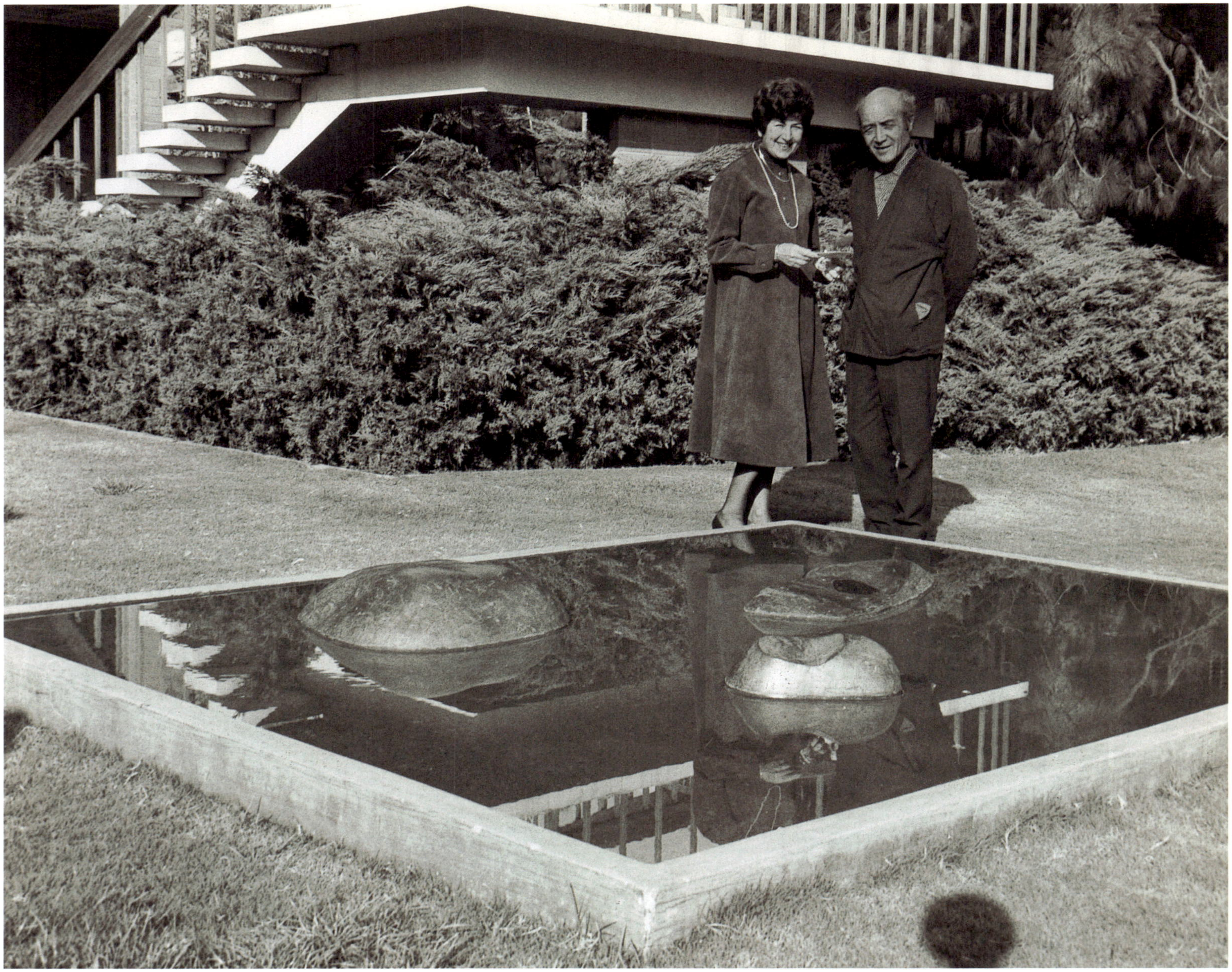

Carmela Speroni and Isamu Noguchi in front of Noguchi's Garden Elements *(1962), Franklin D. Murphy Sculpture Garden, 1967*

Jean Arp's Hybrid Fruit Called Pagoda *(1934), Franklin D. Murphy Sculpture Garden, May 1968*

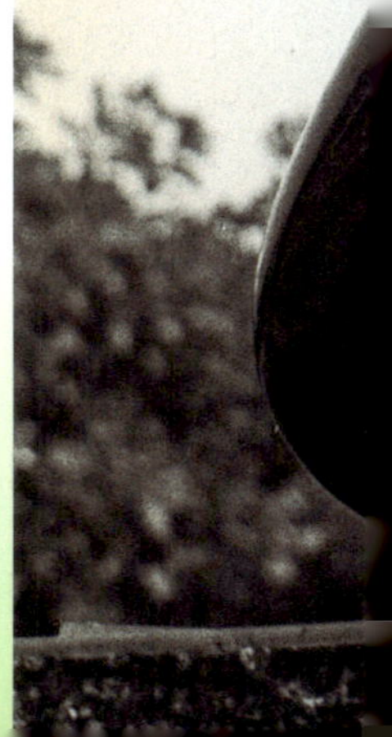

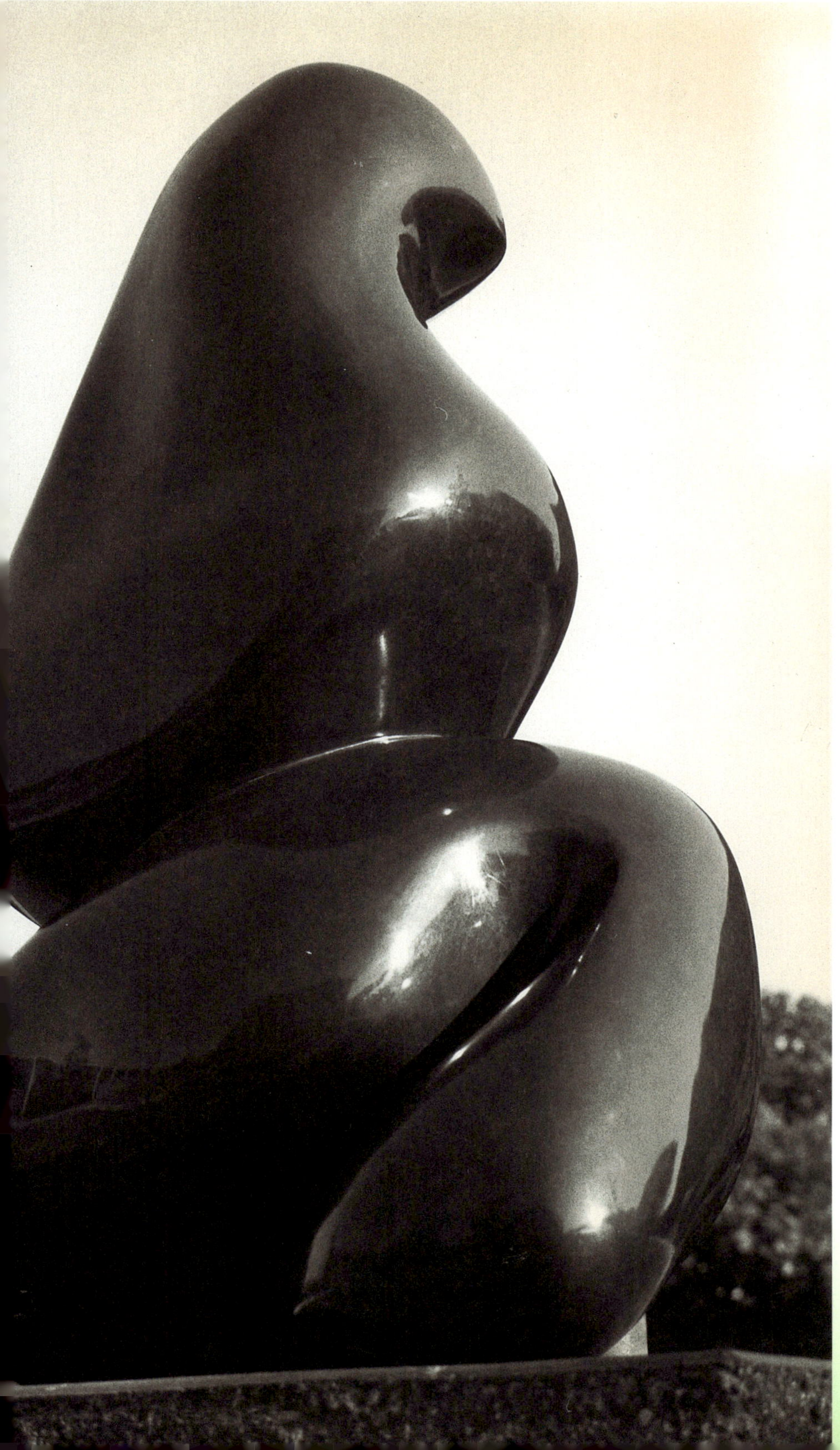

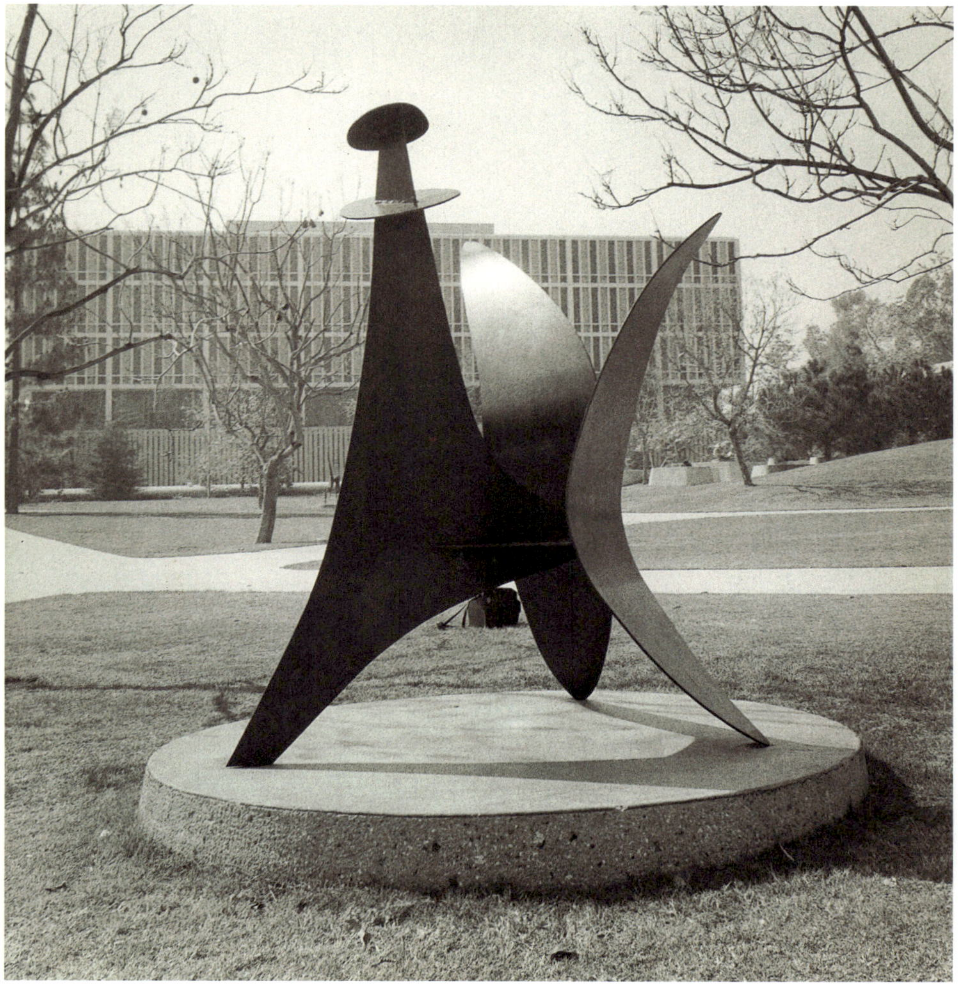

Alexander Calder's Button Flower *(1959), Franklin D. Murphy Sculpture Garden*

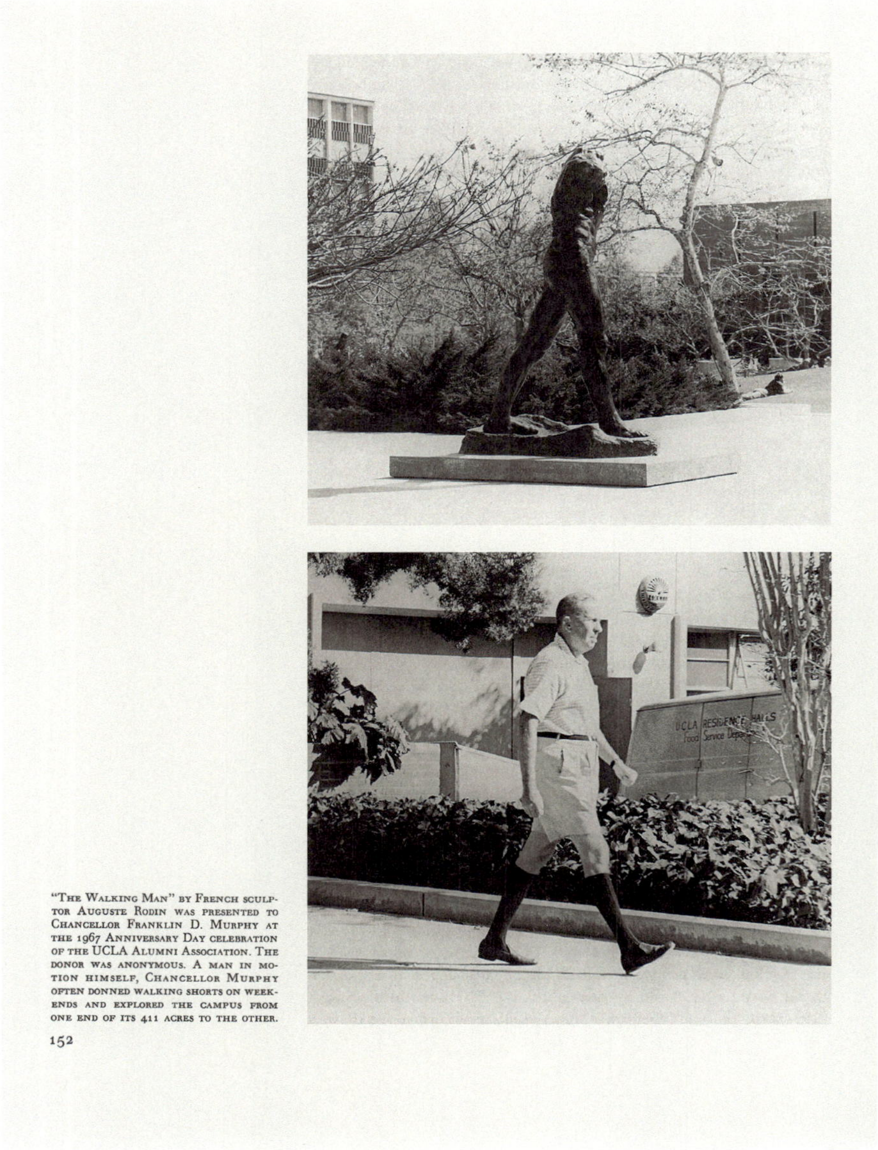

"The Walking Man" by French sculptor Auguste Rodin was presented to Chancellor Franklin D. Murphy at the 1967 Anniversary Day celebration of the UCLA Alumni Association. The donor was anonymous. A man in motion himself, Chancellor Murphy often donned walking shorts on weekends and explored the campus from one end of its 411 acres to the other.

152

Page from Andrew Hamilton and John B. Jackson, UCLA on the Move during Fifty Golden Years, 1919–1969 *(Los Angeles: Ward Ritchie Press and Regents of the University of California, 1969)*

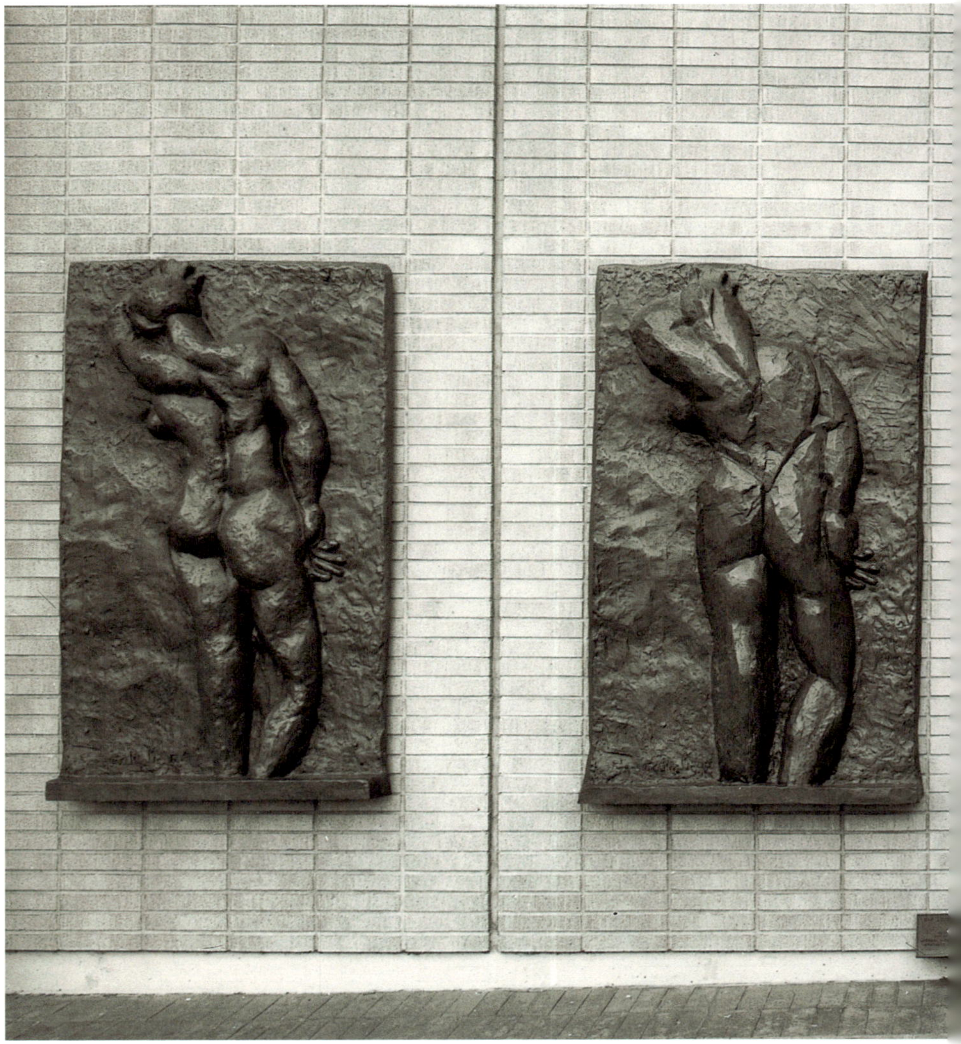

Henri Matisse's Bas-Reliefs I–IV *(1909–30), installed on the Wight Art Gallery exterior wall, Dickson Art Center, UCLA, ca. 1972*

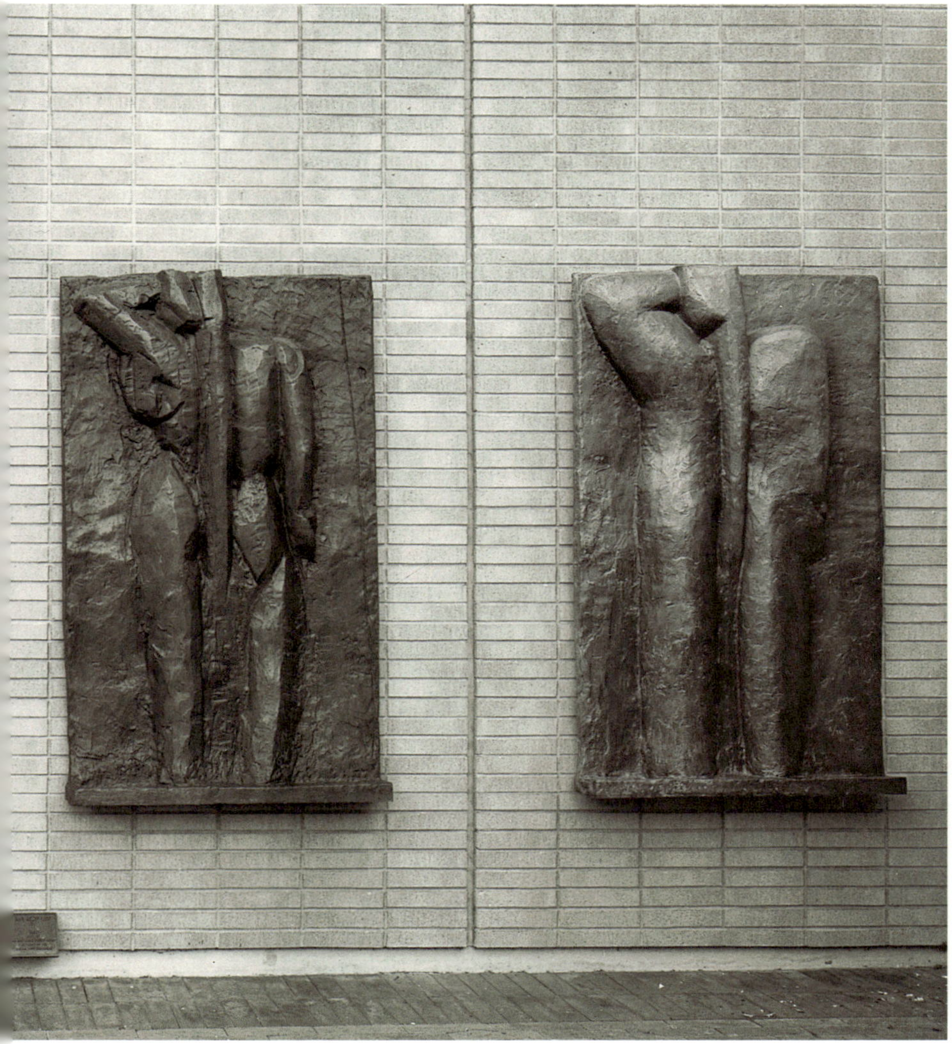

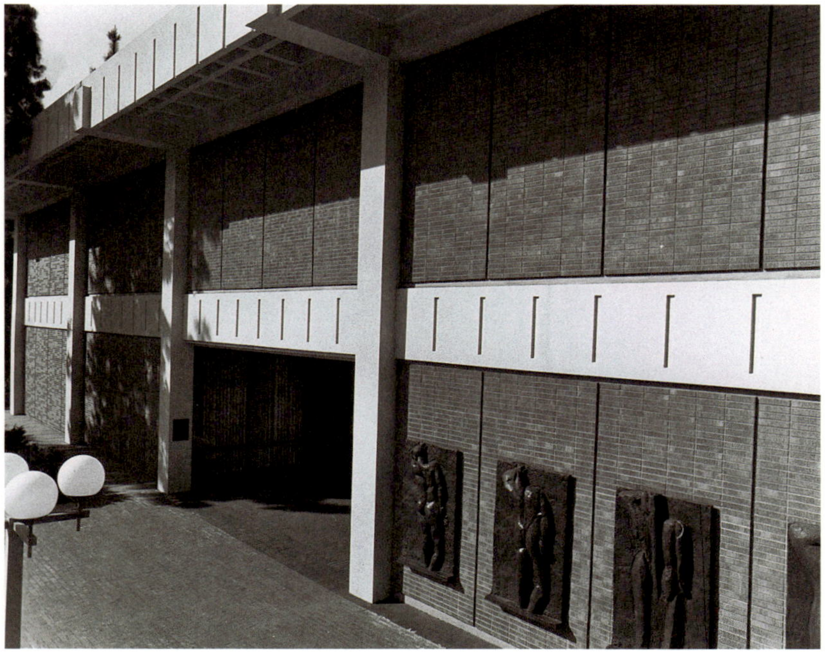

Wight Art Gallery, Dickson Art Center, UCLA, with Henri Matisse's Bas-Reliefs I–IV *(1909–30), ca. 1972*

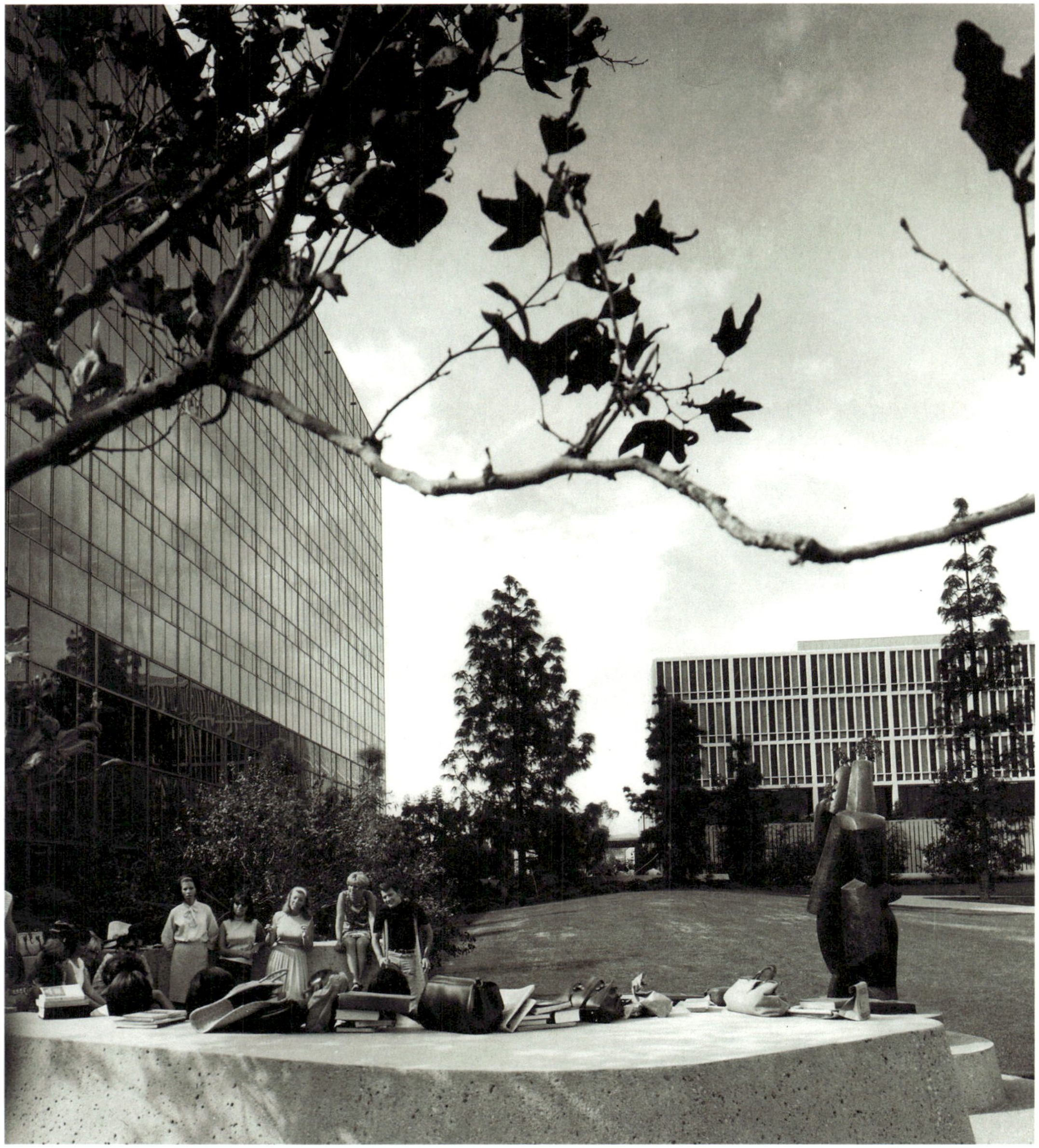

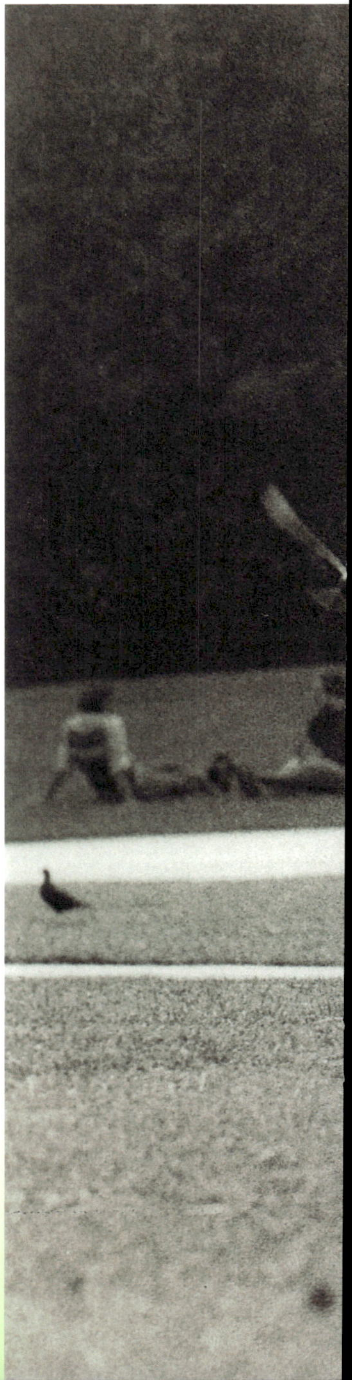

Students with Jacques Lipchitz's Bather *(1923–25),*
Franklin D. Murphy Sculpture Garden, ca. 1970s

Students with Gerhard Marcks's Maja *(1941),*
Franklin D. Murphy Sculpture Garden, ca. 1970s

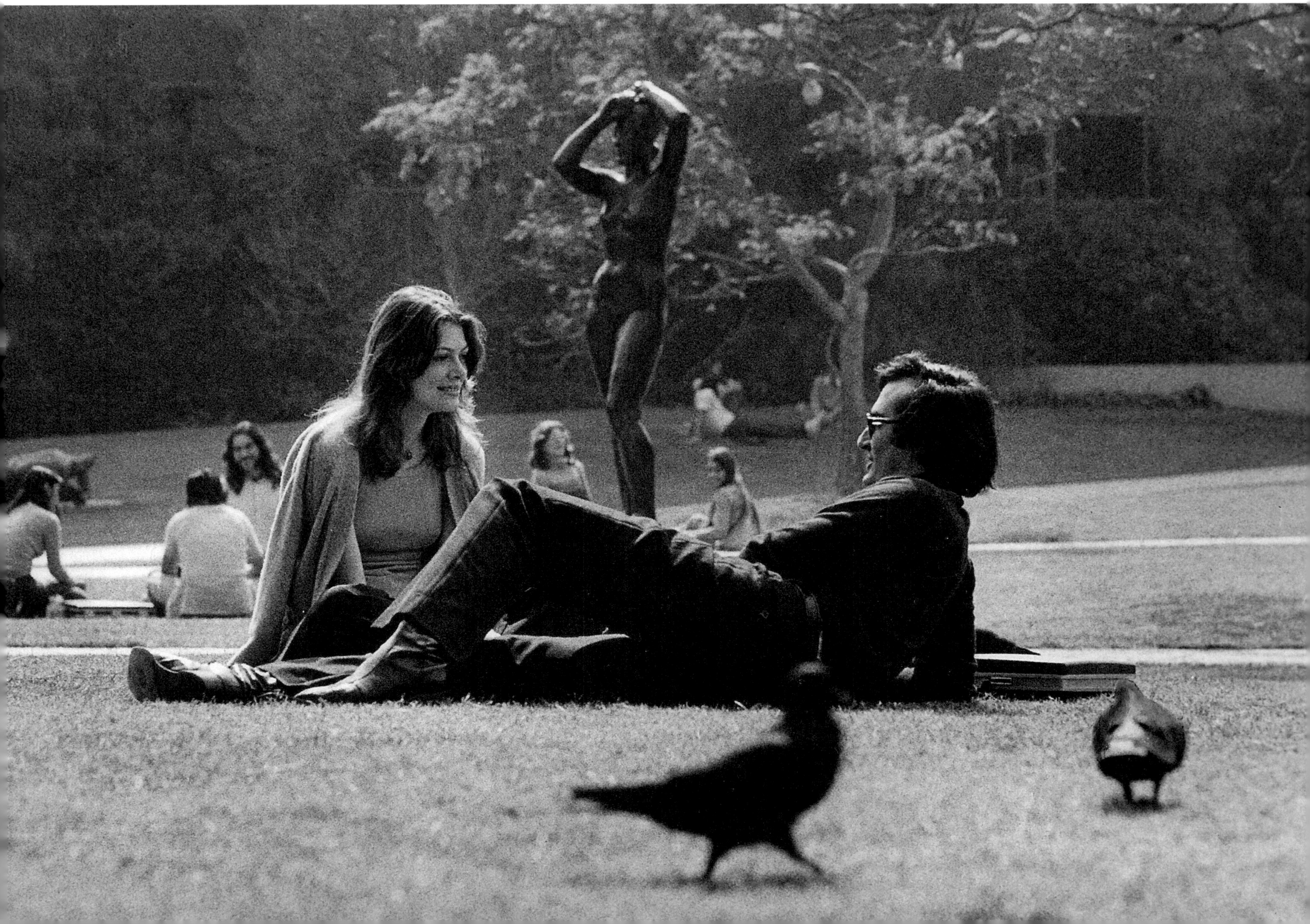

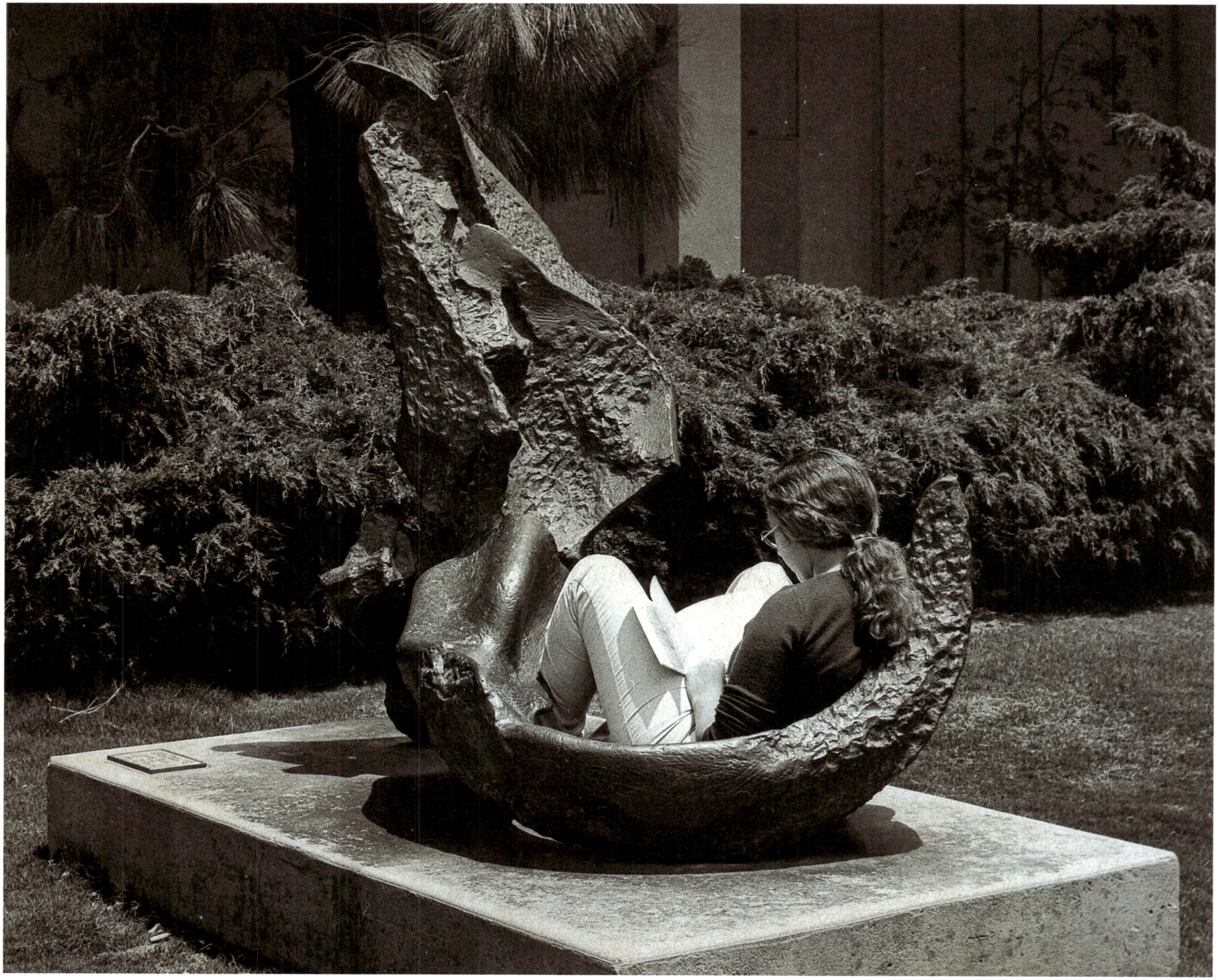

Student with Jack Zajac's Ram Head with Broken Horn, VI *(1963), Franklin D. Murphy Sculpture Garden, ca. 1970s*

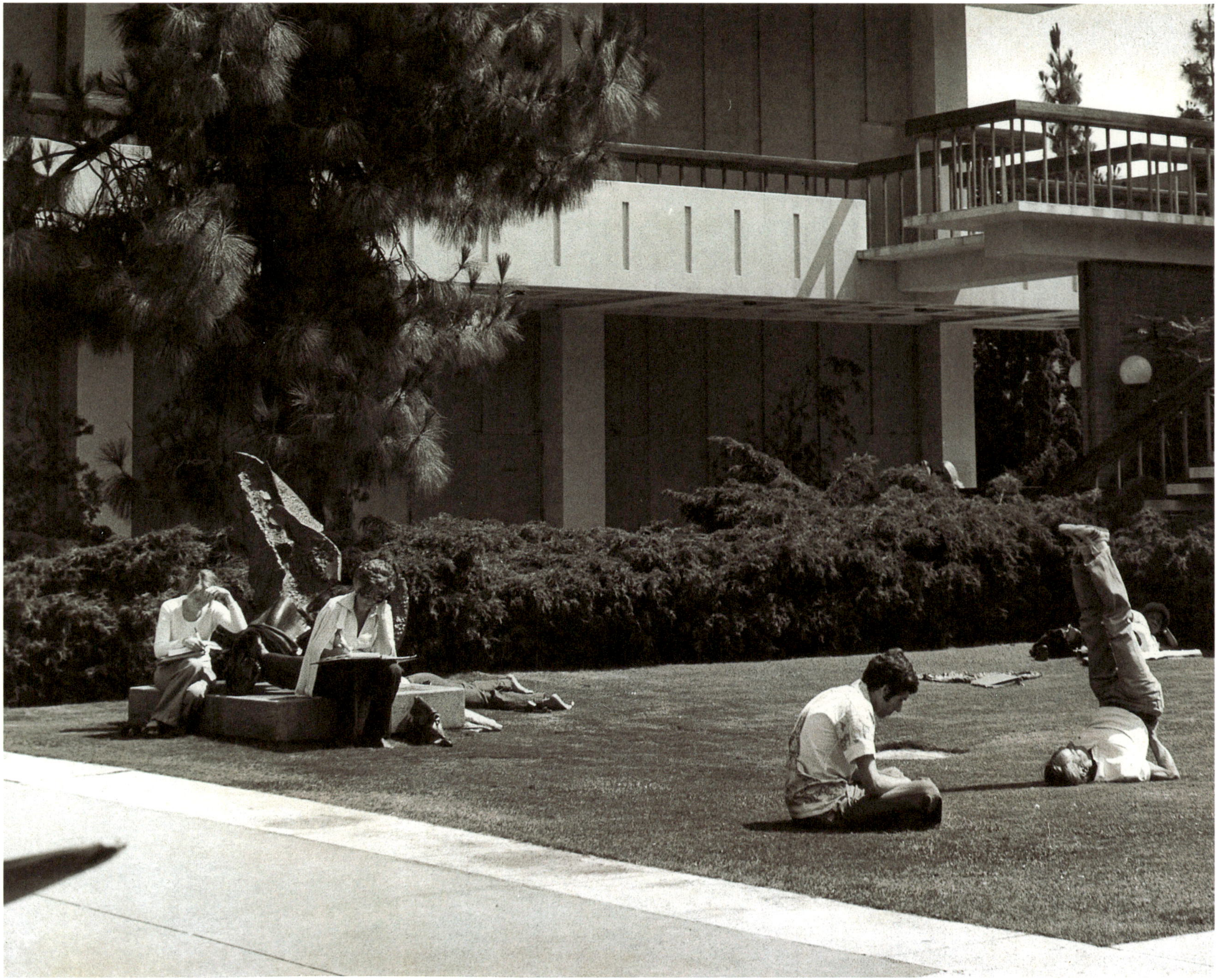

Students with Jack Zajac's Ram Head with Broken Horn, VI *(1963), Franklin D. Murphy Sculpture Garden, ca. 1970s*

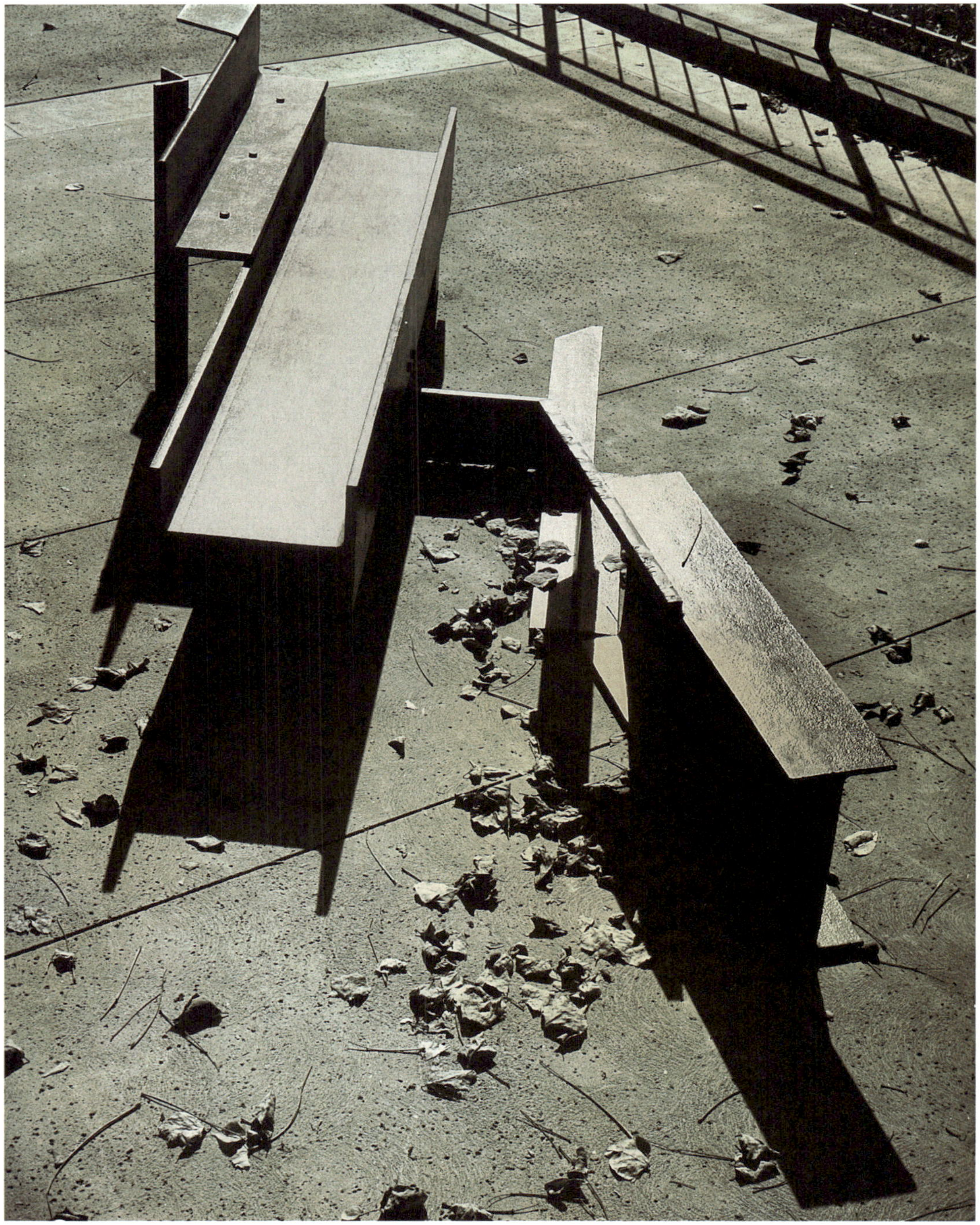

Anthony Caro's Halfway *(1971), Franklin D. Murphy Sculpture Garden, 1973*

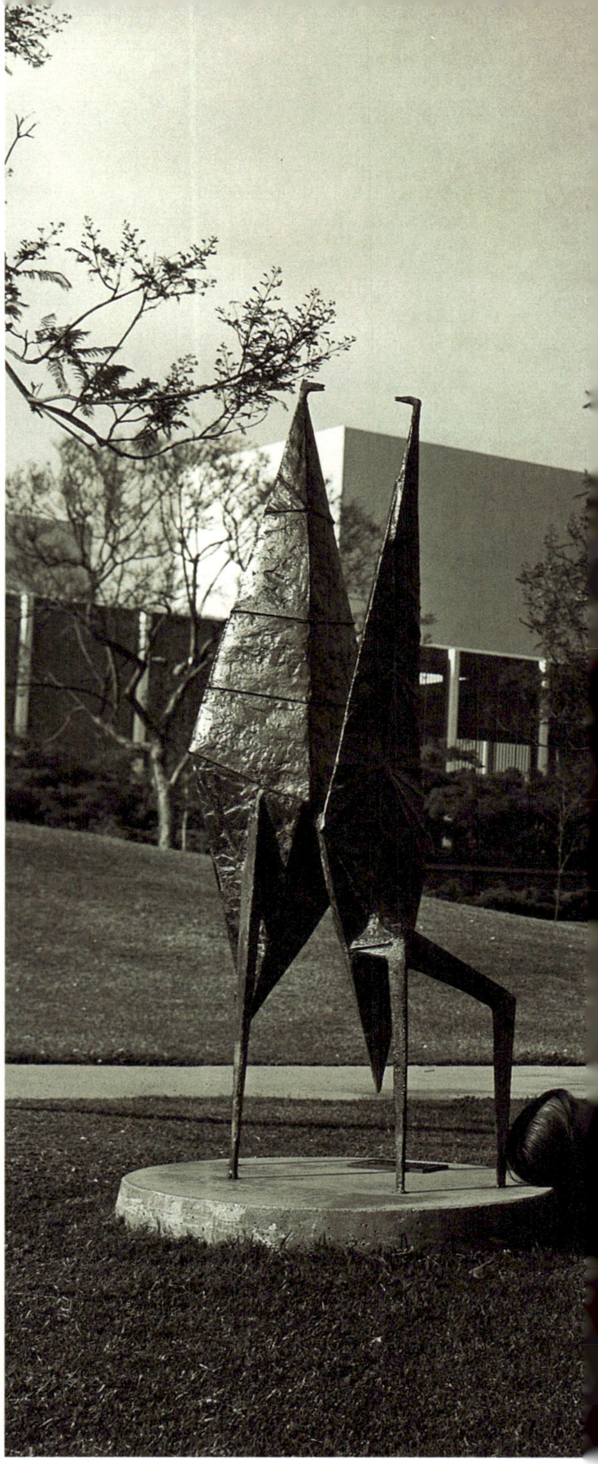

Lynn Chadwick's Encounter VIII *(1957), Franklin D. Murphy Sculpture Garden, ca. 1970s*

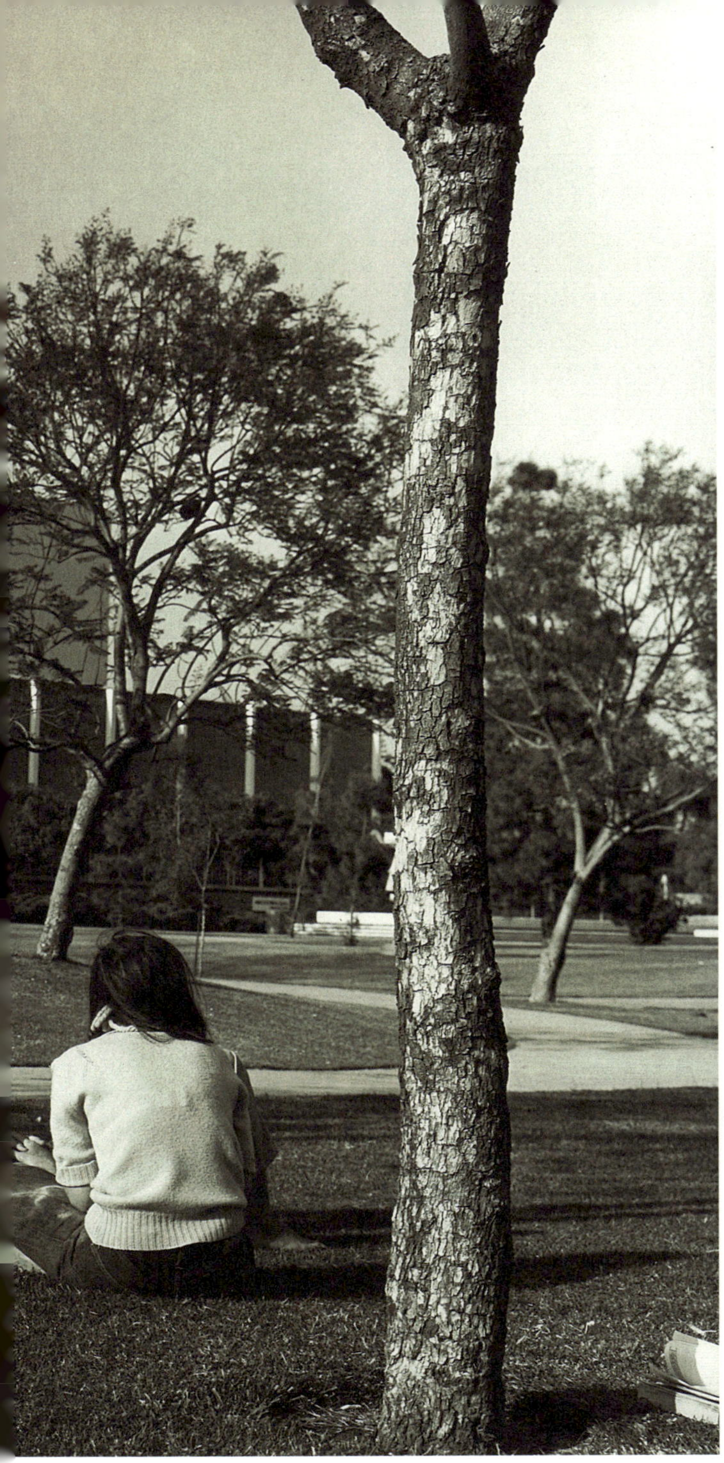

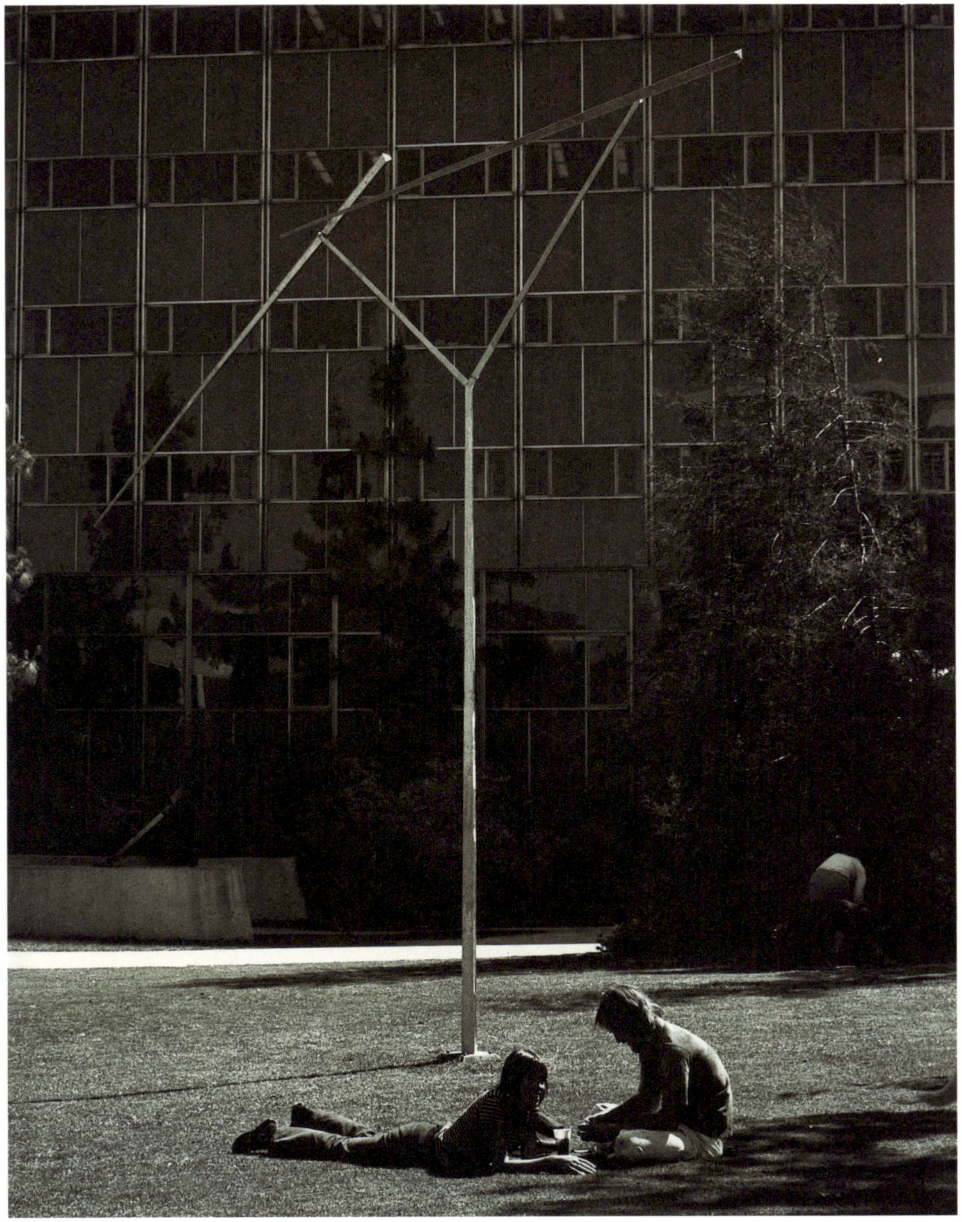

George Rickey's Two Lines Oblique Down (Variation III) *(1970–74), Franklin D. Murphy Sculpture Garden, 1972*

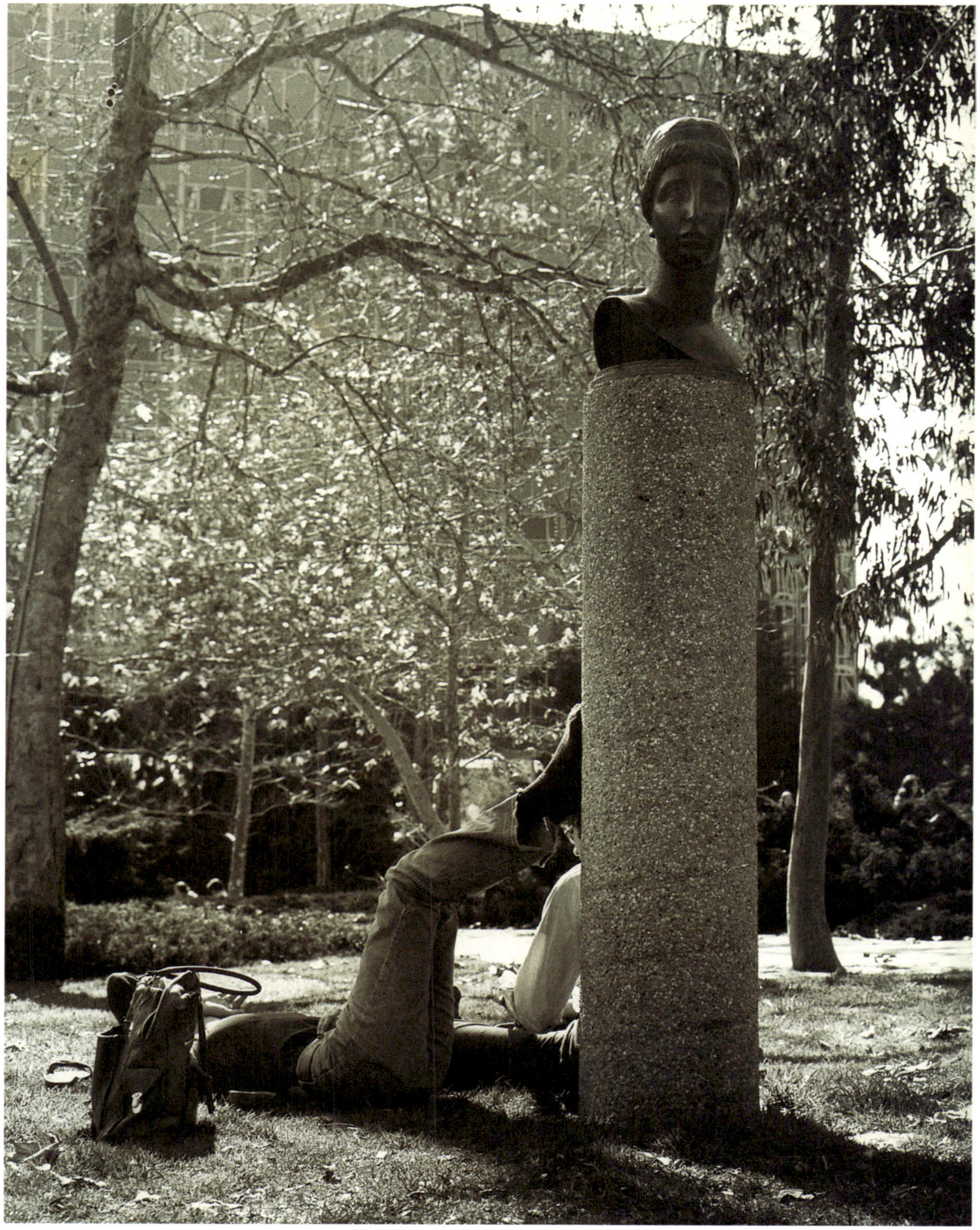

Student with Aristide Maillol's Heroic Head *(1923), Franklin D. Murphy Sculpture Garden, 1974*

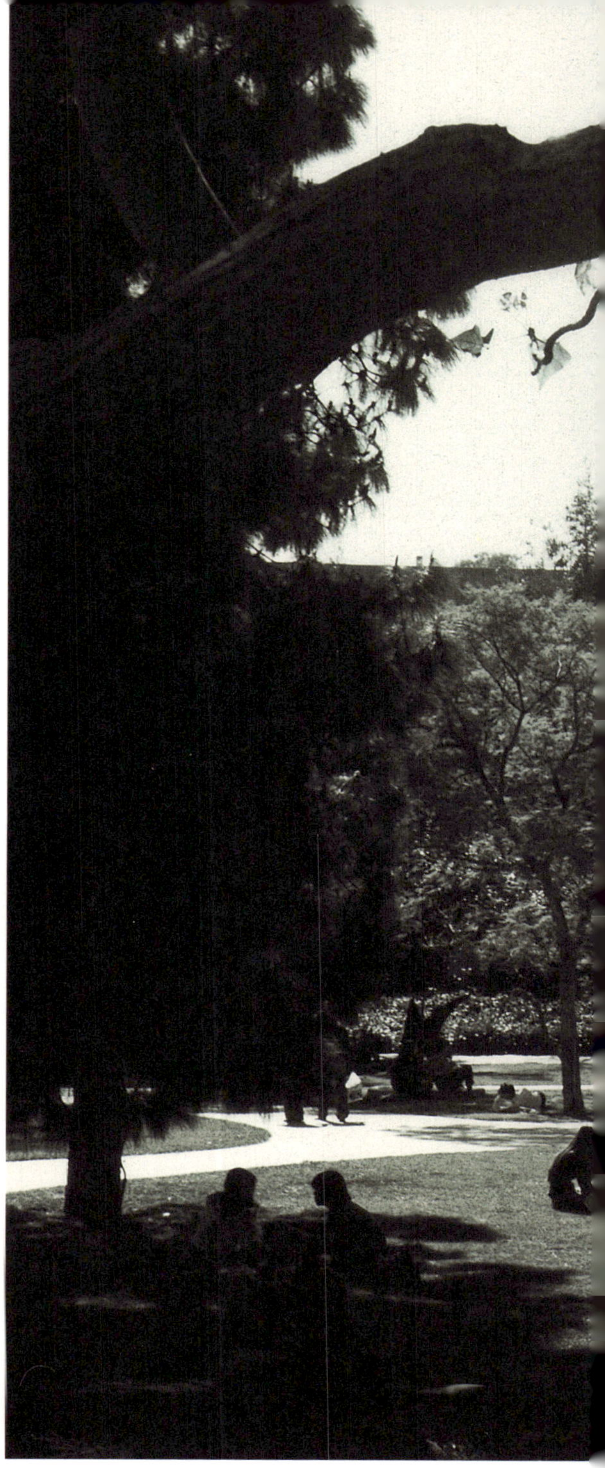

View of the Franklin D. Murphy Sculpture Garden with David Smith's Cubi XX *(1964) and Gerhard Marcks's* Maja *(1941), 1974*

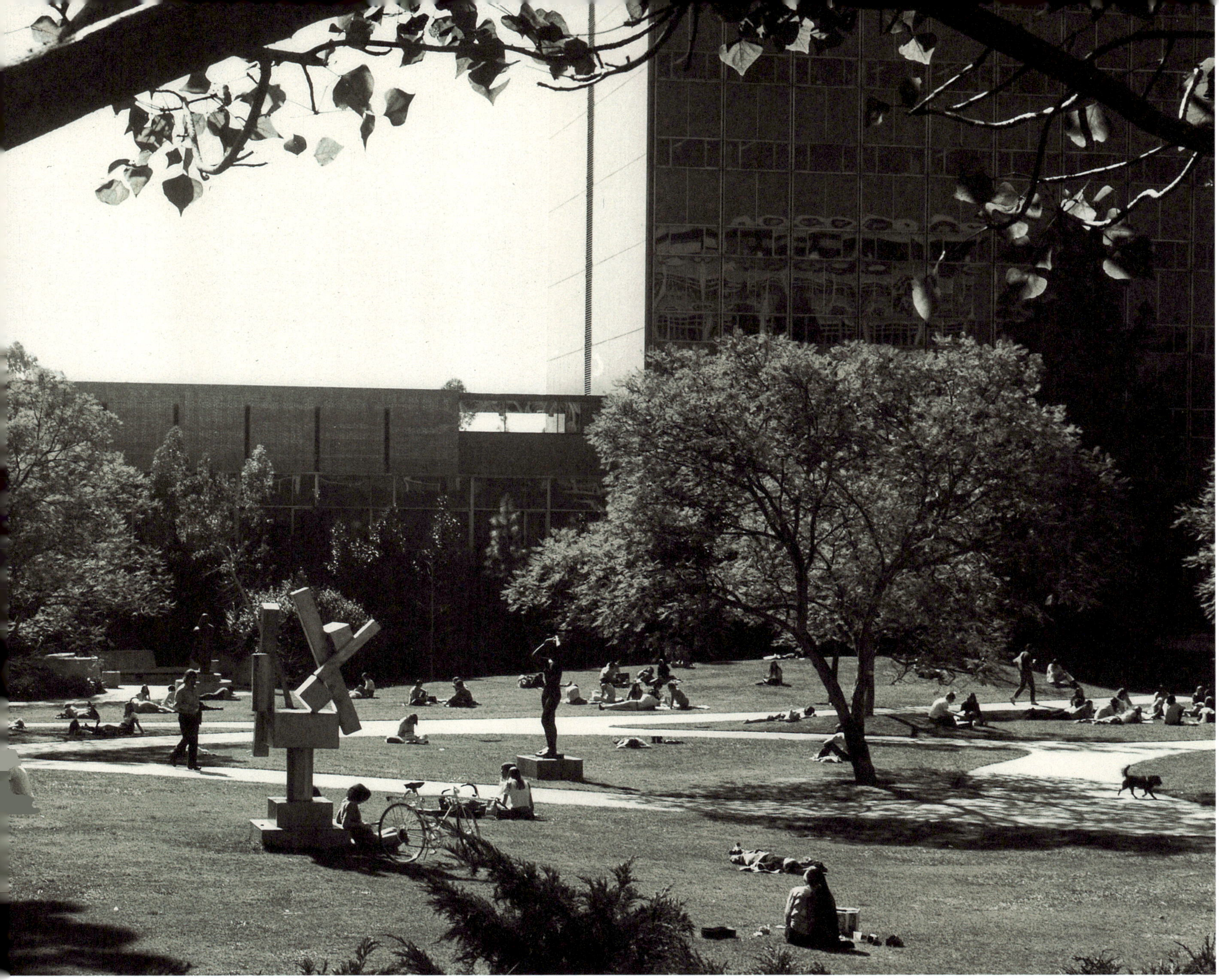

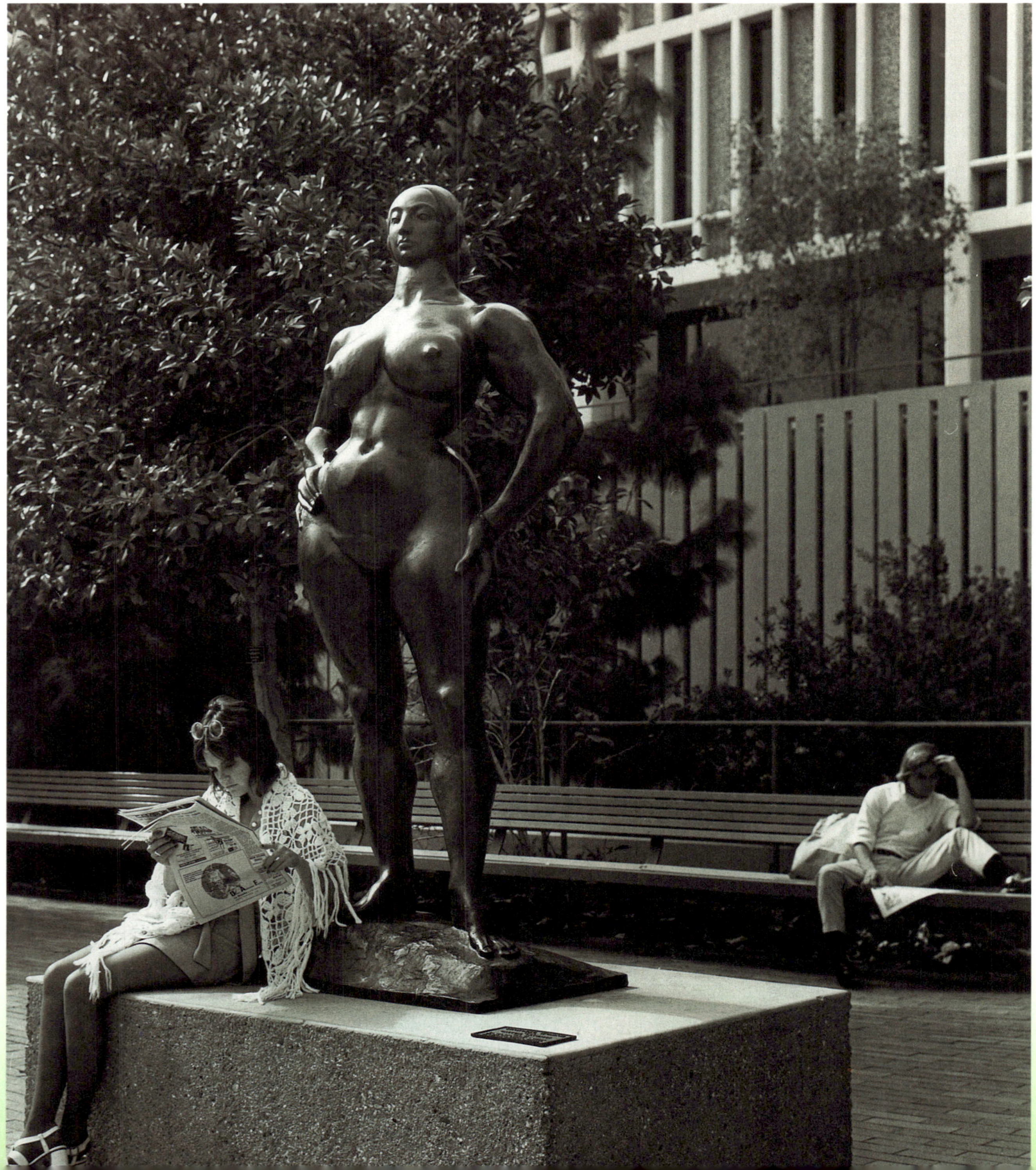

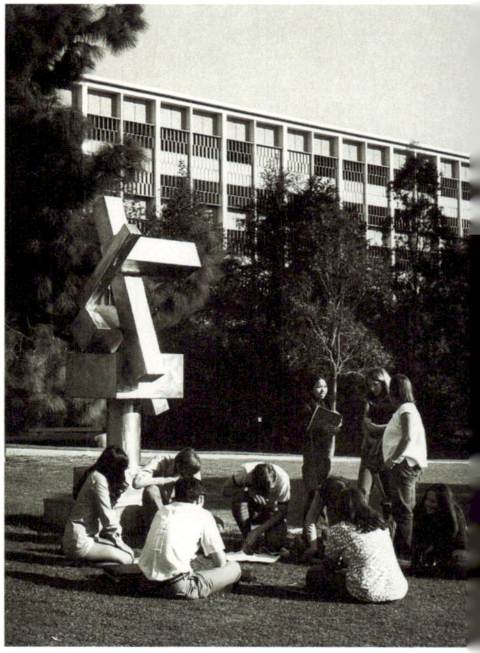

Students with Gaston Lachaise's Standing Woman *(1932), Franklin D. Murphy Sculpture Garden, 1971*

Students with David Smith's Cubi XX *(1964), Franklin D. Murphy Sculpture Garden, 1971*

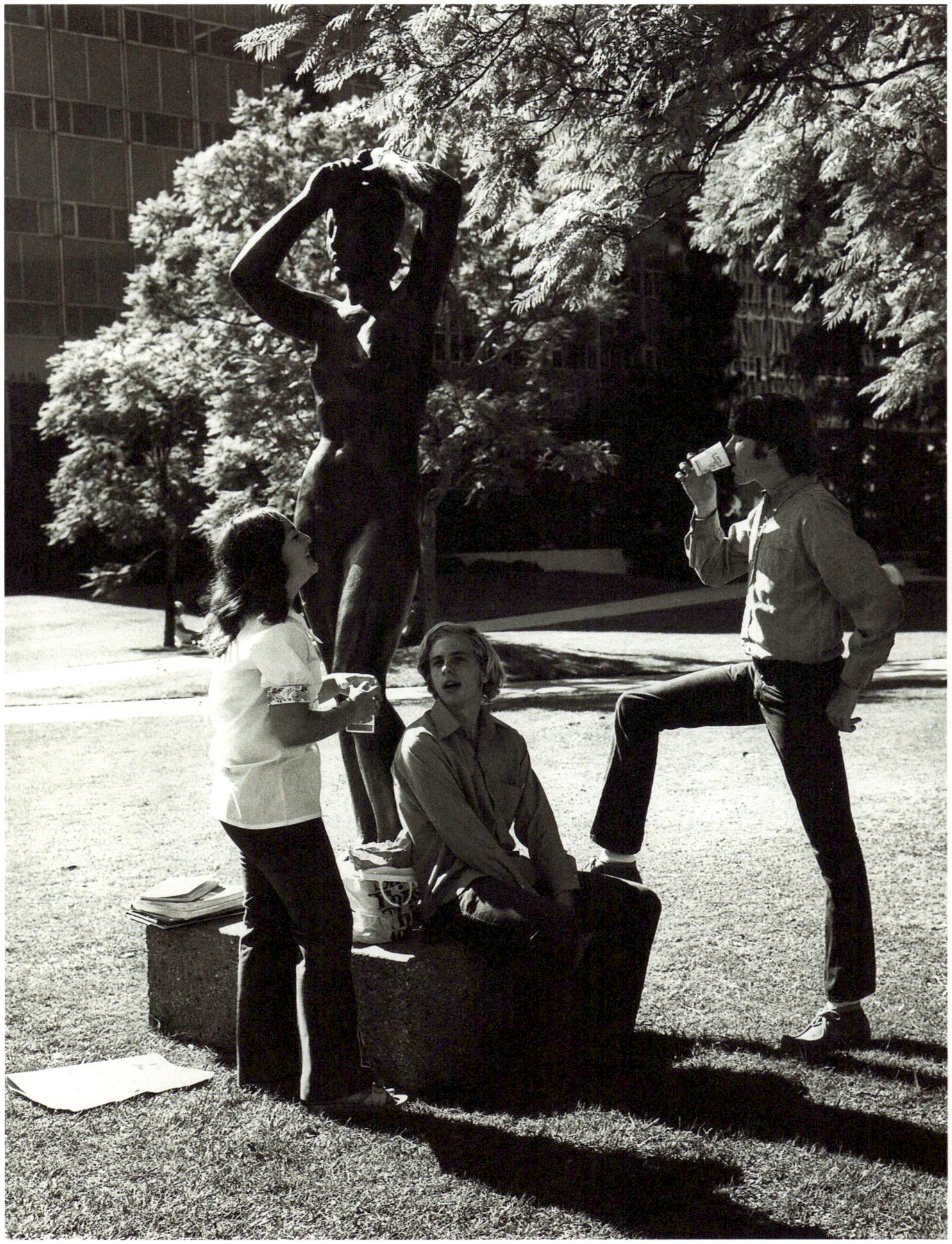

Students with Gerhard Marcks's Maja *(1941),*
Franklin D. Murphy Sculpture Garden, ca. 1970s

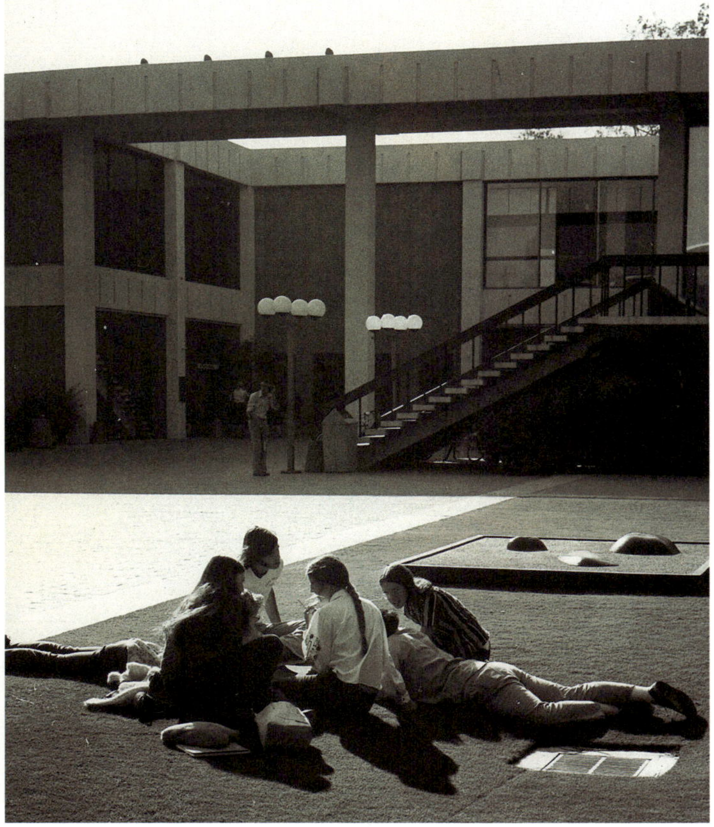

Students with Isamu Noguchi's Garden Elements *(1962),*
Franklin D. Murphy Sculpture Garden, 1971

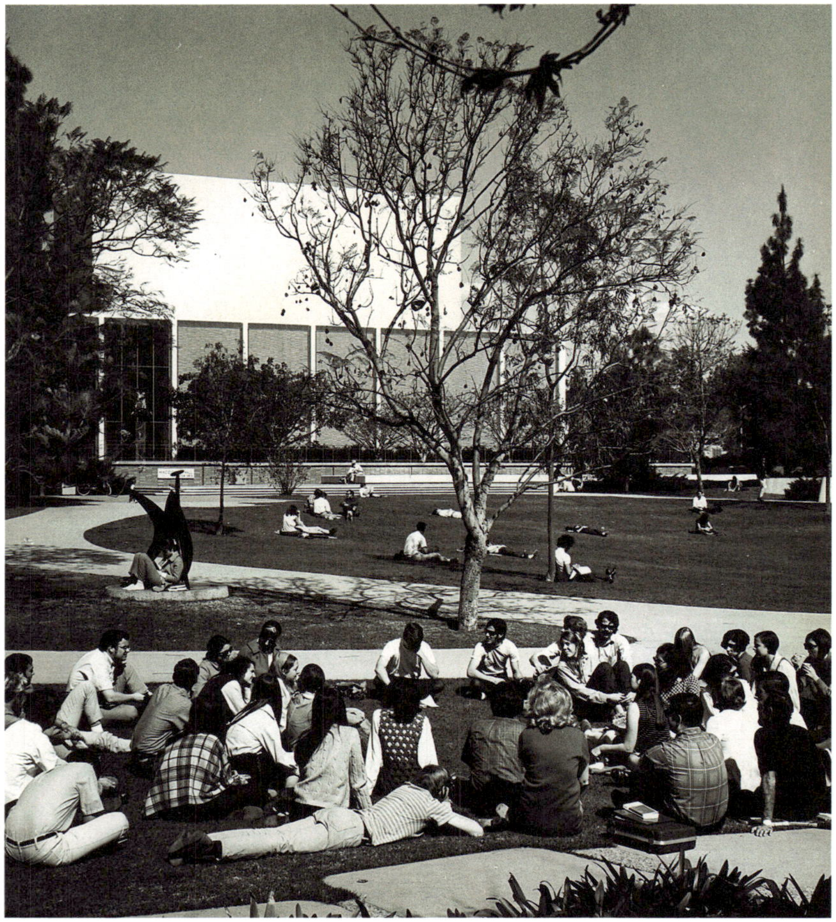

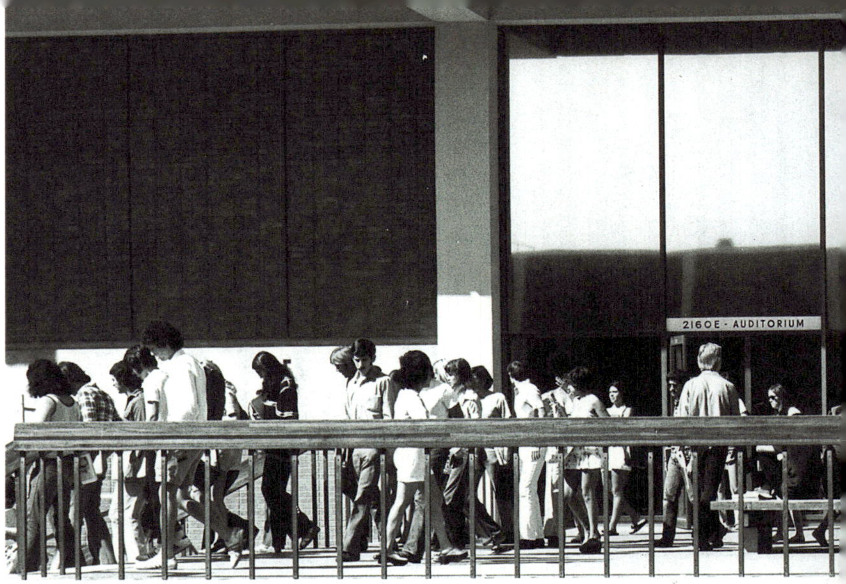

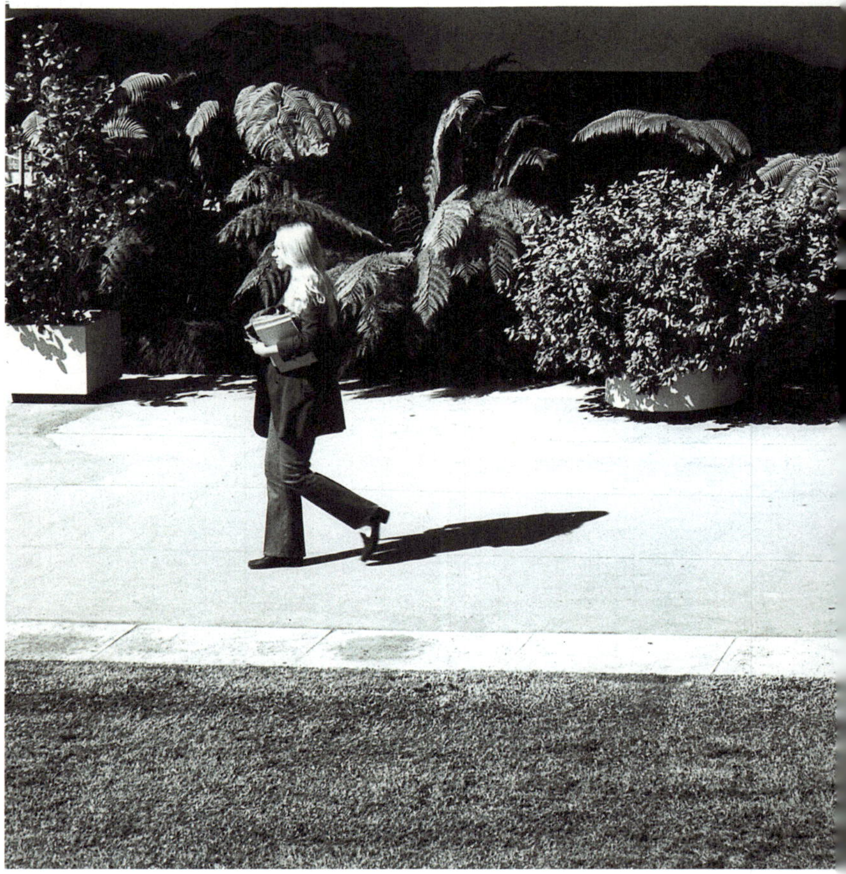

Students in the Franklin D. Murphy Sculpture Garden with Alexander Calder's Button Flower *(1959) in background, February 1970*

Students walking outside Dickson Art Center, UCLA, with Jack Zajac's Ram Head with Broken Horn, VI *(1963) in foreground, 1973*

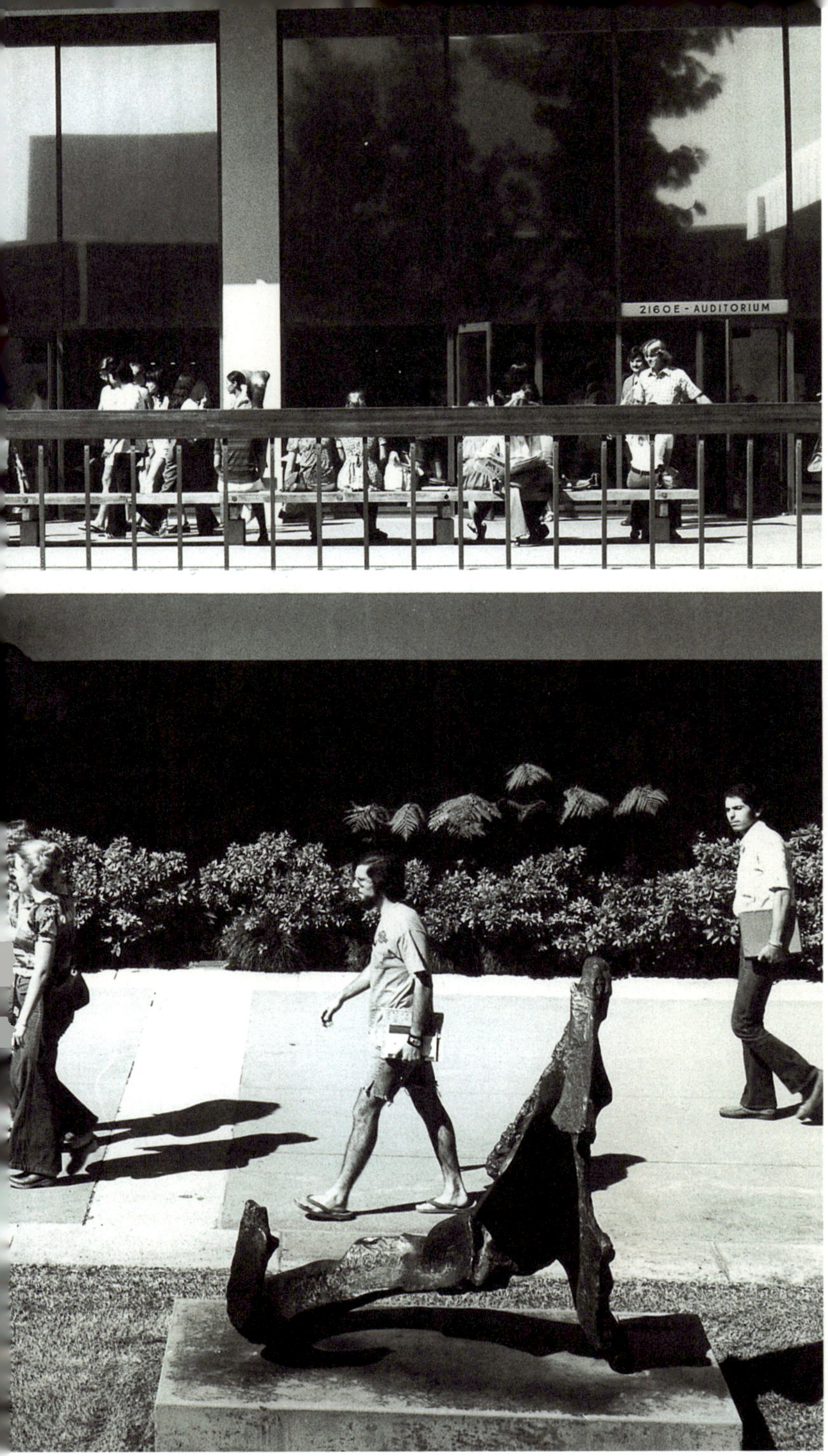

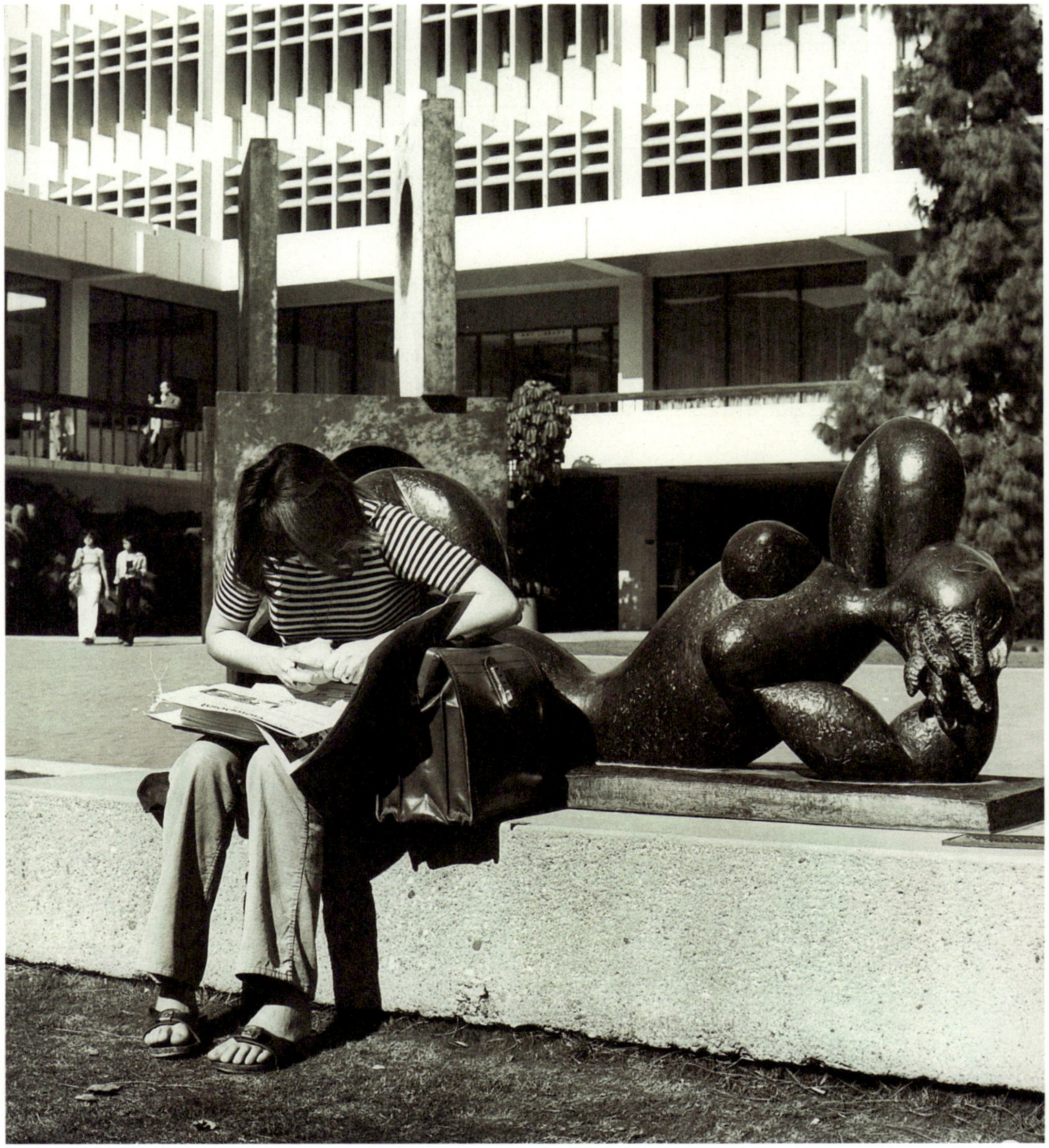

Student with Henri Laurens's Autumn *(1948), Franklin D. Murphy Sculpture Garden, ca. 1970s*

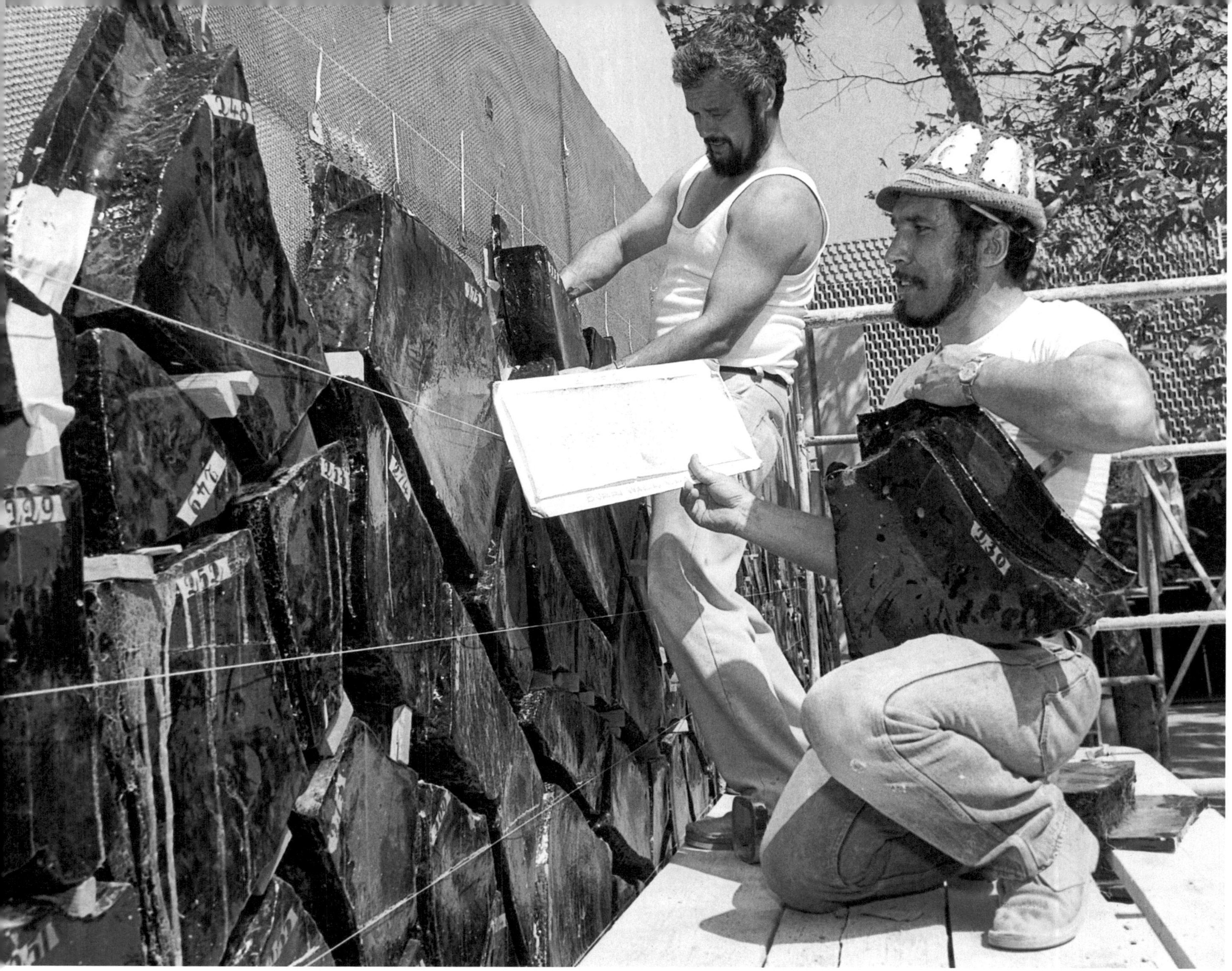

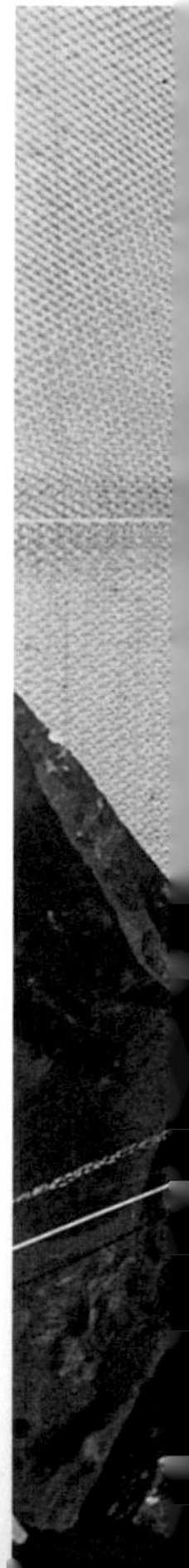

Installation of Alberto Burri's Grande Cretto Nero *(1976–77), Franklin D. Murphy Sculpture Garden, September 9, 1977*

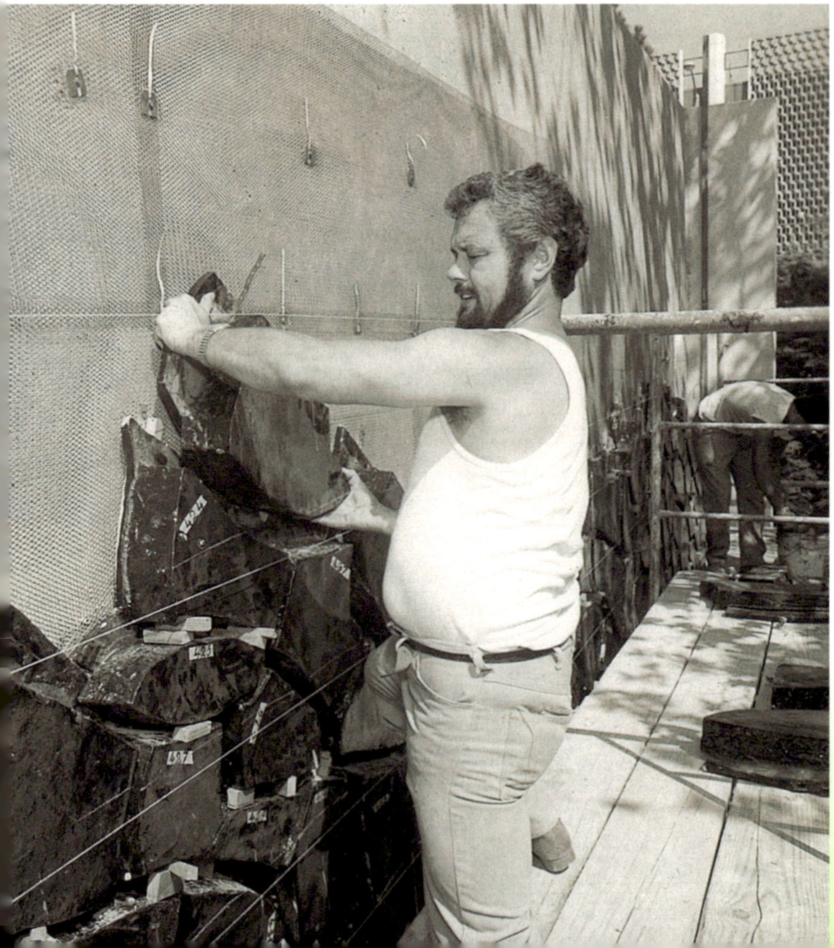

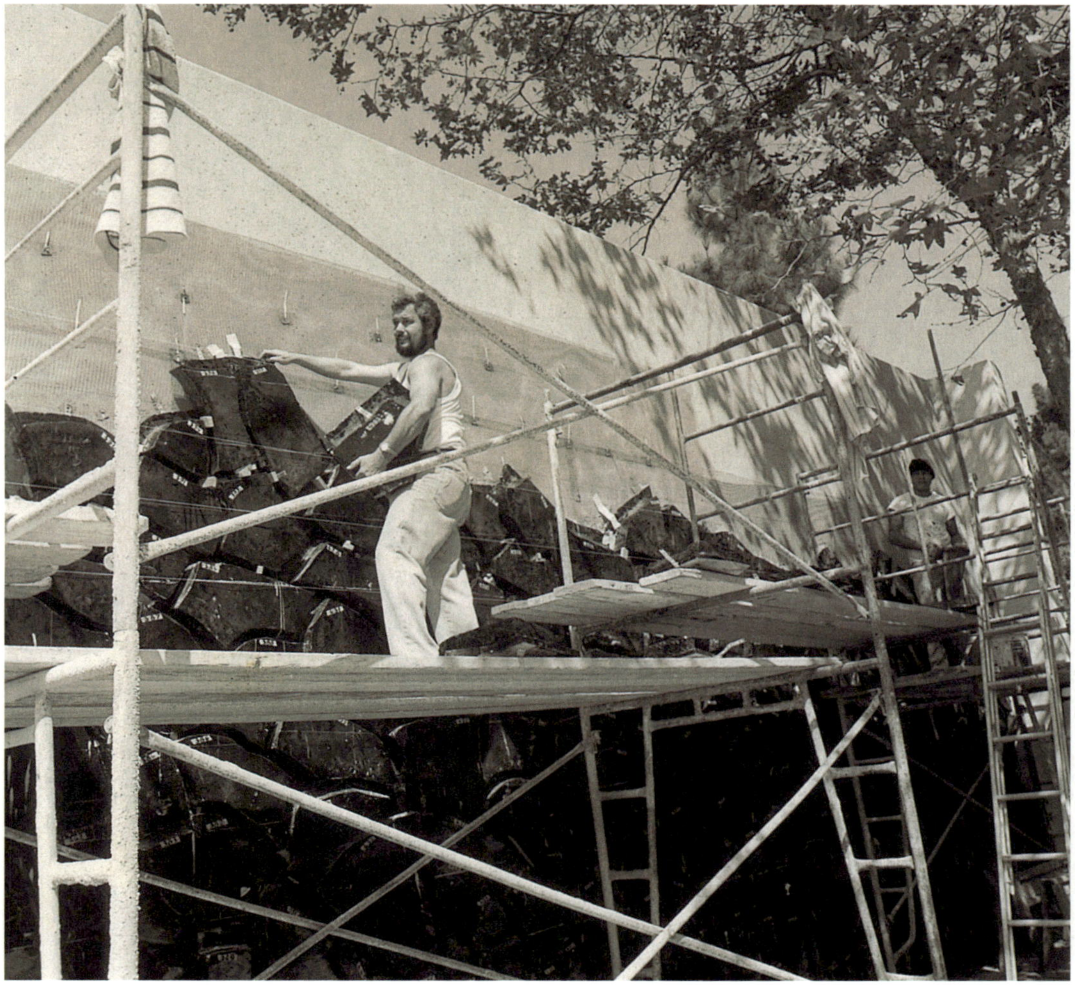

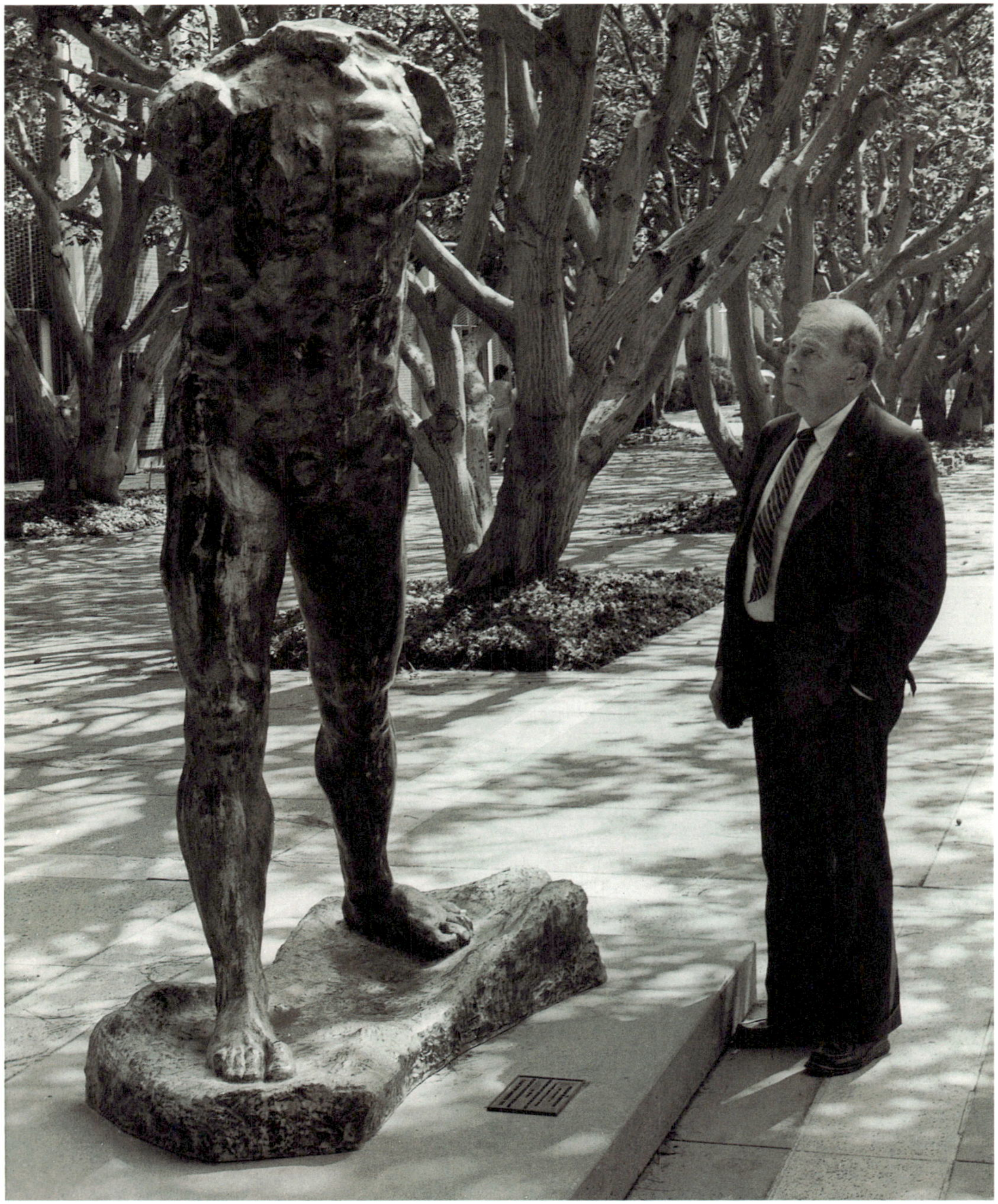

Franklin D. Murphy next to Auguste Rodin's Walking Man *(1878–1907), Franklin D. Murphy Sculpture Garden, ca. 1980s*

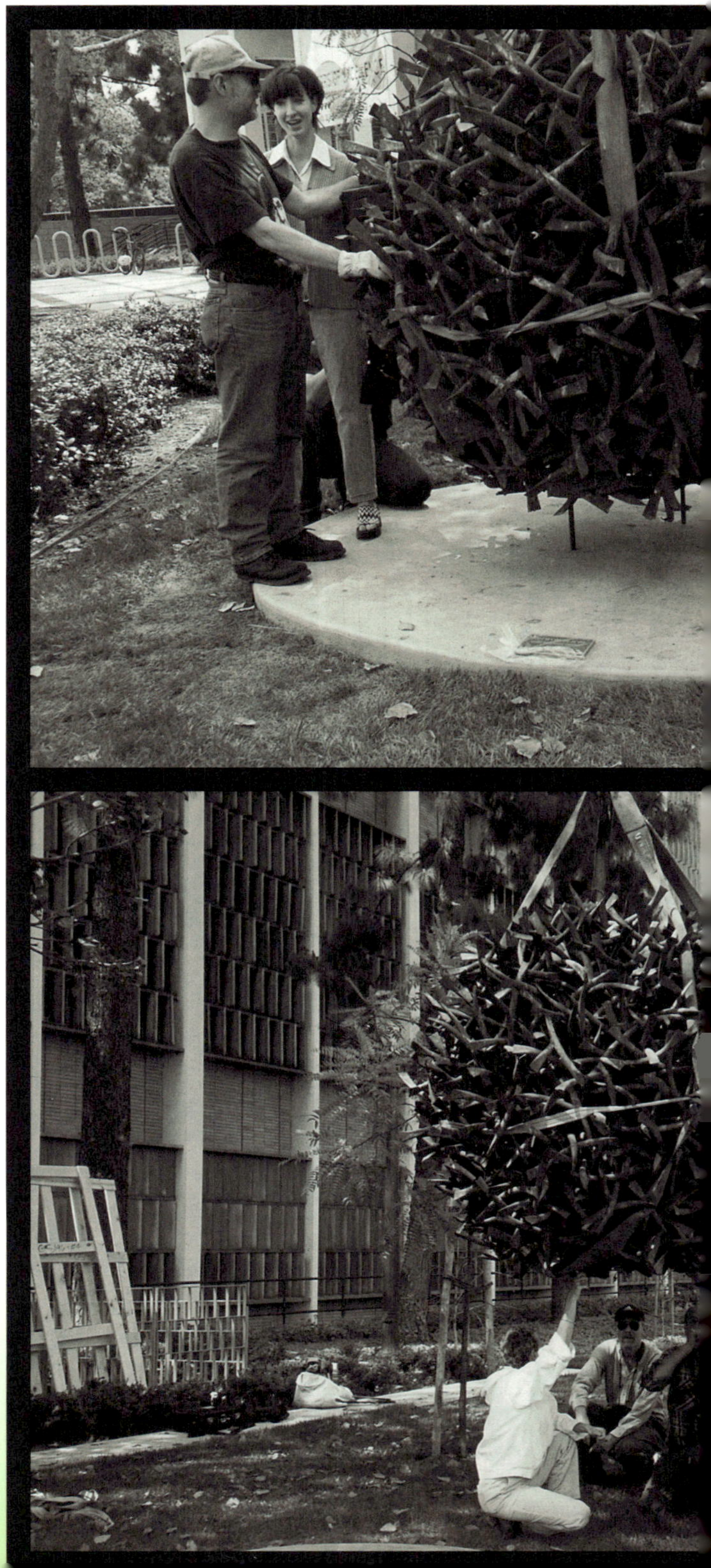

Installation of Claire Falkenstein's Point as a Set No. 25 *(1970), Franklin D. Murphy Sculpture Garden, March 1998*

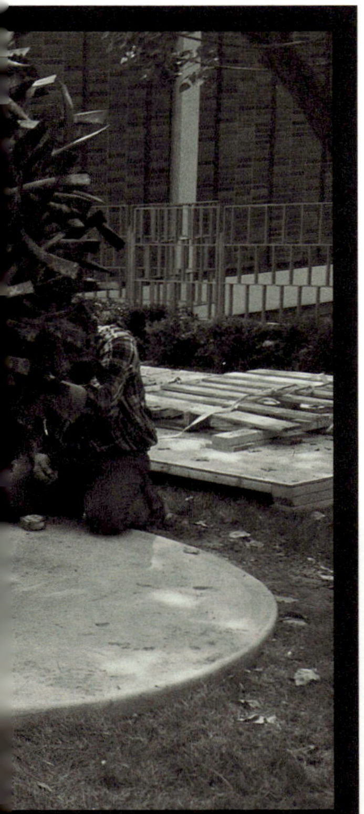

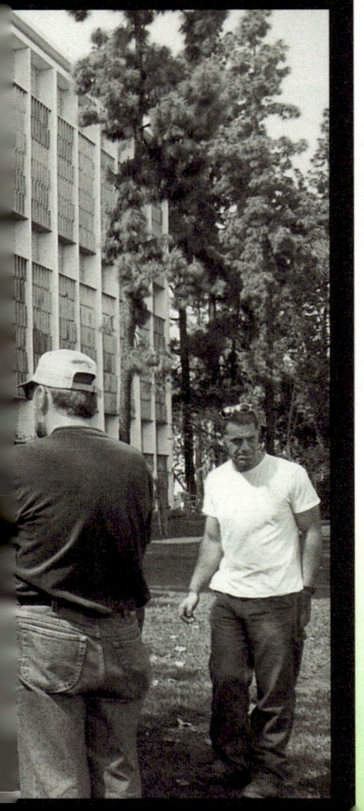

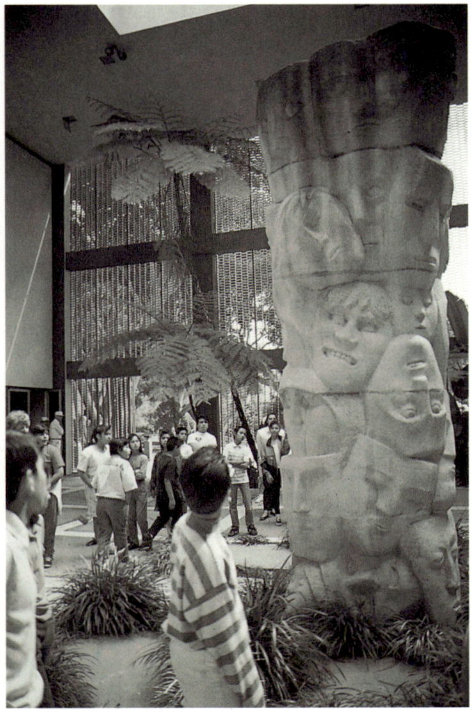

Freud Playhouse Courtyard with Anna Mahler's Tower of Masks *(1961), Franklin D. Murphy Sculpture Garden*

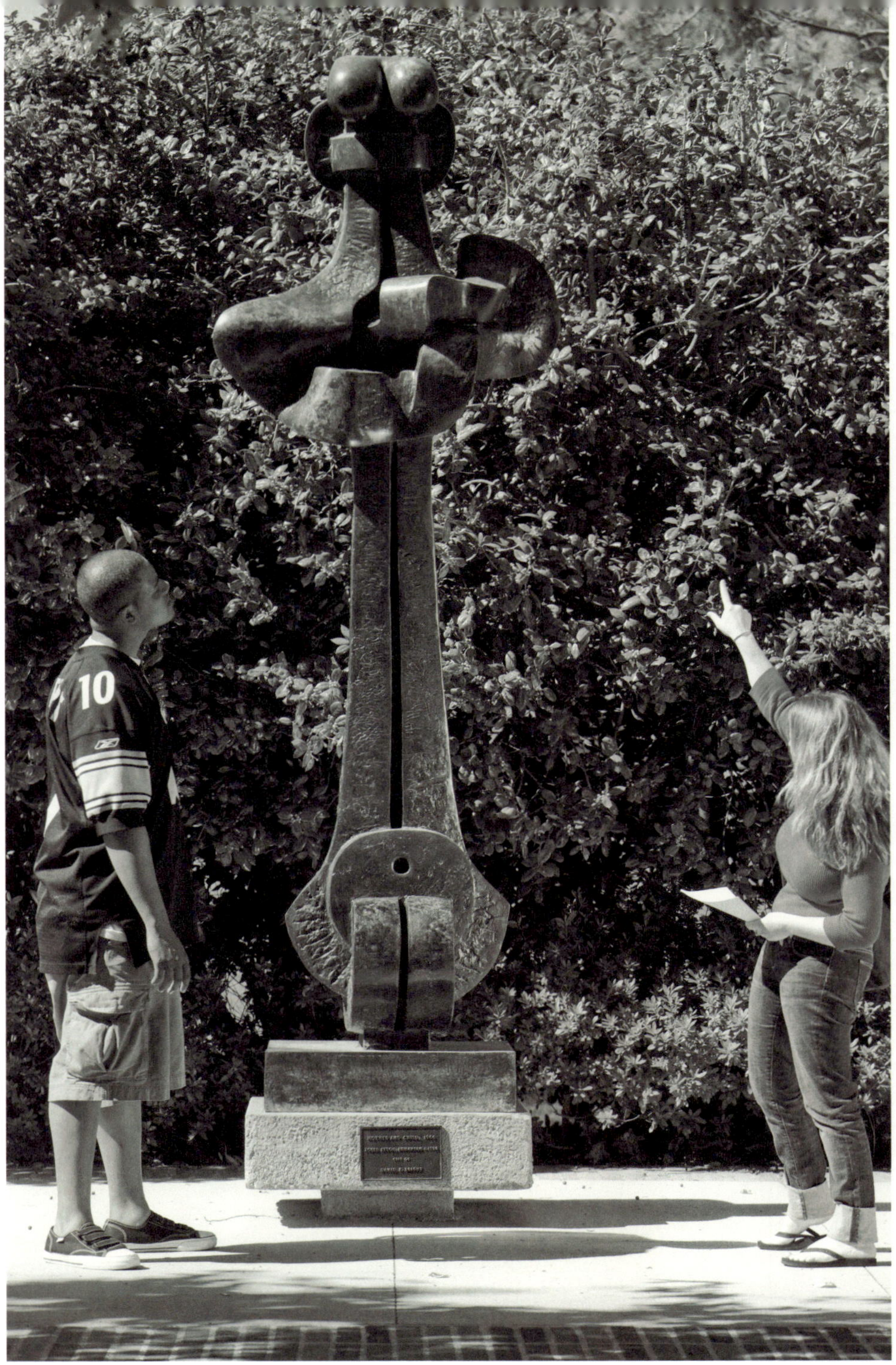

A student docent (right) and a visitor with Sorel Etrog's Mother and Child *(1962–64), Franklin D. Murphy Sculpture Garden, April 2007*

1

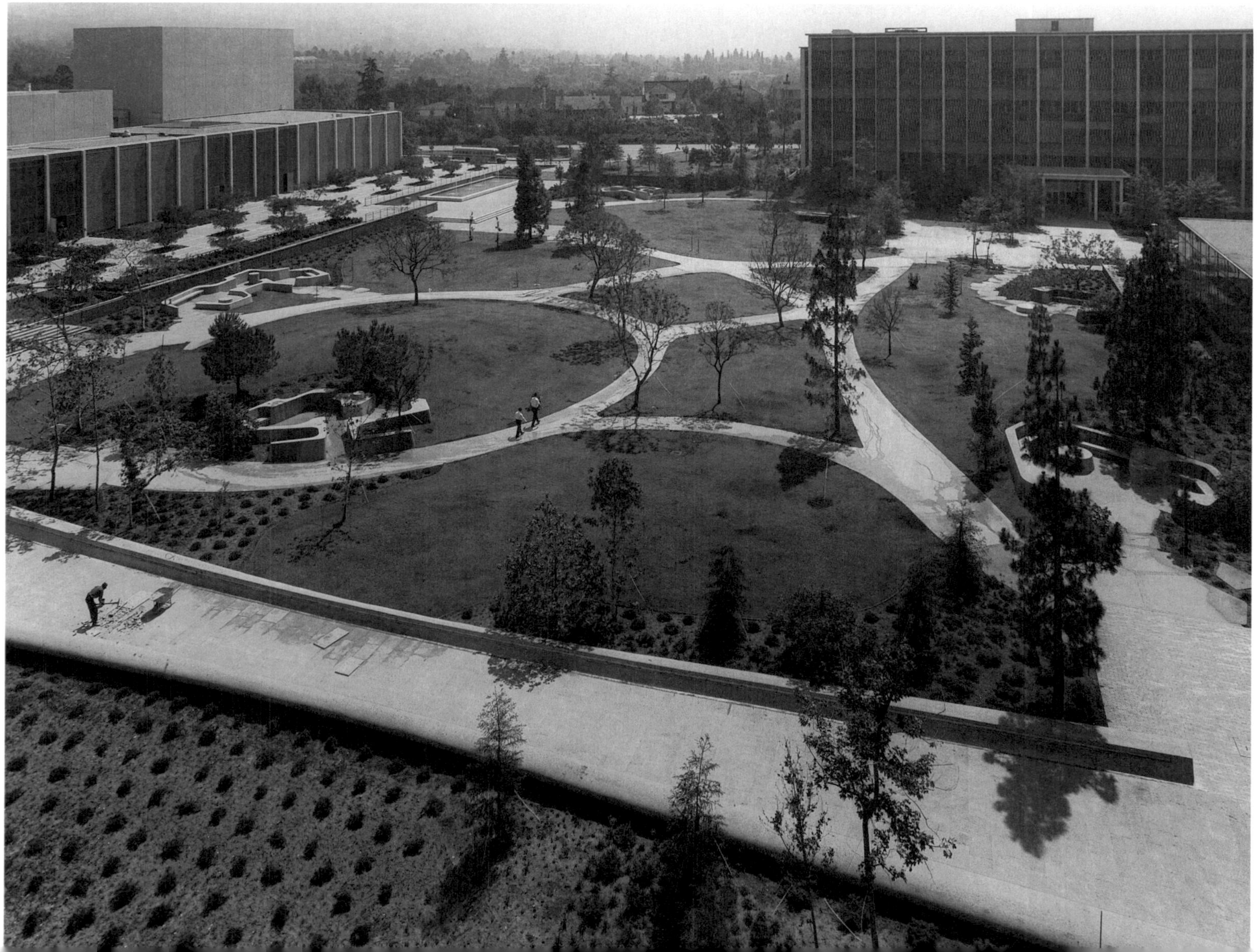

1
View of Franklin D. Murphy Sculpture Garden, June 28, 1965

The Franklin D. Murphy Sculpture Garden was dedicated by UCLA chancellor Franklin D. Murphy on June 11, 1967, before an assembled crowd of some five hundred donors, university and community leaders, faculty, and artists. At that time the garden's collection consisted of thirty-one sculptures, all given by private donors moved to support Murphy's vision to transform a dusty parking lot into "one of the most beautiful sculpture courts in America."[1] The collection would eventually grow to seventy-two works by European and American artists dating from the late nineteenth to the late twentieth century, but both the garden's curatorial focus and its core collection were largely established within a few years of its dedication.

The concept and design of the Murphy Sculpture Garden, one of the most distinguished sculpture gardens of the twentieth century, have their roots in the cultural and artistic milieu of both past and present. For Murphy, the initial model was European, in particular the outdoor sculptures of the great public piazzas and gardens that had so impressed him during his student days.[2] But Murphy's belief in the importance of art as part of everyday life was also allied with a more contemporary American interest in public art. Placement of sculpture outdoors in civic plazas in large urban areas was increasingly popular during the 1960s and 1970s. Outdoor sculpture gardens also became prevalent at American museums during the second half of the century, the earliest and most influential example being the walled garden of the Museum of Modern Art (MoMA) in New York, dating to the original 1939 building and most famously redesigned by Philip Johnson in 1953. The period was marked by the proliferation of rural and urban sculpture parks such as Storm King in New York (established 1960) and the Laumeier Sculpture Park in Saint Louis (established 1976) as well as artist-designed gardens such as Isamu Noguchi's gardens at the Museum of Fine Arts, Houston (commissioned 1978), and at his own museum in Long Island City, New York (begun 1970s). University outdoor sculpture collections, such as that at Princeton University (established 1968) and the site-specific Stuart Collection at the University of California, San Diego (established 1982), also became prevalent throughout the United States, though many of these university collections were not confined to a specific garden but placed throughout the campus, with individual works often commissioned for specific sites.[3]

The Murphy Sculpture Garden incorporates elements from the museum garden, the university sculpture collection, and the sculpture park. Though its location does not have the intensely urban character of an outdoor piazza frequented by a daily working populace, its immediate community is a large urban university with a population the size of a small city. In contrast to a semiprivate museum garden, whose most frequent visitors are those who make it their specific destination, the UCLA garden offers a background to the quotidian lives of students and other members of the university community. With five informal entrances and a variety of paths, it accommodates the passerby and the casual visitor whose primary reasons for visiting are study or relaxation just as readily as it does those who come to view the collection. But unlike many campus-wide sculpture collections, it provides a discrete and purposeful environment designed for the display of works of art.

At UCLA the idea of a campus sculpture garden developed from the timely interest and dedication of the former chancellor, whose remarkable energy and political acumen engaged many members of the campus and greater Los Angeles communities. The development of the garden coincided with an unprecedented period of building on campus just before and during Murphy's tenure as chancellor (1960–68). Enrollment at UCLA was expected to reach 27,500 by 1964, and more than eighteen new buildings, costing more than $100 million, were being erected in previously undeveloped areas of campus.[4] Most of the buildings constructed during this period were built in a modernist style, often uniformly off-white, rather than in the traditional brick of the original 1929 buildings, transforming the appearance of the northern reaches of the UCLA campus from northern Italian Romanesque to Southern California modernism.[5] Somewhat obscured today by mature plants and trees, the clean geometry of the garden's landscape design at first more clearly echoed the modernist lines of the surrounding new buildings by such architects as Welton Beckett and Quincy Jones (FIG. 1). Its semienclosed site and informal but unified components created a sheltered oasis more intimate than the large, formal expanses of lawn befitting the older Romanesque-style structures of the original campus.

CREATING THE MURPHY SCULPTURE GARDEN COLLECTION

Cynthia Burlingham

The sculpture garden also benefited from the university's concurrent commitment to campus-wide landscape design during this period of expansion. A 1959 long-range development plan noted the need for landscaping to preserve UCLA's "campus-like" atmosphere.[6] With characteristic insight, Murphy himself insisted that every new building proposal contain plans for accompanying landscaping. Supervising landscape architect Ralph D. Cornell was an integral part of this process during his lengthy tenure, from 1937 to 1972.[7] Nevertheless, the planning of the sculpture garden presented Cornell with a formidable challenge. With the area of the garden predetermined by the five new buildings surrounding the site, he had to create a plan that not only provided an area that would allow users of the garden to linger but also accommodated pedestrian traffic passing through this busy area of campus. The garden's final tripartite plan included a large plaza and a long allée of trees, providing major thoroughfares that anchored the more pastoral heart of the garden, with its rolling hills and meandering paths (SEE PAGE 27). Perhaps most challenging, the design had to accommodate a growing collection of sculptures not yet selected. Although he was able to finance the project's setting by combining the landscaping budgets of the five surrounding buildings, Murphy had assured university and state officials that no state money would be expended on works of art. And so with characteristic optimism he set about building the garden while also taking responsibility for finding its collection.

Although the gifts were yet to be accumulated, Murphy must have envisioned the kind of sculpture that would populate the garden as the design was being developed, since the collection of the Murphy Sculpture Garden proved to be appropriate to the concept of its landscape design, which was finished before the vast majority of the works were acquired (SEE FIG. 1).[8] As we can see today, both the figurative and abstract sculptures of the garden collection are generally human-scale, neither confrontational nor deliberately imposing. The character of the collection was determined by Murphy's vision of art as an extension of daily life on campus, and how it would offer "a balance between the creativity of nature and the creativity of man."[9] Guided by this classical humanistic inspiration, the collection that Murphy assembled is, as critic Michael Brenson has noted, "defined by a tastefulness and order that is far more French, far more European."[10]

But the European modernism of the collection was also a result of the curatorial vision of UCLA Art Galleries director Frederick S. Wight and his ambitious exhibition program, which directly resulted in many of the garden's most significant acquisitions. In a December 20, 1953, article in the *Los Angeles Times*, Wight noted: "[The UCLA Art Galleries] are dedicated to the principle that students must come in direct contact with the best original works of art, and are open to the community [which in turn] supports the university through its interest and constructive help. . . . There will be an effort to present major exhibitions . . . originating in Los Angeles and circulating through the museums of this country."[11]

The 1950s and 1960s were a heady time for the growth of the arts and culture in Los Angeles. The Los Angeles County Museum of Art (LACMA) was established as a separate entity from the Los Angeles County Museum of History, Science, and Art in 1961, and in 1965 the encyclopedic art museum moved to its current Wilshire Boulevard location. In 1967 LACMA initiated a campaign to raise acquisition funds equal to the $12 million that had funded the new building.[12] The Pasadena Art Museum, founded in 1922 as the Pasadena Art Institute, had assembled a significant collection of works by California and other contemporary artists and mounted extraordinary exhibitions of contemporary art, in 1964 commissioning a new building that would open in 1969. In addition, the new downtown Music Center would open the first of its three performing arts buildings, the Dorothy Chandler Pavilion, in 1965.

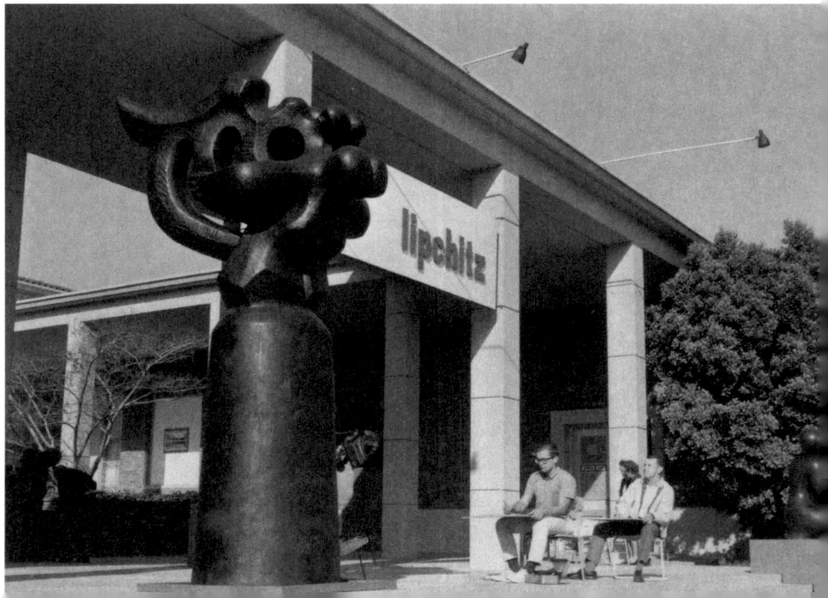

Named head of the LACMA building fund in 1961, shortly after he became chancellor, Franklin Murphy was intimately involved with that museum as well as with virtually every other cultural organization in the city. He developed close relationships with major art collectors and other members of the cultural elite who were determined to put Los Angeles at the forefront of the cultural landscape. These leaders included Howard Ahmanson, Anna Bing Arnold, Sidney and Frances Brody, Edward Carter, Norman and Dorothy Buffum Chandler, and Norton Simon.[13] As chairman of the Kress Foundation (from 1963) and trustee of the National Gallery of Art (from 1964), Murphy also played a prominent role in the national arts scene, a circumstance that would prove advantageous for Los Angeles institutions.[14]

The UCLA Art Galleries' exhibitions of European and American modern and contemporary art occupied a prominent place in the burgeoning Los Angeles art scene of the 1950s and 1960s. Frederick Wight, who served as director from 1953 to 1973, was an artist and museum professional originally trained at Harvard University's Fogg Art Museum. As associate director of the Institute of Contemporary Art in Boston from 1947 to 1953, he organized major exhibitions of work by architects such as Walter Gropius, Louis Sullivan, and Le Corbusier.[15] Hired at UCLA in 1953 as both gallery director and a member of the art department faculty, Wight made his reputation at the university by organizing large-scale exhibitions and retrospectives of modern artists, at first primarily painters, including Charles Sheeler (1954), Morris Graves (1956), Hans Hofmann (1957), Arthur Dove (1959), and Stuart Davis (1965).[16] Between 1963 and his retirement in 1973 Wight organized several retrospectives focusing on modern and contemporary sculptors—among them Jacques Lipchitz (1963), Henri Matisse (1966), Alexander Archipenko (1967), Jean Arp (1968), Gerhard Marcks (1969), and George Rickey (1971)—which resulted in acquisitions for the Murphy Sculpture Garden. Coorganized with or traveling to major museum venues around the country, these exhibitions established a national reputation for the UCLA Art Galleries during these early years.[17] In the words of his successor Gerald Nordland, "[Wight] did things America had to know about, and he did them in Los Angeles."[18] The galleries were conceived of primarily as a *Kunsthalle*, a museum whose programming would be devoted primarily to temporary exhibitions. Dedication to this program precluded the development of an extensive permanent collection of modern and contemporary

3

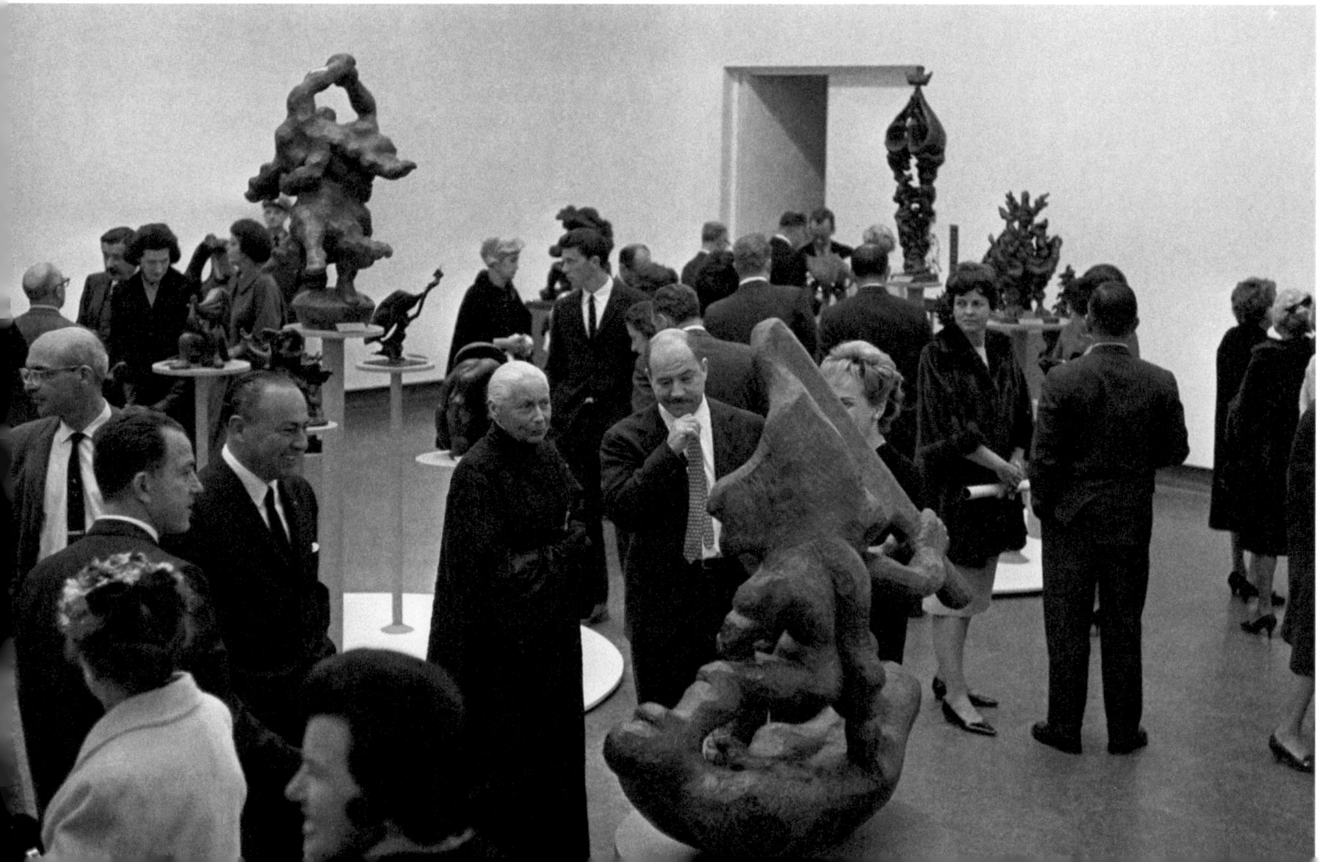

2
View of Lipchitz exhibition and Song of the Vowels *(1931–32) at UCLA Art Galleries, 1963*

3
Opening of Jacques Lipchitz retrospective, March 1963

paintings.[19] The sculpture retrospectives organized by Wight would, however, help create a new permanent collection for UCLA in the form of an outdoor sculpture garden.

As noted, there were few precedents for outdoor collections of modern and contemporary sculpture at museums or university campuses when the north campus area was developed in the 1960s, although similar collections were being developed during the same period. Obviously one major precedent was MoMA's garden, which was populated with a number of works that would also be acquired for the Murphy Garden, such as Henri Matisse's Backs and Gaston Lachaise's *Standing Woman*. In addition, the two gardens would include works by a number of the same artists, among them Alexander Calder, Anthony Caro, Jacques Lipchitz, Aristide Maillol, Joan Miró, Henry Moore, Auguste Rodin, and David Smith. This major modern sculpture collection must have been an important and specific model for Wight and Murphy, who noted that UCLA's garden was comparable only to MoMA's but made a point of adding that there was a difference between a walled and guarded museum and "a place where people lived."[20] The most comparable university outdoor sculpture collection, begun in 1968, just after the Murphy Sculpture Garden, was Princeton's Putnam Collection of Sculpture. The works were selected in 1969 and 1970 by a committee of Princeton alumni, including MoMA director Alfred H. Barr and Metropolitan Museum of Art director Philippe de Montebello. Both the Princeton and UCLA gardens feature works by Calder, Lachaise, Lipchitz, Moore, Noguchi, Rickey, and Smith. Lipchitz's *Song of the Vowels*, the first work acquired for the Murphy Sculpture Garden, was also one of the first works installed on the Princeton campus.[21] The design of the Murphy Sculpture Garden also just preceded that of the Hirshhorn Museum and Sculpture Garden, conceived in 1966–67, though not installed until 1974. The Hirshhorn's collection, drawn from Joseph Hirshhorn's private holdings, includes sculptures by many of the same artists whose works were acquired early on for the Murphy Garden, notably Alexander Archipenko, Jean Arp, Émile-Antoine Bourdelle, Alexander Calder, Barbara Hepworth, Richard Hunt, Gaston Lachaise, Henri Laurens, Jacques Lipchitz, Aristide Maillol, Gerhard Marcks, Henri Matisse, Henry Moore, Auguste Rodin, and David Smith.

The first acquisition for the Murphy Sculpture Garden predated its dedication by several years but established the tenor of the collection.[22] Lipchitz's monumental *Song of the Vowels* of 1931–32 was part of a series of sculpted works that the artist called *transparents*. Designed to endow sculpture with light and air, these later works represented an expansion of his earlier cubist style. *Song of the Vowels* was displayed in front of the art galleries during the 1963 retrospective at UCLA (FIGS. 2, 3), organized by Wight and sponsored by the influential UCLA Art Council.[23] The first bronze cast was originally created as a garden sculpture for the Corbusier-designed home of Madame de Mandrot in Le Pradet, France. Lillian Weiner, president of the UCLA Art Council, approached Murphy about the possible acquisition of *Song of the Vowels* for the proposed sculpture garden.[24] Subsequently the Art Council and University of California regent Norton Simon donated the funds. The leadership of Murphy, together with the curatorial taste of Wight and the support of the UCLA Art Council, had become, and would continue to be, a fortuitous and effective combination.

For Wight, the Lipchitz exhibition represented an opportunity to bring a career survey of the work of a major living sculptor to a new audience in Los Angeles. Lipchitz was in his early seventies at the time, and there had been numerous museum survey exhibitions devoted to his work in Europe as well as in cities throughout the United States, including a retrospective at MoMA in 1954.[25] His work had been shown at the Frank Perls Gallery in Beverly Hills, and he was a favorite of local collectors, but Lipchitz had never been the subject of a major museum exhibition in Los Angeles. Wight often showed an interest in involving artists in their exhibitions. The catalogue text was entirely devoted to Wight's interview with Lipchitz, and the exhibition's title prominently noted that the works were selected by the artist. In another example of the city's close cultural connections, in the same year that the UCLA retrospective took place, the Los Angeles Music Center would commission an even larger Lipchitz sculpture for the plaza facing the Dorothy Chandler Pavilion.

Lipchitz's sculptures would soon become a staple of most museum and university gardens in the country. Another must for an outdoor collection of twentieth-century sculpture was Rodin, and in 1966 Rodin's striding bronze figure, *The Walking Man*, completed in 1907, was given in honor of Murphy (FIG. 4).[26] But the true foundation for the collection was laid four years after the Lipchitz acquisition and shortly before the garden's dedication. In 1967 Murphy was presented with the opportunity to establish a major sculpture collection with the David Bright bequest of eleven important modern and contemporary sculptures. Bright was a member of the UCLA Art Council and had cochaired the building committee for the new Los Angeles County Museum of Art with Murphy. Bright's bequest originally had provided UCLA with 25 percent of his important holdings of modern and New York school paintings, with the other 75 percent given to the Los Angeles County Museum of Art. Bright's sculpture collection—including works by Arp, Calder, Hepworth, Laurens, Lipchitz, Moore, and Smith, among others—was left to his widow, Dolly Bright. Showing his characteristic talent for strategic improvisation, Murphy asked Dolly Bright if she would consider modifying the agreement so that the sculptures would go to UCLA while she would keep the paintings.[27] This arrangement also furthered the goal of maintaining gallery space for an ambitious changing exhibition program by focusing on a permanent collection of outdoor sculpture rather than dedicating gallery space to a permanent collection of paintings.

The Bright bequest confirmed the collection's modernist aesthetic and its focus on established European and American artists. Notable among the works included in the bequest was Lipchitz's *Bather* (1923–25), which provided an earlier cubist counterpoint to *Song of the Vowels*. Henry Moore's iconic *Two-Piece Reclining Figure, No. 3* (1961) was an indispensable component of any midcentury sculpture garden and would form the historical foundation for later acquisitions of other twentieth-century British sculptors. Calder's *Button Flower*, a unique stabile from 1959, provided a point of departure for additions of abstract sculptures. Arguably the most significant and pioneering work of art acquired through the Bright bequest was David Smith's welded-steel *Cubi XX* (1964). Smith's work represented a turning point in the history of twentieth-century sculpture, and this addition created a dialogue between the garden's historical and contemporary works.

Following the Bright gift, major sculpture acquisitions often came in conjunction with the galleries' exhibition program. Again, most of the retrospective exhibitions and the acquisitions that memorialized them were focused on established European and American modern artists, many, like Lipchitz and Matisse, in the latter stages of their careers or recently deceased. Wight himself noted that he purposely focused the exhibition program on the international scene rather than on showing California artists, since California artists were already the focus of exhibitions at the Los Angeles County Museum of Art and the Pasadena Art Museum.[28] The work of European modernists such as Matisse, Archipenko, Arp, and Marcks was compatible with the garden

4

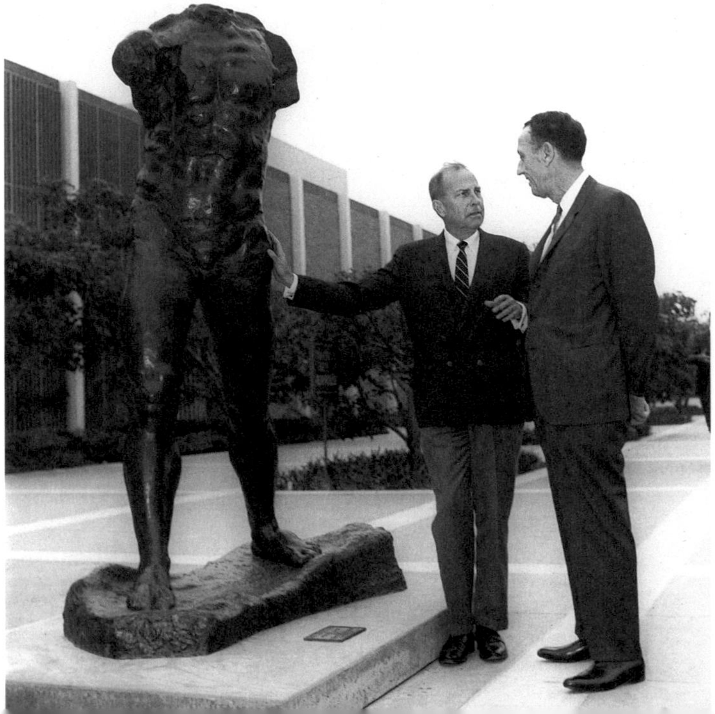

5

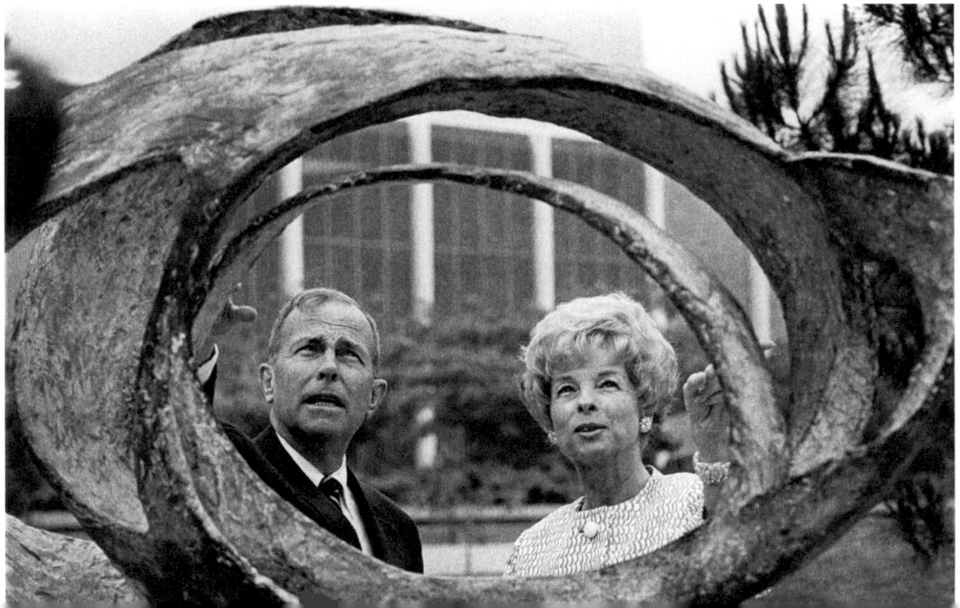

4
Franklin Murphy and Norton Simon with Rodin's Walking Man *(1878–1907)*
5
Franklin Murphy and Dolly Bright with Barbara Hepworth's Oval Form (Trezion) *(1961–63), June 1967*

aesthetic established by the Lipchitz and the Bright gift, as well as the director's and chancellor's interests.

The impressive 1966 Henri Matisse retrospective exhibition was organized by the UCLA Art Galleries and the UCLA Art Council and traveled to the Art Institute of Chicago and the Museum of Fine Arts, Boston. An even more ambitious endeavor than the Lipchitz retrospective, the Matisse exhibition was chosen to open the new Dickson Art Center galleries as a "gala demonstration" of the expansive new role of the arts on campus.[29] Frances Brody (FIG. 6), chair of the UCLA Art Council exhibition committee, and dealer Frank Perls worked closely with Wight on arranging international loans. And with the exhibition the Murphy Garden received all four of Matisse's Backs, a major acquisition that duplicated his largest and most celebrated works in the garden at MoMA and are still among only a handful of those iconic bronzes on public view.[30]

Over the next three years Wight organized three more monographic retrospectives (or "state funerals," as he once called them).[31] Exhibitions of the sculpture of Archipenko (1967) and Arp (1968) resulted in new acquisitions for the garden. In the case of Archipenko, Wight was determined to set right the reputation of an artist who had declined in status in his later career and had no retrospective upon his death in 1964. The *Archipenko Memorial Retrospective* resulted in the acquisition of one of the artist's late works, *Queen of Sheba* (1961).[32] Wight specifically chose one of the late works to make clear that it was the reputation of the late Archipenko that he sought to restore.[33] The Arp exhibition was also instigated in 1966, with Wight calling Thomas Messer, then director of the Guggenheim Museum in New York, immediately after reading of the artist's death to suggest that they jointly organize an exhibition.[34] The Bright bequest had included an Arp bronze, *Hybrid Fruit Called Pagoda*, of 1934. The Arp exhibition in turn led to the donation from the artist's widow of five plaster casts and a large bronze.

Franklin Murphy left UCLA in mid-1968 to assume the post of chairman and chief executive of the Times Mirror Corporation, having served on the company's board since 1965. Charles E. Young became chancellor and continued to support the Murphy Sculpture Garden throughout his twenty-nine-year tenure. But Murphy also remained personally involved with the garden. The Gerhard Marcks retrospective of 1969 resulted in the acquisition of two bronzes, *Maja* (1941) and *Freya* (1950). Murphy was so keen on acquiring a Marcks sculpture that *Freya* was actually acquired in advance of the exhibition.[35] Marcks's modest-scale sculptures of young women represent a continuity of the European tradition of figurative bronze sculptures, with many allies in the garden, such as the bronzes by Matisse, Rodin, and, especially, Maillol.

Wight's exhibition program took somewhat of a detour from these established modern figurative artists during the last couple of years of his tenure as director. Acquisitions of works by younger British sculptors William Tucker and Anthony Caro followed the exhibition *New British Painting and Sculpture* of 1968. The exhibition was organized by the Whitechapel Gallery in London for the UCLA Art Galleries, with Wight contributing an essay to the exhibition catalogue.[36] As noted in the foreword to the catalogue, the idea of the exhibition was "to present a British scene through British eyes," with works by recognized British artists exhibited with those by artists whose work had never been shown in Britain or the United States. Though Caro was already well established, he and Tucker were younger than the sculptors usually featured in Wight's retrospectives. Working in an abstract idiom, they represented a new generation of sculptors succeeding

6

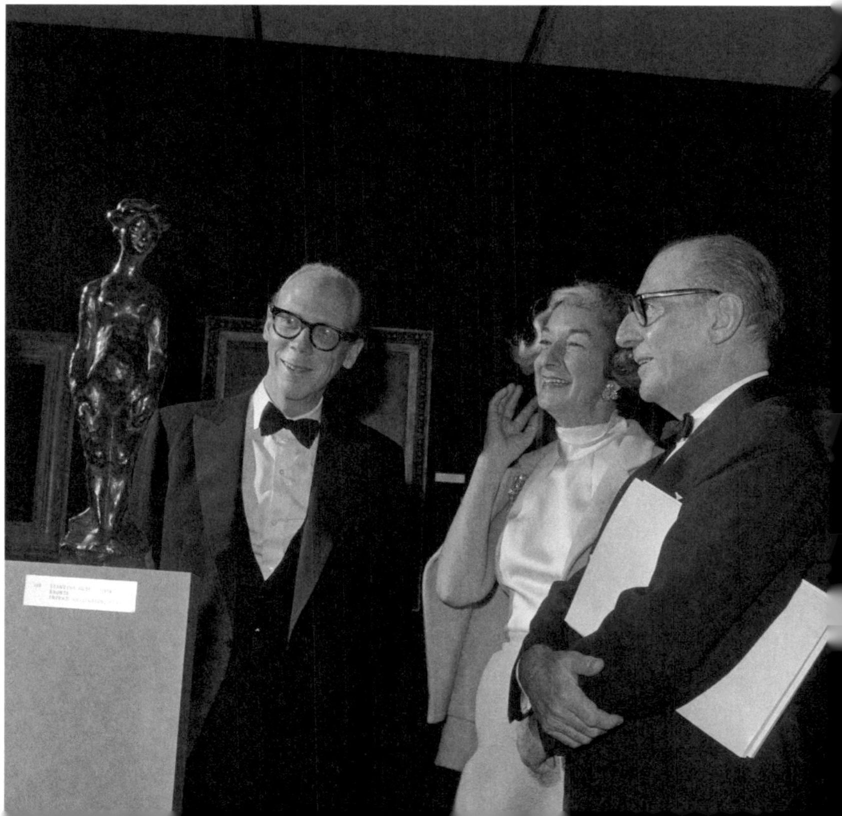

Henry Moore but influenced by the abstract works of David Smith. The relationship of their works to the other sculptures and the garden environment is one that suggests commonality, however, rather than confrontation.[37]

Wight's last monographic retrospective focused on the work of American sculptor George Rickey (FIG. 7). And for the last time as director he "shopped" out of an exhibition, acquiring the large kinetic work *Two Lines Oblique Down (Variation III)* (1970–74).[38] This was Rickey's first retrospective, and as was the case with the Lipchitz exhibition, the works were selected by the artist himself. Wight's notable series of sculpture exhibitions had begun with the established and still-figurative French modernism of Lipchitz and ended with an American artist of a younger generation working with abstract, kinetic forms. Works by both artists would become popular features of sculpture gardens in the United States during the latter half of the twentieth century. Appropriately enough, Wight's last exhibition for the UCLA Art Council was devoted to twentieth-century sculpture from California collections. In the preface to the catalogue, the sponsoring Art Council noted how Wight's vision had "played a vital part in the emergence of the University and Los Angeles as a major center for the arts."[39]

7

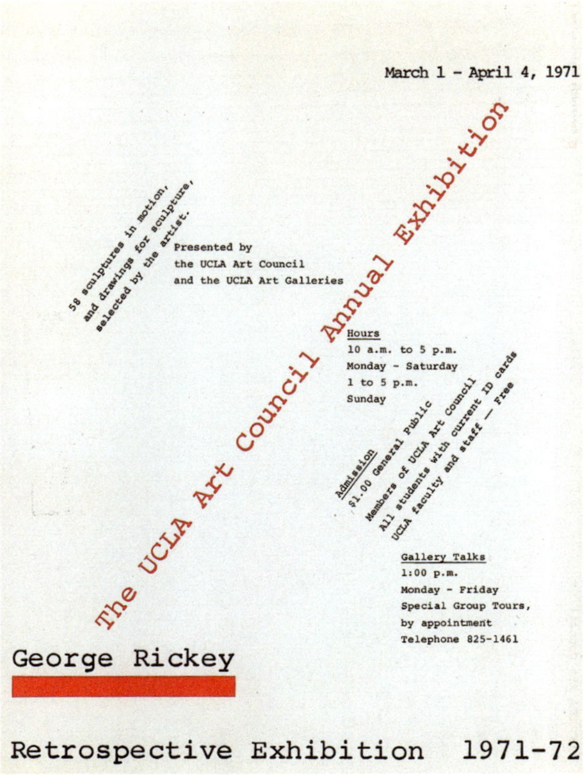

6
Frances Brody (center) with Peter Matisse and Pierre Matisse at opening of Matisse retrospective, January 1966

7
Invitation to opening of George Rickey retrospective, 1971

At the time of Wight's retirement the garden collection comprised fifty-five sculptures. In the years following, director Gerald Nordland acquired a number of important works for the garden, mostly by more contemporary artists but still in keeping with the garden's already-established focus.[40] Notable among these was *Grande Cretto Nero* by Alberto Burri, a gift from the artist at the time of his retrospective in 1977 and the largest work ever made by Burri.[41] Though by far the largest sculpture in the garden, the Burri is relatively unobtrusive due to its discreet placement on a wall along the northern pedestrian walkway. The UCLA Art Council donated a bronze by Joan Miró in 1976, providing a welcoming figure to one of the western entrances. Several other works were acquired by donation in subsequent decades, bringing the total number of works in the collection to seventy-two.[42] The latest acquisition for the Murphy Garden was Deborah Butterfield's *Pensive* (ca. 1997), given with poignant appropriateness by the Marcia Simon Weisman Foundation in memory of Franklin Murphy, who had died in June 1994.

Forty years after its founding, the Murphy Garden remains at the crossroads of campus life. The Dickson Art Center has been re-created by Richard Meier as the Eli and Edythe Broad Art Center, with a new sculpture by Richard Serra in the plaza. The Broad Art Center houses the New Wight Gallery, dedicated to exhibitions of student and faculty work from one of the most important art schools in the country. Historical and contemporary exhibitions are now presented off campus at the Hammer Museum. Though surrounded by change, the garden remarkably has maintained much of the character of its early years. But like the ancient European public spaces that inspired its founder, the Murphy Sculpture Garden still brims with contemporary life. This success is perhaps best explained by an editorial tribute to Franklin Murphy that appeared in the *Los Angeles Times* in June 1994:

> *As the years pass . . . and his memory fades, those who want to know what made his many accomplishments possible should visit the sculpture garden he created at UCLA.... There they may find that the deepest, most fruitful tension in his character was between contemplation and action, the private and the public. The strong, beautiful works in the garden call the viewer inward. But they stand in a public garden and, as his monument, call the viewer outward to a life lived as his was, to the last moment, with splendid and multiplying energy.*[43]

Notes

1 Franklin D. Murphy to Dolly Bright, March 10, 1967, Murphy Sculpture Garden Archives, Hammer Museum.

2 For extensive discussion of the life of Franklin D. Murphy, particularly his years in Los Angeles, see Margaret Leslie Davis, The Culture Broker: Franklin Murphy and the Transformation of Los Angeles, 1960–1994 (Berkeley, Los Angeles, and London: University of California Press, 2007). See also Franklin D. Murphy, "My UCLA Chancellorship: An Utterly Candid View," oral history transcript, interviewed by James V. Mink (Los Angeles: Oral History Program, University of California, 1976). See also Victoria Steele's essay in the present catalogue.

3 For a survey of sculpture gardens in the United States, see Jane McCarthy and Laurily K. Epstein, A Guide to the Sculpture Parks and Gardens of America (New York: Michael Kesend Publishing, 1996).

4 Davis, The Culture Broker, 29, 48, 90.

5 Andrew Hamilton and John B. Jackson, UCLA on the Move during Fifty Golden Years, 1919–1969 ([Los Angeles]: Ward Ritchie Press, [1969]), 144.

6 "Progress Report on the Development Plan for the University of California, April 6, 1959," William G. Young, vice chancellor and chairman of the Committee of Buildings and Campus Development, to Clark Kerr, president, University of California, Franklin D. Murphy Papers, University of California, Los Angeles, 1959. Already in the 1950s Dorothy Chandler, chairman of the Regents Buildings and Grounds Committee, had also lamented the lack of proper landscaping and moved that $50,000 of Regents funds be allocated to acquiring large-specimen trees (see Hamilton and Jackson, UCLA on the Move, 215–16).

7 For more information on Cornell, see Ralph D. Cornell, "Half a Century as a Southern California Landscape Architect," oral history transcript, interviewed by James V. Mink, Enid H. Douglass, and Richard K. Nystrom, 1967 (Los Angeles: Oral History Program, University of California, 1970). Jere Hazlett, campus landscape architect, also oversaw the day-to-day aspects of the landscape design of the campus. For an extended description of the development of the landscape plan for the Murphy Garden, see Laura Cogburn and Farida Baldonado, "Ralph D. Cornell: Designing the Sculptor's Landscape," in In the Sculptor's Landscape: Celebrating Twenty-five Years of the Franklin D. Murphy Sculpture Garden (Los Angeles: UCLA Wight Gallery and Grunwald Center, 1993), 14–20.

8 A photograph dated June 28, 1965, shows the garden largely completed.

9 Franklin Murphy, quoted in Paul Gardner, "Murphy's Secret Garden," Art News 84 (January 1985): 13.

10 Michael Brenson, "Compatibility and Continuity: Franklin D. Murphy's Garden of Humanism," in In the Sculptor's Landscape, 33.

11 Quoted in Twentieth-Century Sculpture from Southern California Collections (Los Angeles: UCLA Art Galleries, 1972), unpaged.

12 Kenneth Donahue, introduction to X: A Decade of Collecting, 1965–1975 (Los Angeles: Los Angeles County Museum of Art), 10.

13 Many of these cultural leaders were also regents of the University of California, including Dorothy Chandler, Norton Simon, and Edward Carter. See Davis, The Culture Broker, 57–65.

14 Murphy was on the boards of a number of major foundations and businesses. See also the section "Trustee," ibid., 71ff.

15 See Frederick S. Wight, "Of Art and Exhibitions," oral history transcript, interviewed by Bernard Galm (Los Angeles: Oral History Program, University of California, 1982).

16 Charles Sheeler: A Retrospective Exhibition (Los Angeles: Art Galleries, 1954); Frederick S. Wight, John I. H. Baur, and Duncan Phillips, Morris Graves (Berkeley: University of California Press, 1956); Frederick S. Wight, Hans Hofmann (Berkeley: University of California Press, 1957); Frederick S. Wight, Arthur G. Dove (Berkeley: University of California Press, 1958); Stuart Davis Memorial Exhibition, 1894–1964 (Washington, D.C.: National Collection of Fine Arts, Smithsonian Institution, 1965).

17 The exhibitions toured to such venues as the Whitney Museum of American Art and the Museum of Modern Art in New York, the San Francisco Museum of Art, the Dallas Museum of Art, the Walker Art Center in Minneapolis, and the Museum of Contemporary Art in Chicago.

18 Gerald Nordland, oral history interview conducted by Susan C. Larsen, Archives of American Art Oral History Program, http://www.aaa.si.edu/collections/oralhistories/transcripts/nordla04.htm.

19 The Art Galleries already housed the important collection of works on paper of the Grunwald Center for the Graphic Arts, donated to UCLA in 1956 by Fred Grunwald and greatly expanded during Murphy's tenure as chancellor. Murphy was also instrumental in the development of the collection of the present-day Fowler Museum at UCLA, particularly in the acquisition of the Wellcome Collection. See Murphy, "My UCLA Chancellorship," 230ff.

20 Hamilton and Jackson, UCLA on the Move, 143; Murphy, "My UCLA Chancellorship," 225.

21 See Valerie J. Fletcher, A Garden for Art: Outdoor Sculpture at the Hirshhorn Museum (Washington, D.C.: Hirshhorn Museum and Sculpture Garden, Smithsonian Institution, in association with Thames and Hudson, 1998).

22 Two works not originally intended for the garden were acquired before 1963; Wilhelm Lehmbruck's Bather I is too fragile for outdoor exhibition, and Anna Mahler's Tower of Masks was originally commissioned by UCLA for the courtyard of the Freud Theater and was moved to the east entrance in 2006.

23 Jacques Lipchitz: A Retrospective Selected by the Artist (Los Angeles: UCLA Art Council and UCLA Art Galleries, 1963–64). The exhibition traveled to several other major institutions, including the San Francisco Museum of Art, the Denver Art Museum, the Fort Worth Museum of Art, the Des Moines Art Center, the Walker Art Center, and the Philadelphia Museum of Art. At that time the UCLA Art Council was the largest support group at the university and played a major role in the organization of exhibitions presented at the UCLA Art Galleries. See Hamilton and Jackson, UCLA on the Move, 198.

24 Murphy, "My UCLA Chancellorship," 223.

25 Henry R. Hope, The Sculpture of Jacques Lipchitz (New York: Museum of Modern Art, 1954).

26 Other works acquired before the garden's dedication include sculptures by Eric Gill, Anna Mahler, and William Zorach (1965); Oliver Andrews, Bruce Beasley, and Louis Sullivan (1966); Aldo Casanova and Isamu Noguchi (1967); and Bourdelle, Lachaise, and Maillol (1968).

27 Murphy, "My UCLA Chancellorship," 224. See also Wight, "Of Art and Exhibitions," 236.

28 Wight, "Of Art and Exhibitions," 203–5.

29 Ibid., 232. Jean Leymarie, Herbert Read, and William S. Lieberman, Henri Matisse Retrospective, 1966 (Los Angeles: UCLA Art Council and UCLA Art Galleries, 1966).

30 The Matisse Backs were donated by the UCLA Art Council, the Michael J. Connell Memorial Fund, and the UCLA Art Council through the generosity of Mrs. Robert Gross, Mrs. Charles E. Ducommun, and Mr. and Mrs. Sidney Brody.

31 Wight, "Of Art and Exhibitions," 279.

32 See Alexander Archipenko (Los Angeles: Ward Ritchie Press, 1967).

33 Wight, "Of Art and Exhibitions," 285.

34 Wight, "Of Art and Exhibitions," 287. See also Herbert Read, The Art of Jean Arp (New York: Harry N. Abrams, 1968), published in conjunction with the exhibition.

35 Ibid., 290; Gerhard Marcks: A Retrospective Exhibition (Los Angeles: UCLA Art Galleries, 1969).

36 New British Painting and Sculpture, organized by the Whitechapel Gallery, London, for the UCLA Art Galleries (Los Angeles: UCLA Art Galleries, 1968).

37 Also in 1970 Wight acquired works by Claire Falkenstein and Gordon Newell.

38. George Rickey: Retrospective Exhibition, 1971–72 (Los Angeles: UCLA Art Council and UCLA Art Galleries, 1971).

39 Twentieth-Century Sculpture from Southern California Collections, an exhibition organized by Frederick S. Wight (Los Angeles: UCLA Art Council and UCLA Art Galleries, 1972).

40 Other acquisitions made during Nordland's tenure included works by Peter Voulkos (1972, 1973); Dimitri Hadzi, Barbara Hepworth, Richard Hunt, and Francisco Zúñiga (1975); Fritz Koenig and Aristide Maillol (1976); and Fletcher Benton, Reuben Nakian, Vladas Vildžiūnas, and Jack Zajac (1977).

41 Alberto Burri: A Retrospective View, 1948–1977 (Los Angeles: Frederick S. Wight Gallery, 1977). In 1974 Nordland also organized an exhibition on Gaston Lachaise. See Gerald Nordland, Gaston Lachaise: The Man and His Work (New York: George Braziller, 1974).

42 Works by Robert Graham and William Turnbull were acquired in 1980.

43 "A Death in the L.A. Family," editorial, Los Angeles Times, June 27, 1994.

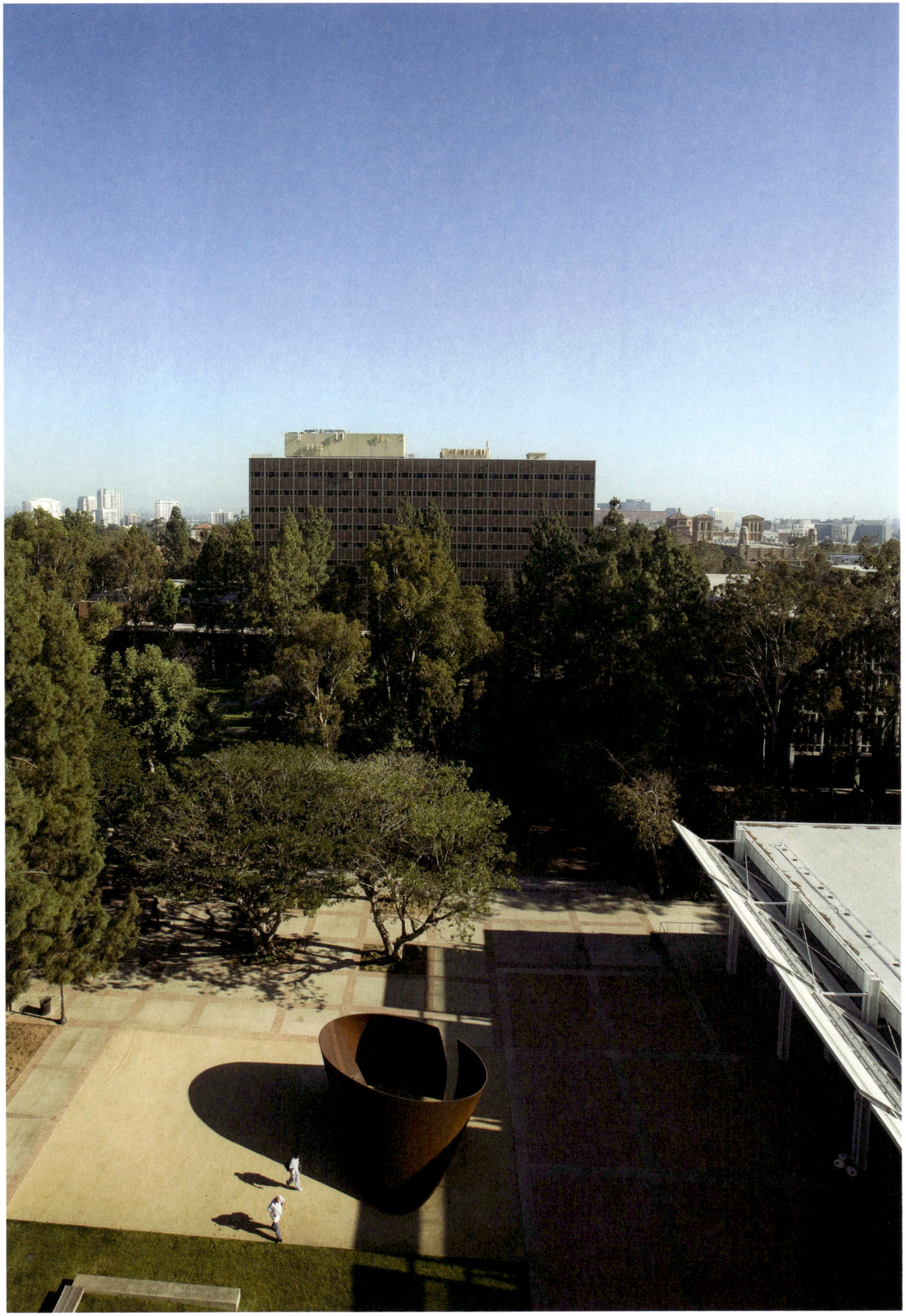

MAP LIST

Note: Works not shown on the map are indicated by the symbol *.

THE FRANKLIN D. MURPHY SCULPTURE GARDEN

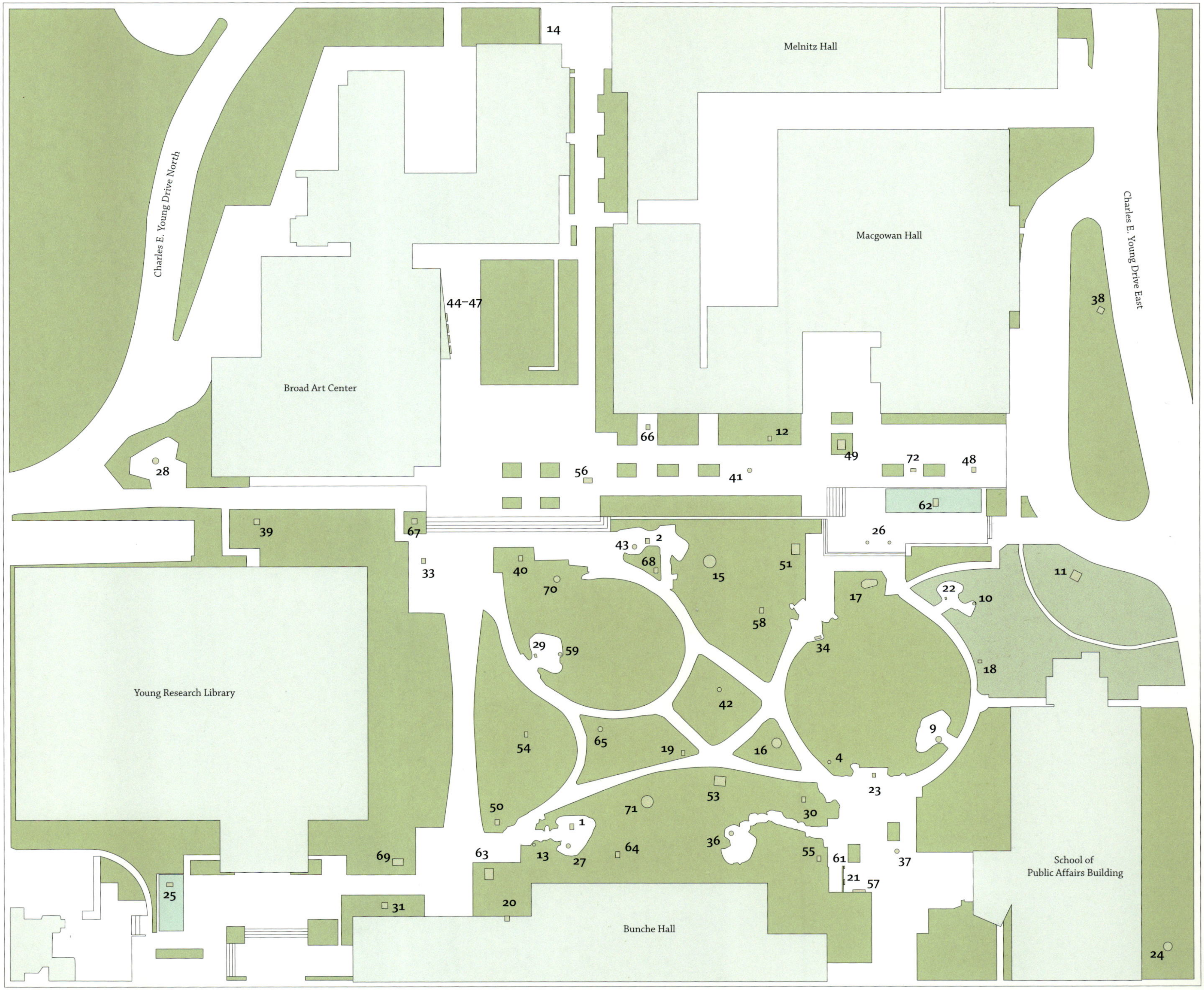
Melnitz Hall
Macgowan Hall
Broad Art Center
Young Research Library
Bunche Hall
School of
Public Affairs Building
Charles E. Young Drive North
Charles E. Young Drive East
1
2
4
9
10
11
12
13
14
15
16
17
18
19
20
21
22
23
24
25
26
27
28
29
30
31
33
34
36
37
38
39
40
41
42
43
44–47
48
49
50
51
53
54
55
56
57
58
59
61
62
63
64
65
66
67
68
69
70
71
72

NOTE TO THE READER

Dimensions are given in inches and centimeters in the following order: height (H), width (W), depth (D). For sculptures that are not unique works, information about edition size is given; the number following the slash (/) indicates the total size of the edition, while the number preceding it indicates the place of the UCLA cast in the edition. Foundry information has been supplied when available. The catalogue entries were written by Cynthia Burlingham, Claudine Dixon, and Allegra Pesenti, who are identified by their initials. Some entries include information based on research conducted for the catalogues of the Murphy Sculpture Garden collection published in 1978 (entries by Gerald Nordland with the assistance of Jan Keller) and in 1984 (research by Katherine Hart and Margaret Nelson), as well as the 1993 exhibition catalogue *In the Sculptor's Landscape: Celebrating Twenty-five Years of the Franklin D. Murphy Sculpture Garden* (entries by Farida Baldonado, Lucinda Barnes, Cynthia Burlingham, Karen Mayers, and Elizabeth Shepherd). Wherever possible, however, the texts have been revised and expanded to reflect more recent scholarship. For further information on these publications, please see the bibliography.

CATALOGUE OF THE COLLECTION

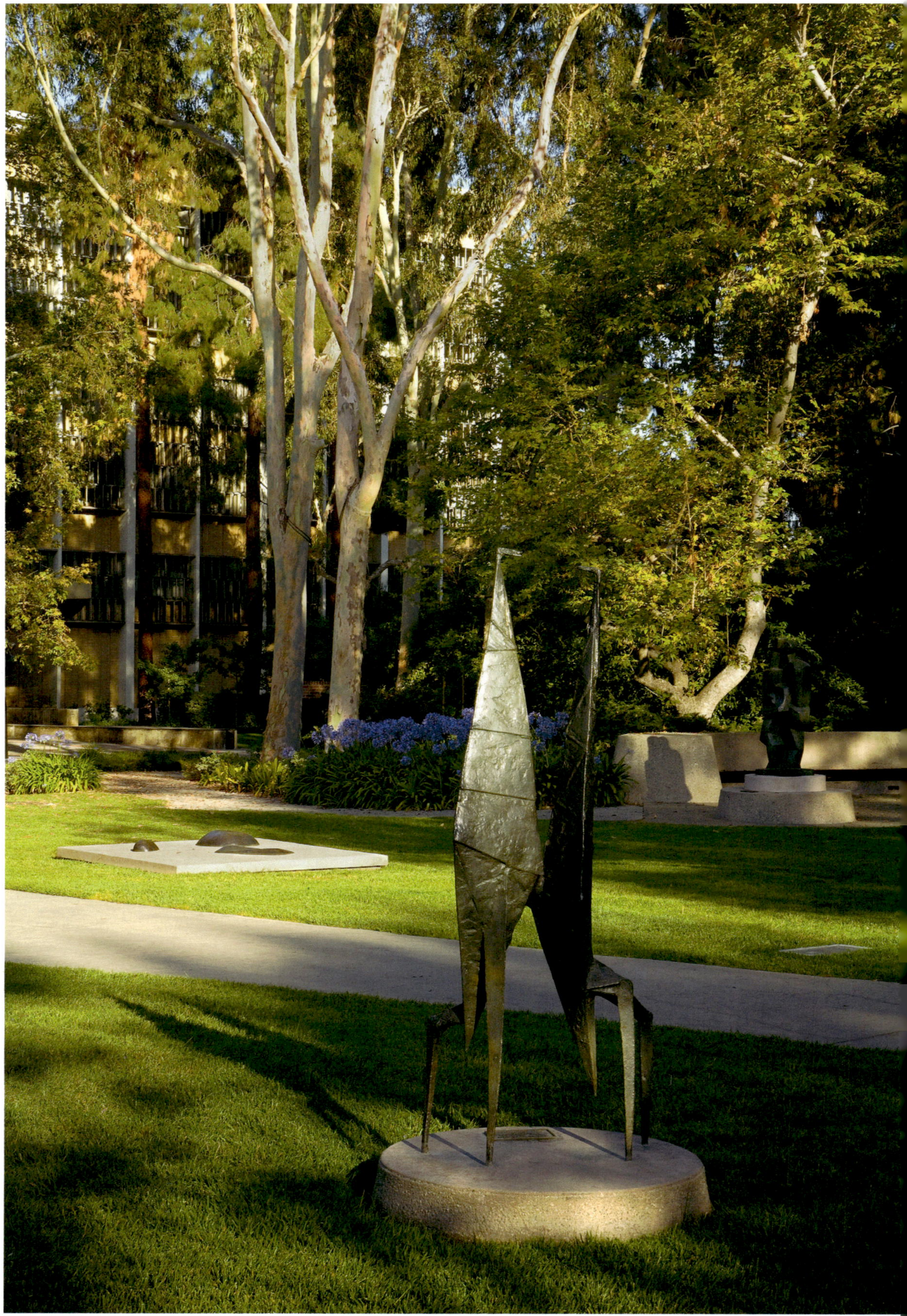

OLIVER ANDREWS

(AMERICAN, 1925–1978)

Oliver Andrews received his BA from Stanford University in 1948. His first solo exhibition took place at the Santa Barbara Museum of Art in 1950. In 1958 he joined the art faculty at the University of California, Los Angeles, where he designed the sculpture studios for the new Dickson Art Center in 1965 and served as head of the sculpture department until his death in a skin-diving accident in 1978. An interest in science and the natural world, particularly the ocean, was an important part of his life and art. In 1972 he created a forty-foot helium-filled Mylar whale for a festival of the American Cetacean Society. This led to a series of Sky Fountains for the cities of Los Angeles, San Diego, and Cincinnati. He later made other large Mylar sculptures for New York's Grand Central Terminal, Shea Stadium, and World Trade Center. Andrews often incorporated elements of electricity, neon, air, and water into his sculptures. He created several fountain sculptures, the first for a shopping center in San Jose, California, in 1963. His book, *Living Materials: A Sculptor's Handbook,* was published after his death.[1]

Architectural Sculpture demonstrates the artist's attempt to combine and harmonize a number of different materials. In an interview in 1977 Andrews commented on his work from this period: "My earlier sculptures had very complicated ways of standing, had multiple legs and sometimes there were different tiers of the sculpture as it moved from stage to stage. The sculptures would seem to have a first story and a second story. Then gradually the main elements of the sculpture came into contact with the ground plane or with the floor and related to it in a much more direct way. As this happened and as the sculpture became more solid, I began to use a more varied combination of materials."[2] C.B.

Notes

1 *Oliver Andrews,* Living Materials: A Sculptor's Handbook *(Berkeley: University of California Press, 1983).*

2 *Oliver Andrews, interview with George M. Goodwin, 1977, Oral History Program, University of California, Los Angeles.*

ALEXANDER ARCHIPENKO

(AMERICAN, 1887–1964)

Alexander Archipenko studied painting and sculpture at the Kiev Art School from 1902 to 1905. After living in Paris and Berlin, he moved to New York in 1923, the year of his first American solo exhibition at the Museum of Modern Art. Archipenko held teaching posts at various American universities and private institutions, including the New Bauhaus in Chicago. The artist, who became an American citizen in 1929, also established several art schools in places where he lived throughout the United States. A major retrospective exhibition on Archipenko, organized by the galleries at UCLA, traveled to ten museums in the United States between 1967 and 1969.[1]

Queen of Sheba is the culmination of Archipenko's exploration of the elongated form that was first demonstrated in his series of elemental "vase" figures made in France in the 1910s, when he experimented with highly abstract sculptures of the female figure. Reminiscent of Cycladic figures of ancient Greece, the slender, corelike form with a handle-shaped head is attired in an expansive gown that is cut away to reveal the figure underneath. Two discs bisect the figure, one slightly below the waist and the other directly below the breasts. This creates a pronounced division of the work into three sections and highlights the implication of the surrounding space, adding dimension to the bronze corporeality of the figure. As Jeanne L. Wasserman has noted: "[Archipenko] discovered the psychological power of the void as a replacement for solidness, and the interchangeability of concave for convex for the sake of form."[2] *Queen of Sheba* is the last of Archipenko's large bronzes to be completed and may be considered the curvilinear feminine counterpart of the artist's last sculpture, *King Solomon*. Cast in bronze in 1964, shortly before the artist's death, *King Solomon* is a more angular masculine figure that was envisioned to be more than sixty feet tall in its final monumental form but was never realized.[3] C.D.

Notes

1 *See* Alexander Archipenko *([Los Angeles]: Ward Ritchie Press, [1967]).*

2 *Jeanne L. Wasserman and James B. Cuno,* Three American Sculptors and the Female Nude: Lachaise, Nadelman, Archipenko *(Cambridge: Fogg Art Museum, Harvard University, 1980), 14.*

3 *For further comparison of these two seminal works, see Katherine Jánszky Michaelsen and Nehama Guralnik,* Alexander Archipenko: A Centennial Tribute *(Washington, D.C.: National Gallery of Art; Tel Aviv: Tel Aviv Museum, 1986), 136–38.*

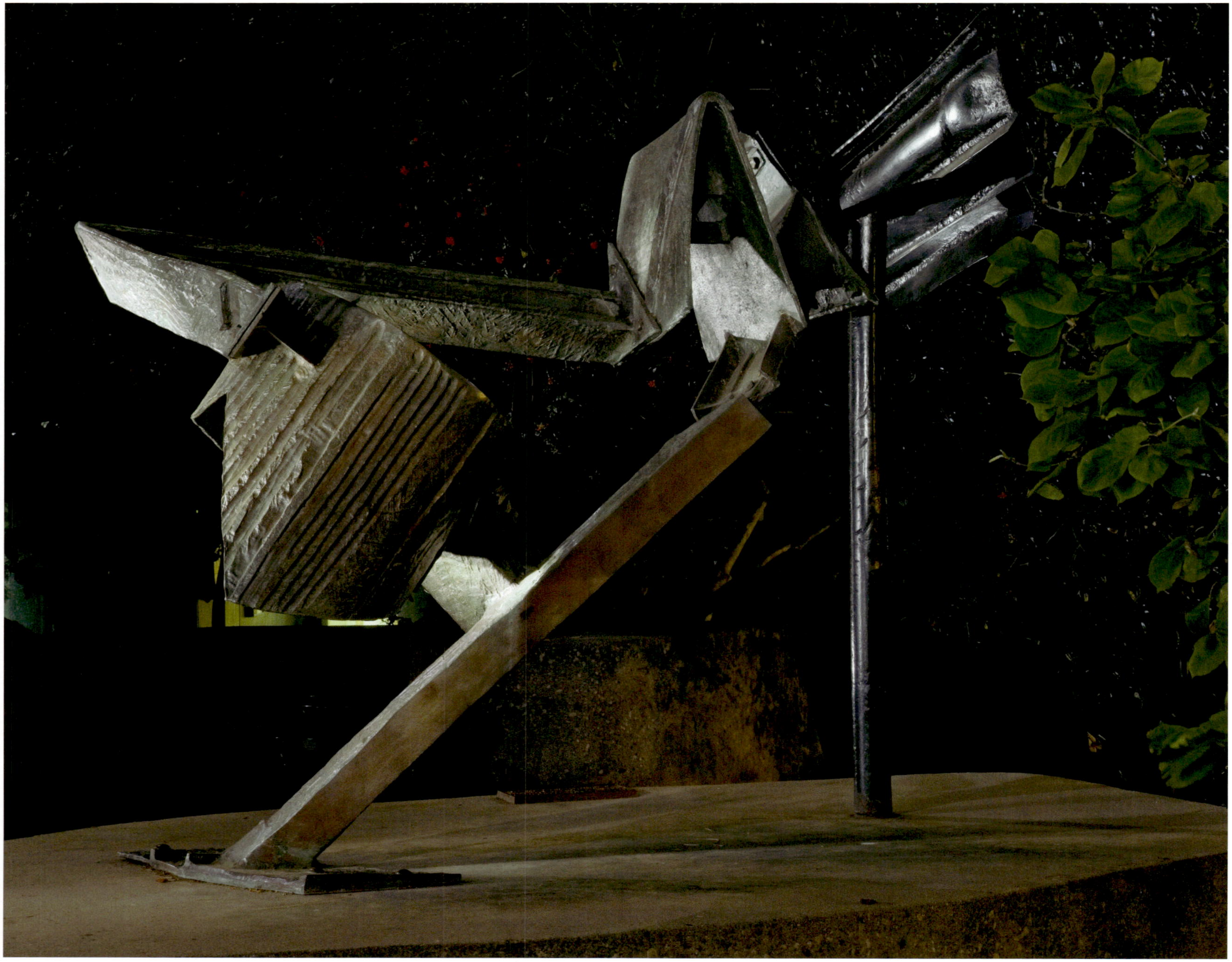

ARCHITECTURAL SCULPTURE
1966
Painted bronze and welded steel
H: 59 IN. (150 CM);
W: 70⅝ IN. (179.4 CM);
D: 35⅜ IN. (89.9 CM)
Acquired through the Michael J. Connell Memorial Fund, 1966

QUEEN OF SHEBA
1961
H: 65½ IN. (166.4 CM); W: 31 IN. (78.7 CM); D: 18 IN. (45.7 CM)
Edition: 3/8
Gift of Donald H. Karshan and an anonymous donor, 1967

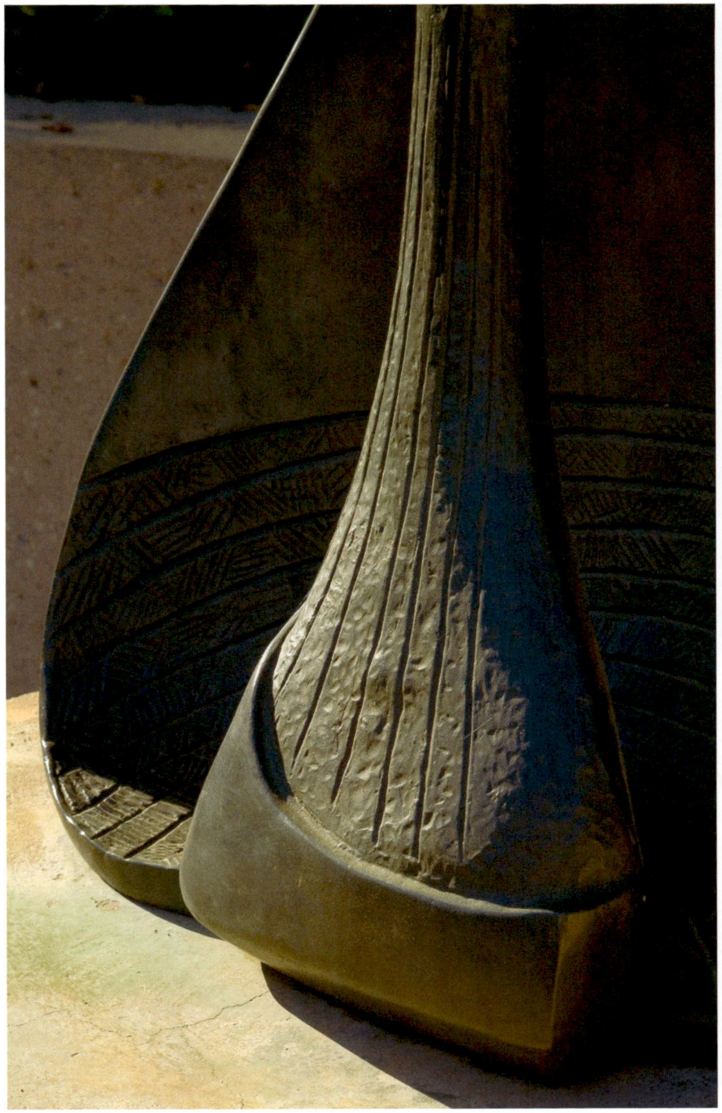

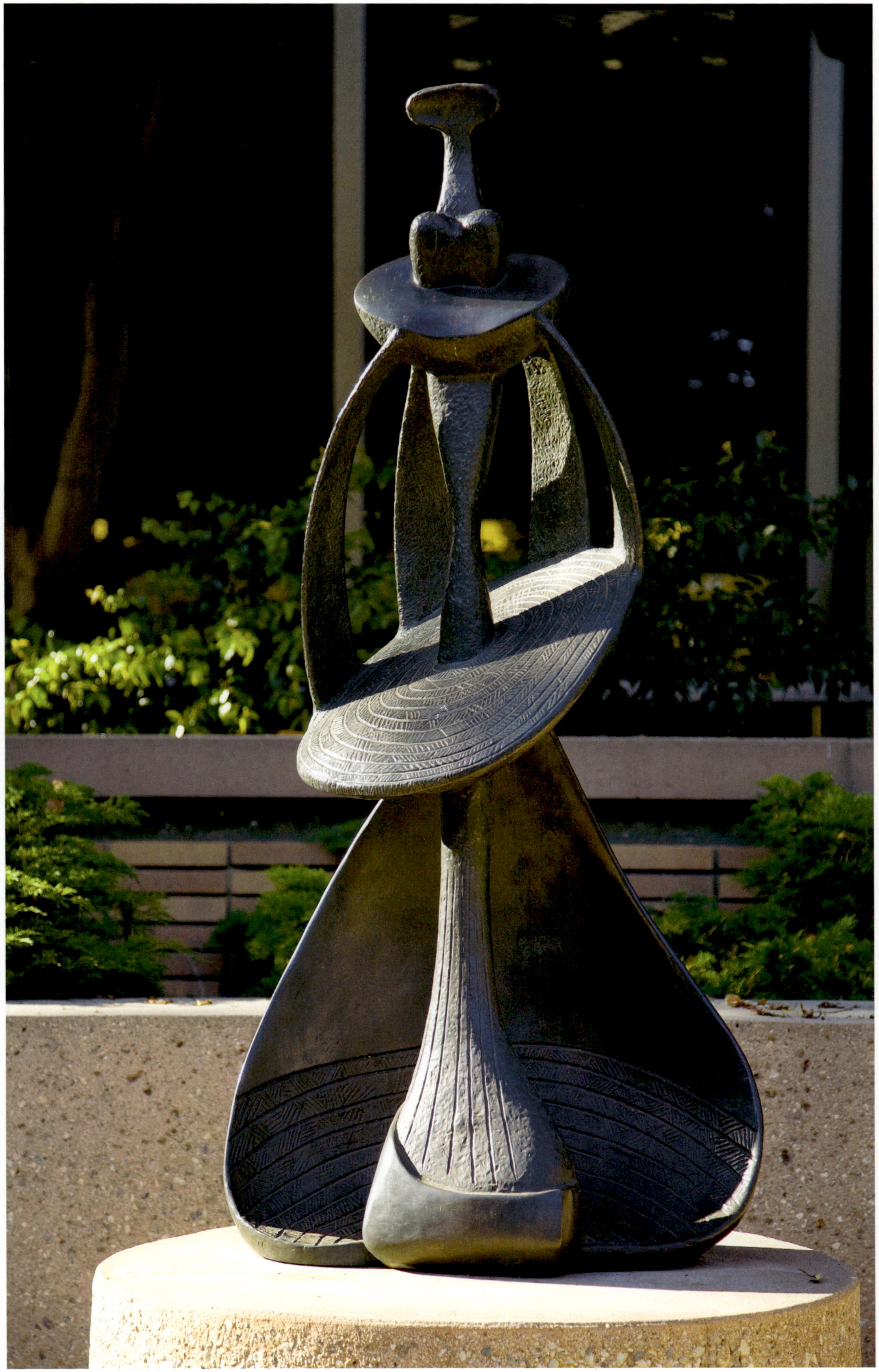

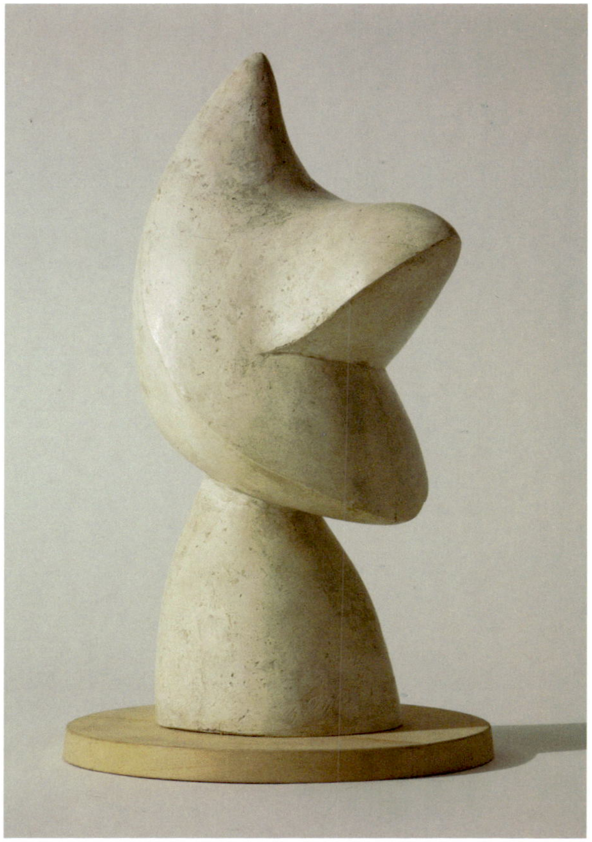

KASPAR
1930
Plaster
H: 19¾ IN. (50 CM); W: 11 IN. (28 CM); D: 7½ IN. (19 CM)
Gift of Madame Marguerite Arp, 1971

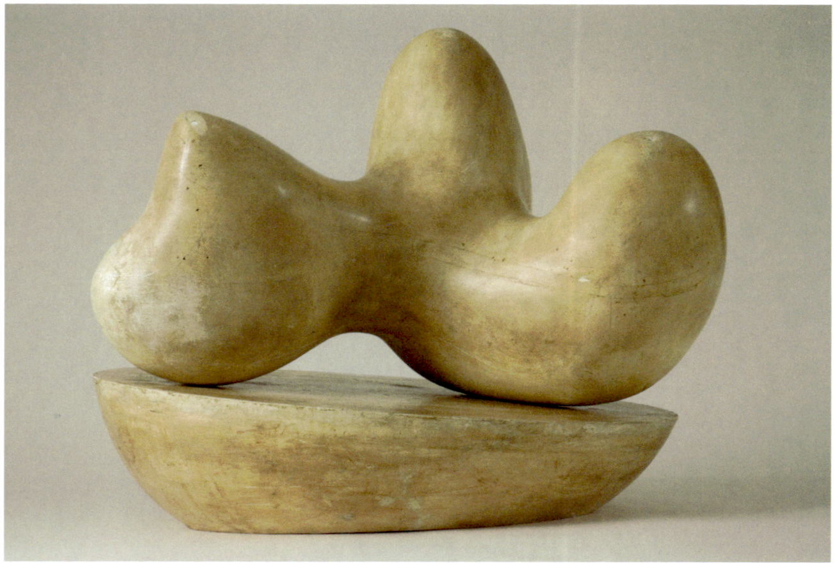

CONCRÉTION HUMAINE SUR COUPE / HUMAN CONCRETION ON OVAL BOWL
1935
Plaster
H: 18½ IN. (47 CM); W: 29 IN. (73.5 CM); D: 17¾ IN. (45 CM)
Gift of Madame Marguerite Arp, 1971

JEAN (HANS) ARP

(FRENCH, 1886–1966)

Jean Arp's formal studies in art began in 1900, when he was only fourteen, but he had a longer-standing passion for poetry, which would remain constant throughout his career. After meeting Vassily Kandinsky in 1912 and participating in the second exhibition of the Blaue Reiter in Munich, Arp began to associate with other artists, including Max Ernst and Paul Klee, as well as poets and writers such as Hugo Ball and Tristan Tzara. Arp was a member of the Dada and surrealist movements in Zurich, Cologne, and Paris and collaborated on projects with Sophie Taeuber, a Swiss artist who became his wife in 1922.

In response to the birth of Dada in 1916, Arp began to experiment with collages, reliefs, and woodcuts for the movement's manifestos. It was not until the 1930s that he began to make works in three dimensions. The five plaster studies in the collection of the UCLA Murphy Sculpture Garden range in date from 1930 (*Kaspar*) to 1953 (*Ptolemy I*), a span of almost twenty-five years. All these plaster casts came from Arp's studio in Meudon, France, and were donated to UCLA by Arp's second wife, Marguerite Arp. Playfulness and whimsy are captured in some of these small-scale works (*Kaspar* and *Tree of Bowls*); others appear as sentient organisms in flux (*Human Concretion*; *Human, Lunar, Spectral*; and *Ptolemy I*).

The sculpture garden also contains two major bronze sculptures by Arp, *Hybrid Fruit Called Pagoda* (1934) and *Ptolemy III* (1961). *Hybrid Fruit Called Pagoda* displays a nonobjective form yet intimates something alive, an organic entity in two parts, the upper "torso" twisting in opposition to the lower "trunk." *Ptolemy III*'s ovoid tubular forms resemble the ventricles of a heart. Arp's biographer Herbert Read considered the Ptolemy series as the "representative piece which seems to concentrate all Arp's formal invention in one coherent image.... It seems to beat with an inner life, and at the same time to rest in eternal stillness."[1] C.D.

Notes
1 *Herbert Read,* The Art of Jean Arp *(New York: Harry N. Abrams, 1968), 101.*

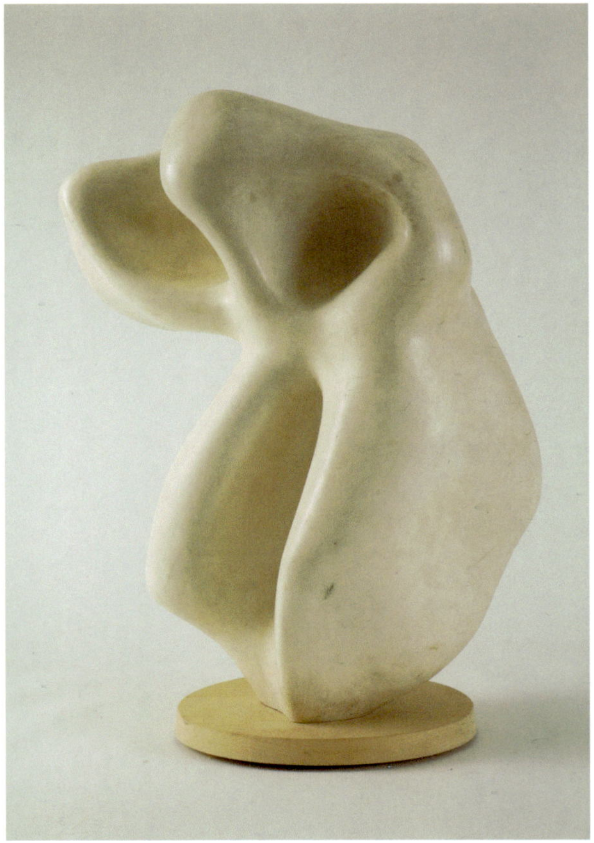

ÉVOCATION HUMAINE, LUNAIRE, SPECTRALE / HUMAN, LUNAR, SPECTRAL
1950
Plaster
H: 32¾ IN. (83 CM); W: 25½ IN. (65 CM); D: 19¾ IN. (50 CM)
Gift of Madame Marguerite Arp, 1971

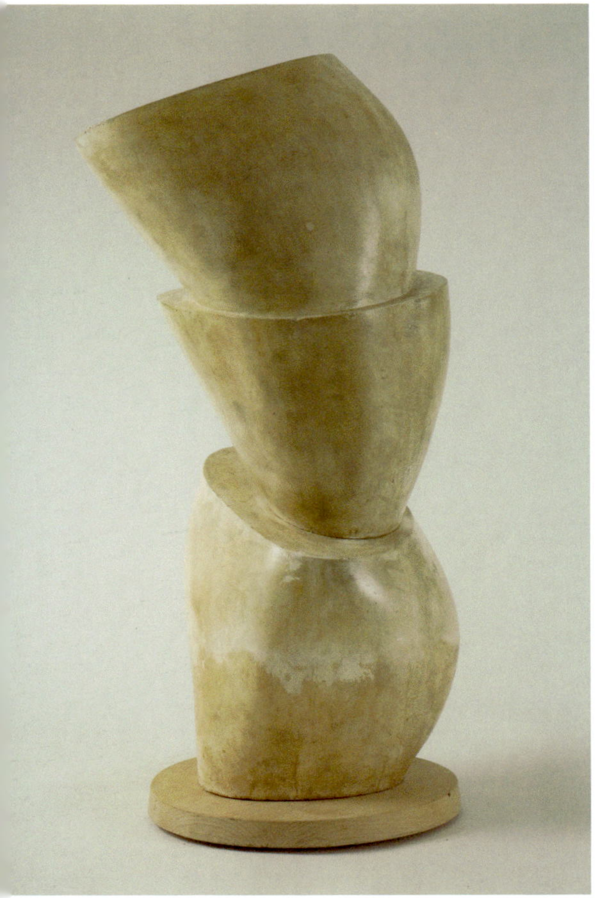

COUPES SUPERPOSÉES / TREE OF BOWLS
CA. 1947
Plaster
H: 38 IN. (96.5 CM); W: 17 ¾ IN. (45 CM); D: 18 ½ IN. (47 CM)
Gift of Madame Marguerite Arp, 1971

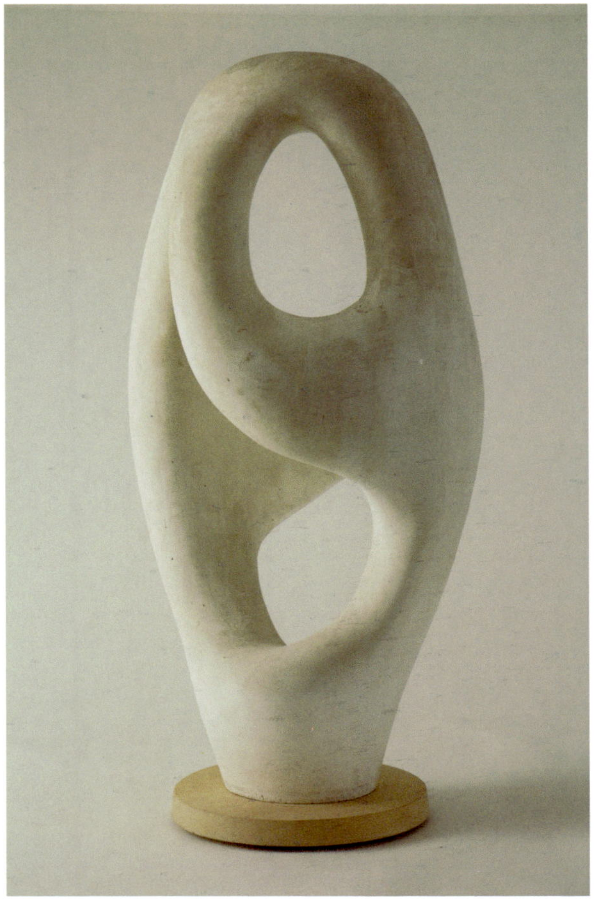

PTOLÉMÉE I / PTOLEMY I
1953
Plaster
H: 40½ IN. (103 CM); W: 20¾ IN. (52.5 CM); D: 17 IN. (43 CM)
Gift of Madame Marguerite Arp, 1971

FRUIT HYBRIDE DIT LA PAGODE / HYBRID FRUIT CALLED PAGODA
1934
Bronze
H: 37¾ IN. (94.6 CM); W: 29½ IN. (74.9 CM); D: 21½ IN. (54.6 CM)
Edition: 3/3
Foundry: unknown
(cast after 1949)
Gift of Mrs. David E. Bright, 1967

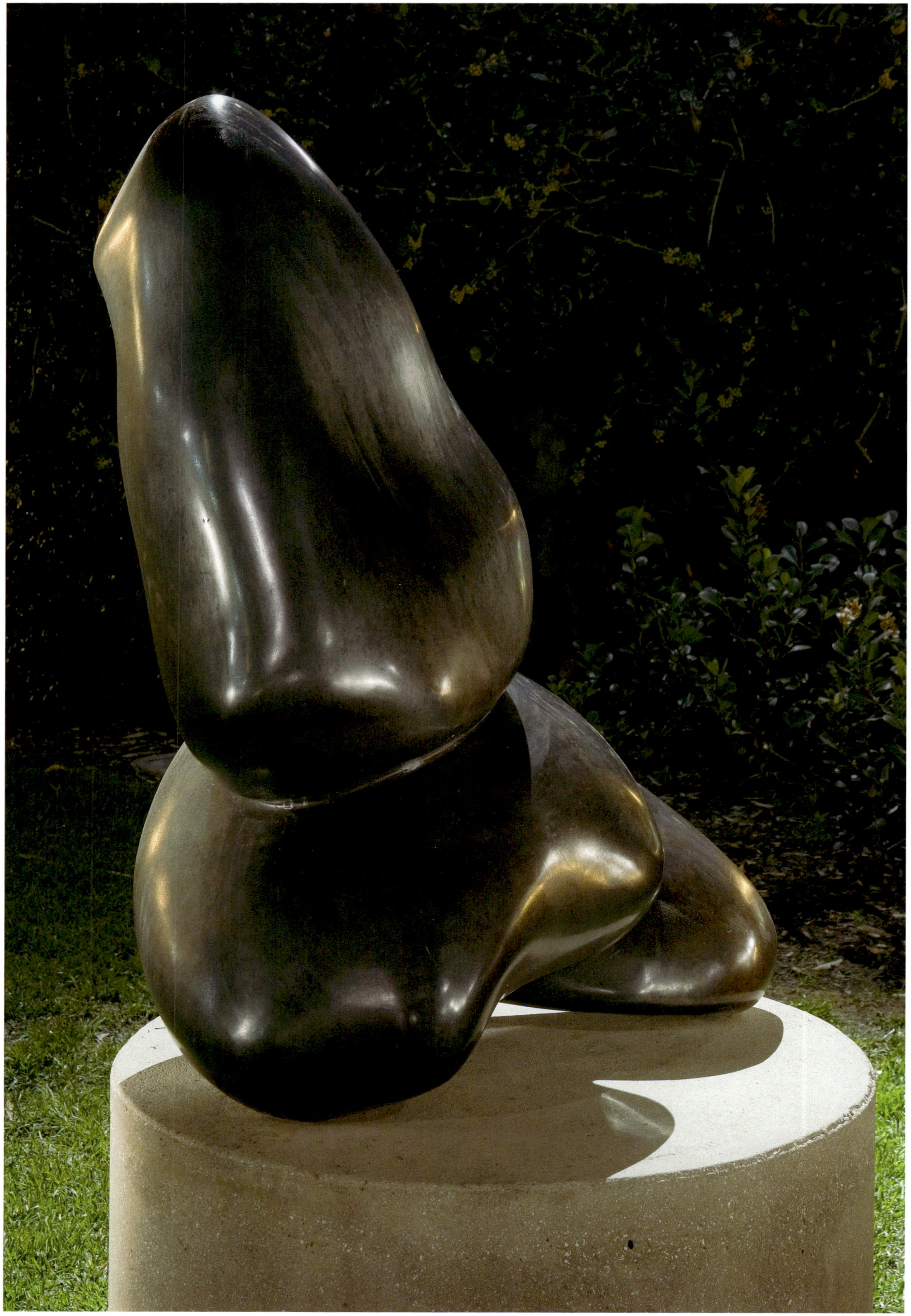

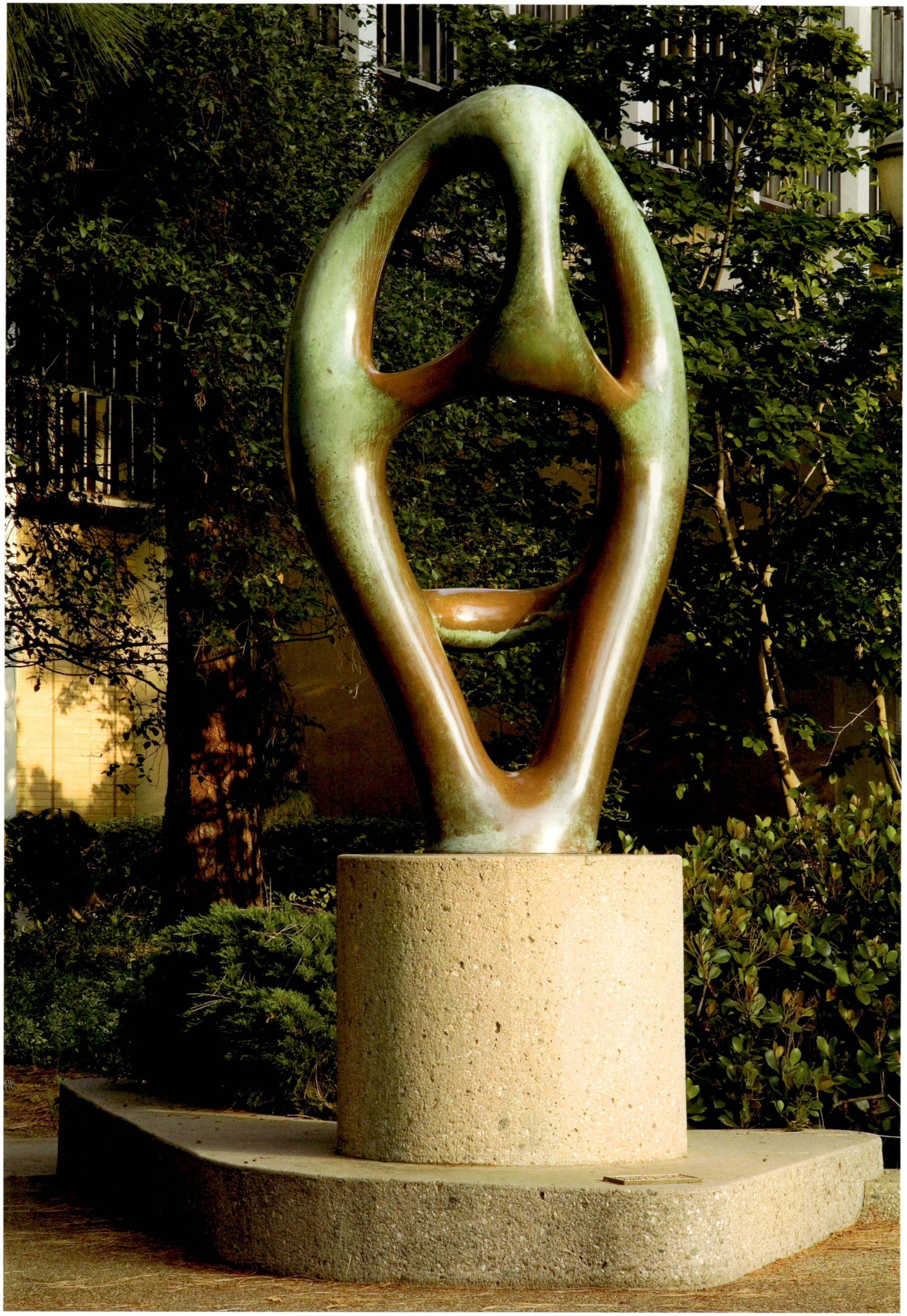

PTOLÉMÉE III / PTOLEMY III
1961
Bronze
H: 79 IN. (201 CM); W: 45 IN. (114.3 CM); D: 30 IN. (76.2 CM)
Edition: /3
Gift of the Hal Wallis Family, 1968

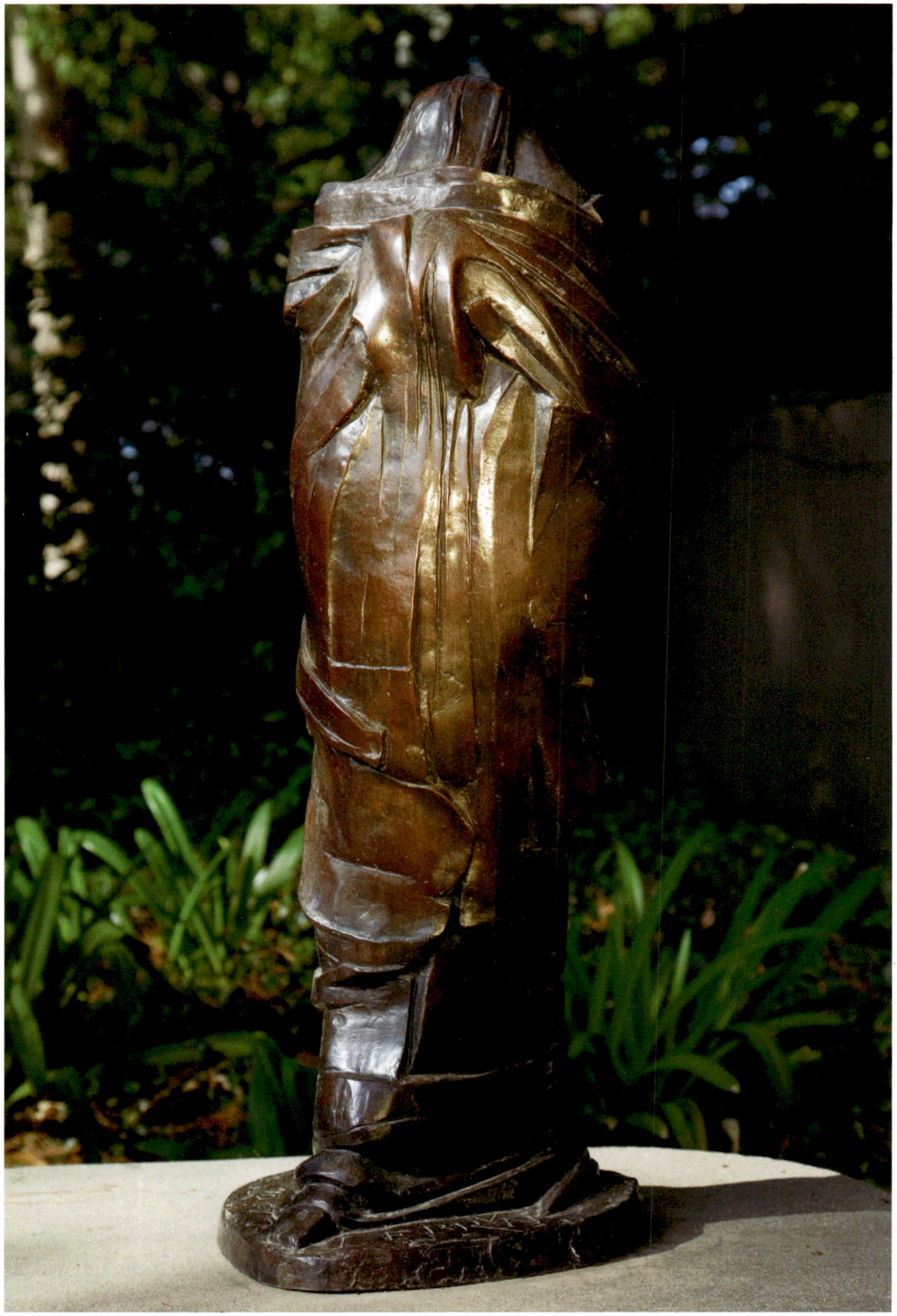

PROPHET: HOMAGE TO RICO LEBRUN
1971
Bronze
H: 35 ⅝ IN. (91 CM); W: 15 IN. (38.1 CM); D: 15 ¼ IN. (38.7 CM)
Edition: /8
Foundry: Bedi-Makky, New York
Given in honor of Dr. Franklin D. Murphy by Michael Hall, Esq., 1977

In addition to his achievements as a sculptor, Leonard Baskin was a prolific graphic artist, book designer, and writer and was director of the respected publishing company the Gehenna Press, which produced artist's books. Baskin studied sculpture in New York from 1937 to 1939 and had his first exhibition there when he was only seventeen. Two of the artist's most renowned public sculpture commissions were the presidential memorials to Franklin Delano Roosevelt and Woodrow Wilson in Washington, D.C.

When Baskin was thirty-five years old, he met the fifty-seven-year-old artist Rico Lebrun. Lebrun and Baskin shared a similar belief in the paramount importance of the human figure as the basis of art. The older artist had a profound influence on Baskin, most markedly on the development of his graphic style.[1] Upon Lebrun's death in 1964 Baskin created *Achilles* as a memorial to his mentor. This work introduced the theme of prophecy, which Baskin felt linked Lebrun's legacy with his own artistic oeuvre, in which the human figure represented the most relevant expression of spirituality.[2] Baskin revered Lebrun, describing him as a "prophet" for himself and for other artists, a moniker that Lebrun himself dismissed.[3] *Prophet: Homage to Rico Lebrun* is a continuation of Baskin's quest to capture Lebrun's "prophetic" quality, to make his influence eternal. The figure is completely submerged under the drapery of the cape, which has essentially been transformed into a shroud. In "A Tribute to Rico Lebrun," Baskin wrote: "The man is inseparable from his work. Bound together are the fire, the tempest and the fury of his trenchant living frame. The physical fabric of his work is his palpable, living monument."[4] C.D.

Notes

1 *See Irma B. Jaffe,* The Sculpture of Leonard Baskin *(New York: Viking Press, 1980),* 52–53.

2 *See Leonard Baskin,* Sculpture Drawings, and Prints *(New York: George Braziller, 1970), 19: "Rico Lebrun, my dear friend and mentor, whose death was ill-timed, robbing his titanic gifts of full development and fruition. Having at last overcome a killing natural brilliance in drawing and the intolerable birthright of all Italian art, when his genius, new-found, was forcing a new vision, wrought of torment and compassion, terror and truth, at that exalted moment he died. A savage stroke leveled at American art and deprived me of my greatest ally in the struggle for a figurative art."*

3 *Baskin wrote of Lebrun, "I once called him a prophet and he with a grimace said 'No'" (Leonard Baskin, "A Tribute to Rico Lebrun," in* Rico Lebrun Memorial Exhibition: Paintings and Drawings, November 5, 1965–January 9, 1966, *Publication no. 230 [New York: American Academy of Arts and Letters, 1966], 6).*

4 *Ibid., 5–6.*

LEONARD BASKIN

(AMERICAN, 1922–2000)

FLETCHER BENTON

(AMERICAN, B. 1931)

Fletcher Benton moved to Northern California from Ohio in 1956 and has taught at the California College of Arts and Crafts in Oakland, the San Francisco Art Institute, and California State University at San Jose. Since 1961 his work has been featured in solo exhibitions at many institutions throughout the United States and Europe, and his sculptures are part of numerous collections.

In the early 1960s Benton began experimenting with kinetic painting, incorporating motorized components. He stopped making kinetic work in 1974 to concentrate on three-dimensional sculptures such as *Dynamic Rhythms Orange (Phase III)*, which dates from this period. Benton first created a painted maquette and cast it in an edition of six (Phase I). He also created a slightly larger version that is in the collection of the de Saisset Museum at the University of Santa Clara (Phase II) and in 1976 cast the first enlarged version in bronze, which was given to the galleries at UCLA by Frederick Weisman. For this work Benton used what he refers to as a "high heat" patina that gives the surface a burnished dull gold color. The painted surfaces of the piece eliminate reflection as an element of the aesthetic, in contrast to the primary role that reflection had in Benton's works prior to this time. As noted by Diane Ghirardo Burke, "The most recent works...fuse color, form, and time, which implies change, in a compelling resolution that appears deceptively simple, but in fact issues from long years of experience and experimentation."[1] Benton continues to be as involved with the fabrication of his sculptures as he is with the design. Many artists habitually turn over the production to technicians at this stage, but Benton oversees this role as well, taking charge of the entire process, from the watercolor study, to the maquette, to the sculpture in its final form. C.D.

Notes
1 *Diane Ghirardo Burke,* Fletcher Benton: Selected Works, 1964–74 *(Santa Clara, Calif.: de Saisset Art Gallery and Museum, University of Santa Clara, 1974), unpaged.*

ÉMILE-ANTOINE BOURDELLE

(FRENCH, 1861–1929)

Émile-Antoine Bourdelle gained experience in wood carving by working first as an apprentice at his father's cabinetry studio in Montauban, in southwestern France. He studied drawing at Montauban's Musée Ingres and then pursued sculpture at the art school in Toulouse. Best known for his commemorative portrait busts of cultural luminaries such as Ludwig van Beethoven, Jean-Auguste-Dominique Ingres, and Frédéric Chopin, Bourdelle was also a prolific designer of large-scale monuments. He was a close friend of Auguste Rodin and was a member of Rodin's workshop in Paris for almost fifteen years. Twenty years after Bourdelle's death, the Musée Bourdelle was established in Paris, and the first retrospective exhibition devoted to the artist took place at the Musée Ingres in Montauban in 1950.

According to Rhodia Dufet-Bourdelle, the daughter of the artist, the subject of *Noble Burdens* was an Italian woman, obviously pregnant, whom Bourdelle had observed walking on a street in Paris, cradling a small child against her body with one hand while using the other hand to balance a large basket of fruit and vegetables on her head.[1] *Head of France* is a cast of a study for Bourdelle's World War I memorial to the fallen, *La France*, of 1923. The physiognomy of the figure depicted in *Head of France* was partially based on the facial features of Fanny Bunand, niece of Cléopatre Sévastos, who was the sculptor's second wife.[2] Instead of a realistic likeness, however, Bourdelle made the features of the sculpted head perfectly symmetrical, creating a symbol of the country rather than a portrait of a woman. C.D.

Notes
1 *Rhodia Dufet-Bourdelle to B. Gerald Cantor, January 8, 1968, Murphy Sculpture Garden Archives, Hammer Museum.*
2 *See* Émile-Antoine Bourdelle (1861–1929): Sculptures *(Montauban: Musée Ingres, 2000), 64, no. 39.*

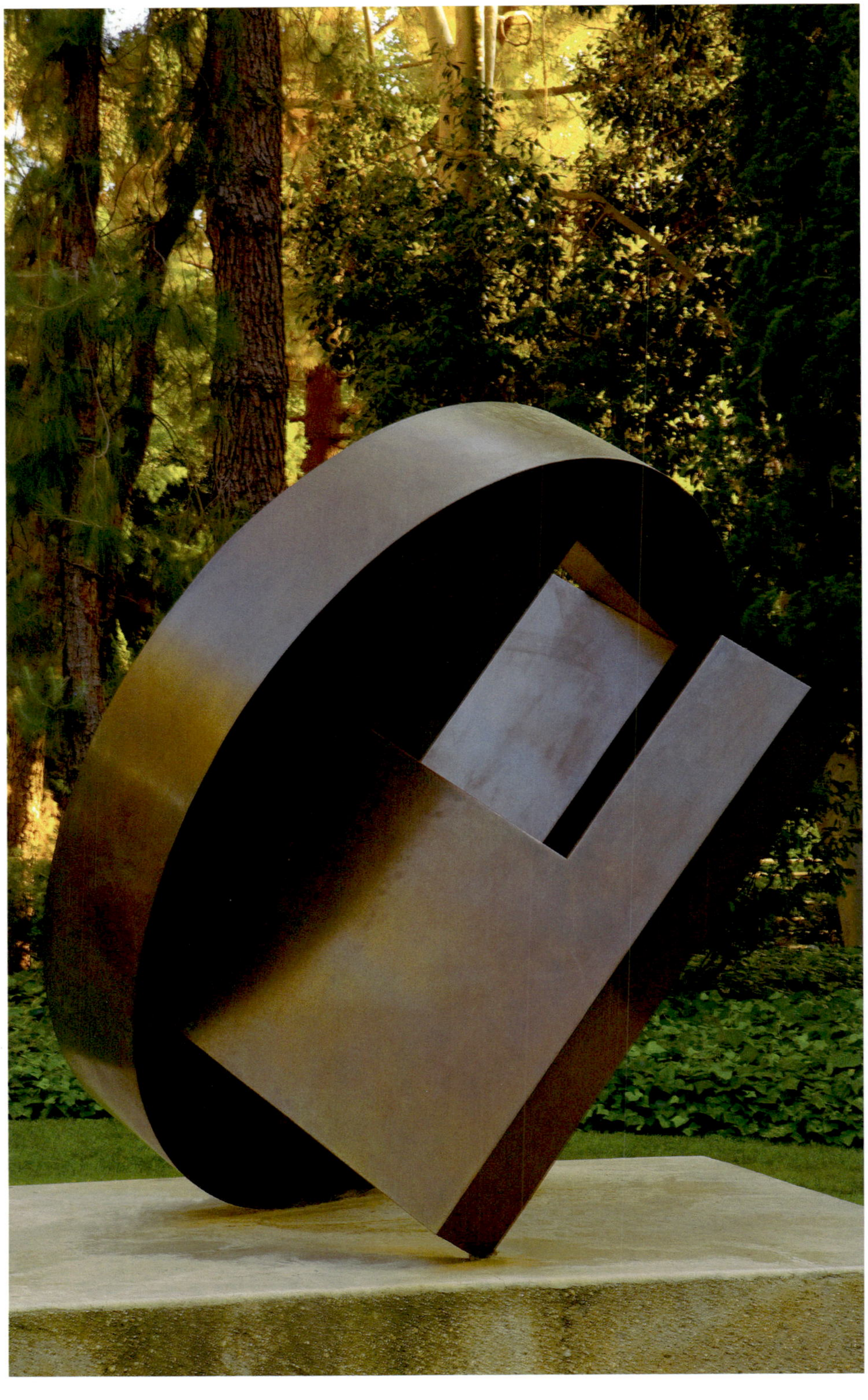

DYNAMIC RHYTHMS ORANGE (PHASE III)
1976

Bronze
H: 84 IN. (213 CM); W: 74 IN. (188 CM); D: 93 IN. (236.2 CM)
Edition: 1/
Foundry: Berkeley Art Foundry
Gift of Frederick Weisman, Inc., in memory of Linda Van Ronkel Simon, 1977

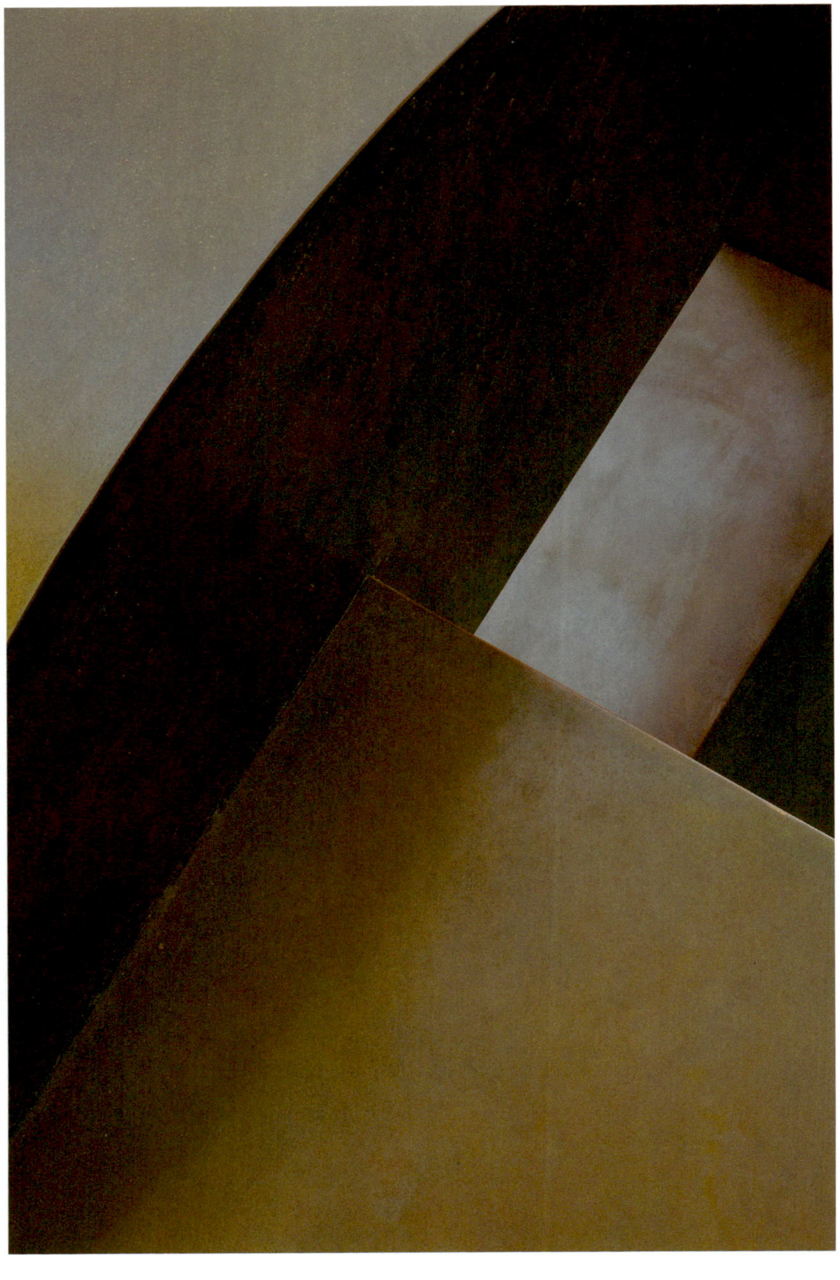

LES NOBLES FARDEAUX / NOBLE BURDENS
1910
Bronze
H: 49½ IN. (125.7 CM);
W: 13½ IN. (34.3 CM);
D: 20¼ IN. (51.4 CM)
Edition: 5/7
Foundry: Susse, Paris
Gift of the B. G. Cantor Art Foundation, 1968

TÊTE DE LA FRANCE / HEAD OF FRANCE
1925
Bronze
H: 18¾ IN. (47.5 CM);
W: 9¾ IN. (24.8 CM);
D: 14½ IN. (36.8 CM)
Edition: 2/4
Foundry: Susse, Paris
Gift of B. Gerald Cantor, 1968

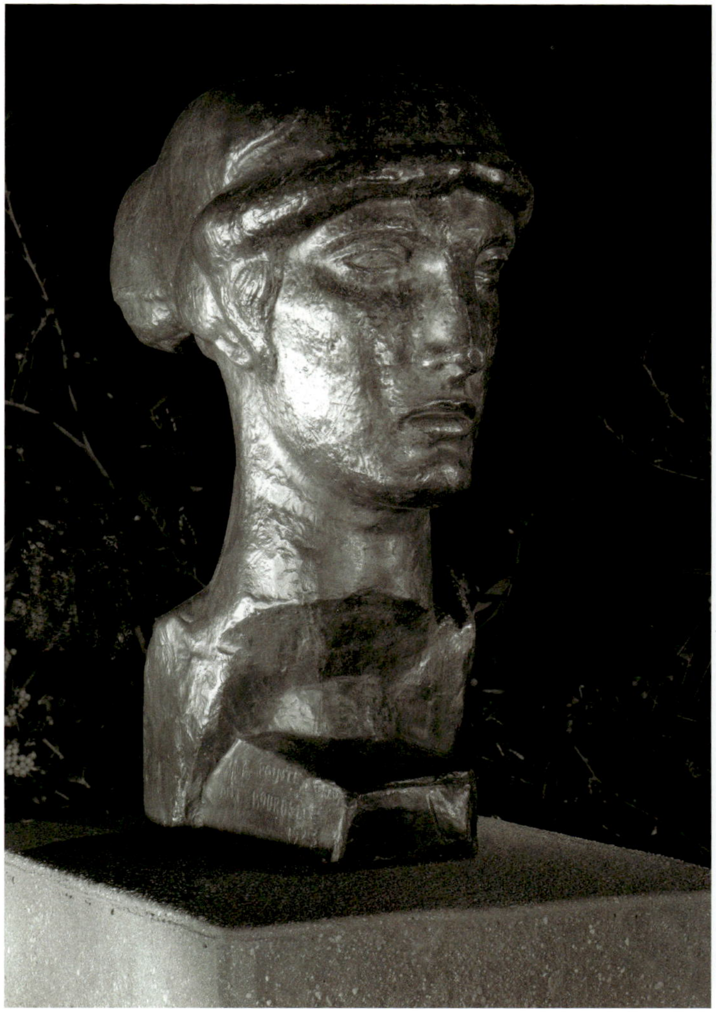

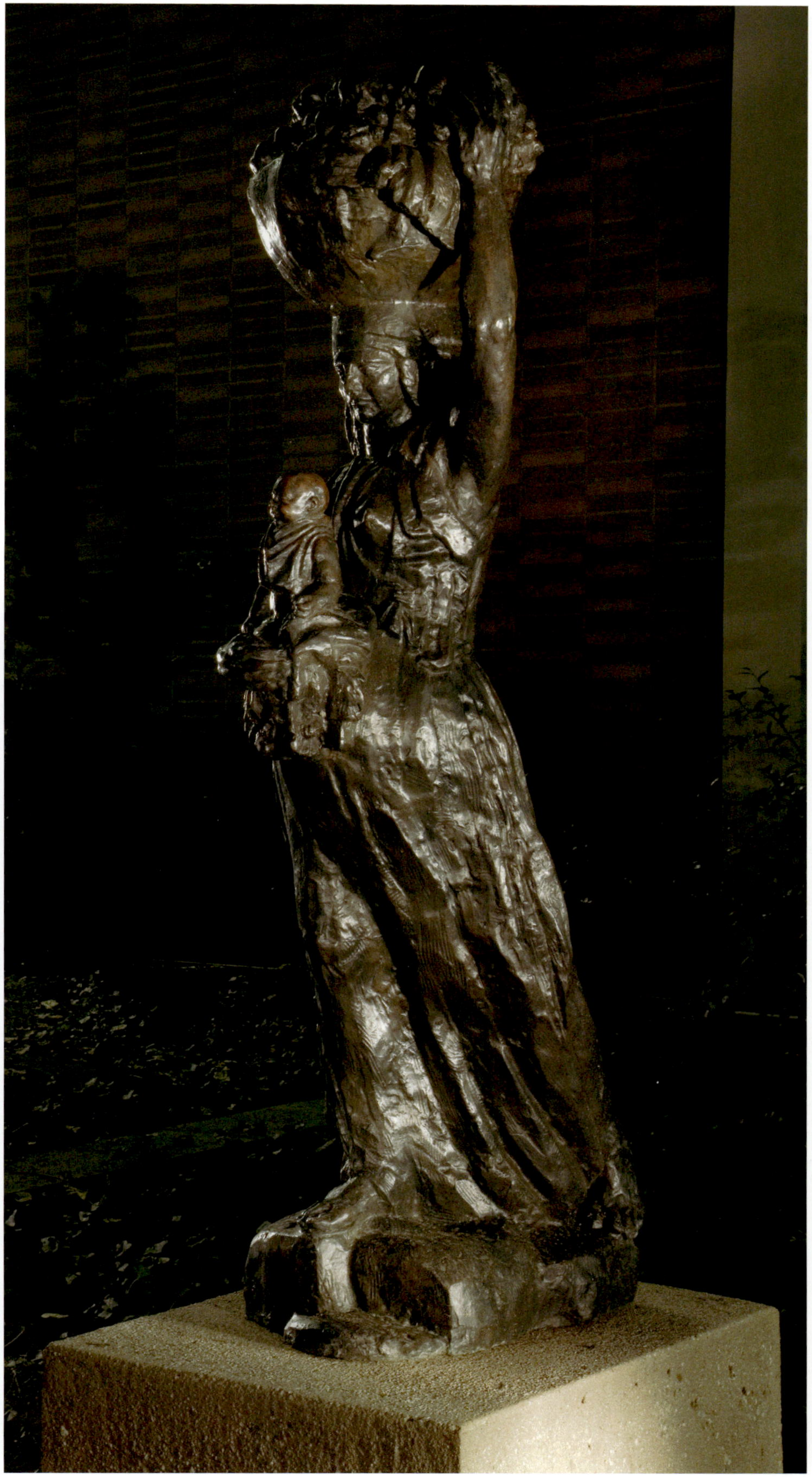

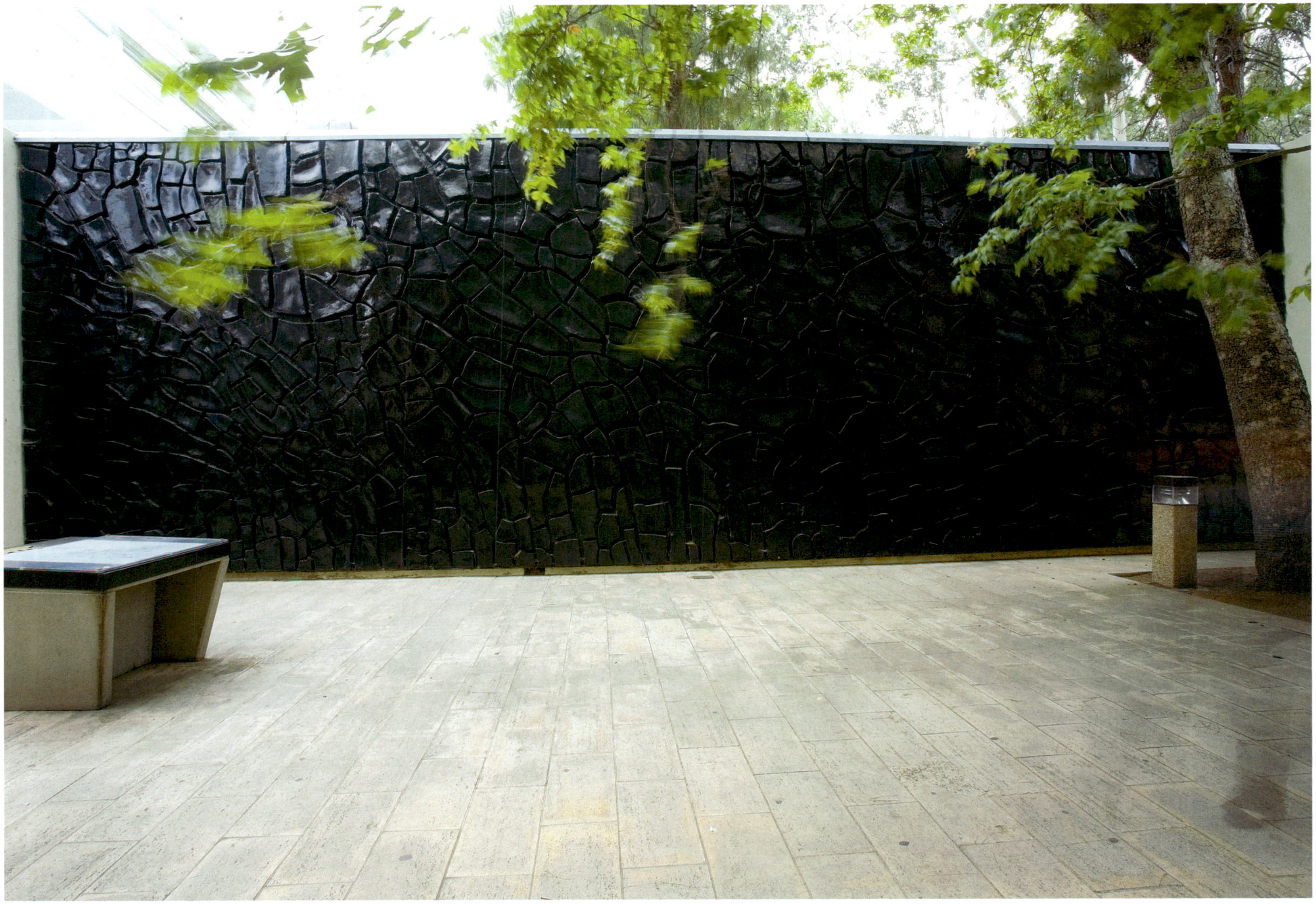

GRANDE CRETTO NERO / LARGE BLACK CRETTO
1976–77
Fired ceramic
H: 198 IN. (503 CM); W: 50 FT. (1524 CM); D: 6 IN. (15.2 CM)
Gift of the artist, 1977

Alberto Burri trained as a doctor, practiced surgery in the Italian army, and was taken prisoner by the British in North Africa in 1944. His first experiments with paint were made in a prisoner-of-war camp in Texas. Upon his return to Rome in 1946 he embraced his generation's pursuit of raw materials and began to assemble pictures out of nontraditional mediums such as pumice, tar, and burned plastic. Burri was among the advocates of art informel who proposed a break with traditional notions of order and composition and pursued spontaneous, nonfigurative, and antigeometric forms. Furthermore, his use of so-called poor materials, like the torn and stained burlap bags in his series of paintings of the early 1950s known as Sacchi (sacks), makes him a precursor of arte povera, Italy's most radical movement after futurism. In 1960 he was awarded the critic's prize for his solo show at the Venice Biennale. Burri's first retrospective in the United States was hosted by the Museum of Fine Arts in Houston in 1963, and another was held at UCLA's Frederick S. Wight Art Gallery in 1977. He received the Italian Order of Merit in 1994, a year before his death in Nice.

Grande Cretto Nero is the largest work made by Burri. It is composed of more than seven hundred pieces of ceramic tile, each one painstakingly assembled by Italian craftsmen. It relates to a series of "cracked" paintings (Cretti) made of white zinc or clay, begun in the early 1970s. When an oil painting ages, the surface of the picture often splits into a web of fine cuts, known as *craquelures*. Burri's Cretti are reminiscent of that effect, except in his case the deformity is intentional. Here the artist magnifies the effect of his paintings by replicating the cut sections in black ceramic tile. Each piece was enlarged to scale by the Baldelli firm of Città di Castello. They are placed side by side, like pieces of a giant puzzle, and recall the dried and wrinkled earth of a desert. The work's verticality, however, accentuates its pictorial quality. As it is, the grooves and slippery planes of the partitions catch the light and create an evocative shimmer. Indeed this work is an ode to Burri's great affinity for the sensuous effects of texture and chiaroscuro. A.P.

ALBERTO BURRI

(ITALIAN, 1915–1995)

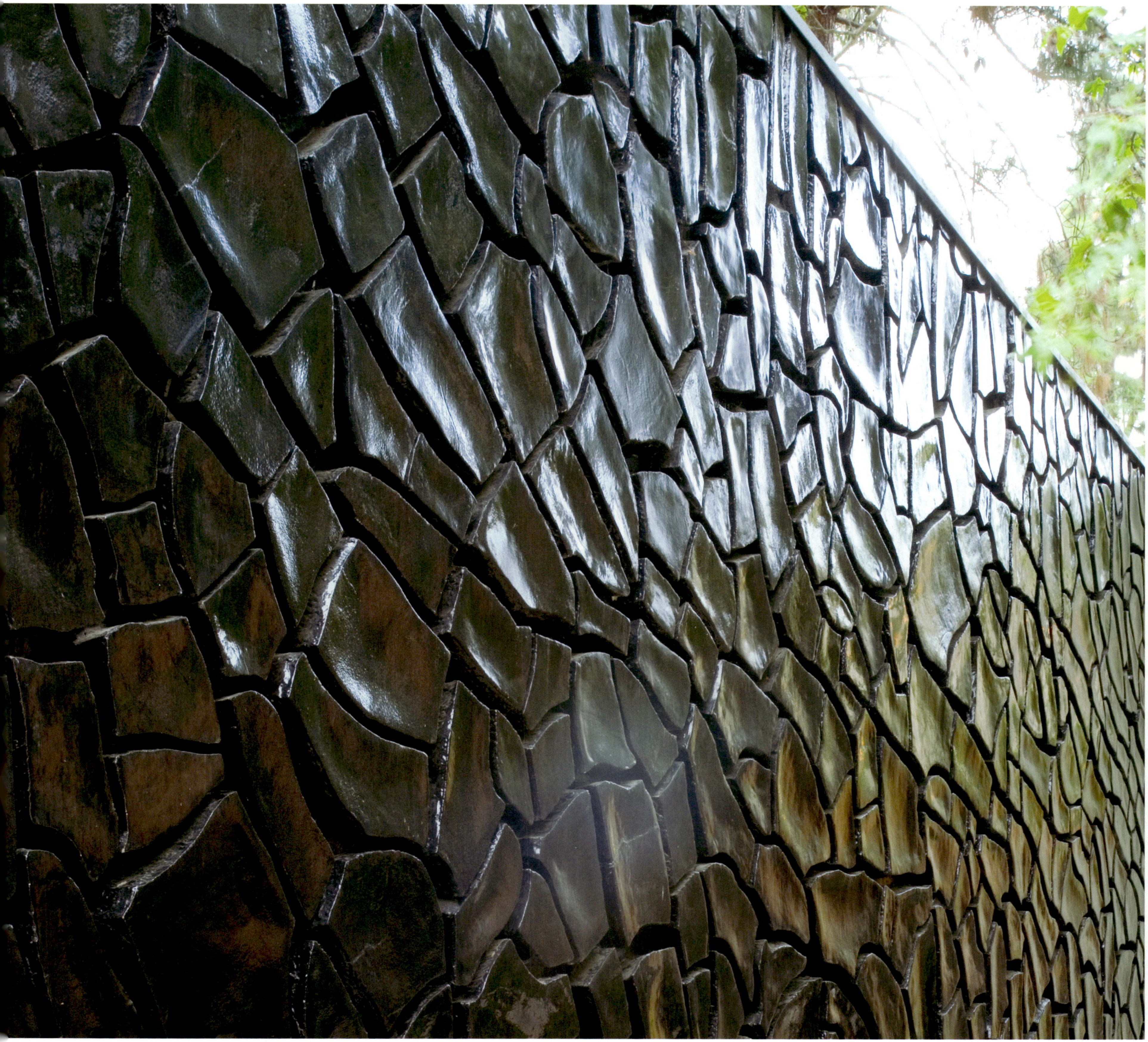

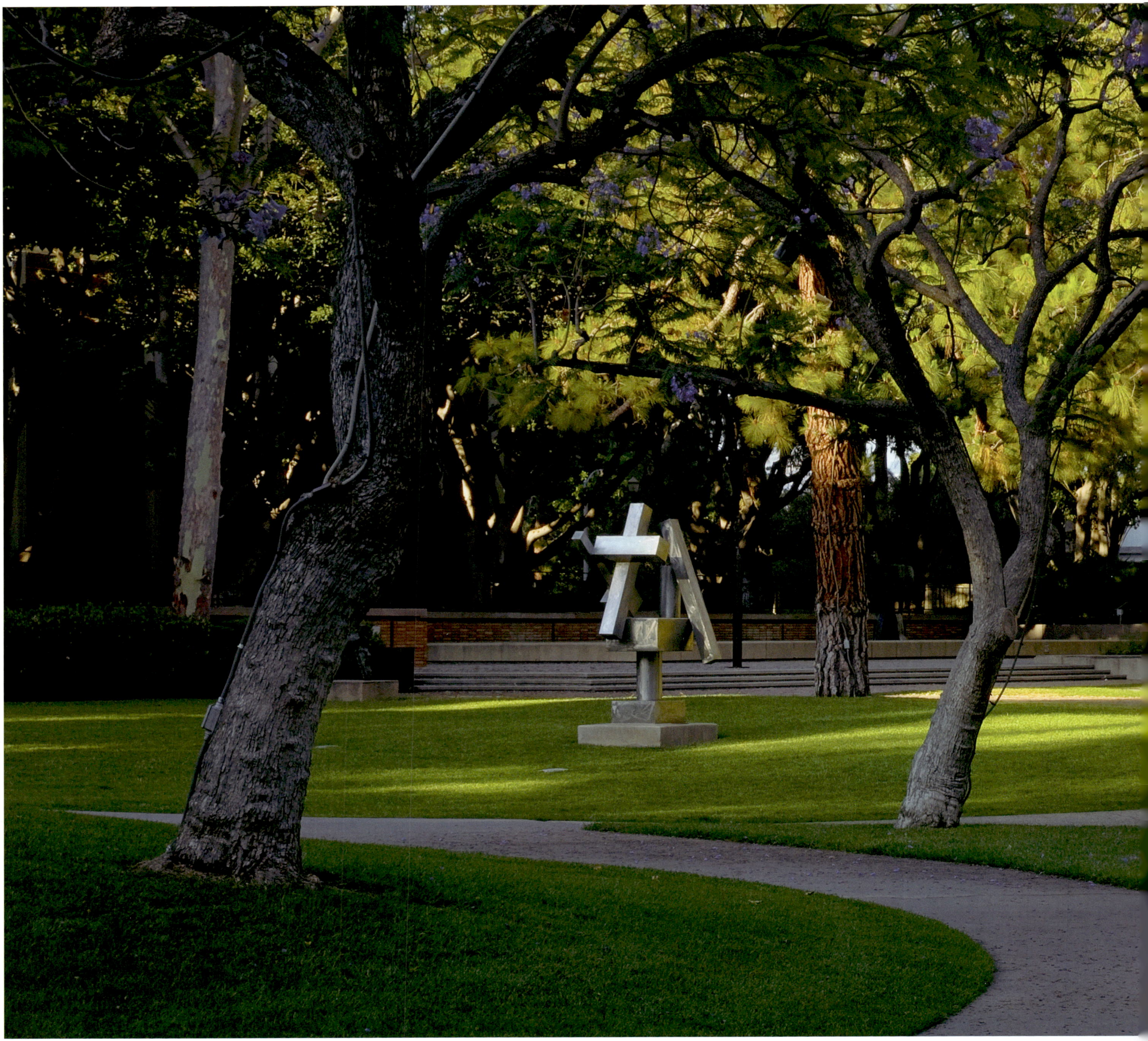

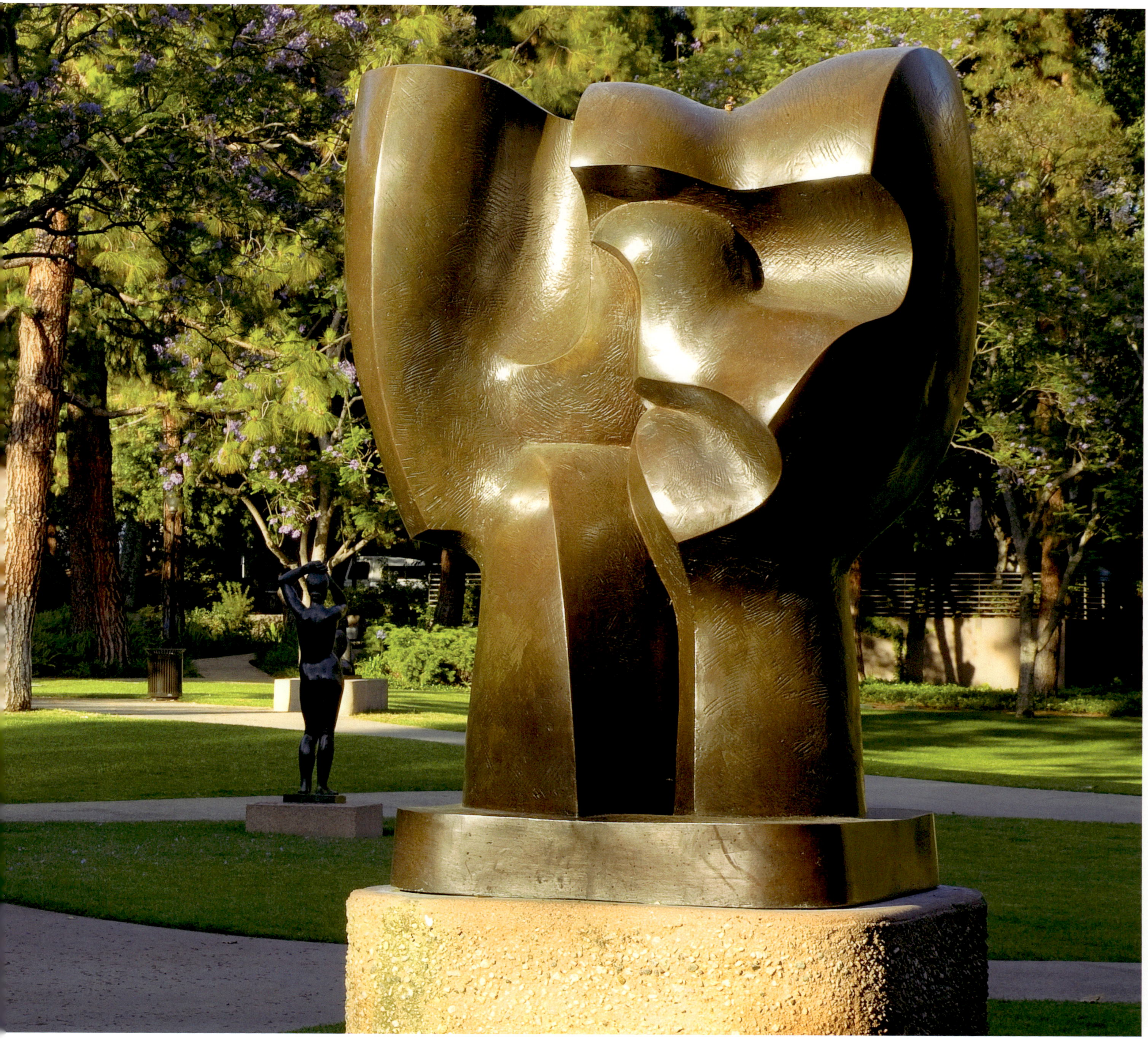

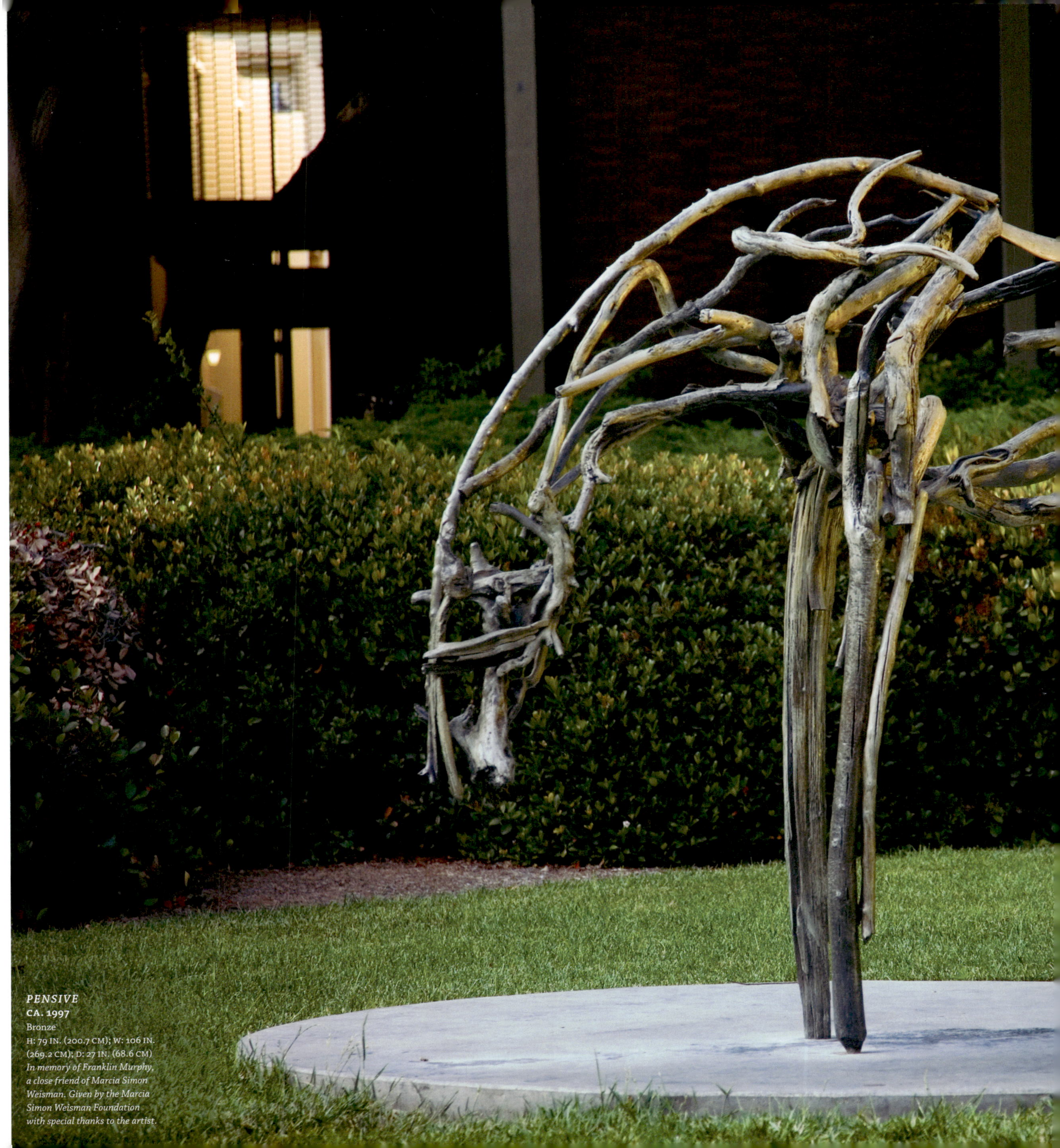

PENSIVE
CA. 1997
Bronze
H: 79 IN. (200.7 CM); W: 106 IN. (269.2 CM); D: 27 IN. (68.6 CM)
In memory of Franklin Murphy, a close friend of Marcia Simon Weisman. Given by the Marcia Simon Weisman Foundation with special thanks to the artist.

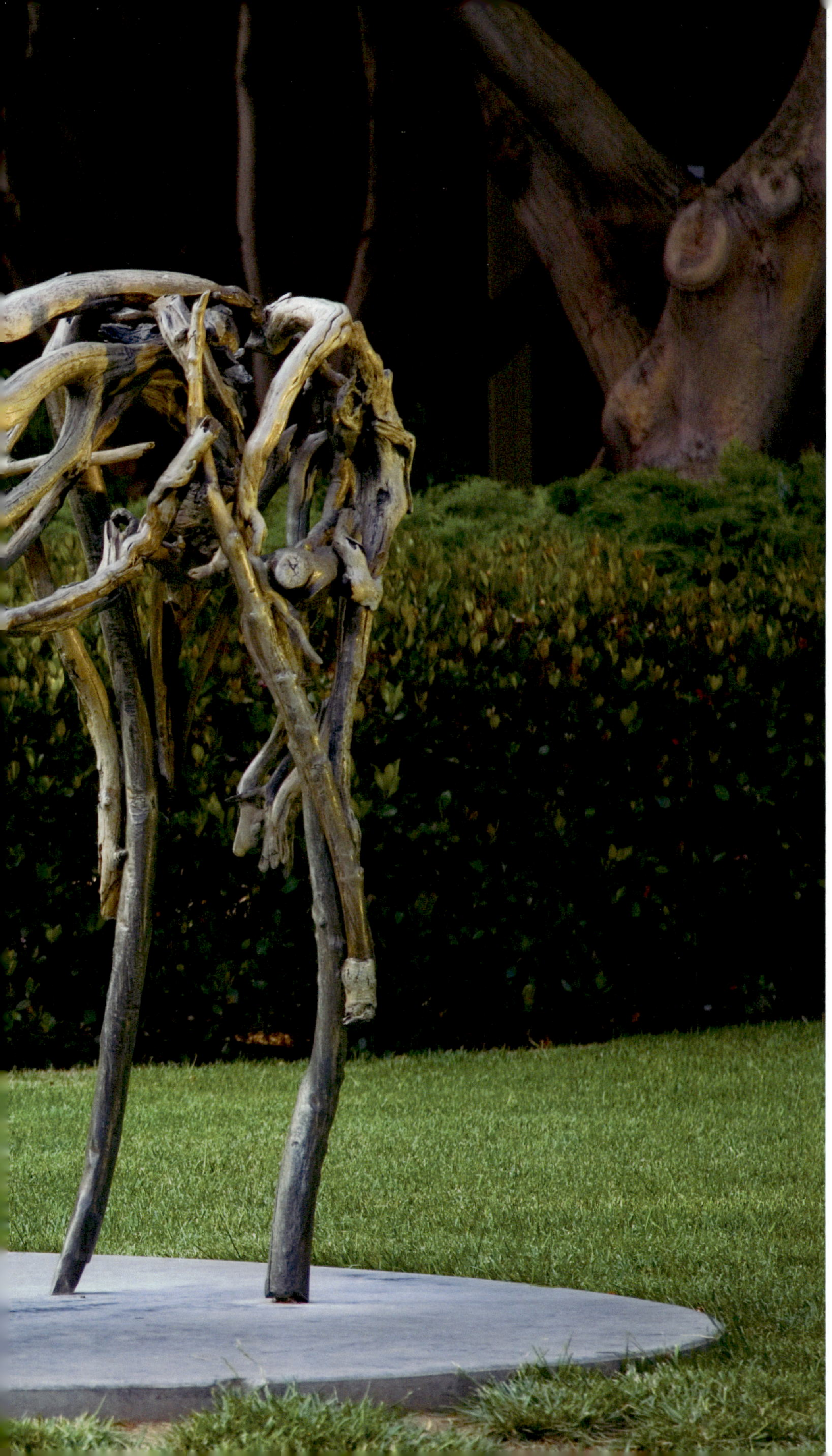

Deborah Butterfield has always been passionate about horses. As a young girl she was an avid horseback rider, played games involving horses, and made drawings of horses. While studying ceramics at the University of California, Davis, in the early 1970s, Butterfield rented a horse farm, rekindling her focus on these animals, which led her to explore the form of the horse through the medium of sculpture. In addition to functioning as metaphoric self-portraits, Butterfield's earliest horse sculptures were also inspired by her reaction to the war in Vietnam. The artist realized that horses throughout art history had universally been depicted as accessories of battle, and she wanted instead to create peaceful mares that were not warhorses. These initial horse sculptures were often composed of plaster, papier-mâché, mud, and sticks—materials that were both unwieldy and impermanent. In 1979 Butterfield began to work with steel, soon adding other metals, wood, and bronze as her preferred materials. As the artist has stated: "Different kinds of metal are like different breeds of horses. . . . Steel reminds me of Thoroughbreds, for example. Each type has its own tensile strength and its own properties."[1] In addition to these materials, Butterfield has also experimented with found objects such as tires, pipes, and corroded scrap metal in the composition of her horses.

Since 1976 Butterfield has lived in Montana, where she continues to create equine sculptures and is surrounded by living horses that inhabit a compound near her studio. *Pensive* is composed of individual bronze pieces formed by casts of driftwood that the artist collected and then welded together to suggest the form of a grazing horse. Although Butterfield created the shape of an actual horse, the components appear more like bones or a skeleton, the structure that lies beneath the skin and muscle of a living creature. *Pensive*, created specifically for the Murphy Sculpture Garden and gifted in 1997, is the most recent addition to the collection. The work's title comes from the name of a horse. Pensive sired Ponder, the horse that won the Kentucky Derby on the exact date of Butterfield's birth: May 7, 1949. C.D.

Notes

1 *Quoted in* Robert Gordon, Deborah Butterfield *(New York: Harry N. Abrams, 2003), 14.*

DEBORAH BUTTERFIELD

(AMERICAN, B. 1949)

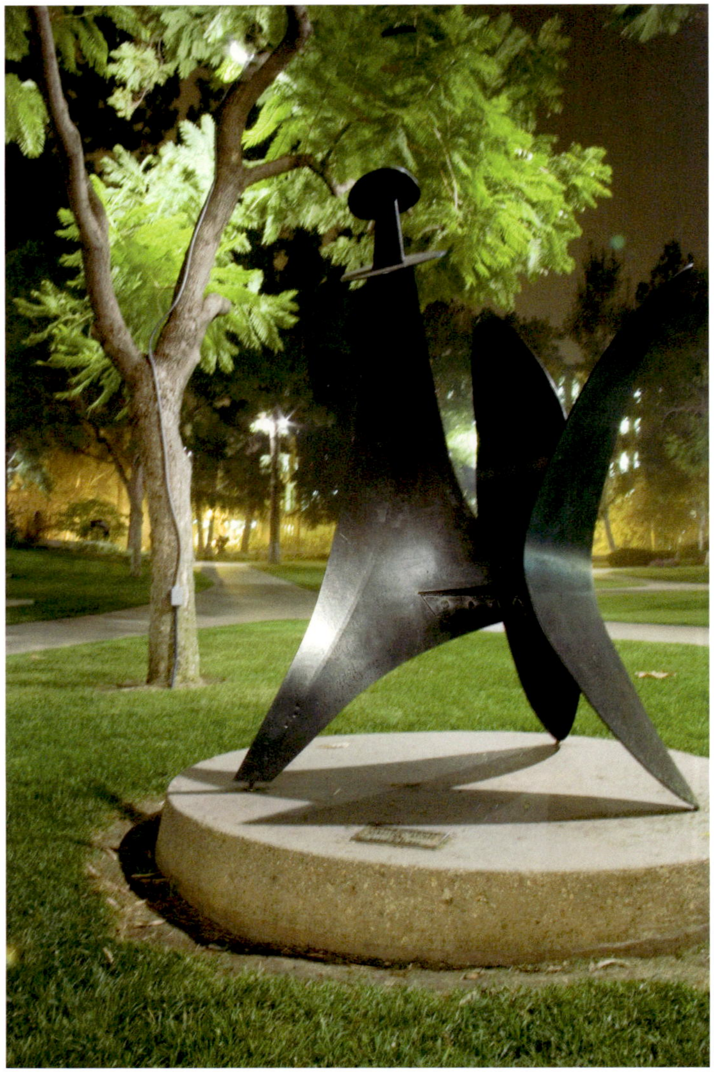

ALEXANDER CALDER

(AMERICAN, 1898–1976)

Born into a family of artists, Alexander Calder initially studied engineering at Stevens Institute of Technology in Hoboken, New Jersey, from 1915 to 1919. Soon after, however, he decided instead to become an artist and studied painting at the Art Students League of New York from 1923 to 1926. In 1926 he began producing movable wood and wire animal figures, his first experiments with moving sculpture and the beginning of his exploration of nontraditional materials. In 1927 he began giving performances of the miniature motorized work entitled *Calder's Circus*. Calder first exhibited his wire sculptures at the Salon des Humoristes in 1927, and in 1932 the Galerie Vignon exhibited his first experimental kinetic sculptures that moved randomly with air currents, named mobiles by Marcel Duchamp.

In the 1930s Calder began working on a number of stationary sculptures made of sheet metal, designated "stabiles" by Jean Arp. Though static, these abstract structures appear different when viewed from varying angles, thus creating a sense of movement similar to that experienced with the mobiles. Calder's first large-scale stabile was *Whale* (1937), a 1964 replica of which is in the Museum of Modern Art, New York. Others included the fifty-nine-foot *Teodelapio* (1962), in Spoleto, Italy, and the seventy-foot *Man*, exhibited at Expo '67 in Montreal. These giant stabiles represented a new type of public sculpture that would become increasingly prevalent in outdoor spaces throughout the world. Although Calder continued to work on giant mobiles and stabiles during the 1950s and 1960s, he also created a number of smaller stabiles such as *Button Flower*. Calder never welded his metal works but rather, as is the case with *Button Flower*, bolted them together, making it easy to disassemble the larger sculptures for shipping. Both large and small stabiles are unique works, initialed and dated by the artist. C.B.

BUTTON FLOWER
1959
Painted sheet steel
H: 70 IN. (178 CM); W: 52 IN. (132.1 CM); D: 43 IN. (109.2 CM)
Gift of David E. Bright, 1967

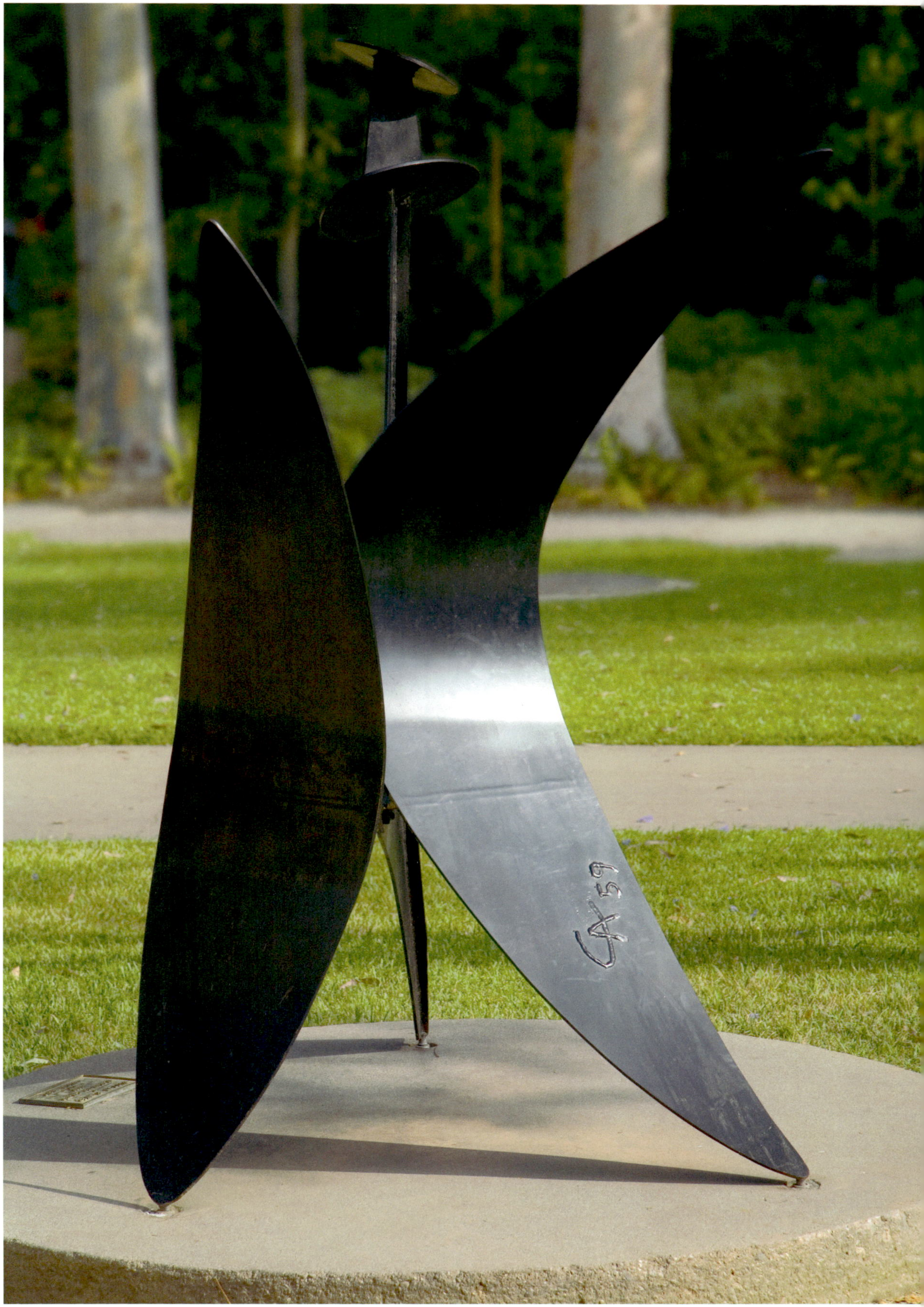

Notes
1 *Anthony Caro, in* Anthony Caro: Drawing in Space: Sculptures from 1963 to 1988, The Last Judgement, 1995–1999 *(Barcelona: Fundació Caixa Catalunya, 2002), 27.*

Anthony Caro gave up his engineering studies at Cambridge in order to attend the Royal Academy of Arts in London in 1947. The greatest impact on his early formation was an apprenticeship in the studio of Henry Moore, the pioneer of modern British sculpture, between 1951 and 1953. As an independent artist, Caro chose to depart from the traditional sculptural practices of modeling and casting in favor of a new type of constructed form. He was particularly affected by a trip to the United States in 1959 and by his encounters with the critic Clement Greenberg and with the artists Kenneth Noland and David Smith. On his return Caro began to create abstract pieces from scrap metal and steel beams. His first major show in England was at the Whitechapel Art Gallery in London in 1963, and his first American exhibition was at the Museum of Modern Art in 1975. Caro's most recent retrospective took place at Tate Britain in 2005. Caro moved forward from the organic tendencies of Moore and his generation, launching a new chapter in the history of British sculpture. He has received countless prizes and honorary degrees, and he continues to produce work today in his Hampstead studio.

The raw, industrial quality of Caro's work is felt in *Halfway*, with its geometrically partitioned girders. Here strong contrasts of light and shade accentuate the sweeping lines of the sculpture and define its changing perspectives. The sharply defined shadows are integral elements of the composition. They join the cut abstract forms, which alternately intersect and run parallel to one another, as they would in a cubist painting. A uniform coat of brown paint blends the individual parts of the sculpture and distinguishes them from basic building material. By placing *Halfway* so low on the ground, Caro intentionally defies the traditional laws of sculpture, inviting the onlooker to walk around and encapsulate the sculpture's mutating design. In his own words: "I wanted to give my sculpture the immediacy one feels in talking one-to-one with another person. It was for this reason that I eventually did away with the plinth, and placed my figure on the same ground as the spectator and sat it on a bench."[1] A.P.

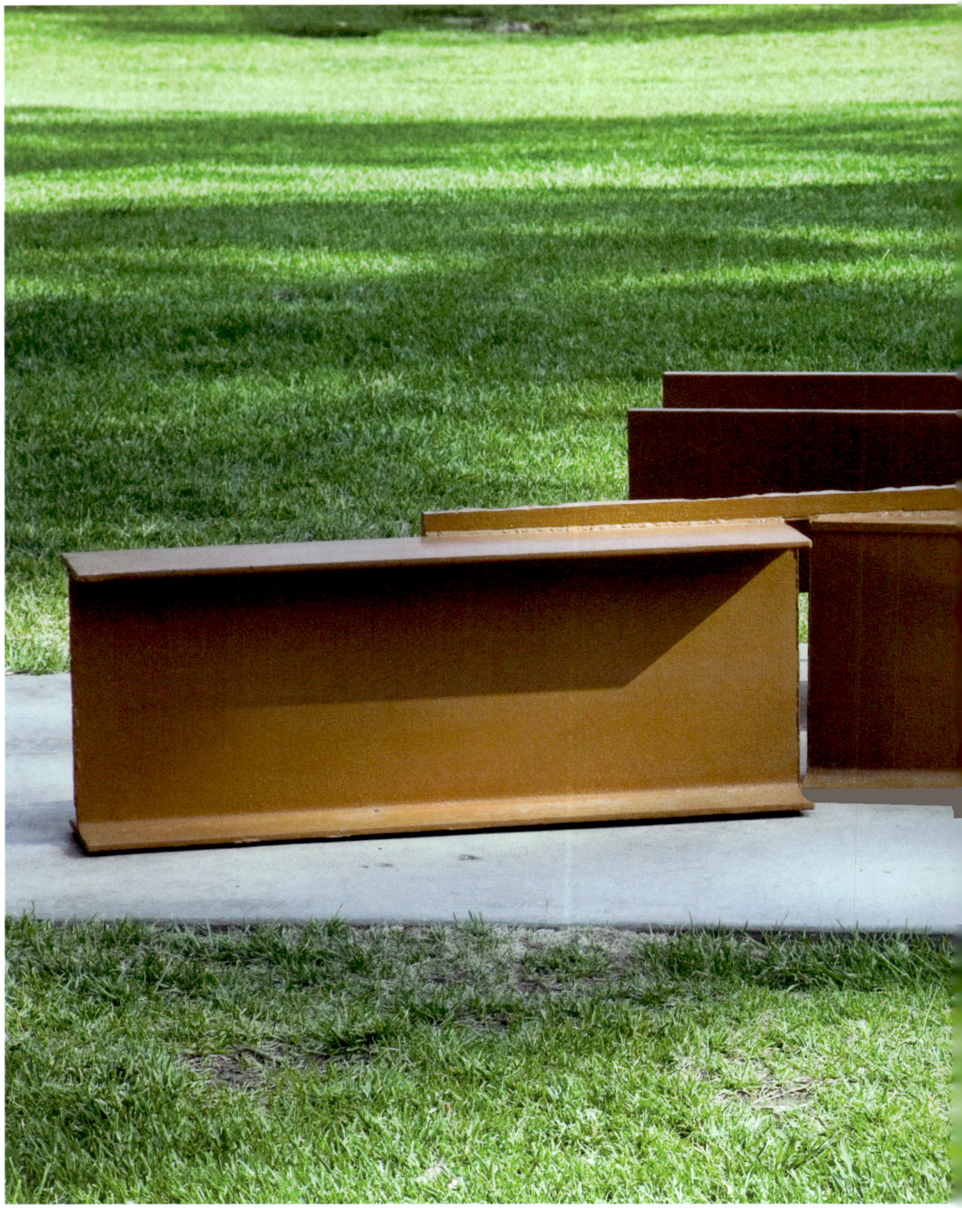

ANTHONY CARO

(BRITISH, B. 1924)

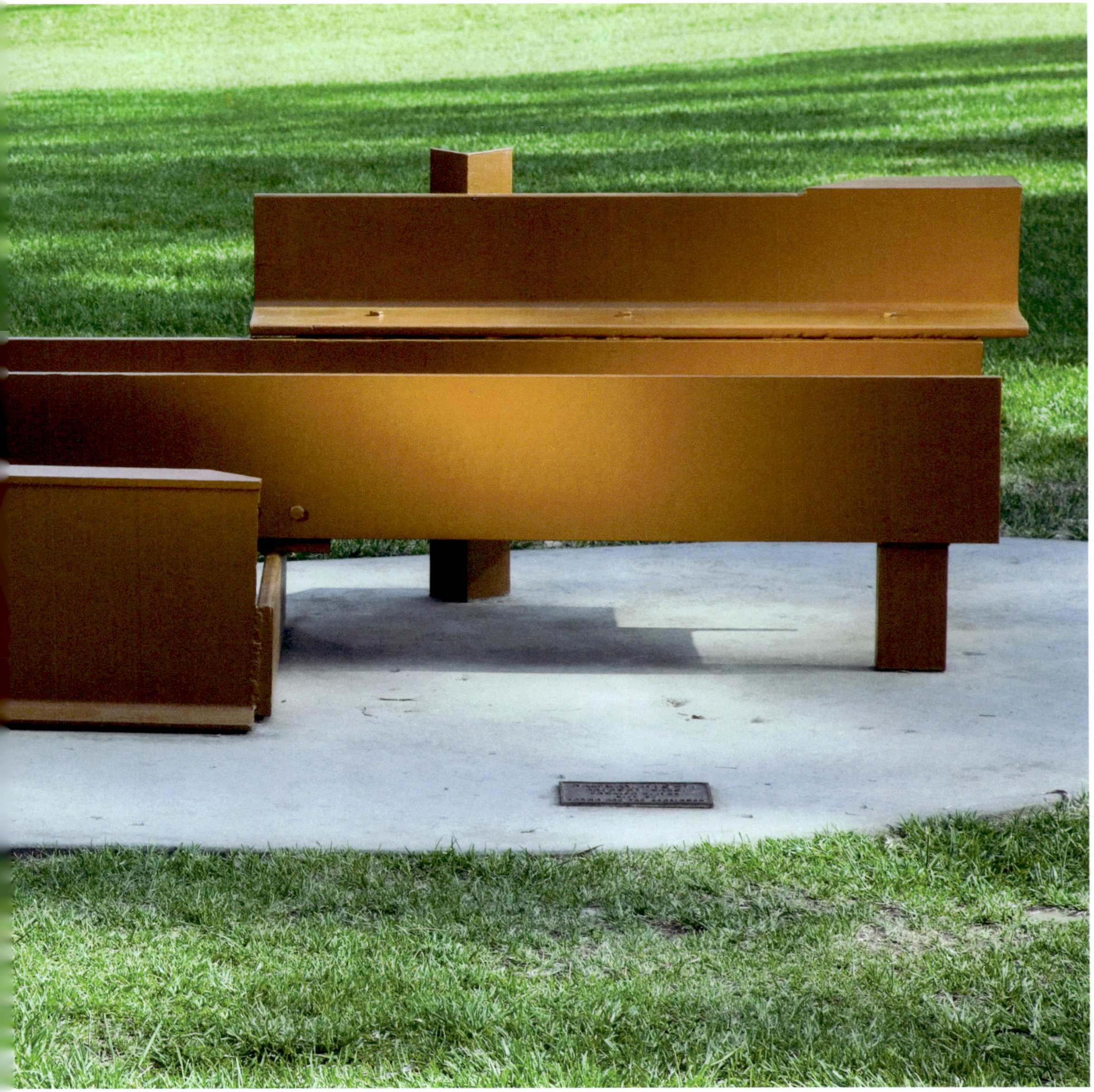

HALFWAY
1971
Painted mild steel
H: 29 IN. (73.5 CM); W: 109 IN.
(272.5 CM); D: 55 IN. (137.5 CM)
Gift of Ted and
Jarma Bensinger, 1973

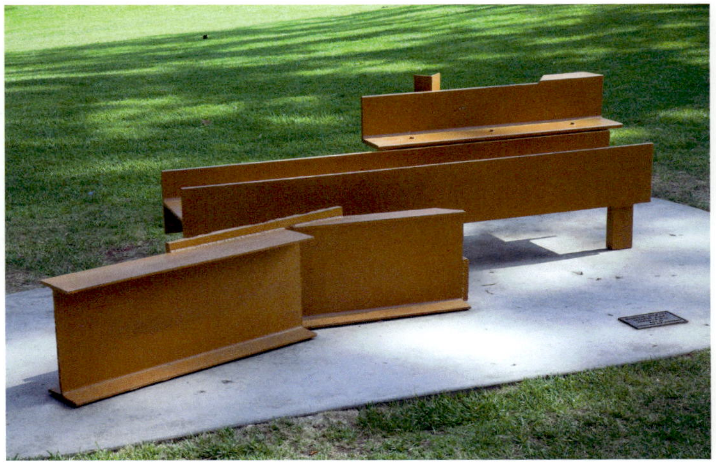

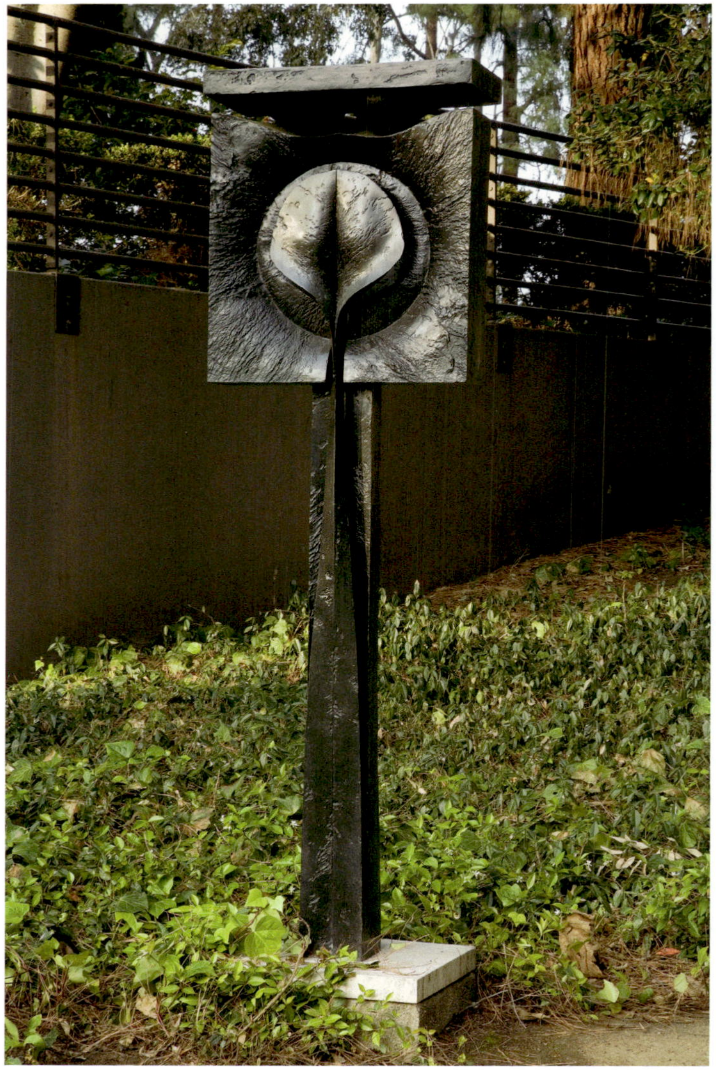

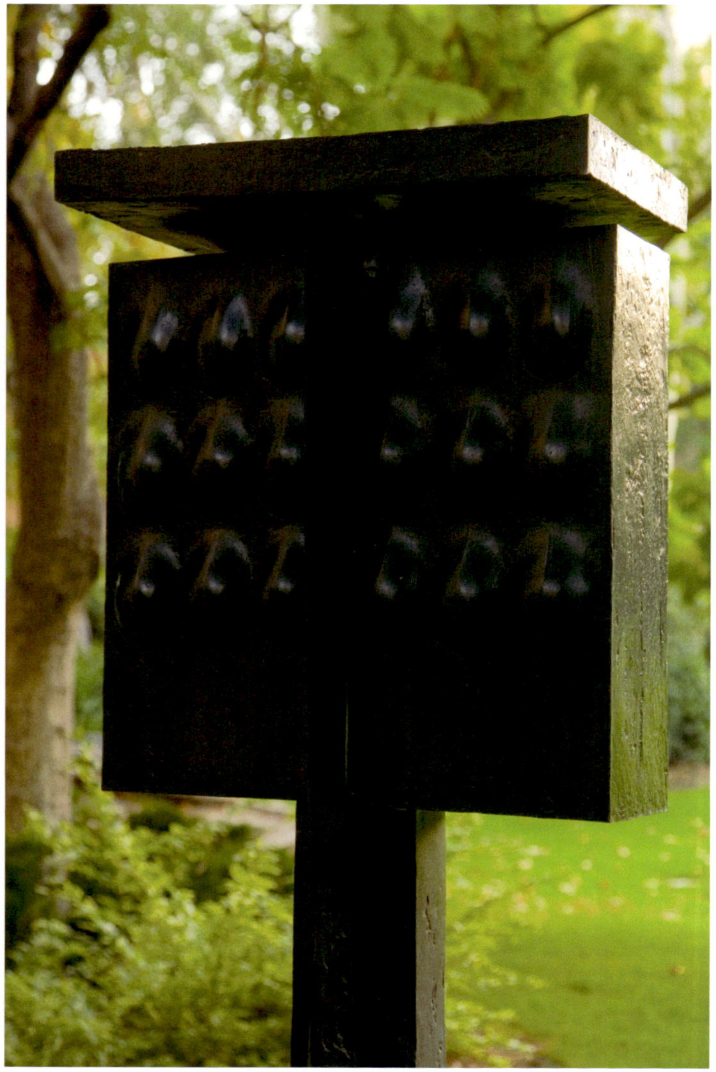

ARTEMIS OF EPHESUS
1964–66
Bronze
H: 84 IN. (213.4 CM); W: 24¾ IN. (62.9 CM); D: 14¼ IN. (36.2 CM)
Edition: 1/6
Foundry: Nicci, Rome
Gift of Nathaniel and Margaret Wentworth Owings Foundation, 1967

ALDO CASANOVA

(AMERICAN, B. 1929)

Rome and its classical heritage are an underlying source in the work of Aldo Casanova. After he received his PhD from Ohio State University in 1957, he was awarded the Prix de Rome Fellowship in sculpture for study at the American Academy in Rome. *Artemis of Ephesus* was made on a subsequent sojourn in Rome between 1964 and 1966, as part of a series of mythology-inspired bronze sculptures. After returning to the United States, he taught at universities throughout the country. In 1992 he was elected to the National Academy of Design, and in 1994 he was made a fellow of the National Sculpture Society. For more than thirty years, Casanova has taught at Scripps College in Claremont, California, where he is now emeritus professor of art. A retrospective of his work at the college in 2002 paid tribute to his life as an artist and his legacy as a teacher.[1]

In *Artemis of Ephesus* the warrior goddess Artemis, who was worshipped at an ancient temple at Ephesus, is conceived as a combination of human and organic form. Viewed from the front, the "face" consists of an open leaf, enclosed in a circle or Artemis's symbolic moon. The curvaceous lines and sensual design of this central motif are framed in a comparatively severe boxlike structure, as if to insinuate a parallel between the feminine and masculine sides of the goddess. The back of the frame contains a set of multiple breasts, which also appear on the ancient sculpture of Artemis in Ephesus (a version of this cult image is in the Vatican Museums). Here the surface is polished, while at the front it has the coarse quality of bark. Casanova's sculpture has the geometry and perfection of a plant. An emblem of femininity and fertility combined, it springs from the ground like the trees that surround it in its current environment. A.P.

Notes
1 Aldo Casanova: A Retrospective, *essay by Suzanne Muchnic (Claremont, Calif.: Ruth Chandler Williamson Gallery, Scripps College, 2002), 74, fig. I.31.*

ENCOUNTER VIII
1957
Bronze
H: 73 IN. (185.4 CM); W: 28½ IN. (72.4 CM); D: 21 IN. (53.3 CM)
Edition: /4
Gift of Mrs. David E. Bright, 1967

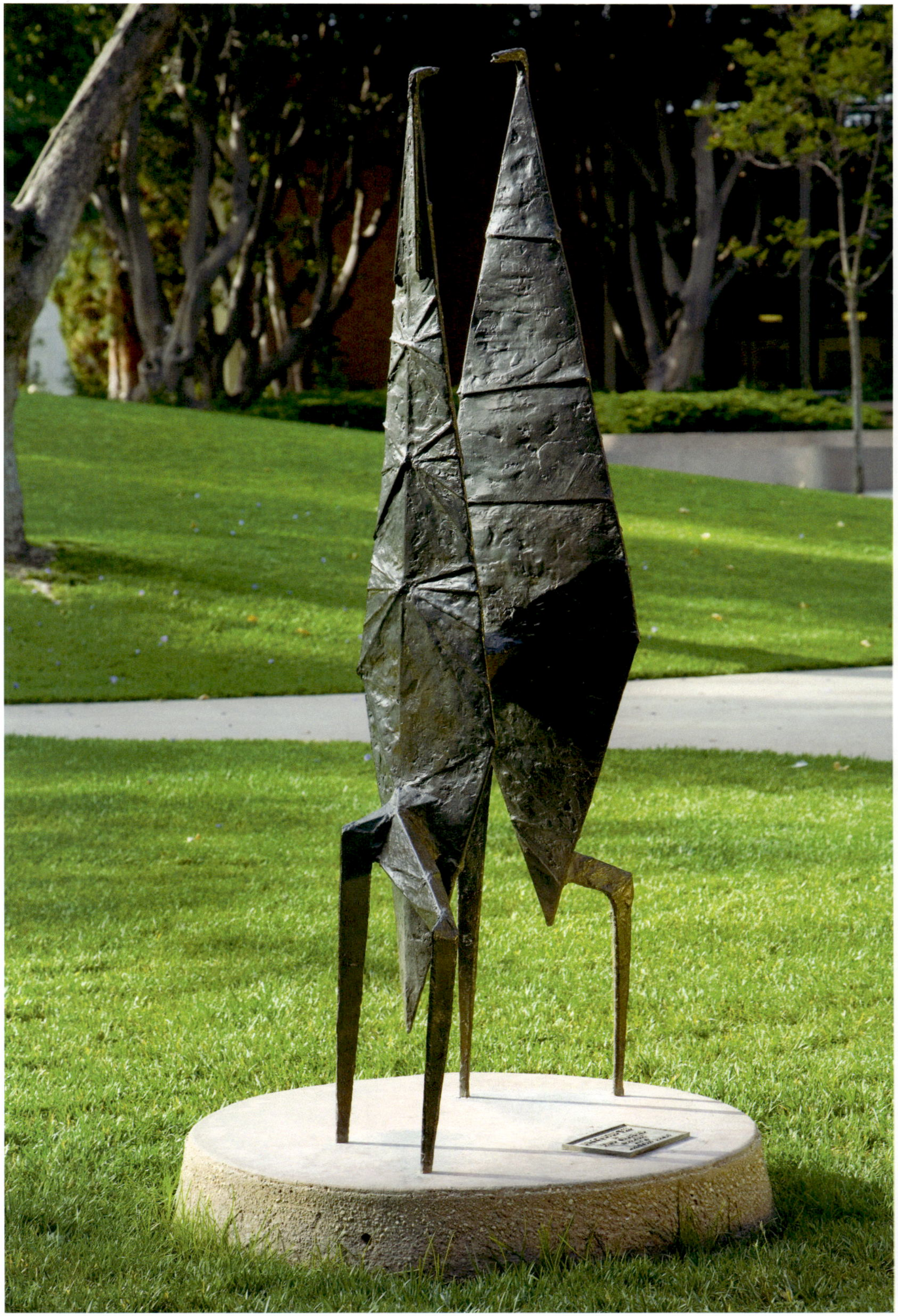

British sculptor Lynn Chadwick trained as an architect and served as a naval aviation pilot in World War II. Between 1946 and 1952 he was based in Gloucestershire and produced designs for textiles, furniture, and buildings, thus combining his interests in art and architecture. He began to experiment with sculpture at this time and held a first exhibition of mobiles at Gimpel Fils Gallery in London in 1950. Subsequently, after learning how to weld, he began to tackle large-scale works in the form of abstracted figures. His earlier experiences in architecture and aviation are reflected in the calculated equilibrium of his sculptures and in their frequent references to avian creatures. He was chosen to represent Great Britain at the Venice Biennale in 1952 and again in 1956, when he was awarded the International Sculpture Prize. Chadwick produced much of his work at Lypiatt Park, a medieval enclave in Gloucestershire and his home until his death in 2003. Among Britain's most respected artists, he was named a Commander of the Order of the British Empire in 1964 and was also honored by the French when he was created an Officier de l'Ordre des Arts et des Lettres in 1985.

In *Encounter VIII* two beaked figures stand face-to-face, as if silently acknowledging each other's presence. They coexist as different yet balanced forms, bound at the hip and supported on four thinly tapered legs. Undulated stellar patterns catch the light across the surface of their triangular bodies. Chadwick's complex assemblage is based on a model made in 1955 out of pieces originally created for an architectural project. The construction combines the balance of a geometric structure with the character of a surrealist beast. A.P.

LYNN CHADWICK

(BRITISH, 1914–2003)

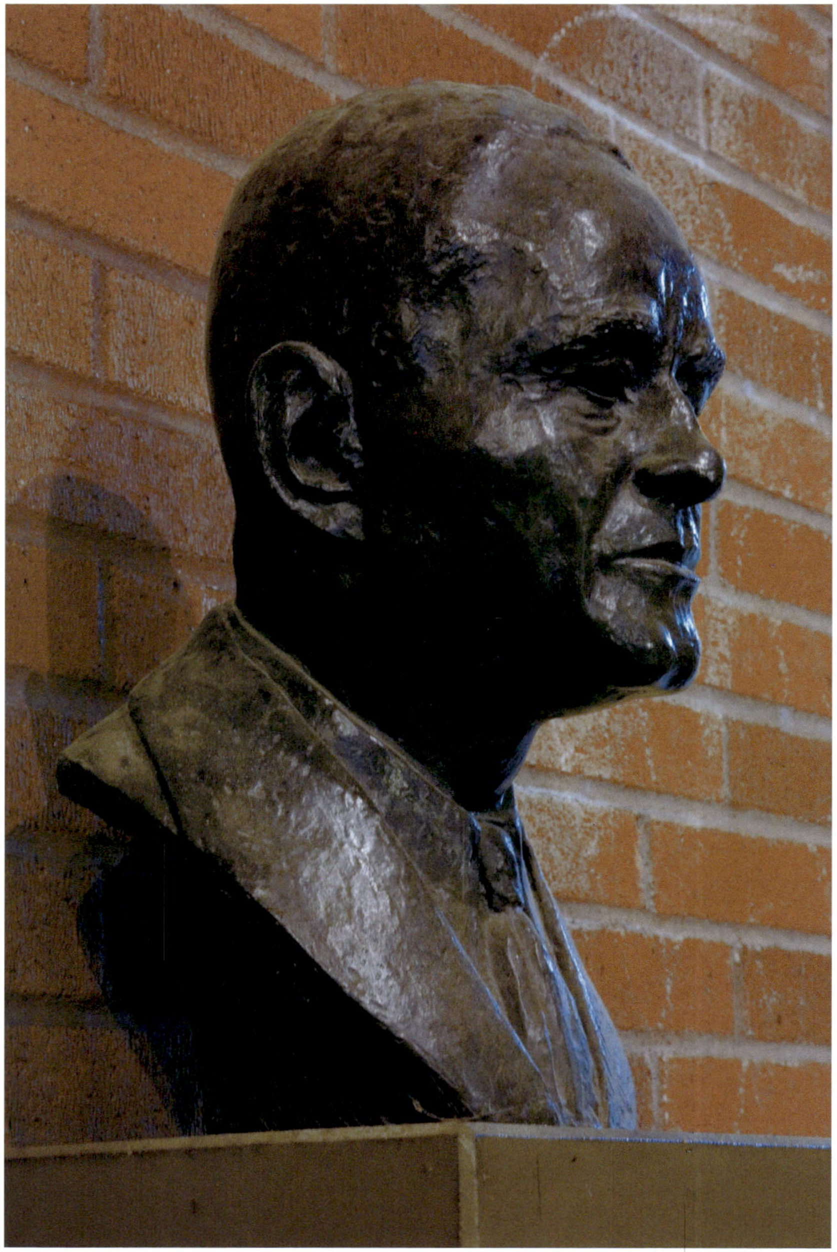

RALPH J. BUNCHE
1958
Bronze
H: 17 IN. (43 CM); W: 9 IN. (22.9 CM); D: 11 IN. (27.9 CM)
Gift of Leo Cherne, 1969

Leo Cherne was an economist who served as executive director of the Research Institute of America, chairman of the executive committee of Freedom House, and chairman of the International Rescue Committee (IRC). Under Cherne's leadership the IRC, which grew out of efforts to save endangered people in Nazi Germany and Vichy France, became the world's largest organization for the relief and resettlement of refugees. He served on various presidential commissions and boards and was awarded the Presidential Medal of Freedom in 1984.

Cherne began making sculpture in 1954, while still actively working for the IRC and serving as an economic consultant and analyst. He created portraits of many distinguished and well-known public figures, including a bust of Albert Schweitzer at the Smithsonian Institution and a bust of Abraham Lincoln for the Lincoln Museum (now Ford's Theatre) in Washington, D.C. Ralph J. Bunche (1904–1971) studied political science at UCLA, where he received his undergraduate degree in 1927, and at Harvard University, where he received a PhD in 1934. In 1950 Bunche was awarded the Nobel Peace Prize for his efforts in mediating the conflict in the Middle East. UCLA's Bunche Hall was dedicated on May 23, 1969, and the university's Ralph Bunche Center for African American Studies also bears the name of its distinguished alumnus. C.B.

LEO CHERNE

(AMERICAN, 1912–1999)

COLLOQUIO DURO / DIFFICULT DIALOGUE
1959
Bronze
H: 53 IN. (134.5 CM); W: 43 IN. (109.2 CM); D: 4½ IN. (11.5 CM)
Gift of David E. Bright, 1967

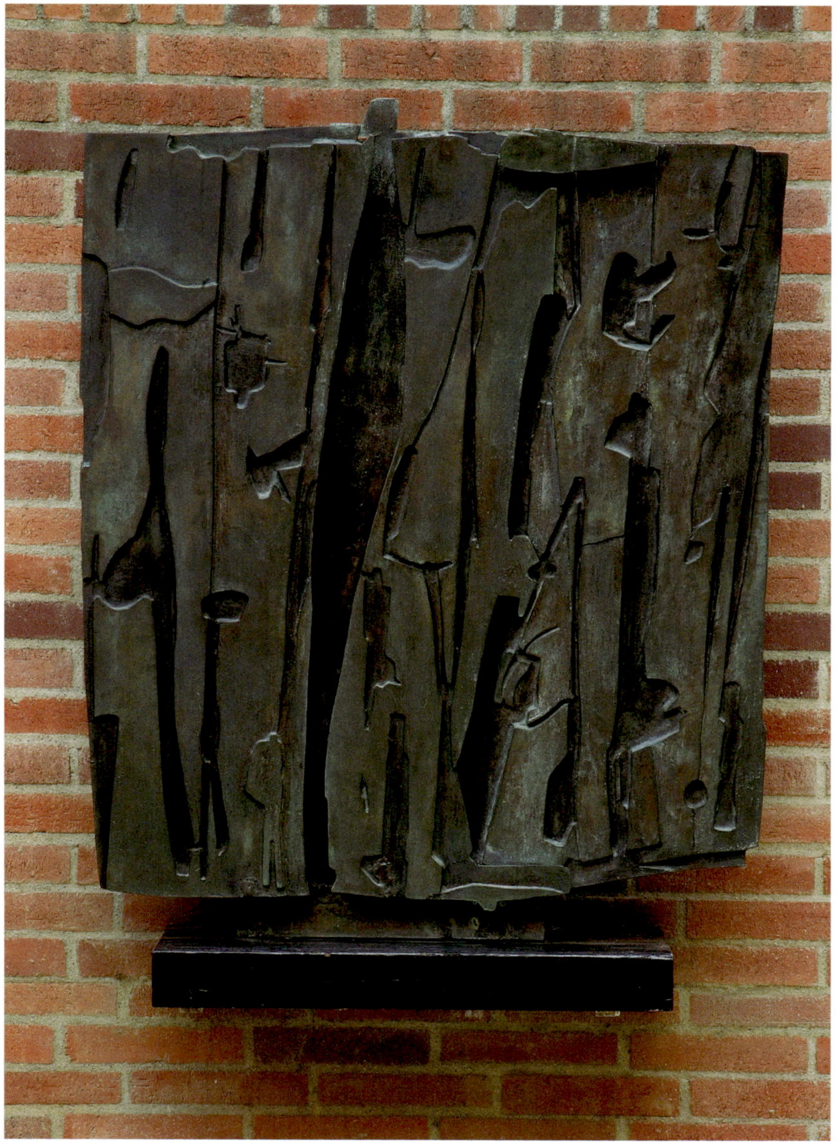

The Sicilian artist Pietro Consagra studied at the Accademia di Belle Arti in Palermo between 1941 and 1944, then proceeded to Rome, where he joined the Italian avant-garde. By 1947 he had produced his first abstract sculptures and developed explorations of form in relief. Consagra published a number of polemics, such as *Necessità della scultura*, of 1952. His activist pursuits led him to found the artists' groups Forma, in 1947, and Continuità, in 1961. Although he pushed his art in new directions, he worked in the traditional manner, beginning with small preparatory sketches on paper, followed by a model and then the final work. Consagra's creations were fixtures at Venice Biennales from 1952 to 1972. Throughout his career he received numerous public commissions, such as the bronze sculptures for the Garden of Pinocchio in Collodi in 1963, and a sculpture for the Foreign Ministry in Rome in 1966.

The title of the work presented here translates as *Difficult Dialogue*, and it is in effect a platform for visual discourse. It is part of a series of Dialogues made between 1954 and 1962, which share an underlying recognition of the role of humankind within a changing world. The sculpture is reminiscent of a carved woodblock, with its slightly primitive shapes that overlap and move in and out of the surface. A wooden model probably formed the basis for the cast bronze. Consagra's skill is particularly appreciated when the work is viewed from the side: what appears as a textured array of forms from the front is actually a very thin, undulated sheet of metal. A.P.

PIETRO CONSAGRA

(ITALIAN, 1920–2005)

MOTHER AND CHILD
1962–64
Bronze
H: 111 ⅝ IN. (283.5 CM); W: 37 IN. (94 CM); D: 37 IN. (94 CM)
Edition: 1/5
Gift of David E. Bright, 1967

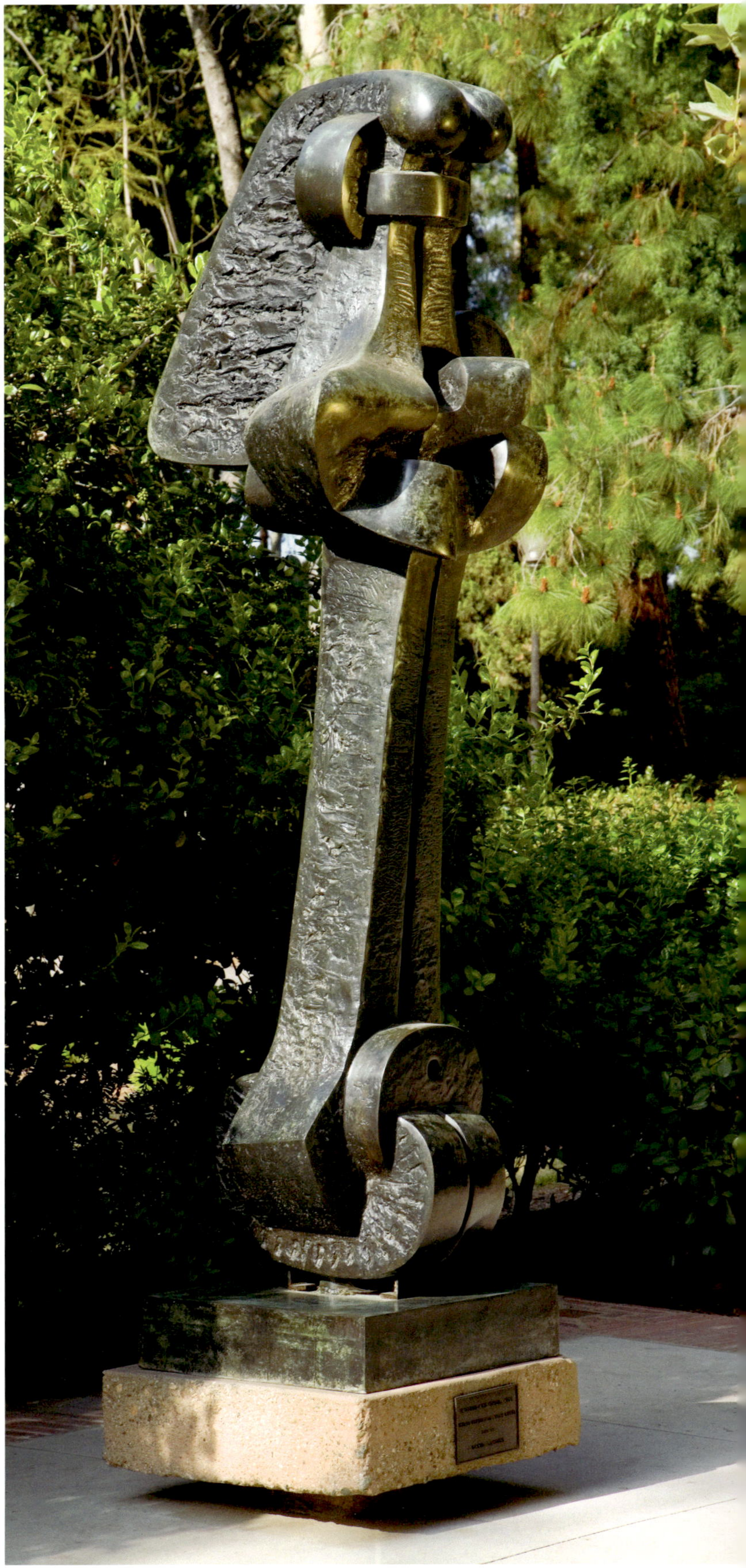

In 1950 Romanian-born Sorel Etrog immigrated with his family to Israel, where he studied drawing, painting, sculpture, graphics, and scenic design at the Tel Aviv Art Institute. In 1958 Etrog had his first solo exhibition in Tel Aviv and was awarded a scholarship to study at the Brooklyn Museum Art School. In New York, Etrog met Sam Zacks, an art collector from Toronto, who purchased one of the artist's painted constructions and offered him a studio in Ontario for the summer of 1959. Etrog continued to commute between New York and Canada until 1963, when he decided to close his New York studio and settle in Toronto, where he continues to live to this day. In addition to making wood, marble, and bronze sculptures and two-dimensional painted constructions, he has also illustrated books, practiced printmaking and painting, designed sets and costumes for plays, written and directed films, and choreographed and composed electronic music for the 1984 public performance of *The Bodifestation of the Kite*, a tribute to his friend Samuel Beckett.[1]

The multifaceted breadth of Etrog's work manifests itself from one medium to another. The artist credits the Brooklyn Museum's collection of African, pre-Columbian, and Oceanic sculpture as profoundly influential in the development of his own sculpture, since he had to pass by it every day while he attended school there in the late 1950s. *War Remembrance,* of the early 1960s, includes the pronounced arrow-shaped motif that Etrog employed in wood constructions of the late 1950s. The arrow image harks back to a prehistoric age, revealing his fascination with form at its most elemental. As the 1960s progressed, Etrog's sculpture shifted to an emphasis on individual figures with a prominent vertical alignment. Frequently these figures involved themes of women and fertility, as in *Mother and Child*. Although formally abstract, the sculpture embodies a contemporary view of a motif that has remained constant throughout the history of art and within all cultures. C.D.

Notes
1 *See Pierre Restany,* Sorel Etrog *(Munich: Prestel, 2001), 10–11, for discussion of this performance piece.*

SOREL ETROG

(CANADIAN, B. 1933)

WAR REMEMBRANCE
1960–61
Bronze
H: 17 IN. (43.2 CM); W: 41 IN. (104.1 CM); D: 22 ½ IN. (57.2 CM)
Edition: 5/5
Gift of Anna Bing Arnold, 1965

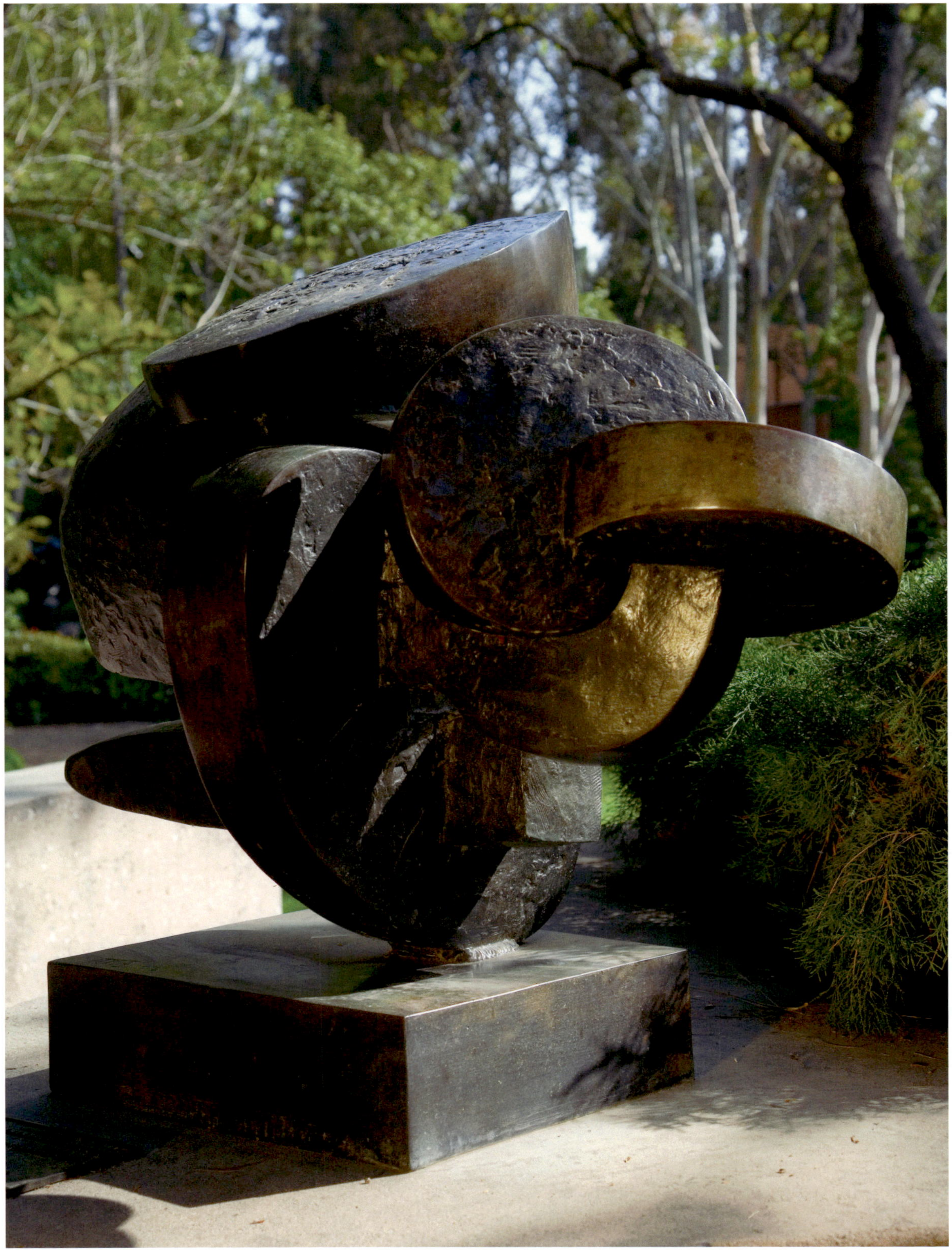

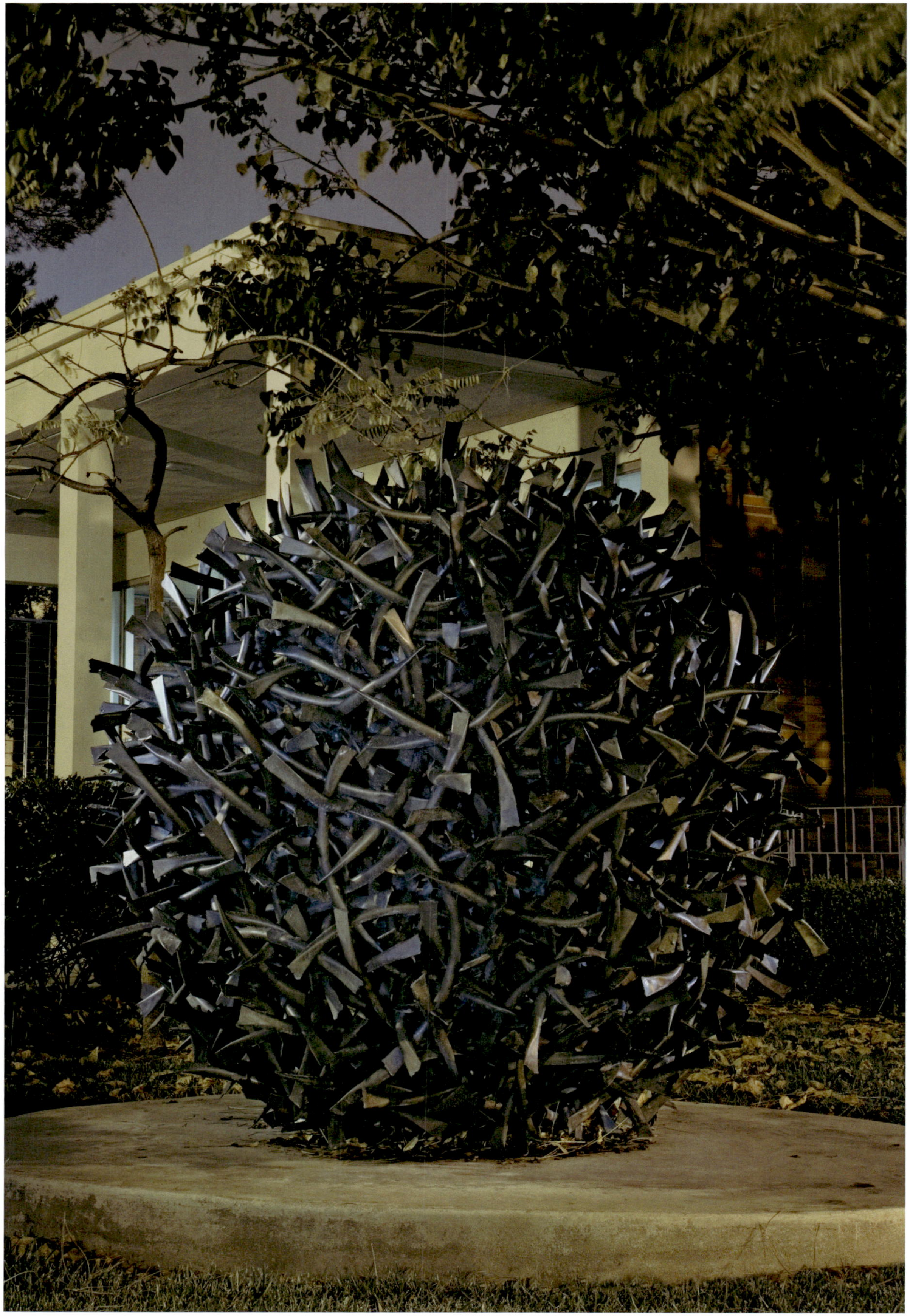

POINT AS A SET NO. 25
1970
Copper
DIAM: 74 IN. (188 CM)
Gift of Mr. and Mrs. Arthur Spitzer, 1970

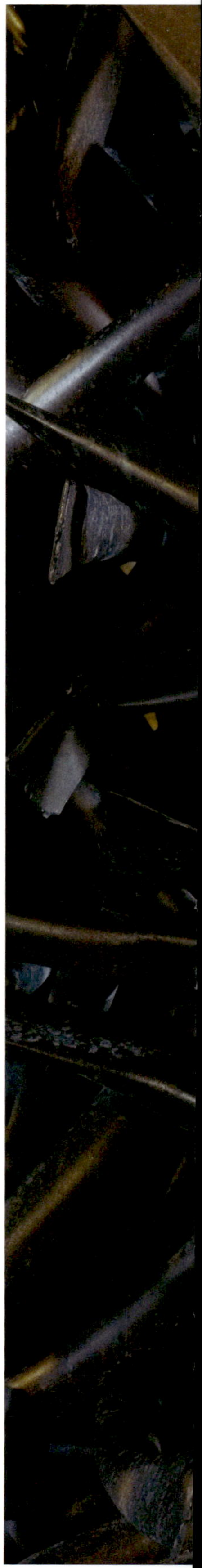

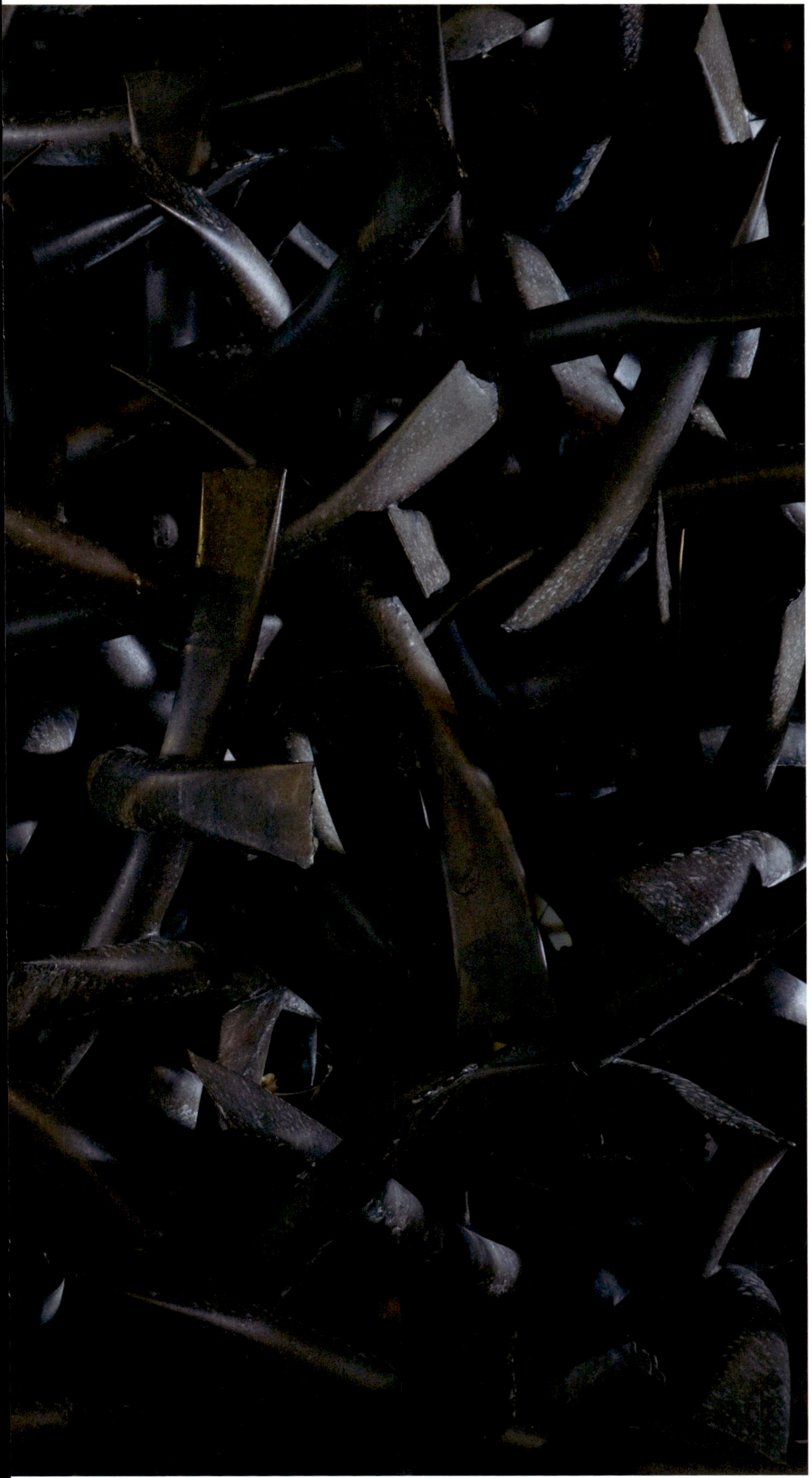

CLAIRE FALKENSTEIN

(AMERICAN, 1908–1997)

Claire Falkenstein received her BA from the University of California, Berkeley, in 1930. In 1933 she received a grant to study at Mills College with the sculptor Alexander Archipenko. Over the next decade she produced ceramic works that fused painting and sculpture. After completing her studies, she moved to San Francisco, where she exhibited regularly and taught at the California School of Fine Arts until 1950. In 1950 she moved to Paris, returning to California in 1962. During these years she increasingly experimented with nontraditional tools and processes, including power saws and readymades, and her work became almost entirely abstract. In 1979 she received the John Simon Guggenheim Fellowship Award for public art in Los Angeles. She lived and worked in Venice, California, until her death in 1997.

Falkenstein worked with a variety of materials throughout her long career, producing large-scale sculpture in addition to paintings, ceramics, stained-glass windows, and prints. Her major commissions include the steel and glass *Garden Gates* (1961) for the Guggenheim Residence in Venice, Italy; stair sculptures for the Galerie Stadler in Paris and Galleria Spazio in Rome; fifteen three-dimensional stained-glass window screens and eight doors for the Saint Basil Church, Los Angeles (1968–69); and her Structure and Flow fountains at the California Federal Savings and Loan, Los Angeles (1965, now destroyed), the Fresno Mall (1966), and the Long Beach Museum of Art (1970), all in California.

In 1958 Falkenstein began to use lightweight copper tubing, utilizing short, curved lengths of it to create her first Point as a Set sculpture the following year. Ultimately the series would comprise forty-one sculptures produced over a period of twenty-five years. The sculptures range from small tabletop pieces to large-scale outdoor works such as the UCLA sculpture. Describing *No. 26* (1970–71), a similar work in the Tate Gallery, London, Falkenstein writes: "When one contemplates this work, energy seems to flow through the space intervals between the copper boundaries. Moving from interval to interval, from the interior to the exterior.... A visceral communication is resolved in total involvement. The observer should have re-enacted in himself the meaning of the structure."[1] C.B.

Notes

1 *Claire Falkenstein, artist's statement (1971), Tate Online, "Collection," http://www.tate.org.uk/servlet/ViewWork?cgroupid=999999961&workid=4219&searchid=8947&tabview=text.*

MULIER
CA. 1912
Portland stone
H: 84 IN. (213.4 CM); W: 22 IN. (55.9 CM); D: 19 IN. (48.3 CM)
Acquired through the Michael J. Connell Memorial Fund, 1965

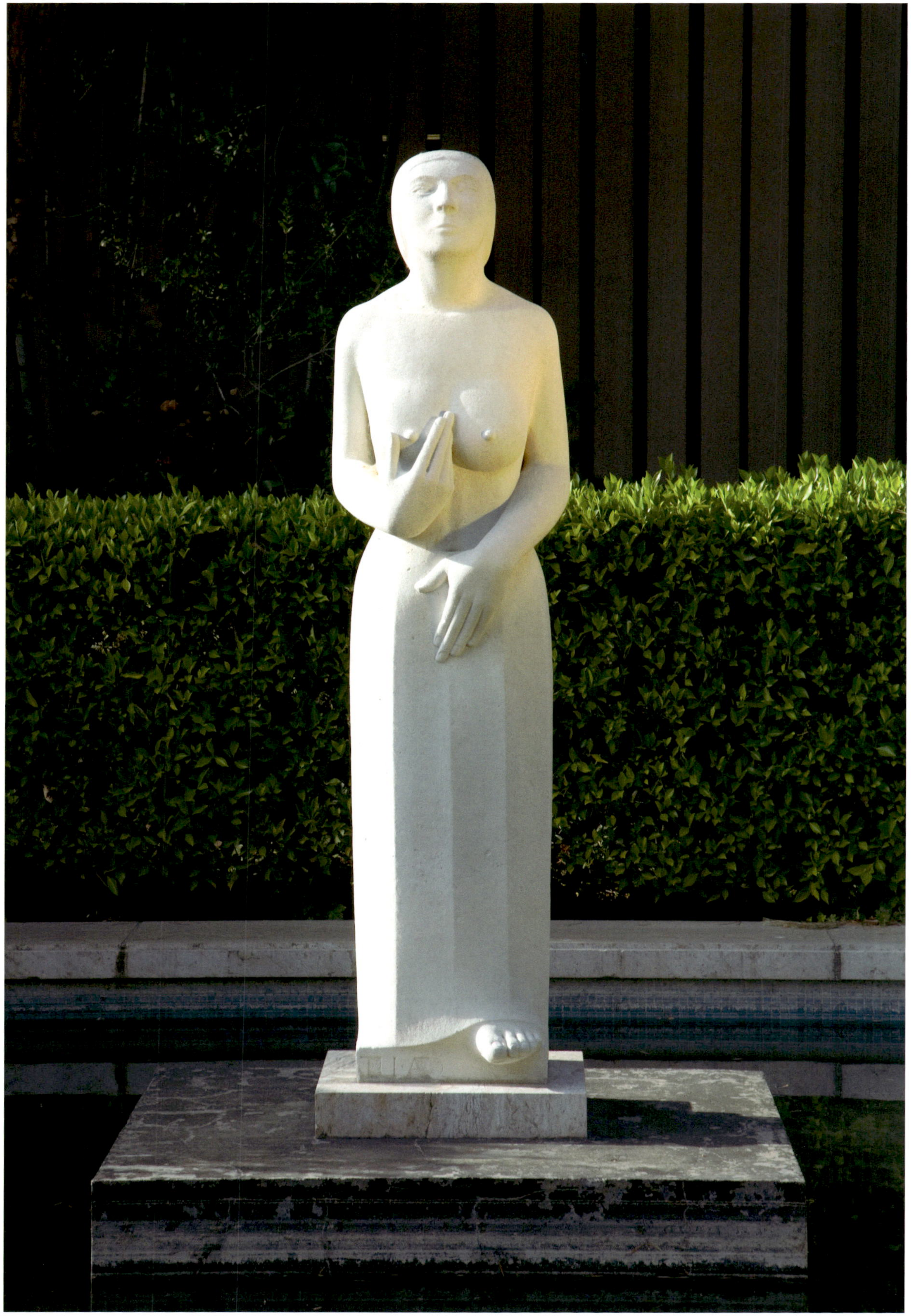

Eric Gill is one of the most compelling figures in the history of modern British sculpture, if a somewhat enigmatic one. He was born in the coastal town of Brighton, the son of a minister, and displayed a precocious affinity for the arts. He trained at Chichester Technical and Art School from the age of fifteen, before moving to London to work as an apprentice to an architect while attending classes in stone carving and lettering. These early years of design training formed an essential background for Gill's expertise in typography. He made great strides in this field, and some of his fonts are standard options on computers today. While in London, Gill married, mingled with the arts and crafts community of Hammersmith, and flirted with social activism. In 1907, however, he chose a more rural environment for his family and retreated to the countryside of Sussex. Here, in the small town of Ditchling, he embraced the local artisanal lifestyle and developed a strong religious fervor. His autobiography describes his spiritual zeal and eventual conversion to Catholicism on his thirty-first birthday, in 1913.[1]

It was around this time that *Mulier* was created. The title is a Latin term for "woman" or "wife," and the sculpture itself is a monument to female form and fecundity. This tall, columnar figure, with large breasts and an upright stance, is at once strong, sexual, and maternal. Her most distinctive features are her oversize hands, one pointing upward between her breasts and the other evocatively placed between her hips, pointing toward the ground. The abstraction of features such as the straight geometric plait that falls down the center of her back, or the vertical pleats of her skirt, endows the work with a stern yet powerful sense of nobility. The viewer cannot miss the wide foot that comes forward from beneath *Mulier's* skirt either. She is as firm as a caryatid, but she is not immobile.

For this work Gill used his preferred medium of carved stone. He was devoted to the practice of carving because it required the total participation of the artist from conception to completion, without any mechanical form of production. His process of creation developed in the traditional way, employing preparatory sketches and finished drawings, some squared for transfer.[2] The singular quality of a hard but versatile material retrieved from a quarry was appealing to Gill. In his own words: "I just wanted to make in solid stone, round and smooth and lovely images of the round and smooth and lovely things which filled my mind."[3] *Mulier* epitomizes his thoughts. A.P.

Notes

1 *Eric Gill,* Autobiography *(London: J. Cape, 1940), 192.*

2 *See Cynthia Burlingham and Elizabeth Shepherd, eds.,* In the Sculptor's Landscape: Celebrating Twenty-five Years of the Franklin D. Murphy Sculpture Garden *(Los Angeles: Wight Art Gallery and Grunwald Center for the Graphic Arts, University of California, 1993), 52, figs. 35–36.*

3 *Gill,* Autobiography, *163.*

ERIC GILL

(BRITISH, 1882–1940)

Born in Mexico City, Robert Graham studied art at San Jose State College (now San Jose State University) and the San Francisco Art Institute. His initial sculptures were miniature wax figures encased in Plexiglas boxes, composing small, self-contained environments. When he moved to Los Angeles in 1971 and created his first sculpture in bronze, Graham discovered that few foundries could provide the precision and control he required of the casting process, so he set up a foundry at his studio. Civic commissions in Los Angeles include the Olympic Gateway for the 1984 Olympic Games, depicting monumental fragmentary nude male and female statues modeled after two athletes, and the Great Bronze Doors of 2002 for the Cathedral of Our Lady of the Angels. Graham's works are consistently based on the human figure, and as they are figurative, the artist prefers to describe them as statues rather than sculptures.

Viewed from a distance, *Dance Columns I and II* may remind the viewer of ancient monuments such as Trajan's Column in Rome, but upon closer inspection the richly appliquéd surfaces, with their relief fragments composed of a multitude of studies of the human form, show evidence of Graham's fascination with the formal possibilities of human anatomy. The figures delicately perched upon the columns are modeled after Lise, one of four women who worked as a model for the artist in the 1970s. Placement and environment function as integral parts of Graham's work: it is important to view the components of *Dance Columns I and II* in terms of their relationship to each other. One other work from this edition is currently on public view in front of the Wright Runstad Building in Seattle. C.D.

ROBERT GRAHAM

(AMERICAN, B. 1938)

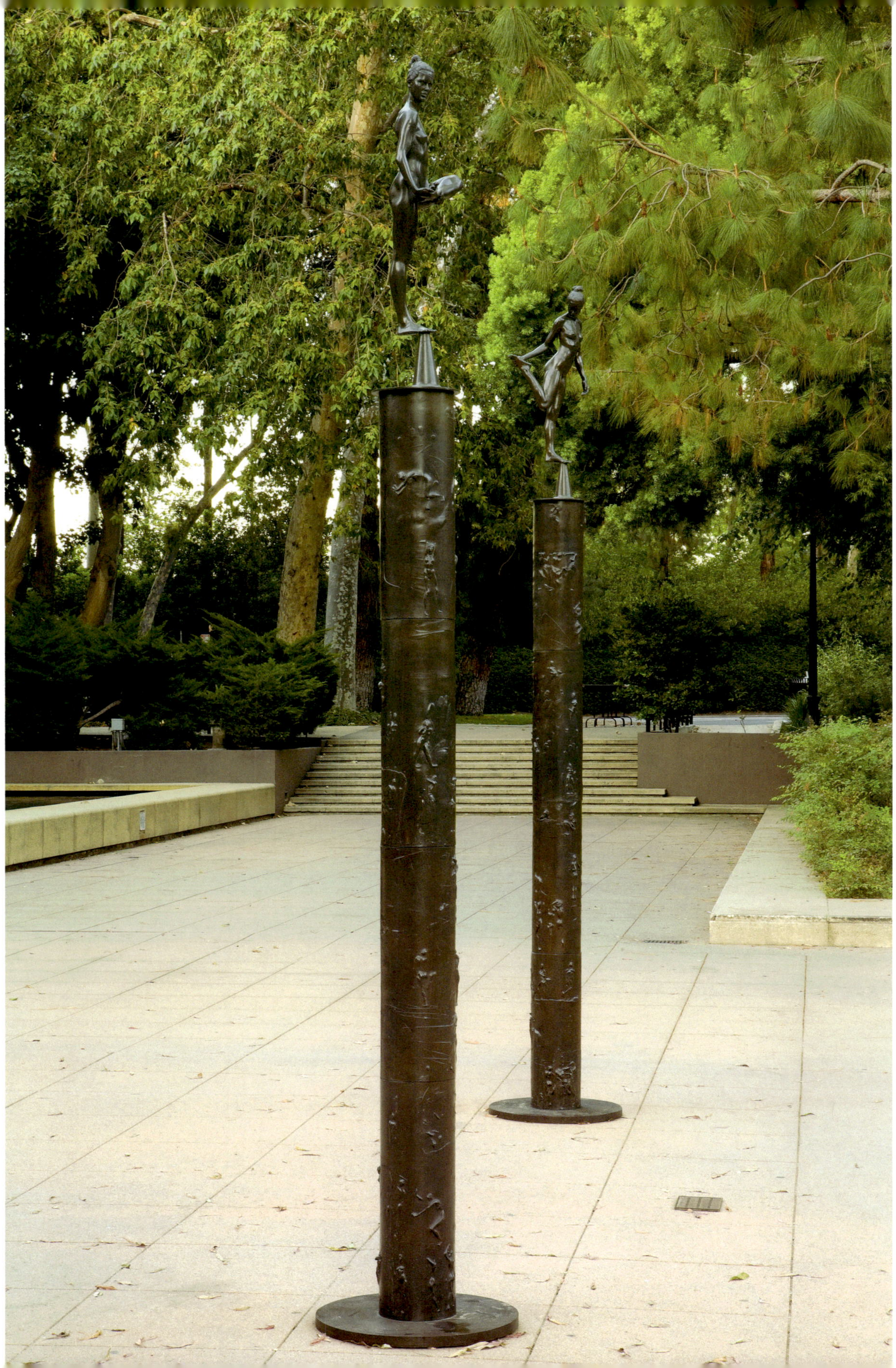

DANCE COLUMNS I AND II
1978
Bronze
H: 102 IN. (259.1 CM); W: 164 IN. (416.6 CM); D: 15 IN. (38.1 CM)
Edition: 1/7
Foundry: Robert Graham Studio
Gift of Carol and Roy Doumani, 1980

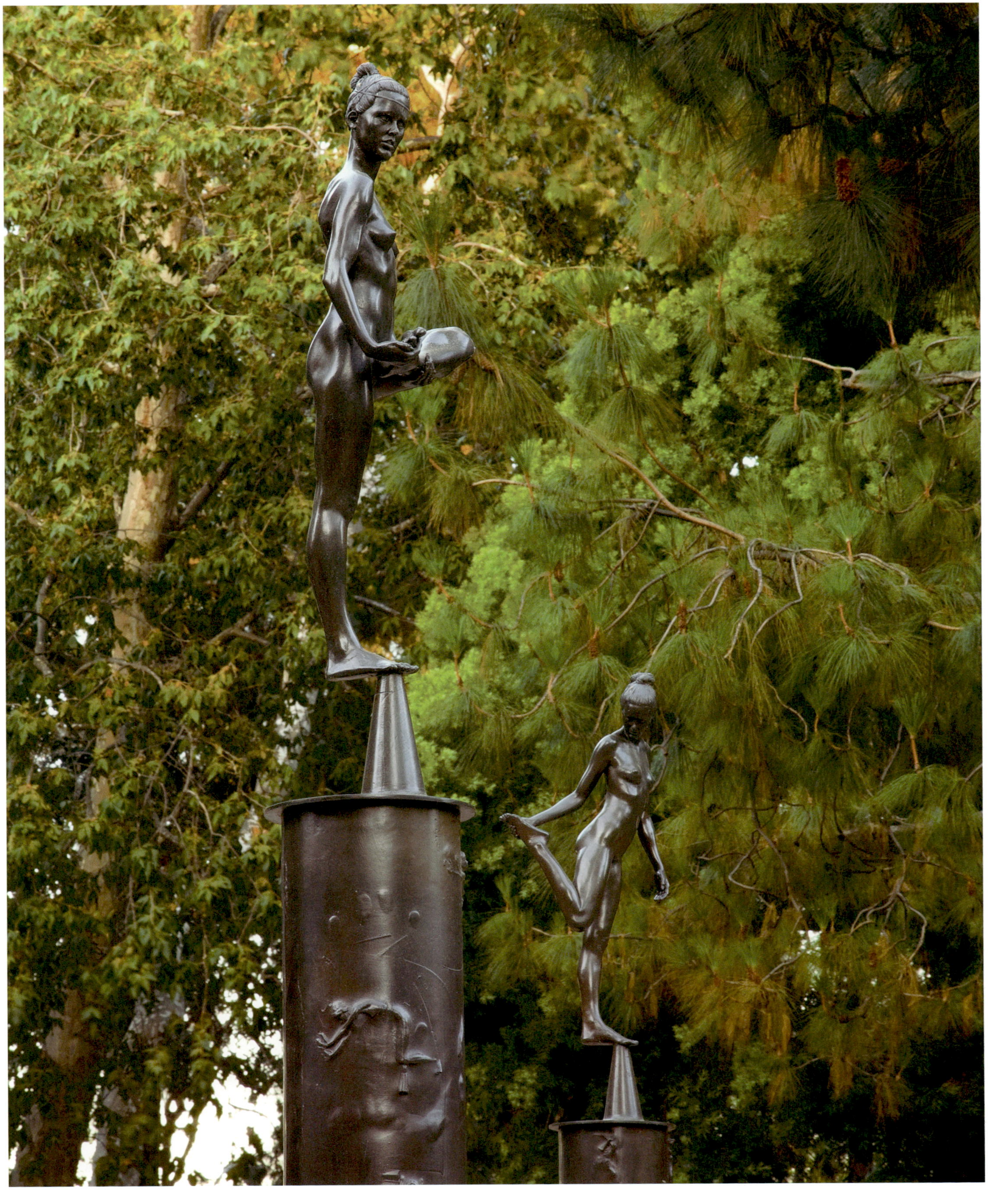

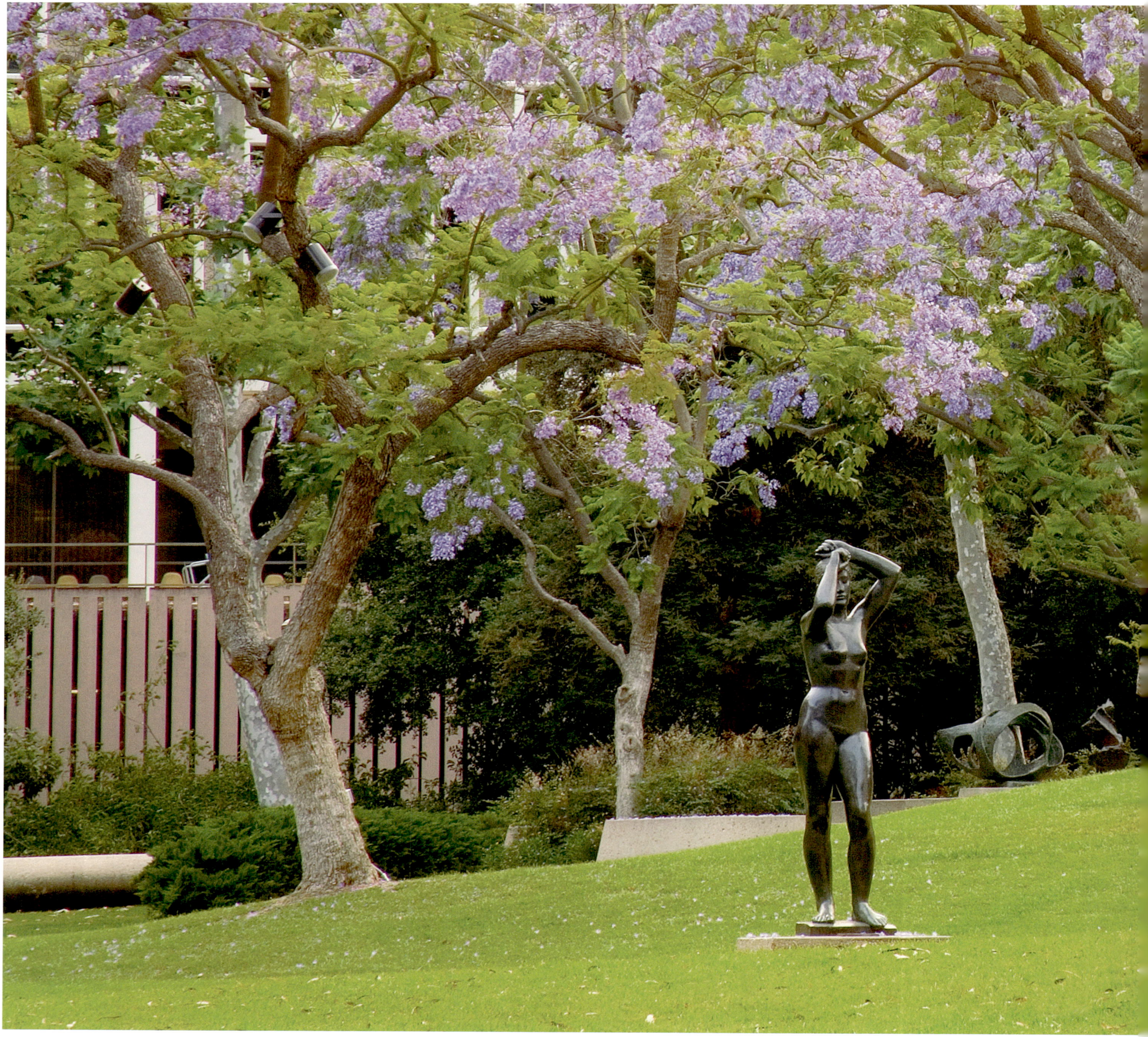

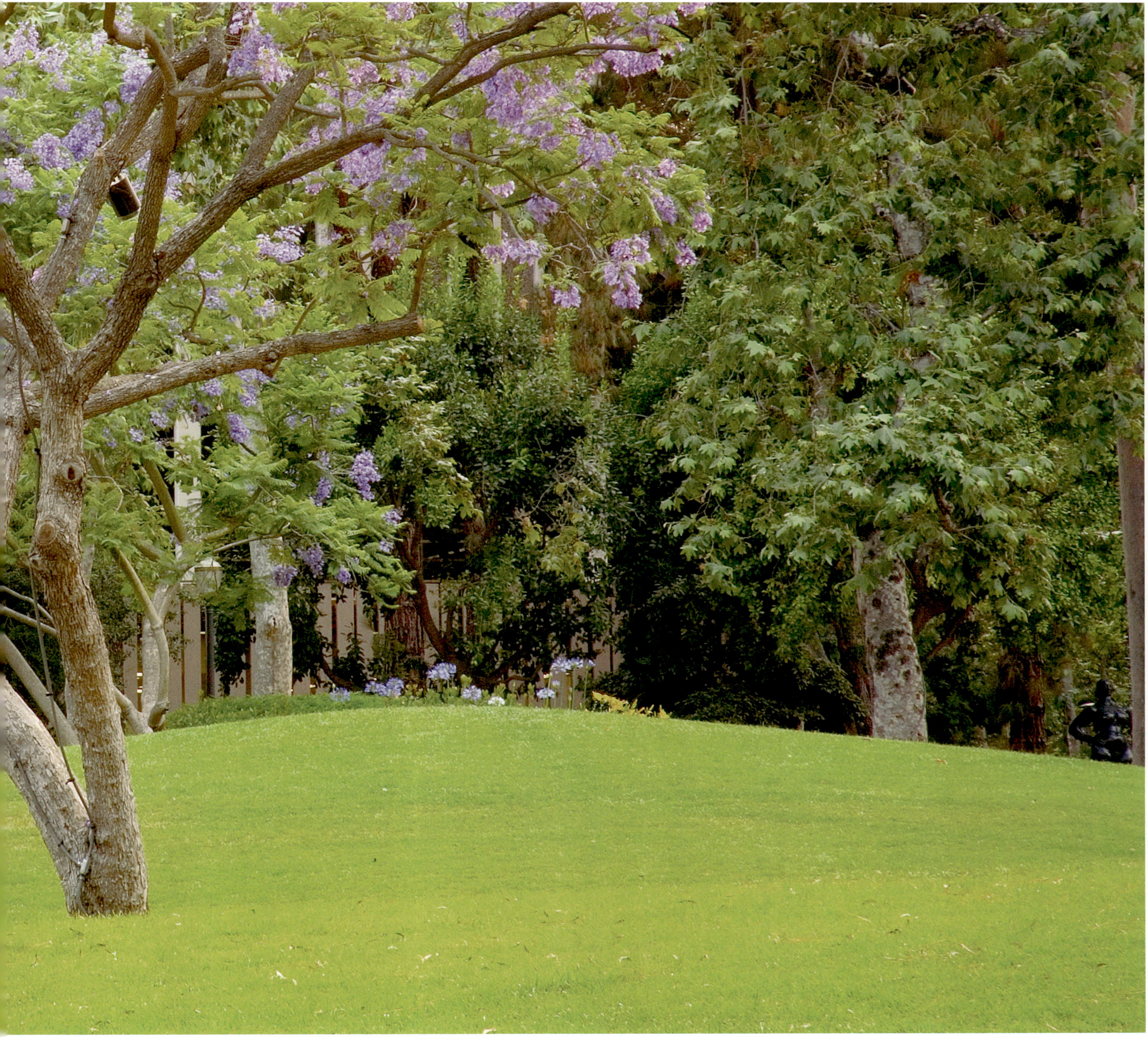

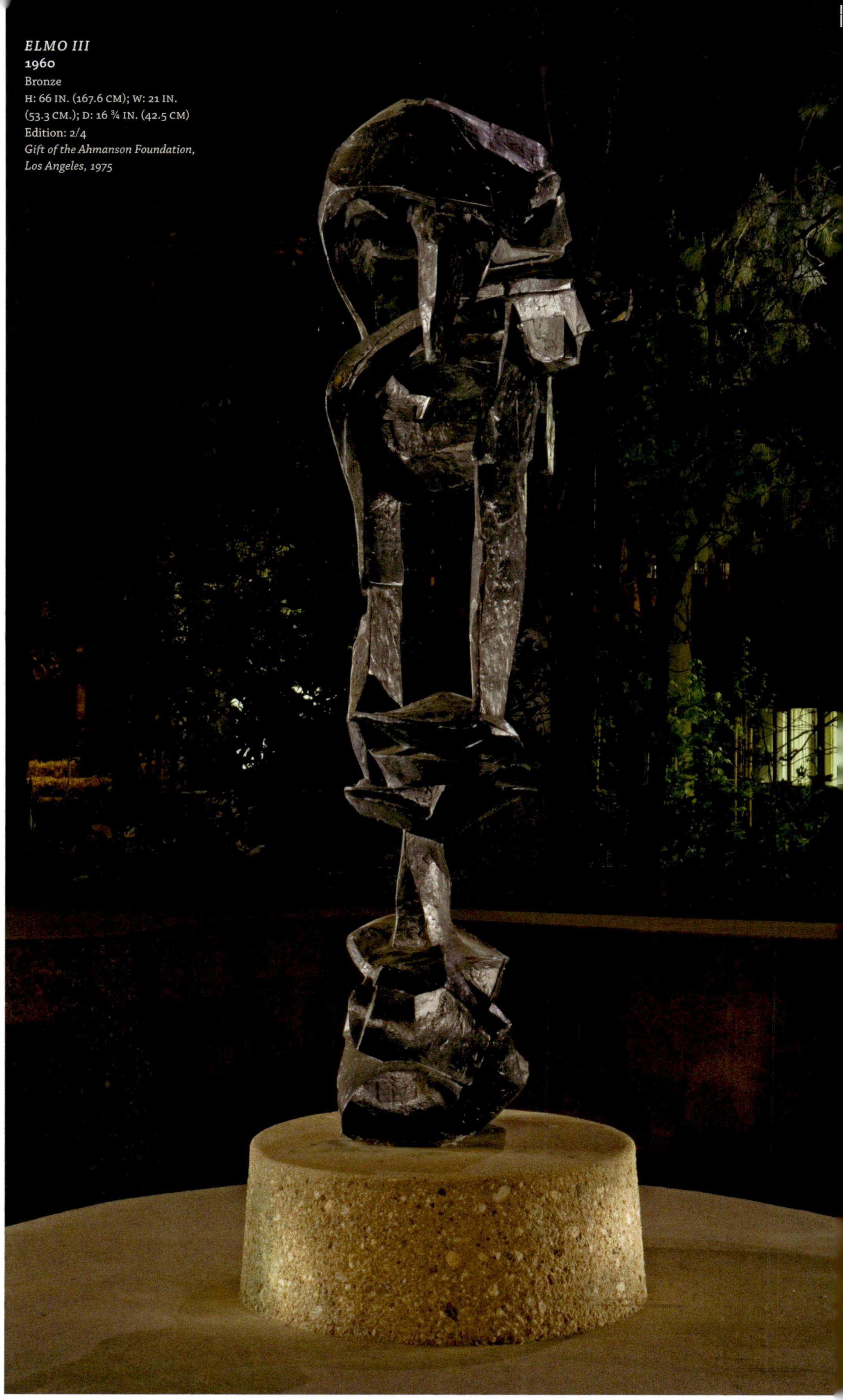

ELMO III
1960
Bronze
H: 66 IN. (167.6 CM); W: 21 IN. (53.3 CM.); D: 16 ¾ IN. (42.5 CM)
Edition: 2/4
Gift of the Ahmanson Foundation, Los Angeles, 1975

Dimitri Hadzi attended art school at the Cooper Union, New York, from 1946 to 1950. From 1950 to 1951 he studied carving at the Polytechnion, Athens, through a Fulbright Fellowship and later attended the Museo Artistico Industriale, Rome. He lived and worked in Greece for many years, returning to the United States in the mid-1970s. He received numerous awards, including the Tiffany Foundation Fellowship for sculpture (1955); a Guggenheim Fellowship (1957); and a National Academy of Arts and Letters Grant (1962). His public commissions include the bronze doors of the American Episcopal Church in Rome (1962–76) and sculptures in Avery Fisher Hall at Lincoln Center, New York (1962–66); the Dallas Centre (1978–80); and Harvard Square, Cambridge (1979). From 1975 until his retirement in 1989, Hadzi was professor of visual and environmental studies at Harvard University, and he lived and worked in Cambridge until his death in 2006.

References to ancient Greek art and mythology are found in much of Hadzi's work. Both his UCLA pieces belong to the Elmo series, also referred to as "helmets." Discussing this series, art historian Albert Elsen writes: "The moving solemnity of several major pieces takes its tone from the artist's reflections of tragedies, contemporary and ancient, of Auschwitz and Agamemnon. It was while competing for the memorial at the notorious concentration camp in 1958 that Hadzi first directed his abstract art toward the tragedies of war."[1] C.B.

Notes
1 *Albert Elsen, introduction to* Dimitri Hadzi: Recent Sculptures *(New York: Gruenebaum Gallery, 1978), 4.*

DIMITRI HADZI

(AMERICAN, 1921–2006)

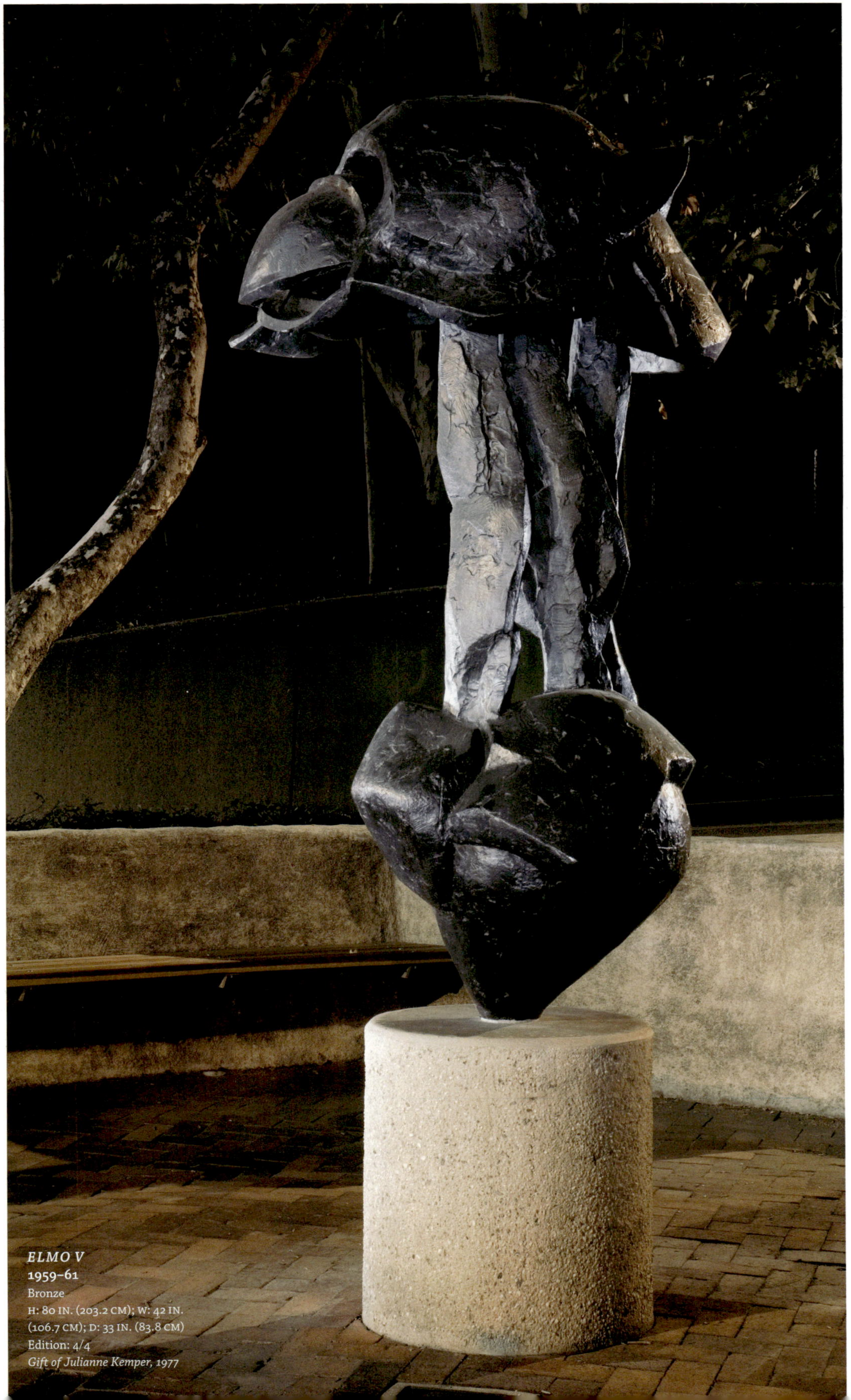

ELMO V
1959–61
Bronze
H: 80 IN. (203.2 CM); W: 42 IN. (106.7 CM); D: 33 IN. (83.8 CM)
Edition: 4/4
Gift of Julianne Kemper, 1977

ELEGY III (HOLLOW FORM WITH COLOR)
1966
Bronze
H: 51 IN. (129.5 CM);
W: 25 IN. (63.5 CM);
D: 19 IN. (48.3 CM)
Edition: 6/6
Foundry: Morris Singer
Foundry, London
Gift of Jean and Irving Stone, 1975

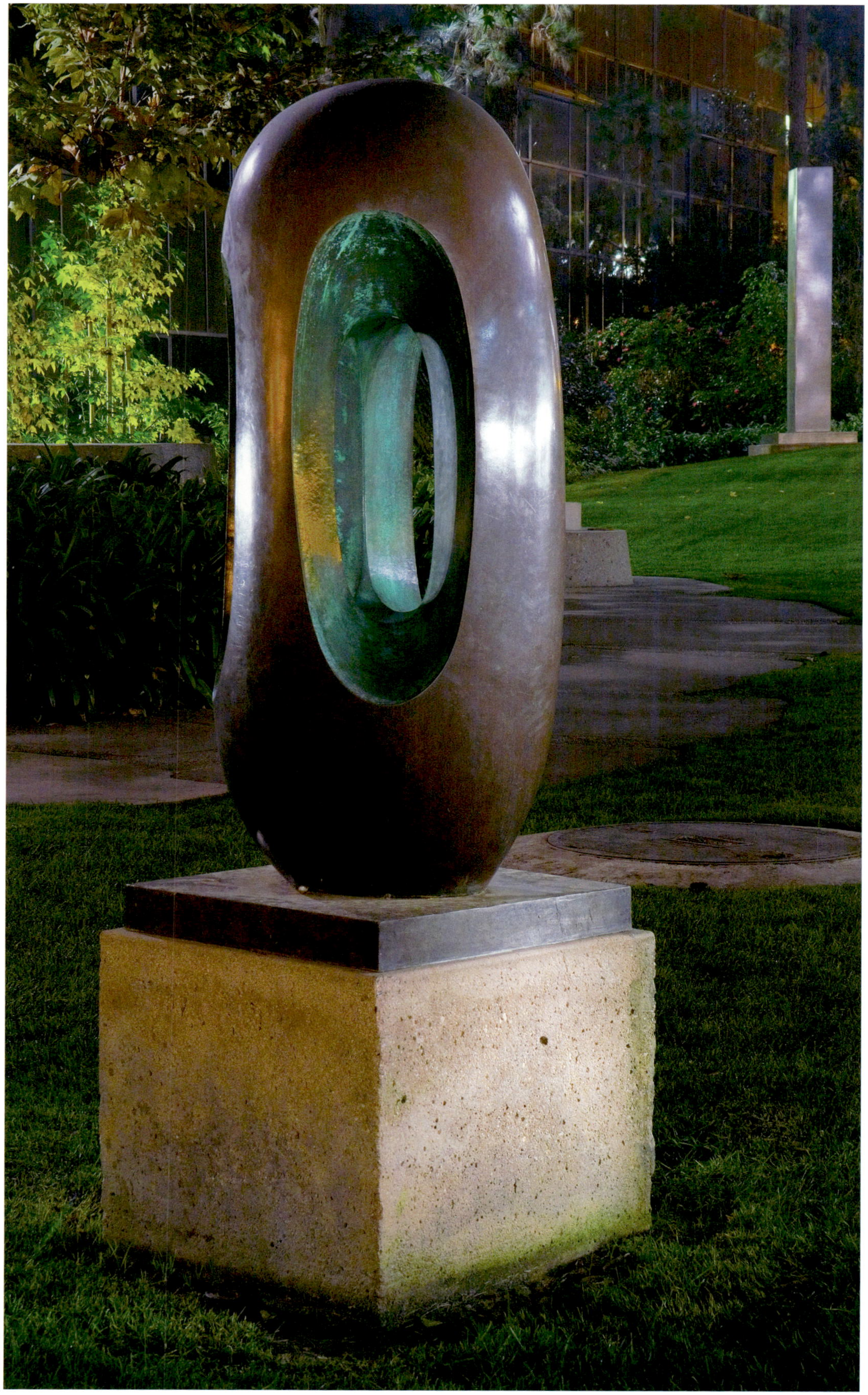

OVAL FORM (TREZION)
1961–63
Bronze
H: 33 ½ IN. (85.1 CM); W: 55 IN. (139.7 CM); D: 35 IN. (88.9 CM)
Edition: 1/7
Foundry: Morris Singer Foundry, London
Gift of David E. Bright, 1967

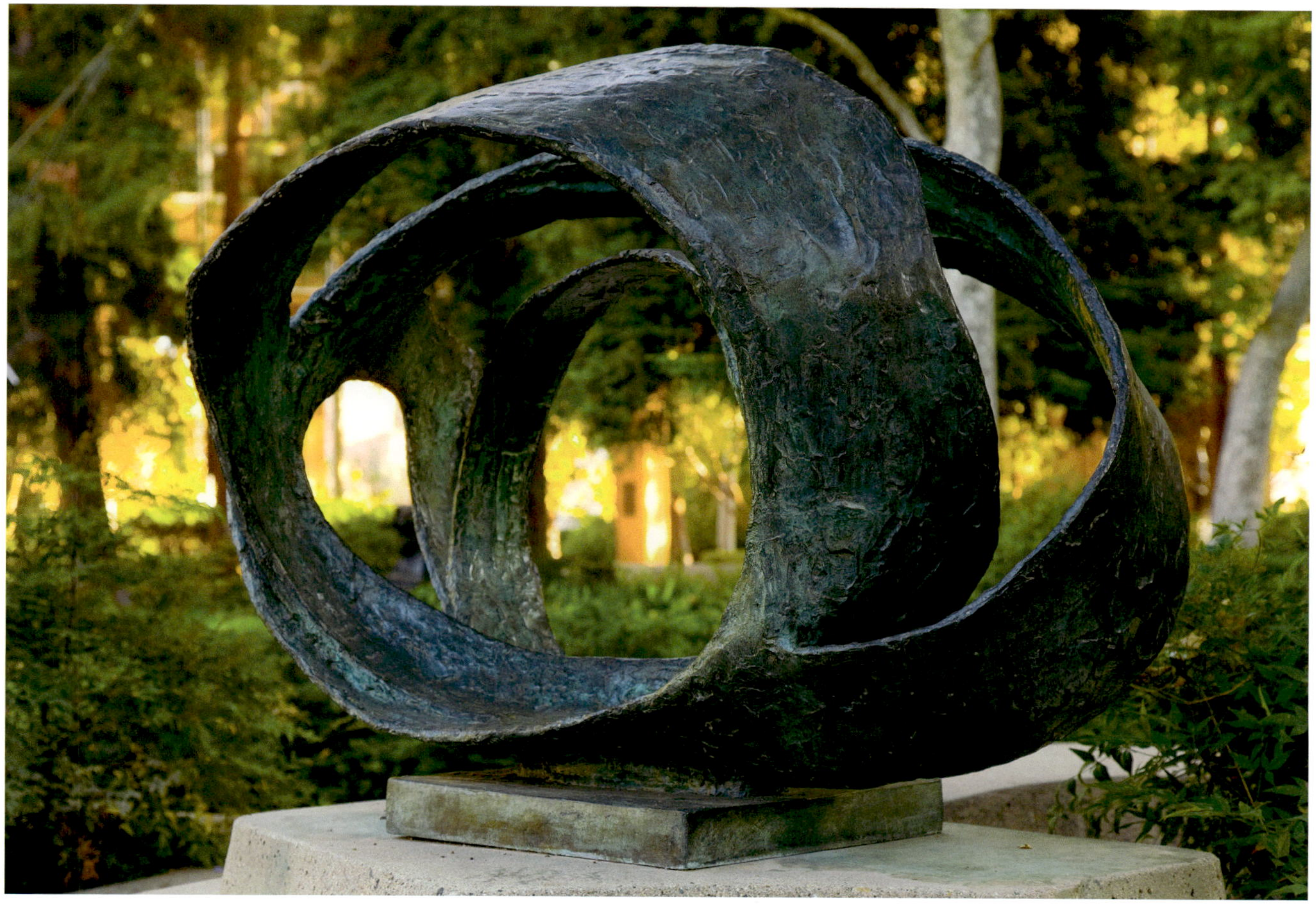

BARBARA HEPWORTH

(BRITISH, 1903–1975)

Barbara Hepworth is among Britain's leading twentieth-century sculptors and was the first British woman artist to achieve worldwide fame in her field. Her life was as turbulent as it was rewarding. Born in Yorkshire, she began her studies at Leeds School of Art and then proceeded to London's Royal College of Art. A scholarship for study in Italy in 1924 made a lasting impression on her and exposed her to various forms of sculpture and stonecutting. Throughout her life she surrounded herself with mutually stimulating friends and colleagues. Her first husband was the sculptor John Skeaping, and her second was the highly acclaimed avant-garde painter Ben Nicholson. Henry Moore was among her close acquaintances and vacation companions. Hardship hit her in the prewar period, when she and Nicholson struggled to afford their studios in Hampstead, in North London. She gave birth to triplets but had to place them in foster care during the first three years of their lives. Eventually, just before World War II broke out, the family moved to the coast of Cornwall. Hepworth was an avid worker through good and bad times. When domestic chores and lack of funds and materials kept her from making sculptures, she found solace in drawing. The fisherman's village of Saint Ives and its alluring seascape became her home and inspiration. Here Hepworth's work picked up and evolved in the many directions we witness today. Her great abstract forms in wood, stone, and metal were like mutated reflections of the sweeping views and geologic formations that surrounded her in Cornwall. They granted her fame and prestigious commissions such as the memorial to Secretary-General Dag Hammarskjöld at the United Nations building in New York of 1963 and a major retrospective at the Tate Gallery in 1968. In 1965, ten years before her tragic death in a fire at her home in Saint Ives, she was named Dame Commander of the Order of the British Empire. Today her studio is a museum and a tribute to her unique talent and passionate dedication to her sculpture.

Although she had a predilection for wood and stone carving, Hepworth produced some outstanding works in bronze as well. The medium allowed her to work at a larger scale and to experiment with the relationship between form and space in outdoor sculpture. *Oval Form (Trezion)* demonstrates her mastery of this medium and her skill in creating frameworks for a natural setting like that of the Murphy Sculpture Garden. It is part of a sequence of sculptures made in the early 1960s that focus on the ocean, caves, rocks, and cliffs of Cornwall. Its rounded shapes and stretched, overlapping bands of bronze do recall gushing waves and the cavernous formation of a marine environment. To some, however, this piece is simply a comforting, womblike form that lulls the senses. It is particularly inviting to children, who are often found cradled in its arched base. Hepworth would have enjoyed this sight, as she herself noted that "there is a stronger sense of participating in the form—you want to go in and out as you look at a sculpture like 'Trezio' or 'Porthcurno.'"[1]

Elegy III is also a bronze, although it has the smooth, polished surface of Hepworth's wooden sculptures. Here is her signature organic form, like a large nut with intersecting openings through its center. Light slips off its glossy exterior but is captured by the coarser vertical slits within. Again Hepworth's work melds easily into the landscape and suits its current environment. Its tactile quality invites touch, and its versatile viewpoints encourage the onlooker to navigate around it. She said: "I particularly love to have things related in a friendly and near way to human beings, so that they can be touched. The patina of people's hands is a wonderful thing in sculpture, and I really believe that through touching they can be deeply expressive to people."[2] A.P.

Notes
1 *Penelope Curtis and Alan Wilkinson,* Barbara Hepworth: A Retrospective *(London: Tate Gallery Publications, 1994), 105.*
2 *Warren Forma,* Five British Sculptors (Work and Talk): Henry Moore, Reg Butler, Barbara Hepworth, Lynn Chadwick, Kenneth Armitage *(New York: Grossman Publishers, 1964), 27.*

ELEGY III (HOLLOW FORM WITH COLOR)
(DETAIL)

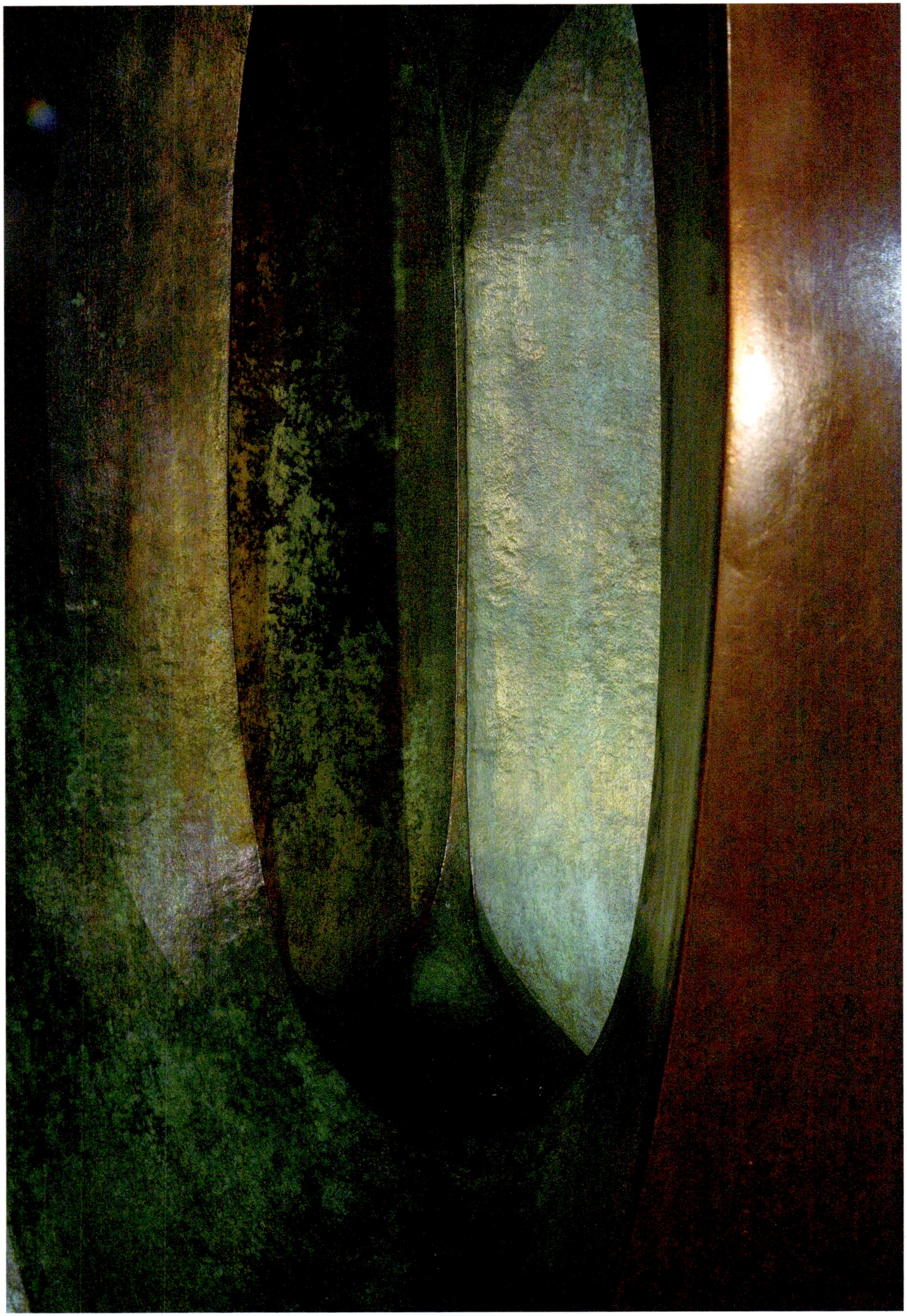

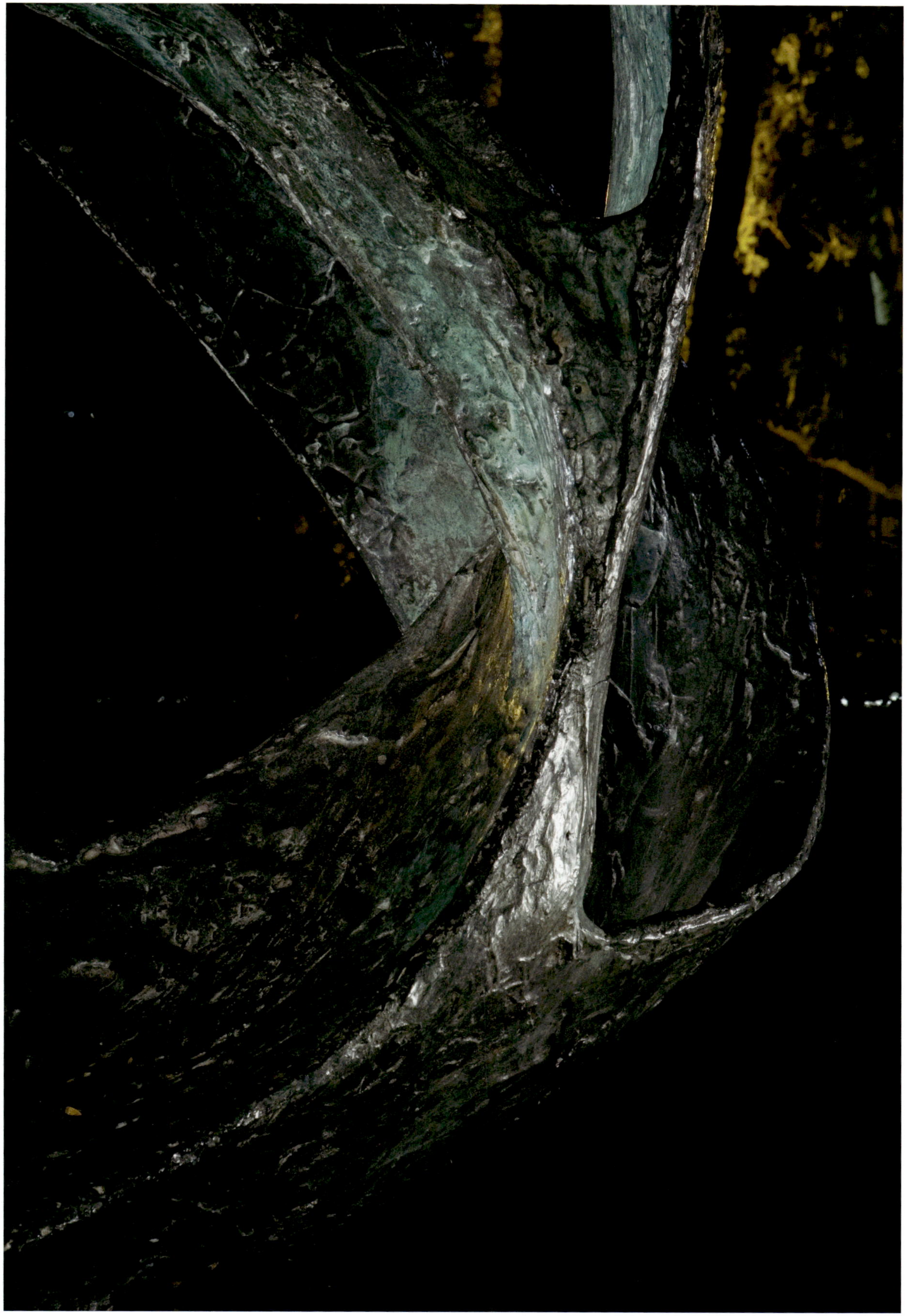

OVAL FORM (TREZION)
(DETAIL)

RICHARD HUNT

(AMERICAN, B. 1935)

WHY?
1974
Bronze
H: 86 IN. (218.5 CM); W: 48 IN. (121.9 CM); D: 44 IN. (111.8 CM)
Edition: 2/3
Foundry: Aesthetic Systems (operated by the artist and J. Henry)
Given in memory of Samuel H. Nerlove, 1975

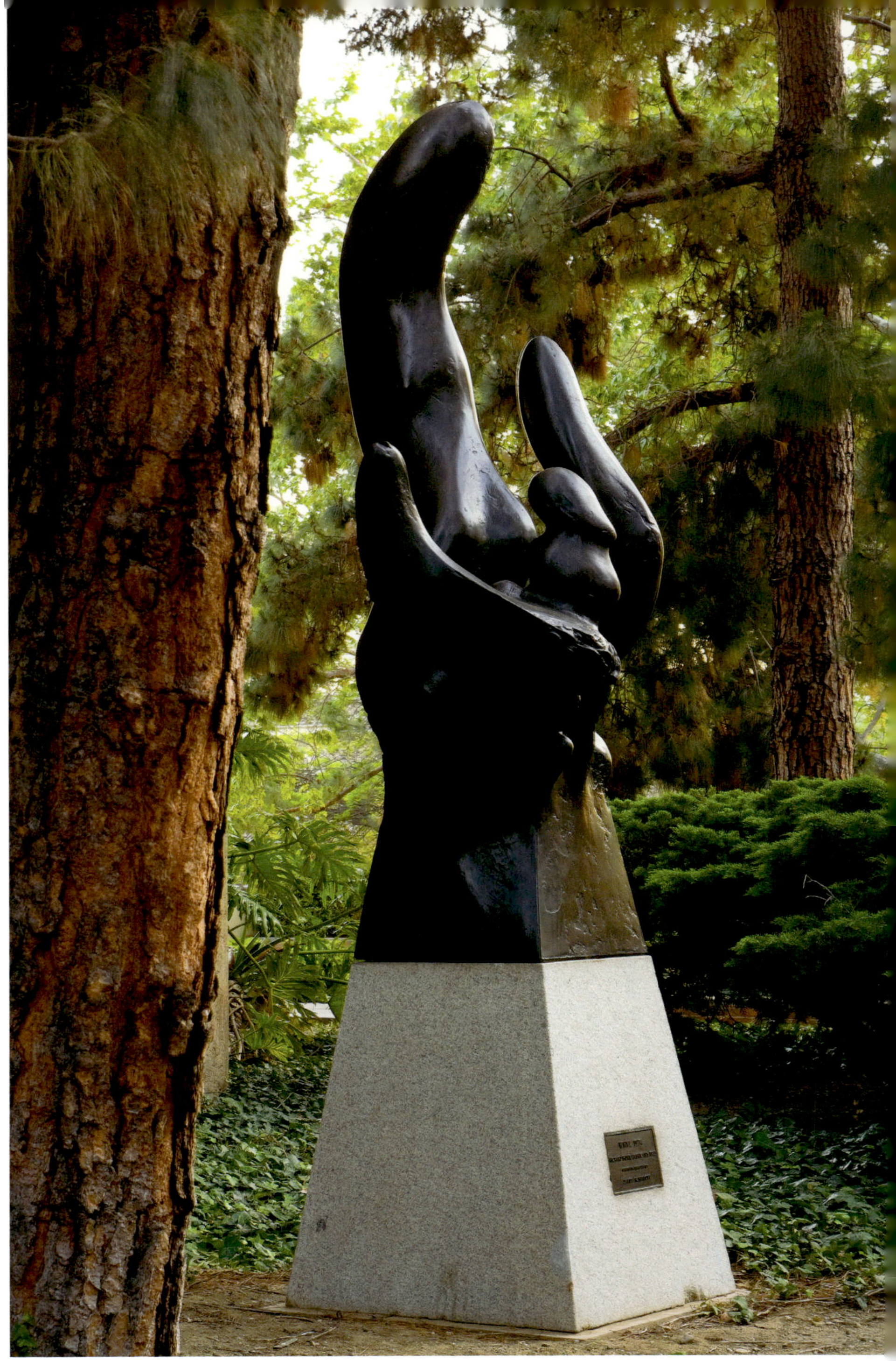

Richard Hunt studied at the Art Institute of Chicago from 1948 to 1953 and taught at several institutions, including Yale University (1964), Northwestern University (1968–69), Southern Illinois University (1969), and Washington University in Saint Louis (1977–78). His work was featured in a retrospective exhibition at the Museum of Modern Art, New York, in 1971. Hunt was a member of the National Council on the Arts (1968–74) and served on the board of trustees for the American Academy in Rome (1980), the board of governors of the School of the Art Institute of Chicago (1985–91), and the National Board of Directors of the Smithsonian Institution (1994–97). He has executed many public commissions across the United States, including a memorial to Martin Luther King Jr. in Memphis in 1977, and his work is represented in numerous museum collections.

In the 1950s Hunt began to work in direct metal welding in response to the art of Julio González, the Spanish sculptor who, with Pablo Picasso, fabricated abstract metal sculpture in the 1920s. Hunt has worked in a variety of media—including industrial copper, iron, and steel—and has experimented with the incorporation of found objects into his sculpture. In the 1970s the artist installed a bronze foundry in his Chicago studio, where the sculpture *Why?* was cast. It was commissioned by Mrs. Evelyn A. Nerlove as a memorial to her husband, Samuel H. Nerlove, who taught economics at the University of Chicago (1923–65) and at UCLA (1962–69). Hunt has traced his ideas and the title for *Why?* to discussions with the professor's widow and associates.[1] Nerlove's questioning personality suggested the vertical form of a question mark, which evolved into an organic abstraction rising out of a central form. Two other casts of this work were made and installed in the Law and Business Quadrangle at the University of Chicago and at the Northwestern University School of Law, Chicago. C.B.

Notes

1 *Richard Hunt, telephone interview with S. Livingston, April 30, 1984, notes in Murphy Sculpture Garden Archives, Hammer Museum.*

VOTIVE S
1963
Bronze
H: 59 IN. (150 CM); W: 64 IN. (162.5 CM); D: 8¾ IN. (22.2 CM)
Edition: 1/3
Gift of Robert W. Sarnoff, 1976

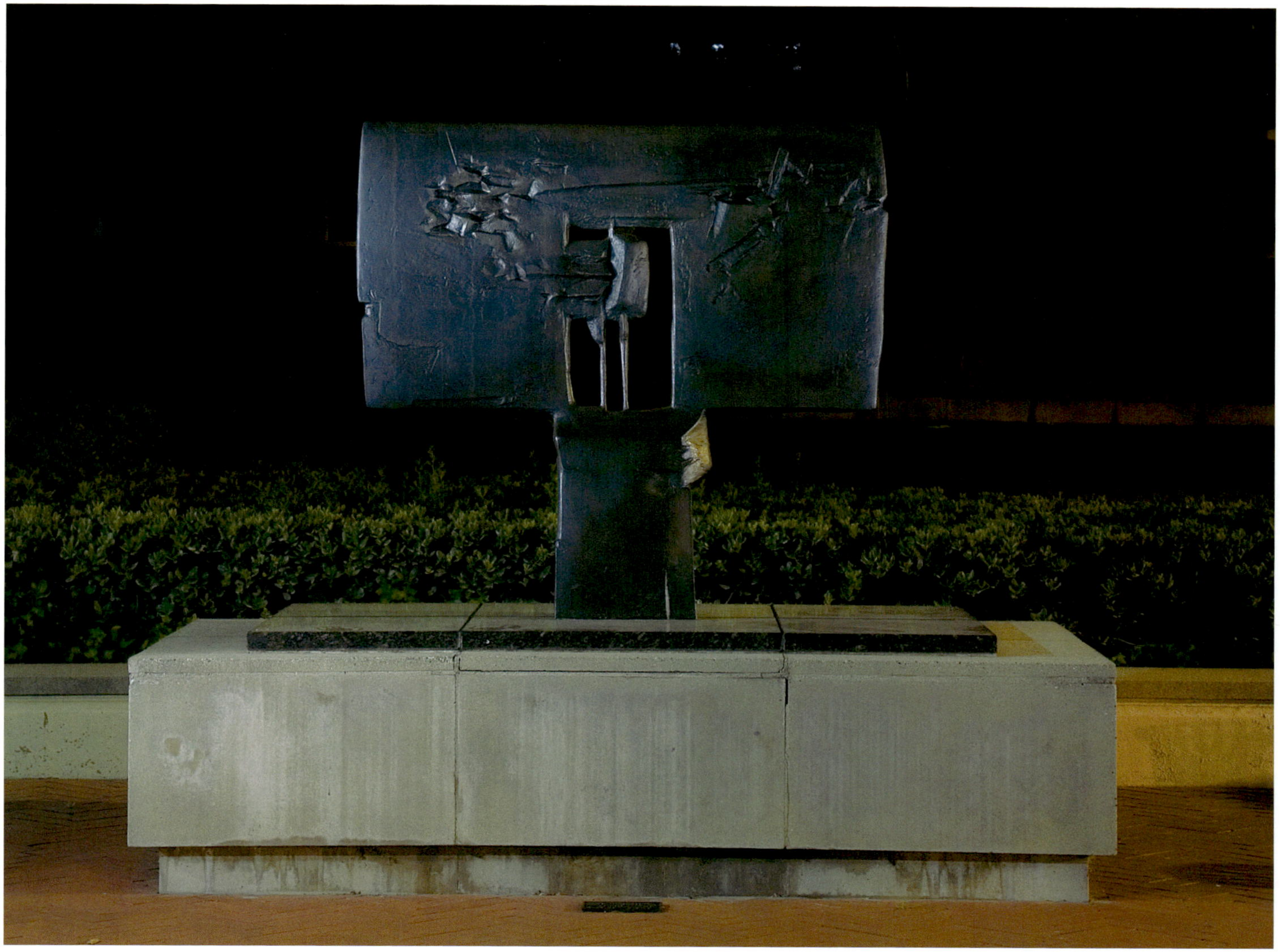

After World War II Fritz Koenig went to the Academy of Fine Arts in Munich to study sculpture under Anton Hiller, completing his training there in 1952. He received stipends that allowed him to continue his studies in France (1951) and at the Villa Massimo in Rome (1957) and participated in such international exhibitions as the Venice Biennale (1958, 1964) and Documenta, in Kassel (1959, 1964). In 1964 Koenig joined the faculty of architecture at the Technical University in Munich, teaching in the area of plastic arts. He works primarily in bronze but also sculpts in wax, plaster, and stone. His sculptures and drawings have been shown in numerous exhibitions throughout Germany since the 1970s. The recipient of many significant commissions for public buildings and plazas, Koenig created *Spherical Caryatid* (1967–71) for the fountain complex of the World Trade Center in New York. Although badly damaged on September 11, 2001, this large, globelike sculpture was the only work of art known to have survived the attacks and has since been resited at a memorial installation in Battery Park, on the lower tip of Manhattan. In 1993 Koenig and his wife donated works to the Bavarian city of Landshut, which established a museum of sculpture, the Skulpturenmuseum im Hofberg. Koenig continues to work as a sculptor in Ganslberg, near Landshut.

Part of a series of abstract bronze works dating from 1959 to 1969, *Votive S* exemplifies Koenig's concern with both defining and restraining the space surrounding the sculpted form. The three powerful geometric sections of the sculpture shape a coherent whole and are complemented by the textural incisions inlaid in the patina of the bronze surfaces. This work is a unique cast and was commissioned by Robert W. Sarnoff (1918–1997), former president of NBC, who saw the plaster model for this work in the artist's studio in Ganslberg. The title of this piece incorporates the first initial of the donor's last name for identification. C.D.

FRITZ KOENIG

(GERMAN, B. 1924)

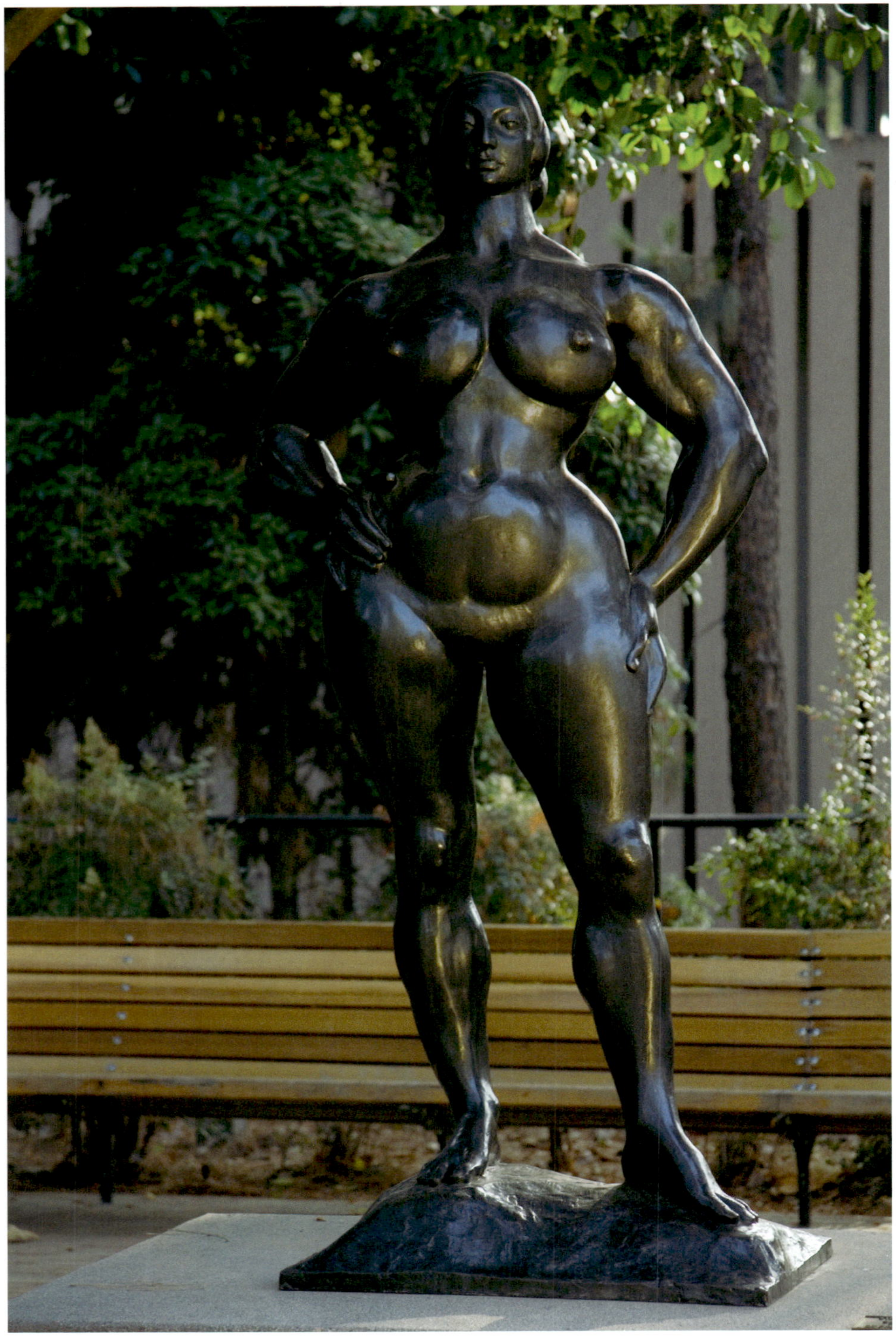

STANDING WOMAN (HEROIC WOMAN)
1932
Bronze
H: 88½ IN. (225 CM); W: 41 IN. (104.1 CM); D: 15 IN. (38.1 CM)
Edition: 1/6
Foundry: Modern Art Foundry, New York
Gift of Mr. and Mrs. Arthur C. Caplan, Mr. and Mrs. Donald Winston, and Mr. and Mrs. Walter McC. Maitland, 1968

Gaston Lachaise studied sculpture at the École Bernard Palissy and the Académie Nationale des Beaux-Arts. While a student he met a Canadian American woman, Isabel Nagle, who would have a profound impact on his life and work. After following Isabel to the United States in 1906, Lachaise worked for the sculptors Henry Hudson Kitson and Paul Manship. Lachaise's major subject was the heroically proportioned female figure, usually modeled on Isabel, who became his wife in 1917 and remained his main source of inspiration. Lachaise's friends and patrons included prominent members of literary and artistic circles, such as Alfred Barr, E. E. Cummings, John Dos Passos, Lincoln Kirstein, Gilbert Seldes, and Edward Warburg. Lachaise exhibited at Alfred Stieglitz's Intimate Gallery in New York in 1927 and at the Joseph Brummer Gallery in New York in 1928. In 1935 he became the first living sculptor to be given a retrospective exhibition at the Museum of Modern Art, New York, held just four months before his unexpected death from leukemia. A large retrospective of his work was held at the Los Angeles County Museum of Art and the Whitney Museum of American Art, New York, in 1963 and 1964.

Like Auguste Rodin and Constantin Brancusi, Lachaise cast a number of partial figures from existing full-scale sculptures, concentrating primarily on the torso. Lachaise also created several variations of the standing female nude. The life-size *Standing Woman (Elevation)* of 1912–27 is his earliest major work on the subject. After 1928 Lachaise's sculptures began to feature distorted and exaggerated body parts, particularly female breasts and genitalia. The sculpture in the UCLA collection, *Standing Woman*, also referred to as *Heroic Woman*, is his last life-size figure. According to art historian Gerald Nordland, it "is surely the triumph and fulfillment of all Lachaise's small studies, statuettes and fragments. . . . The sculpture is the embodiment of Lachaise's lifelong effort to express the imperious goddess quality in heroic scale."[1] C.B.

Notes
1. *Gerald Nordland,* Gaston Lachaise: The Man and His Work *(New York: George Braziller, 1974), 82.*

GASTON LACHAISE

(AMERICAN, 1882–1935)

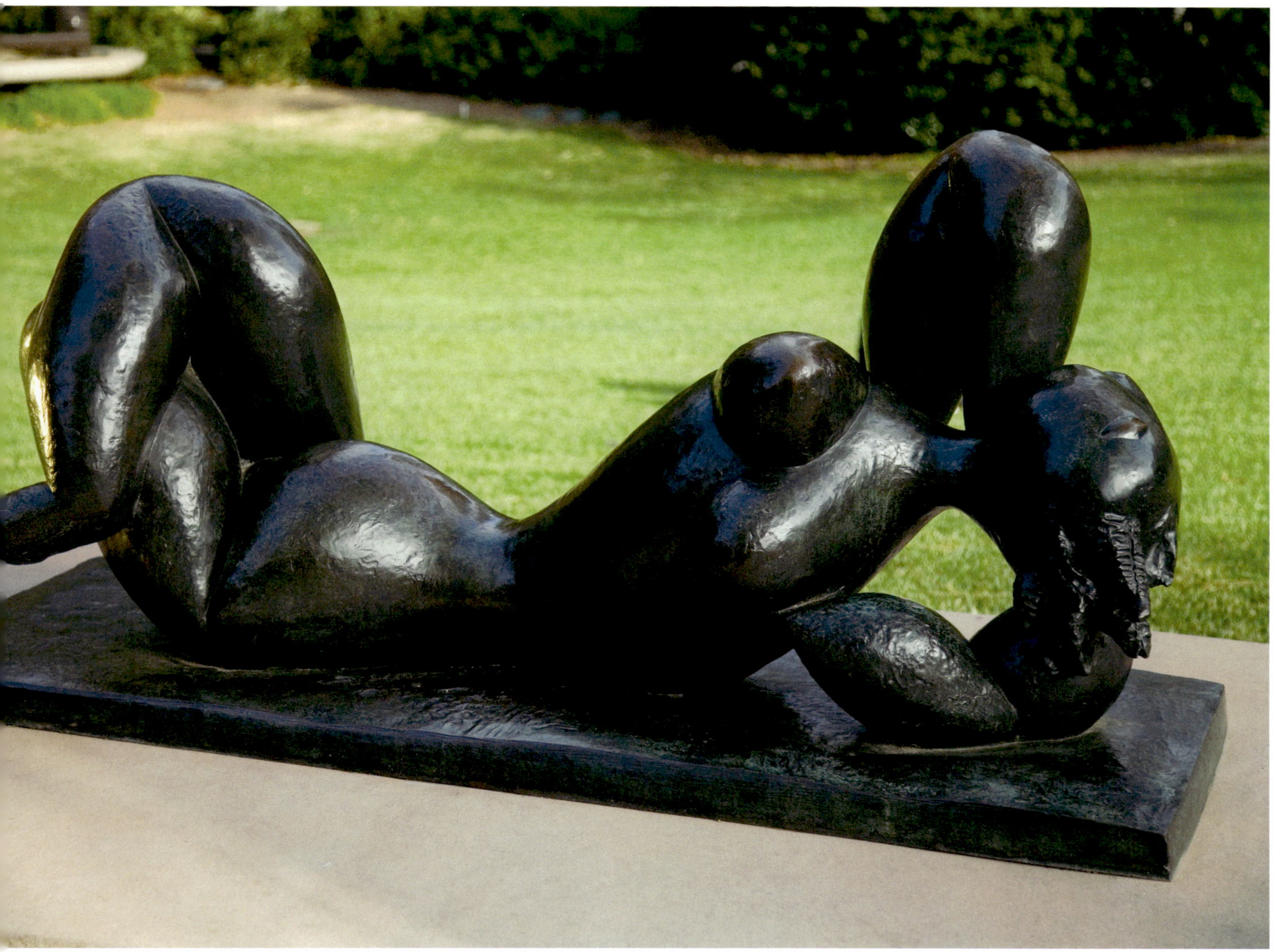

AUTOMNE / AUTUMN
1948
Bronze
H: 20½ IN. (52 CM); W: 68 IN. (173 CM); D: 22 IN. (56 CM)
Edition: 2/6
Foundry: Valsuani, Paris
Gift of David E. Bright, 1967

HENRI LAURENS

(FRENCH, 1885–1954)

During his early career Henri Laurens studied architectural drafting and ornamental stonecutting. His early friendship with Georges Braque, whom he met in 1913, led to experiments with mixed-media constructions employing materials such as clay, steel, plaster, and wood, often polychromed. In 1913 Laurens exhibited with the cubists at the Salon des Indépendents in Paris. His first extant work dates from 1915, as Laurens destroyed some of his earliest constructions. In addition to sculpture he produced paper collages, engravings, and illustrations for books by Pierre Reverdy and Cécile Arnaud. Although he continued to create two-dimensional work, for most of his career he concentrated primarily on sculpture. By the mid-1920s he drew away from the more angular forms of cubism, focusing instead on graceful curvilinear forms, particularly that of the female nude. He typically modeled in clay and cast plaster maquettes before carving or casting the final work in stone or bronze. An important exhibition of Laurens's work was organized by the Palais des Beaux-Arts in Brussels in 1949, and he was given a major retrospective at the Musée National d'Art Moderne in Paris in 1951.

Autumn is one of the last of the artist's large-scale bronzes. Laurens had focused on the subject of the odalisque, or reclining woman, as early as 1913 and continued to explore it frequently from the 1920s until the end of his career. Although *Autumn* is an example of the artist's curvilinear style, it also exemplifies how cubism remained an important influence. As Werner Hofmann noted, "Laurens makes the two poles of *Autumn* into equal growth centers and thus is able to rely upon one of the most important achievements of cubism—that 'deductive' method which allows the artist to free the arrangement of his formal vocabulary from its subordination to empirical reality."[1] C.B.

Notes
1 *Werner Hofmann, introduction to* The Sculpture of Henri Laurens *(New York: Harry N. Abrams, 1970), 29.*

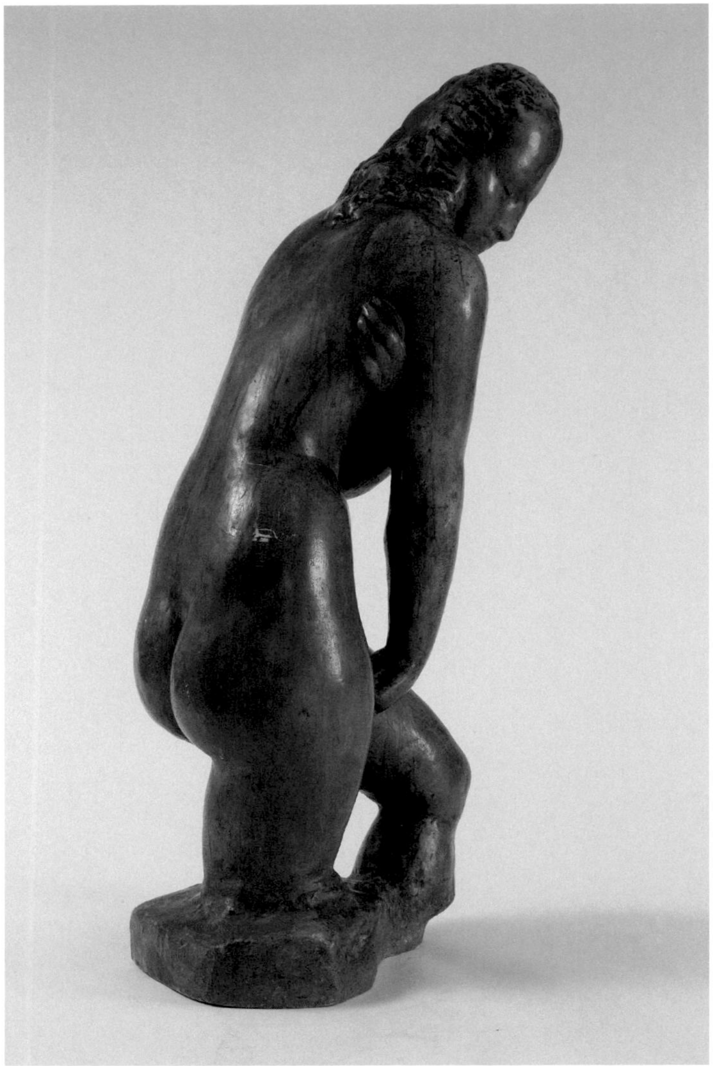

DIE BADENDE I / THE BATHER I
1913
Cast stone
H: 36 IN. (91.4 CM); W: 13¾ IN. (34.9 CM); D: 18 ¼ IN. (46.4 CM)
Gift of Mr. and Mrs. Donald Winston, 1957

WILHELM LEHMBRUCK

(GERMAN, 1881–1919)

Wilhelm Lehmbruck's art training took place in Düsseldorf, not far from his native Duisburg, between 1895 and 1906. Although always figurative, Lehmbruck's sculptures are different from the classical precedent of human depiction that was expounded at the more conservative German art academies during the late nineteenth and early twentieth centuries. His figures, according to biographer August Hoff, "express a melancholy reverie and meditative withdrawal."[1] From 1910 to 1914 Lehmbruck lived in Paris, where he first met Aristide Maillol and Auguste Rodin and later Constantin Brancusi and Alexander Archipenko. In the aftermath of World War I, Lehmbruck's work focused on themes of human suffering and alienation. In 1919, unable to cope and struggling with despair following the cataclysm of the war years, the sculptor committed suicide in Berlin.

Executed in Paris and exhibited at the Salon d'Automne there in 1913, *The Bather I* was one of many female torso figures created by Lehmbruck in the period just before World War I. Hoff notes that his work of the Paris years differs from his earlier work done in Germany, comparing a Bather of 1905 with the UCLA rendition, executed eight years later: "The former is a pleasant example of superb technique, while the latter is quietly concerned with itself, is complete in itself, mass, and contour. Her movements veil rather than reveal.... The bold breaking off at the calves emphasizes the forward thrust even more strongly. The line of the back, noble and unified, is counterbalanced by a more agitated treatment of the front view."[2] All the versions of *The Bather* made during Lehmbruck's lifetime were in cast stone; casts in bronze were made posthumously by the artist's family. This sculpture is not currently on public view because the fragile nature of the cast-stone material prohibits its permanent installation in the Murphy Sculpture Garden. C.D.

Notes
1 *August Hoff,* Wilhelm Lehmbruck: Life and Work *(Berlin: Rembrandt Verlag, 1961), 22.*
2 *Ibid., 31.*

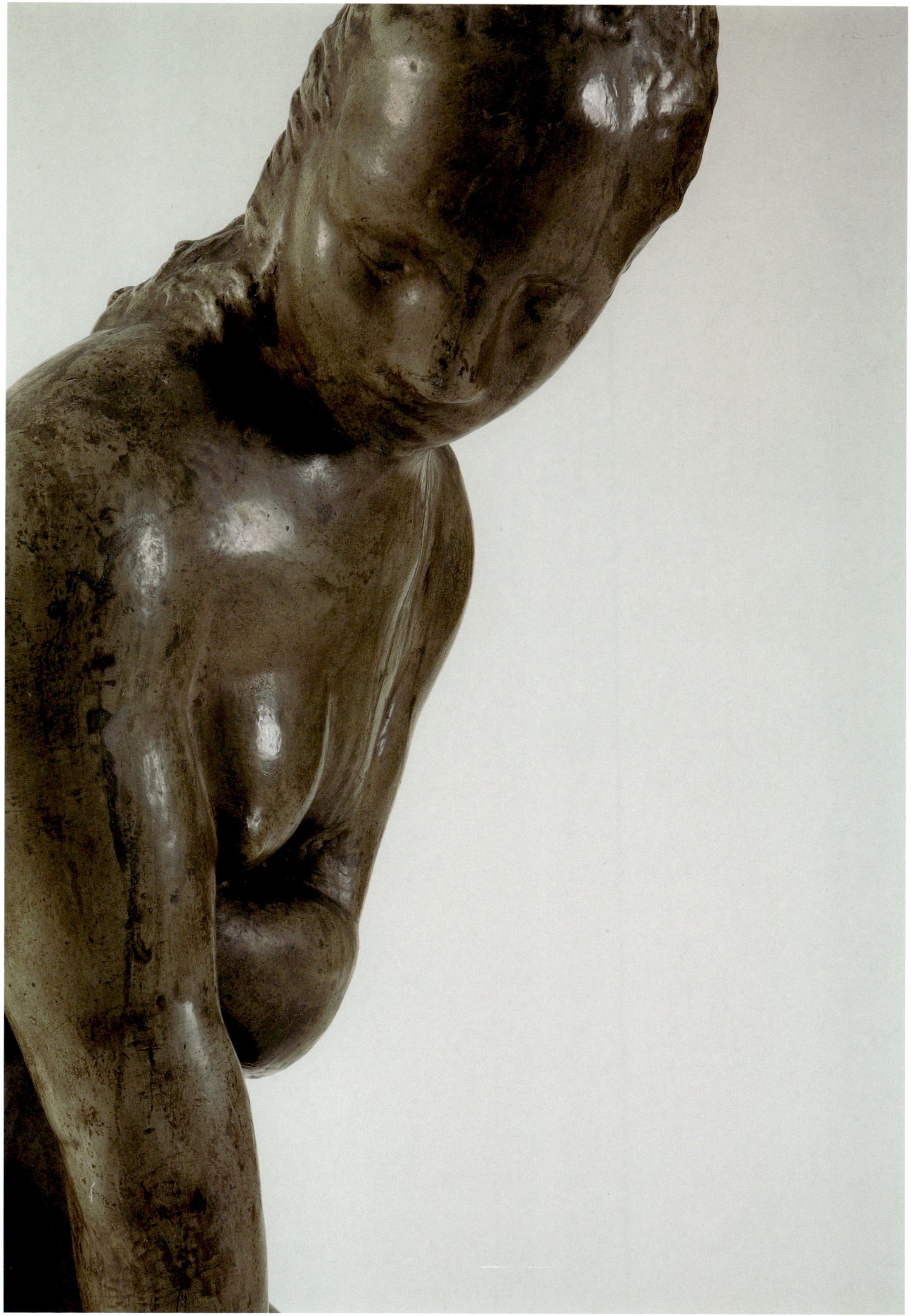

JACQUES LIPCHITZ

(FRENCH, 1891–1973)

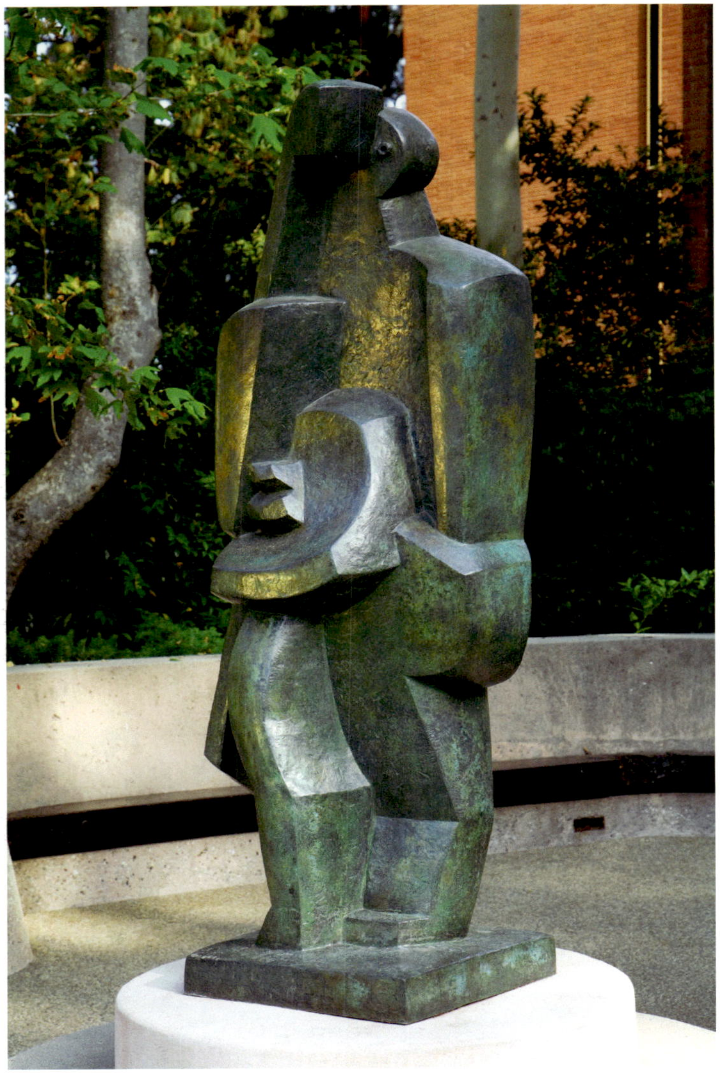

BAIGNEUSE / BATHER
1923–25
Bronze
H: 76¾ IN. (195 CM); W: 30⅛ IN. (76.5 CM); D: 25½ IN. (64.8 CM)
Edition: 6/7
Foundry: Modern Art Foundry, New York
Gift of David E. Bright, 1967

In 1909 Jacques Lipchitz left Lithuania for Paris, and for the next few years he studied at the École des Beaux-Arts and the Académie Julian. He soon developed friendships with important artists and writers working in Paris, including Jean Cocteau, Juan Gris, Max Jacob, Amedeo Modigliani, and Diego Rivera, who introduced him to Pablo Picasso in 1913. Though his earliest works reflected his academic training and the influence of Aristide Maillol, after meeting Picasso, Lipchitz began to more fully explore the cubist idiom in sculpture. In the mid-1920s his cubist style gave way to his exploration of new ways to produce transparent forms, which he designated *transparents*. With the Nazi occupation of France, Lipchitz, who was of Jewish heritage, was forced to flee, and in 1941—at the invitation of a number of American friends, including Alfred Barr, director of the Museum of Modern Art in New York—he moved to the United States, where he would remain for the rest of his life. His work was the subject of major retrospectives at the Museum of Modern Art in 1954, at UCLA in 1963, and at the Metropolitan Museum of Art in New York in 1972.

The Murphy Sculpture Garden's *Bather* dates from the latter part of Lipchitz's cubist period. The work was one of a number commissioned by American collector Alfred Barnes to adorn the facade of his museum outside Philadelphia and was designed to be placed in a niche. The artist said of this work: "I was returning to the problem of creating a cubist figure, free-standing in surrounding space, creating that space by its axial pivot.... It was in a sense my farewell to literal cubism, the record of the moment when it was no longer necessary for me to concentrate on the vocabulary of forms, when I could move on to a sculpture of themes and ideas."[1]

Song of the Vowels is one of the artist's *transparents*, works marked by open spaces in a framework of thin bands of metal. The subject of the harpist first appeared in Lipchitz's work in 1928 the same year that the artist and his wife bought a subscription to the Paris Symphony Orchestra. A few years later Lipchitz created the first cast of this monumental sculpture for the garden of Madame de Mandrot at her house in Le Pradet, France, designed by Le Corbusier. The work is one of the few sculptures in the Murphy Garden originally commissioned for a garden setting. The base of the sculpture in Le Pradet is concrete, but in subsequent editions it was cast in bronze. The artist took the title from an Egyptian papyrus that contained a song composed only o vowels, which was performed to subdue the forces of nature.[2] C.B

LE CHANT DES VOYELLES / SONG OF THE VOWELS
1931–32
Bronze
H: 145 IN. (369.6 CM); W: 63 IN. (160 CM); D: 78¾ IN. (200 CM)
Edition: 7/7
Foundry: Modern Art Foundry, New York
Gift of the UCLA Art Council and Mr. and Mrs. Norton Simon, 1963

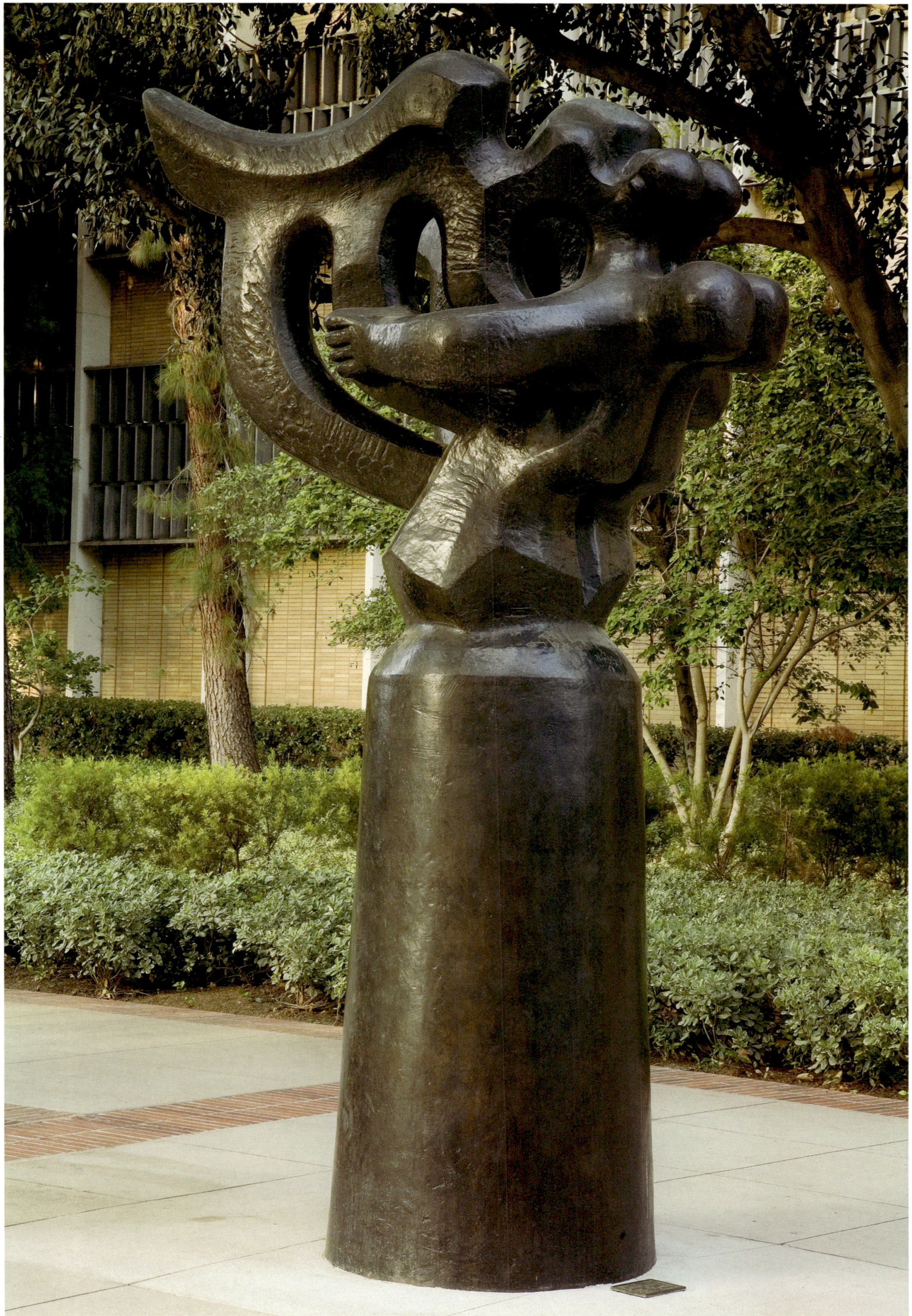

Notes
1 *Jacques Lipchitz,* My Life in Sculpture *(New York: Viking Press, 1972), 74.*
2 *Ibid., 123.*

TOWER OF MASKS
1961
Indiana limestone
H: 183 IN. (465 CM); W: 54 IN. (137.2 CM); D: 54 IN. (137.2 CM)
Gift of Anna Bing Arnold, 1962

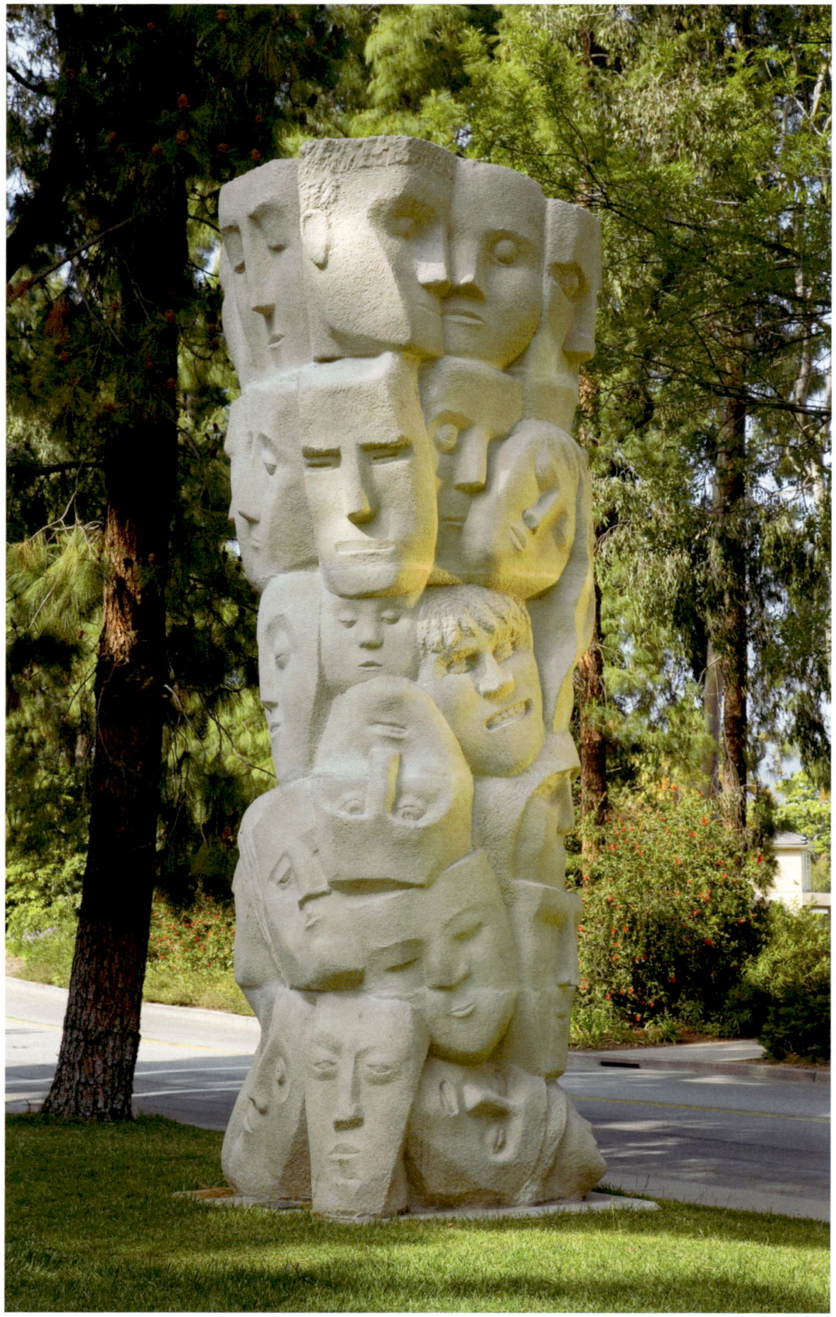

Anna Mahler's initial studies in art began in Italy, where she admired the sculptural formalism of early Renaissance painters such as Masaccio, Andrea Mantegna, and Andrea del Castagno and studied painting with Giorgio de Chirico in Rome. Upon Mahler's return to Vienna, the sculptor Fritz Wotruba induced her to forgo painting and concentrate upon working in three dimensions, especially through the method of direct carving. This was a technique to which Mahler readily adapted; she seldom used models in her art, and she generally carved her sculptures from large blocks of limestone and marble, the materials of the two works in the Murphy Sculpture Garden collection. Between 1950 and her death in 1988 she spent several months each year in Los Angeles, where she often worked in her open-air studio and received many local commissions.

The angular form of the marble block is retained in *Night*, in which the sculpted female figure emerges from the white block, looking over her shoulder as she confronts the viewer—almost like Lot's wife turning into a pillar of salt before our eyes. This technique of blending a finished form with a portion of the unfinished material base is one that Mahler used frequently in her sculpture. *Tower of Masks*, the largest work created by the artist, was composed of Indiana limestone blocks, carved into five sections, placed one atop the other through a central structural core, each section containing a variety of human faces that express "physiognomic force with [great] intensity.... The finished work imparts to the masks an air of finality that is truly monumental."[1] The totemic structure of the piece also invites the viewer to experience it in the round, the diversity of the more than forty masked faces clearly apparent as one circumnavigates the sculpture. Originally commissioned for the courtyard of the UCLA theater auditorium, the Freud Playhouse, in Macgowan Hall, the sculpture was reinstalled in a different location in the Murphy Sculpture Garden after conservation work to repair it following damage sustained in the 1994 Northridge earthquake. C.D.

Notes
1 *Ernst Gombrich, introduction to* Anna Mahler: Her Work *(Stuttgart and Zurich: Belser, 1975), 8.*

ANNA MAHLER

(AUSTRIAN, 1904–1988)

NIGHT
1963
Marble
H: 65 IN. (165 CM); W: 20 IN. (50.8 CM); D: 22 IN. (55.9 CM)
Gift of Anna Bing Arnold, 1965

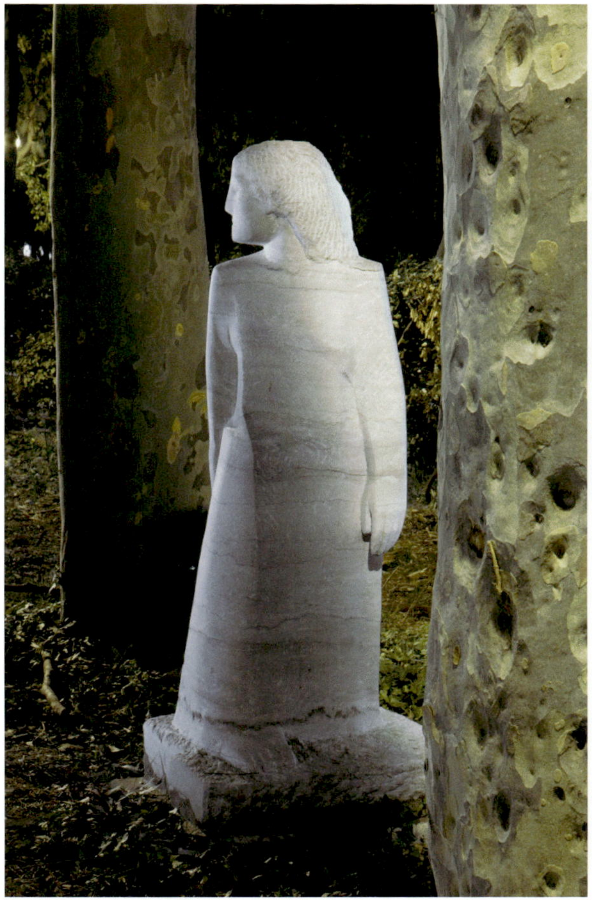

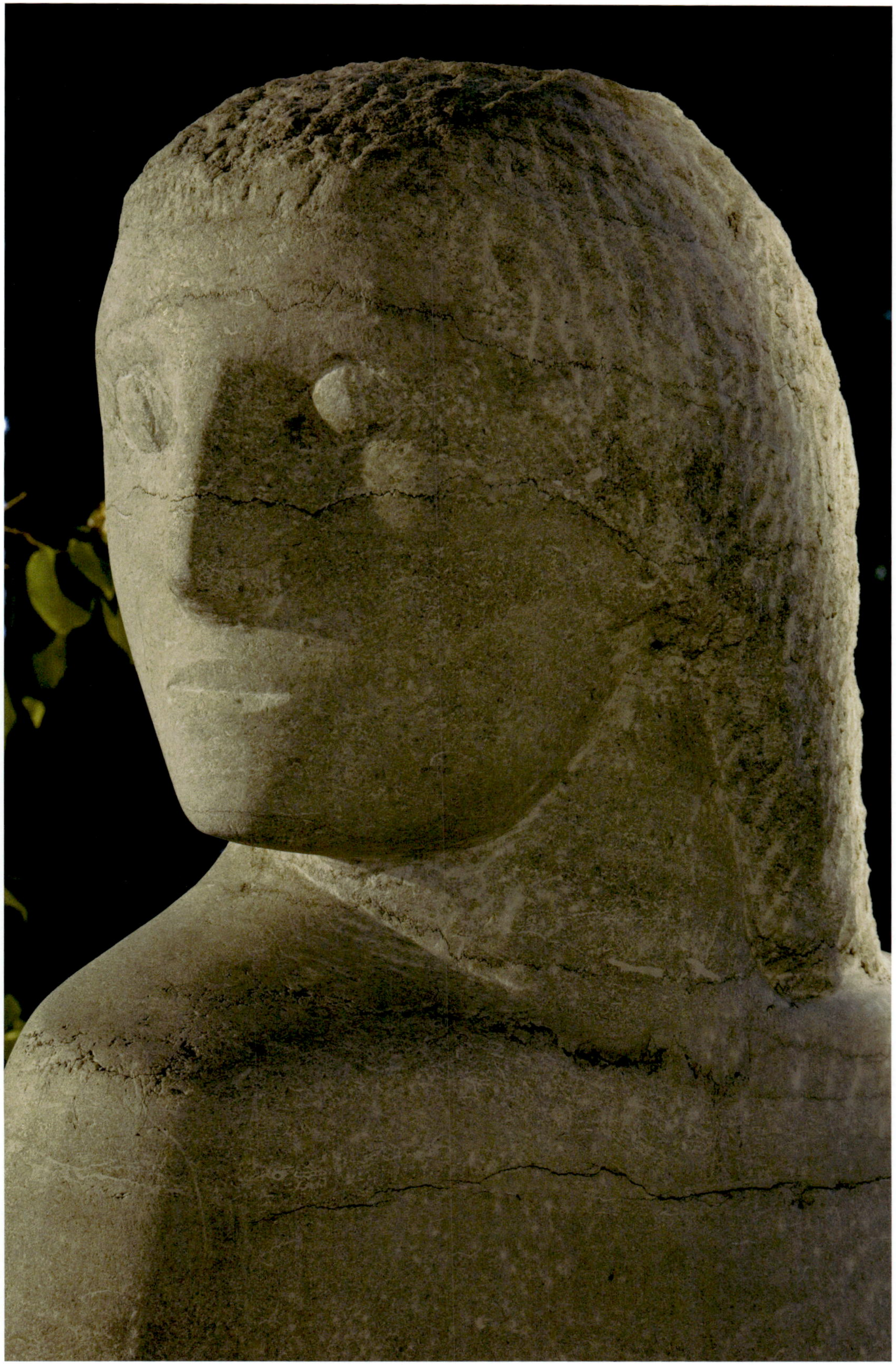

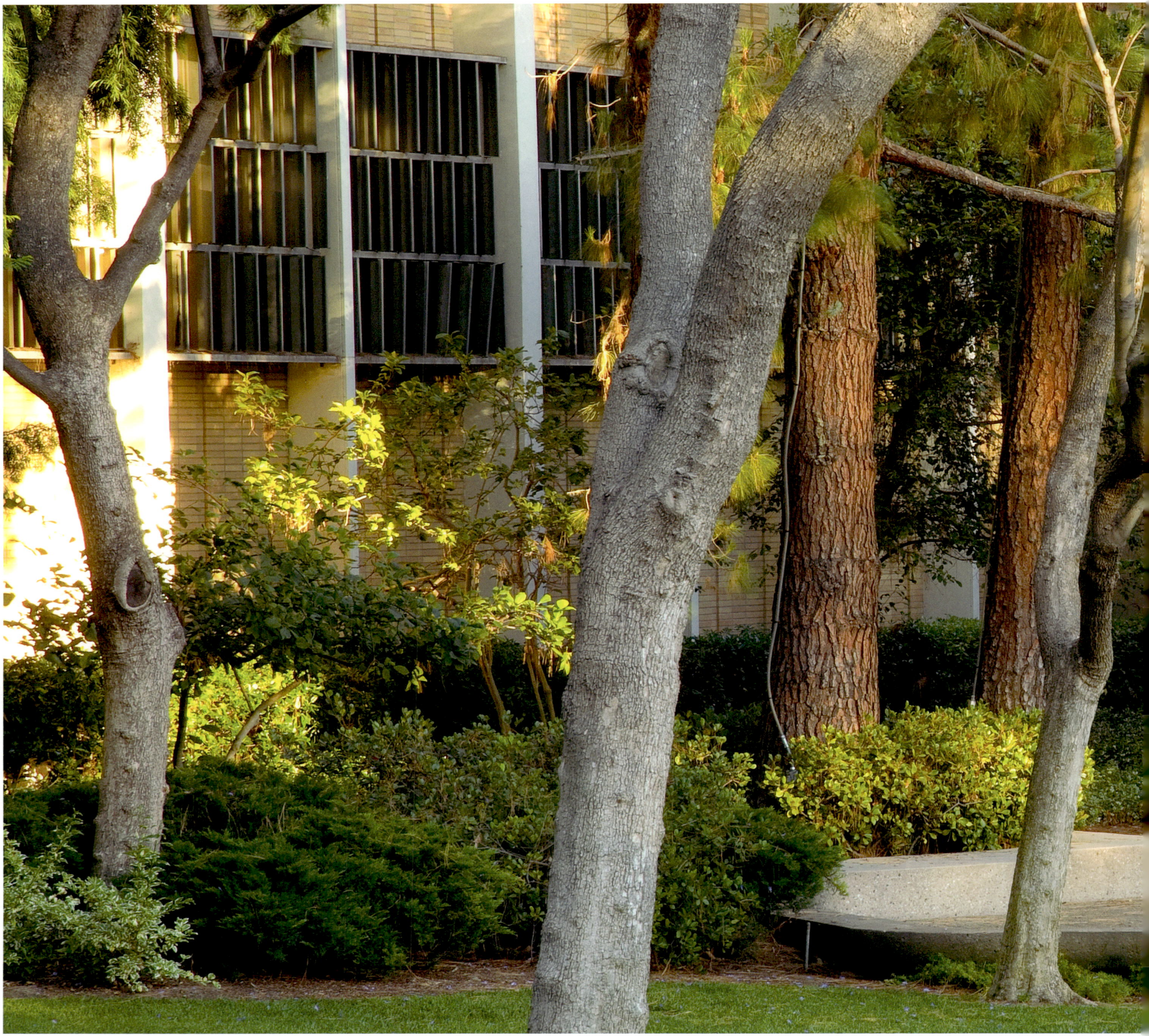

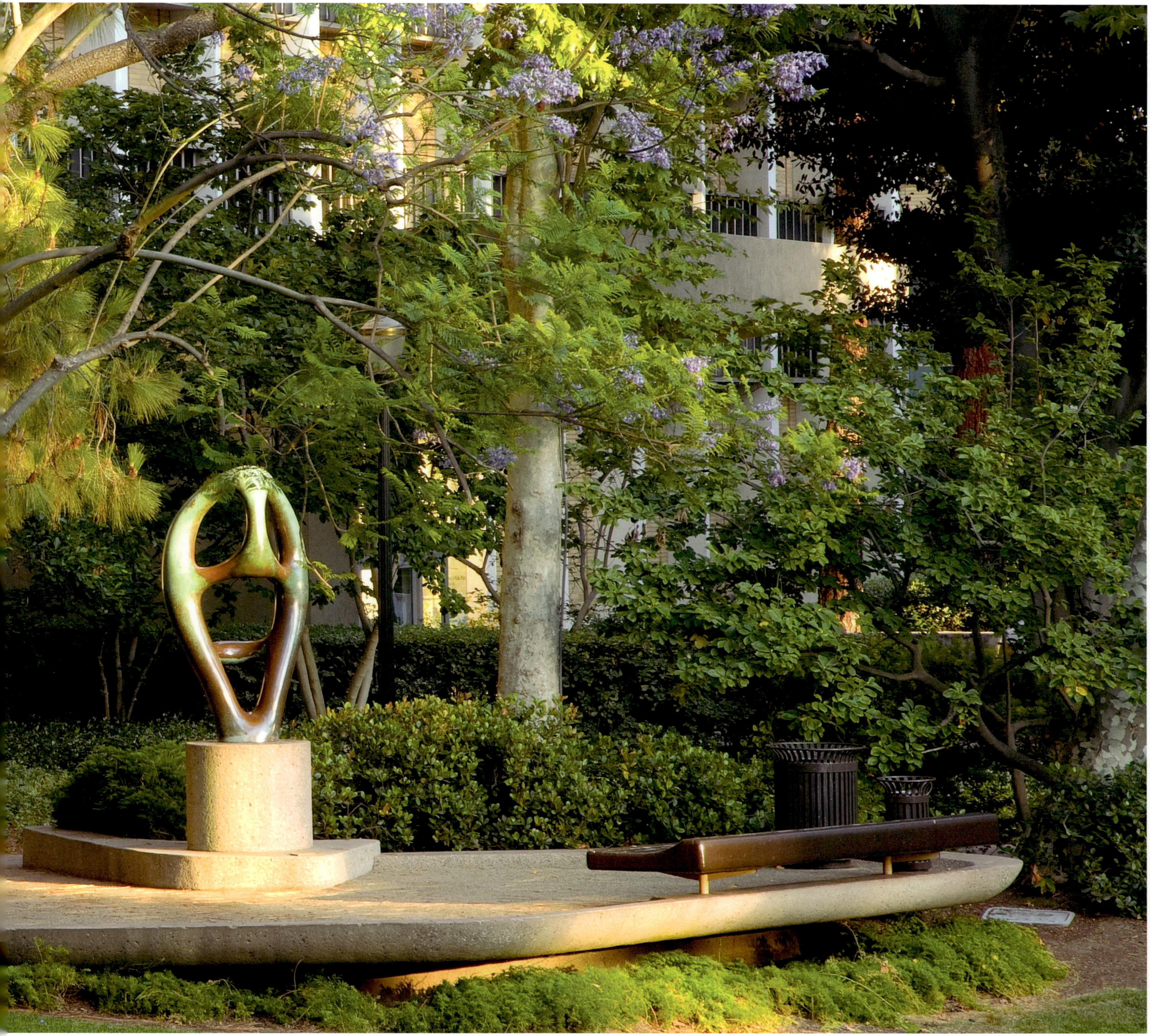

TÊTE HÉROÏQUE / HEROIC HEAD
1923
Bronze
H: 23 IN. (58.4 CM); W: 17 IN. (43.2 CM); D: 18 IN. (45.7 CM)
Edition: 5/6
Foundry: Valsuani, Paris, cast 1962–63
A gift in memory of Mary E. Freiberg from her family, her friends, and the members of the UCLA Art Council, 1968

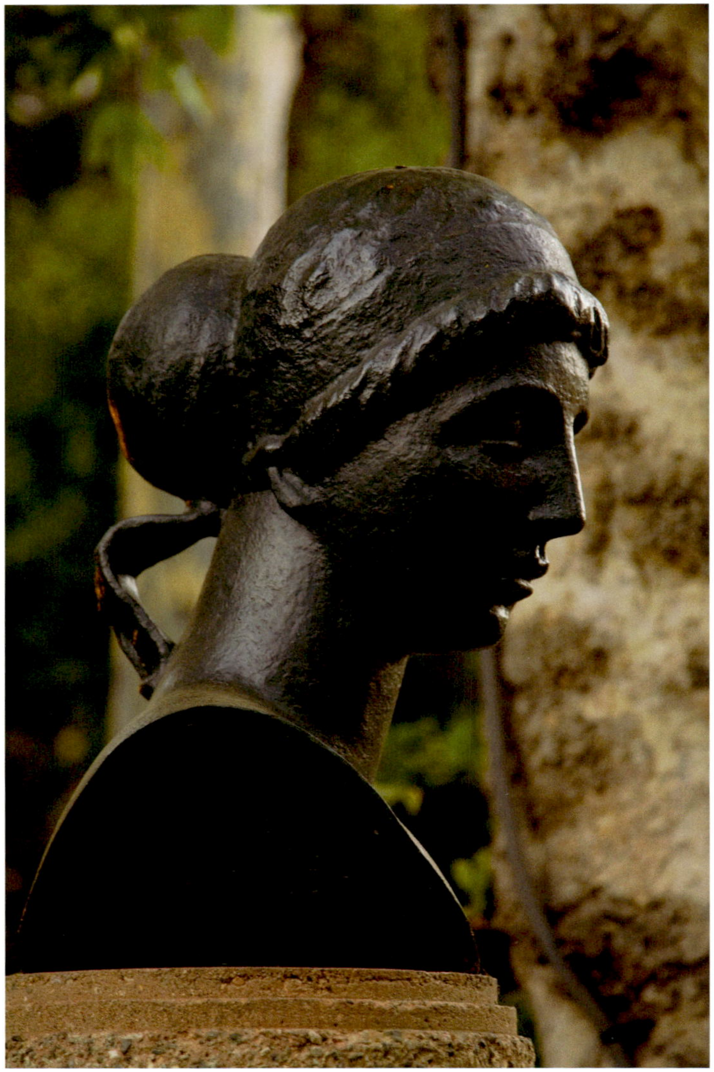

Aristide Maillol began his artistic training in his native Perpignan, in southwest France. At the age of twenty he traveled to Paris, where he studied first at the École des Arts Décoratifs and then, after numerous attempts to pass the entrance exam, at the École des Beaux-Arts. Disenchanted with his academic training, he put aside his original goal of becoming a painter and turned to tapestry design. He did not take up sculpture until he was nearly forty, encouraged by his successful affiliation with the Parisian art dealer Ambroise Vollard, who purchased a number of smaller clay figurines and later cast them in bronze. A trip to Greece in 1908, which brought renewed contact with archaic and early classical sculpture, reinforced the artist's long-standing interest in the nude female form. He continued to work in a variety of media, including woodcuts and book illustration, though large-scale sculpture would remain his primary artistic activity.

Maillol's *Heroic Head* is a posthumous cast from a study for the head of the reclining female form of *Monument to the Dead, Port Vendres*, also from 1923, one of several commissions awarded to the artist to honor those who died in World War I.[1] Representing a young, grieving woman, it bears comparison with Bourdelle's *Head of France* in the Murphy Garden, which is also based on a figure from a World War I memorial dating to 1923. *Torso* is a fragment of the right figure of Maillol's *Three Nymphs*. It is one of a number of full- and partial-figure female nudes, including each of the figures from *Three Nymphs*, that the artist continued to rework and create variations of over the years. It is quite similar to a bronze at the Montreal Museum of Fine Arts, also considered a unique work, as well as the terra-cotta *Torso of a Young Girl* (Indiana University Art Museum).[2] C.B.

Notes
1 *The edition of six was authorized by the Maillol estate and cast in 1962–63 by Valsuani in Paris.*
2 *See Kathleen A. Foster,* Maillol: Sculpture and Drawings in the Indiana University Art Museum Collection *(Bloomington: Indiana University Art Museum, 1991), 2, and* The Montreal Museum of Fine Arts: Painting, Sculpture, Decorative Arts *(Montreal: Montreal Museum of Fine Arts, 1960), 123. See Cynthia Burlingham and Elizabeth Shepherd, eds.,* In the Sculptor's Landscape: Celebrating Twenty-five Years of the Franklin D. Murphy Sculpture Garden *(Los Angeles: Wight Art Gallery and Grunwald Center for the Graphic Arts, University of California, 1993), 73n6, for descriptions and further discussion of these sculptures.*

ARISTIDE MAILLOL
(FRENCH, 1861–1944)

TORSO
CA. 1938
Bronze
H: 42 IN. (106.7 CM); W: 16 IN.
(40.6 CM); D: 11 IN. (27.9 CM)
Edition: possibly unique cast
Foundry: Alexis Rudier,
Paris, ca. 1938–44
Gift in honor of Franklin D.
Murphy from Henry Ford II, 1976

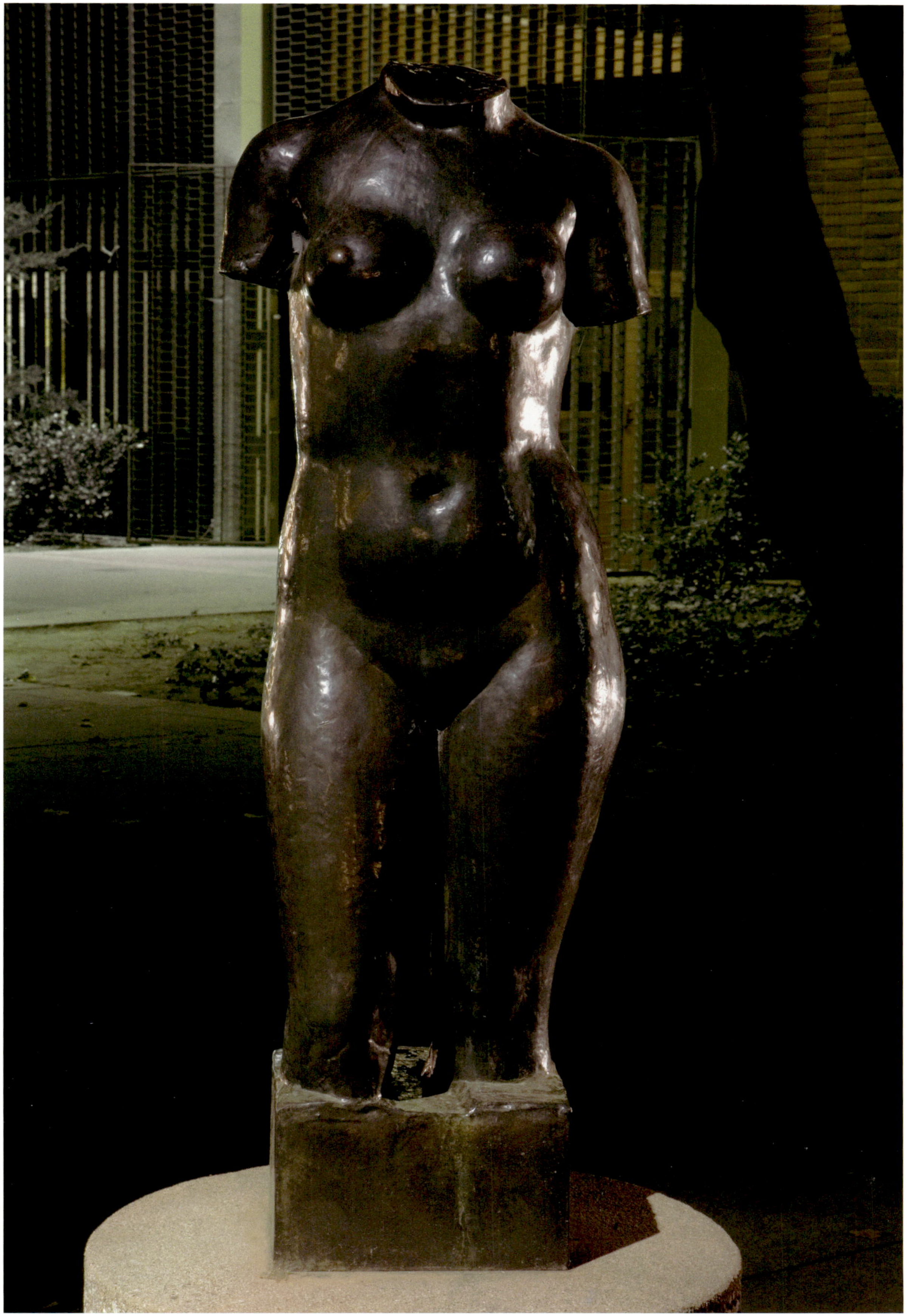

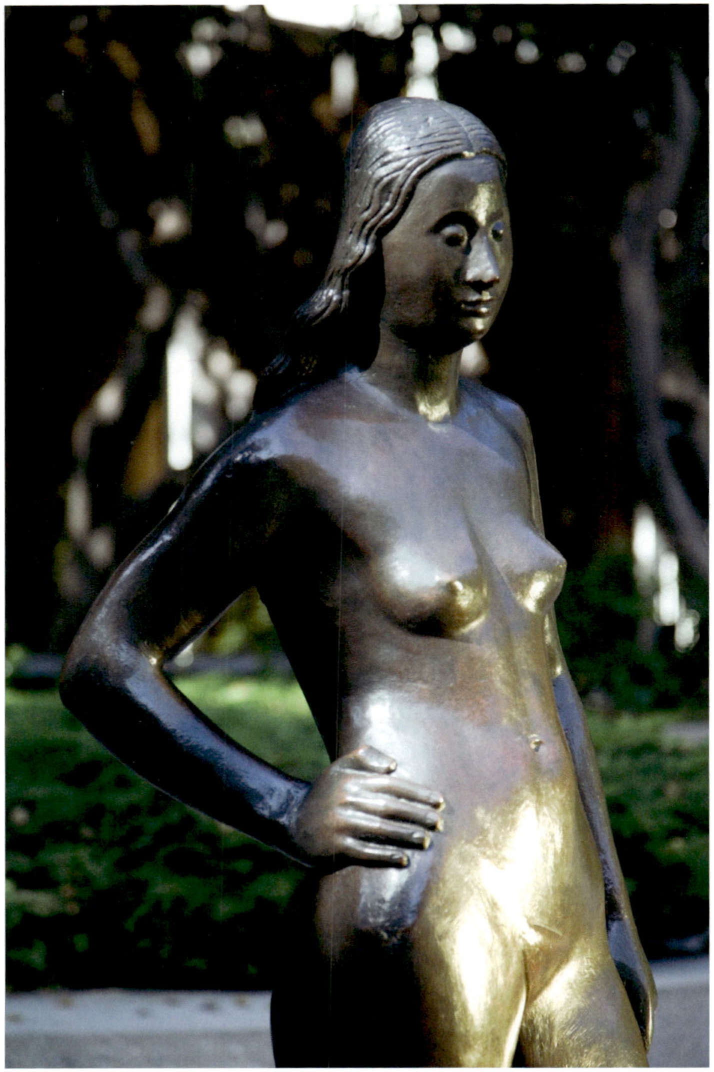

FREYA
1950
Bronze
H: 65 ½ IN. (166.5 CM); W: 21 IN. (53.3 CM); D: 14 IN. (35.6 CM)
Edition: 7/10
Foundry: Barth, Berlin
Gift of the UCLA Art Council in honor of Franklin D. Murphy, 1968

Although he never received a formal art education, Gerhard Marcks learned about sculpture from his friend Richard Scheibe, whose studio he entered in 1907. After military service during World War I, Marcks was employed in 1918 at the Berlin School of Applied Arts (Kunstgewerbeschule). The following year, Walter Gropius invited Marcks to supervise the pottery division at the Weimar Bauhaus, where the artist worked until 1925. When the Weimar Bauhaus closed, Marcks obtained a teaching post at the Kunstgewerbeschule near Halle, where he worked until his dismissal by the National Socialists in 1933. Despite government orders that forbade him to work as an artist, as well as the inclusion of his work in the "Degenerate Art" exhibition of 1937, he continued to create art clandestinely in his Berlin studio and traveled to Italy during World War II. Marcks was later appointed professor at the State Art School in Hamburg and received important public commissions from various German cities, including Hamburg, Lübeck, and Mannheim. In 1950 he moved to Cologne, and in 1966 he established the Gerhard Marcks Foundation in Bremen, which is still active today.

Created during the middle of World War II, *Maja* was modeled after Marcks's daughter Ute, whose portrait bust he executed in 1945. The original plaster cast of *Maja* survived the Allied bombing of the artist's studio at the end of the war and was one of his few works that were left undamaged; the bronze versions of the sculpture were cast after the war. The later work, *Freya*, was derived from Marcks's *Melusine III* of 1948, and bronze casts were made in 1950. These female figures reflect Marcks's ability to idealize the human form while imbuing it with a tranquil serenity and quietude, based on a classical rather than an avant-garde aesthetic sensibility. C.D.

GERHARD MARCKS

(GERMAN, 1889–1981)

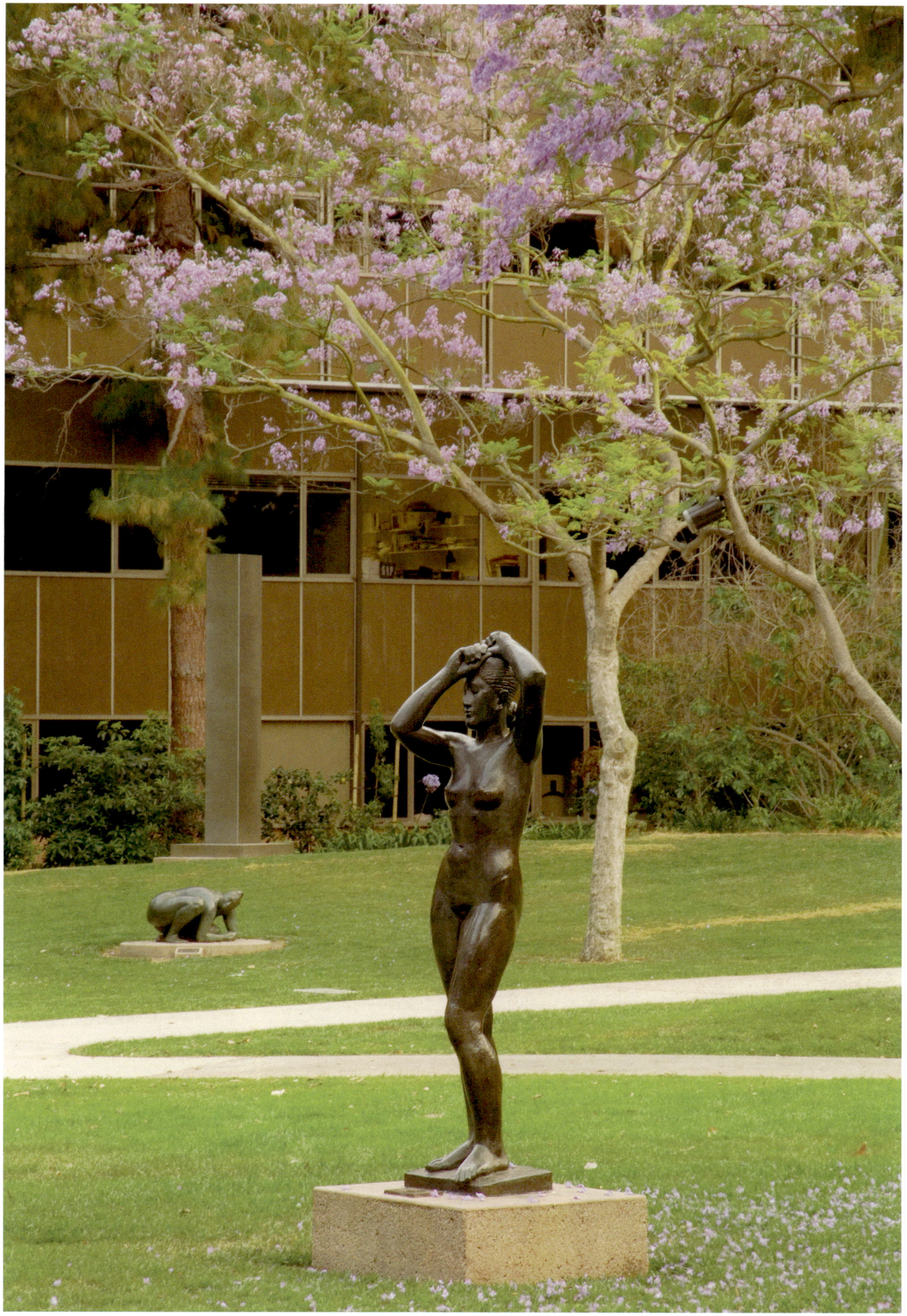

MAJA
1941
Bronze
H: 88 IN. (223.5 CM); W: 25 IN. (63.5 CM); D: 23 IN. (58.4 CM)
Edition: /8
Foundry: H. Noack, Berlin
Gift of Mr. and Mrs. Jack Warner and the UCLA Art Council, 1970

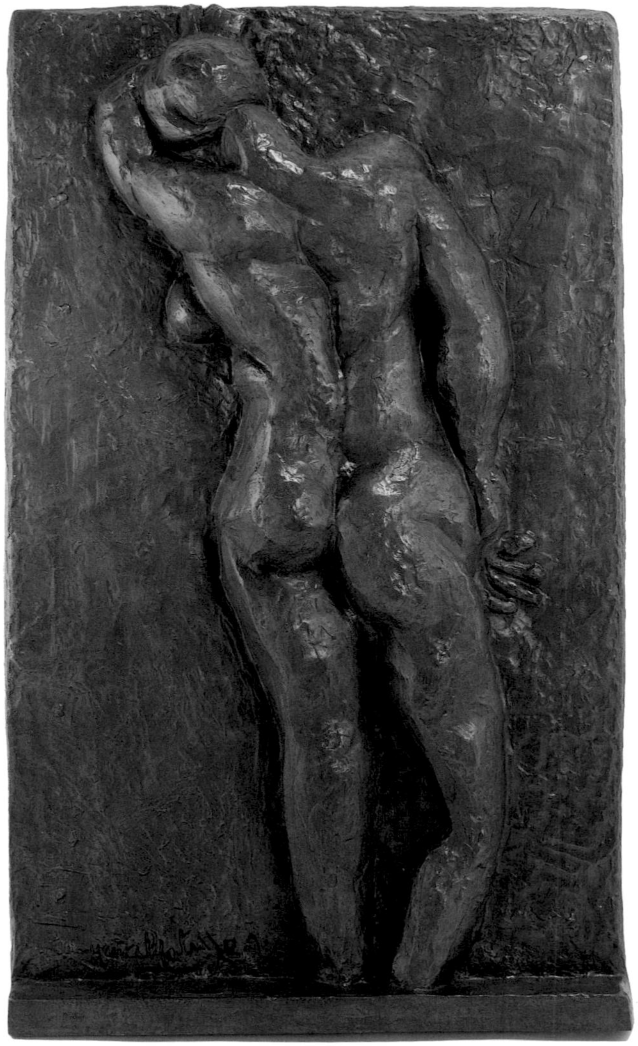

BAS-RELIEF I
1909
Bronze
H: 75 IN. (190.5 CM); W: 46 IN. (117 CM); D: 6½ IN. (16.5 CM)
Edition: 6/10 (posthumous cast)
Foundry: Georges Rudier, Paris
Gift of Michael J. Connell Memorial Fund, 1967

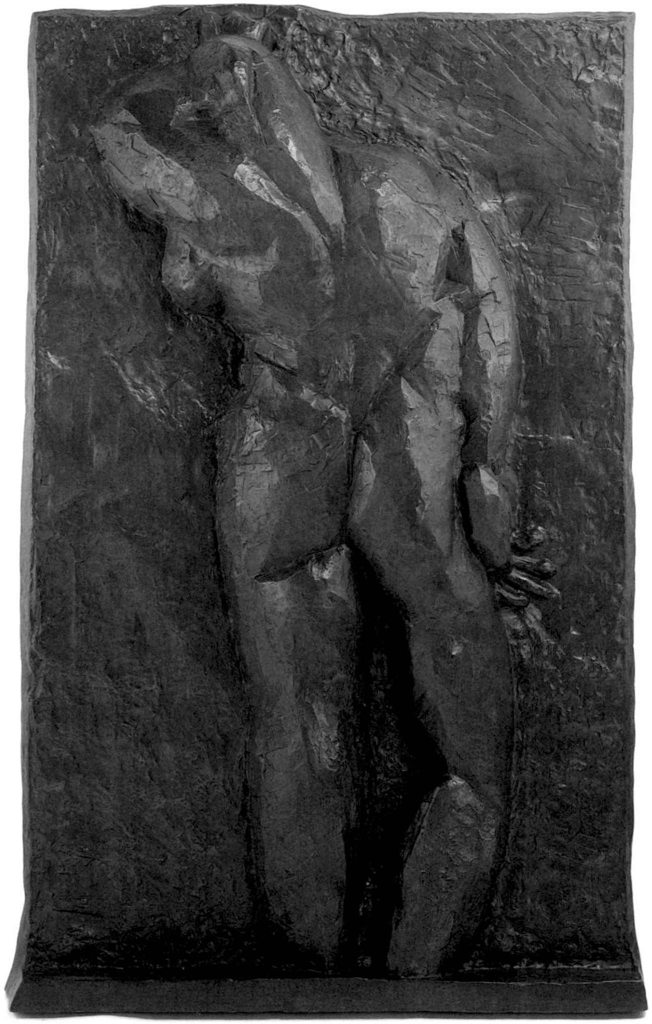

BAS-RELIEF II
1913
Bronze
H: 75 IN. (190.5 CM); W: 48 IN. (122 CM); D: 6¾ IN. (17.1 CM)
Edition: 6/10 (posthumous cast)
Foundry: Georges Rudier, Paris
Gift of the UCLA Art Council Fund, 1966

HENRI MATISSE

(FRENCH, 1869–1954)

Henri Matisse began his career as a lawyer and first discovered painting during a period of convalescence in 1890. A year later he subscribed to the Académie Julian in Paris and began one of the most successful artistic careers of the twentieth century. His early work is marked by the impact of postimpressionist painters Paul Cézanne, Paul Gauguin, Vincent van Gogh, and Paul Signac. After his first solo show at Ambroise Vollard's gallery in Paris in 1904, he visited the French Riviera, where he explored the rich color palette that characterizes his paintings of this period. Bright, expressive color and flat compositions were common attributes in the work of the Fauves, a group Matisse formed with André Derain and Maurice Vlaminck, among others. Matisse lived and worked among the creative community of Montparnasse until 1917. Here, as the fauvist movement declined, his work developed independently and granted him continuing critical success. Thereafter he returned to the coast, settling in the town of Cimiez, near Nice, where he remained until his death in 1954. Here again, his style took fresh turns in the natural and more organic environment of the South of France. He and Pablo Picasso were friends as well as rivals in terms of the many directions they pushed their art in and the diverse mediums they experimented with.

Matisse's sculptures, numbering just over eighty in all, have until recently been relegated to a subordinate status by critics. Research has shown that he labored on them intensely, however, and that he considered them as complements rather than adjuncts to his two-dimensional works. The large-scale reliefs known as Backs I–IV are landmarks in modern sculpture and among Matisse's most intriguing creations. They were produced over a twenty-one-year period, and although they are certainly connected in style, size, and iconography, there is no evidence that Matisse himself considered them a series.

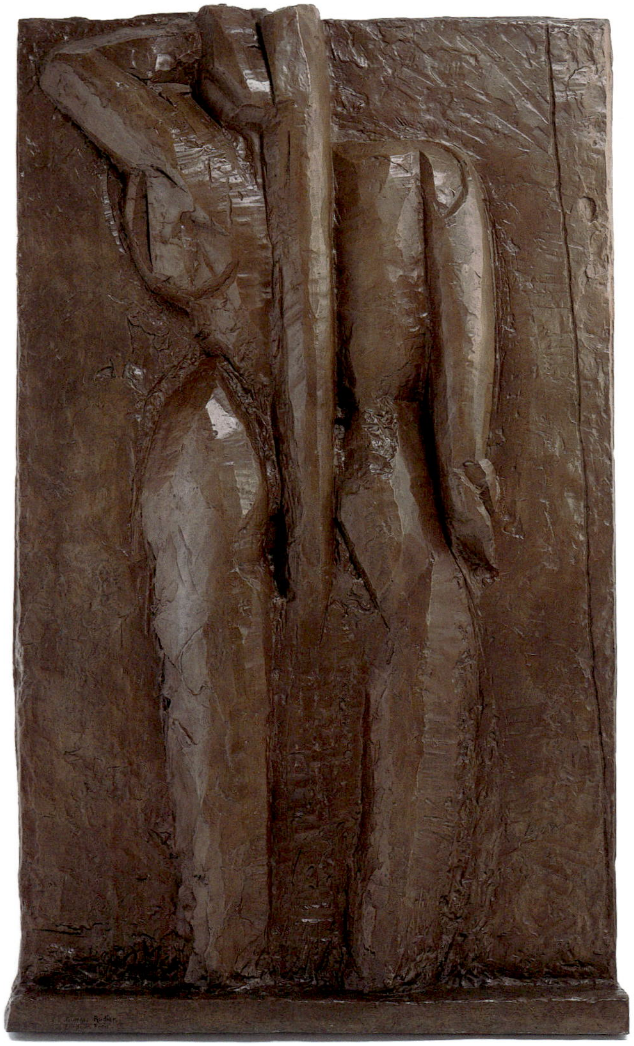

BAS-RELIEF III
1916–17
Bronze
H: 75 IN. (190.5 CM); W: 45 IN. (114 CM); D: 6 ¼ IN. (15.9 CM)
Edition: 6/10 (posthumous cast)
Foundry: Georges Rudier, Paris
Gift of the UCLA Art Council through the generosity of Mrs. Robert E. Gross and Mrs. Charles E. Ducommun, 1966

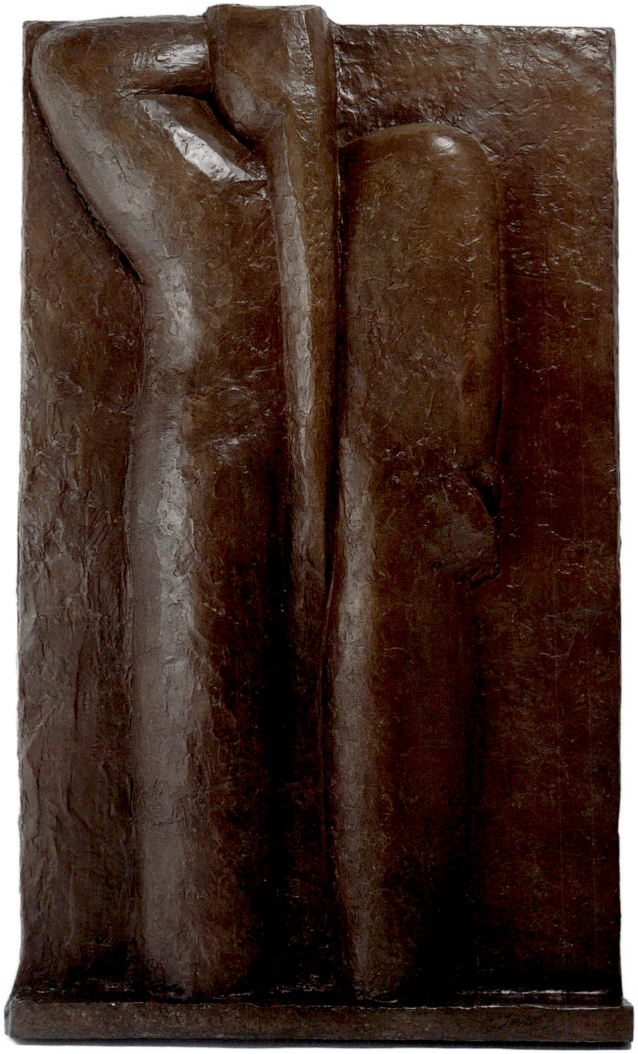

BAS-RELIEF IV
1930
Bronze
H: 75 IN. (190.5 CM); W: 45 IN. (114 CM); D: 6 ¼ IN. (15.9 CM)
Edition: 6/10 (posthumous cast)
Foundry: Georges Rudier, Paris
Gift of Mr. and Mrs. Sidney F. Brody in honor of the UCLA Art Council, 1966

Rather, they are evolving interpretations of the same theme: a nude model viewed from the back in a traditional *contrapposto* studio pose. The preliminary version in clay, known as *Back 0*, was made in 1909 and survives today only in a photograph.[1] *Back I* was made the same year, probably by reworking the same clay model. It is the most naturalistic of the group. Subsequently the figure was progressively simplified into geometric forms until it was reduced to bold, abstract blocks in *Back IV* of 1930. The hair, at first in a conservative knot, was let down in stages until it reached the figure's hip in the form of a single plait that splits the body in two halves. The evolution marks a release in Matisse's style, and the continuing development of his artistic expression. In all versions the feet are masked by a horizontal band along the lower frame, possibly referring to a pool of water. This rigid lower line is integral to the composition. In *Back I* it acts as a balancing ground for the figure, and by *Back IV* it is a counter-poise to her vertical outlines. The pose remains the same, with the figure's weight balanced on the left leg, and the limbs hanging loose on the right.

The Backs are explorations of mass in space and as such can be considered in parallel to paintings Matisse was making simultaneously. They have been linked to the large-scale paintings *Dance* and *Music* of 1910, commissioned by his Russian patron Sergei Shchukin, which both deal with the relationship between figure and background.[2] In the Backs the relief of the figure is gradually reduced so that it increasingly melds with the textured background. Indeed Matisse's three-dimensional panels are as pictorial as they are sculptural. *Back I* and *Back II* have also been linked to *Bathers by a River*, another painting commissioned by Shchukin, dated 1916–17.[3] While Matisse's paintings are about the illusion of form, his sculptures, in contrast, are about its raw physicality. Thus, what may have started as a simple exercise in modeling and casting developed into a complex challenge, involving numerous preparatory drawings. The Backs certainly kept Matisse's inquisitive mind alive and presented him with endless challenges. While inspired by the antique, the great masters of the Renaissance, and more recent heroes such as Cézanne, these works are unique reflections of the evolving facets of Matisse's art and of modern art in general. A.P.

Notes
1 *Archives Matisse, Paris; see Dorothy Kosinski, Jay McKean Fisher, and Steven Nash,* Matisse: Painter as Sculptor *(Baltimore: Baltimore Museum of Art; Dallas: Dallas Museum of Art and Nasher Sculpture Center; New Haven: Yale University Press, 2007), 9, fig. 9.*
2 *Ibid., 160.*
3 *Ibid.*

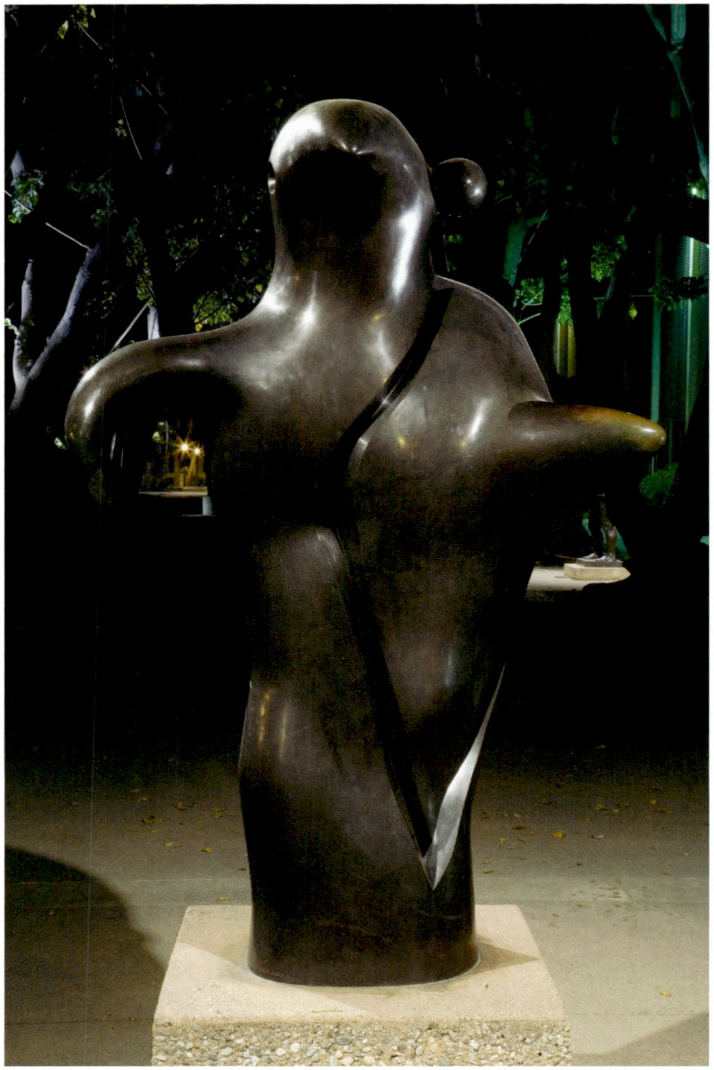

MÈRE UBU
1975
Bronze
H: 67 IN. (170.2 CM); W: 45 IN. (114.3 CM); D: 35 IN. (88.9 CM)
Edition: 2/4 (posthumous cast)
Foundry: Susse, Paris
Gift of the UCLA Art Council in honor of the Thieves Market Volunteers, 1976

Joan Miró joins Pablo Picasso and Salvador Dalí as one of Spain's greatest and most revered twentieth-century masters. He pursued his studies and encountered his first success as an artist in Barcelona, a city he would remain devoted to throughout his life. Greater strides in his work were made in Paris, where he was invited to participate in a Dada festival in 1920. He found his place in the thriving artistic community there and drew inspiration from contemporary experimental movements. The kinetic work of Alexander Calder, for instance, made a particular impression on Miró. In 1926 he held his first show in America, organized by Marcel Duchamp's and Katherine Dreier's Société Anonyme at the Brooklyn Museum of Art. His art was embraced by the surrealists. Nevertheless Miró retained his artistic autonomy and a unique and instantly recognizable style. He was highly prolific in all media: printmaking, drawing, painting, sculpture, and ceramics. Today we envisage him at work in the remote tranquillity of the island of Majorca, near Barcelona, to which he retreated, remaining there in the company of his family until his last days.

The UCLA sculpture is connected to a play by Alfred Jarry called *Ubu Roi* (1896), which is often cited as a forerunner of the theater of the absurd. Miró developed a fascination with the characters in the play, in particular with Mère Ubu, the lusty wife of Jarry's protagonist, Père Ubu. She appears in the collector's edition of *Ubu Roi* illustrated by Miró in 1966, and recurs in drawings by the artist from the 1940s to the 1970s.[1] This anthropomorphic creature, and the woman-bird iconography in particular, returned in various forms in Miró's work. Here short wings branch out from Mère Ubu's side, and a beak protrudes from the tip of her head. She is simultaneously bold and endearing. A sharp incision traces the edge of the figure from front to back, piercing her rotund forms. Seen from the front, the figure seems young and motherly, positioned as if she were about to embrace an invisible child, while from the back her large, lopsided hump makes her resemble an old woman. A.P.

JOAN MIRÓ

(SPANISH, 1893–1983)

Notes
1 Drawings by Miró from the Artist's Studio and the Joan Miró Foundation, Barcelona *(London: Arts Council of Great Britain, 1979), nos. 229–78.*

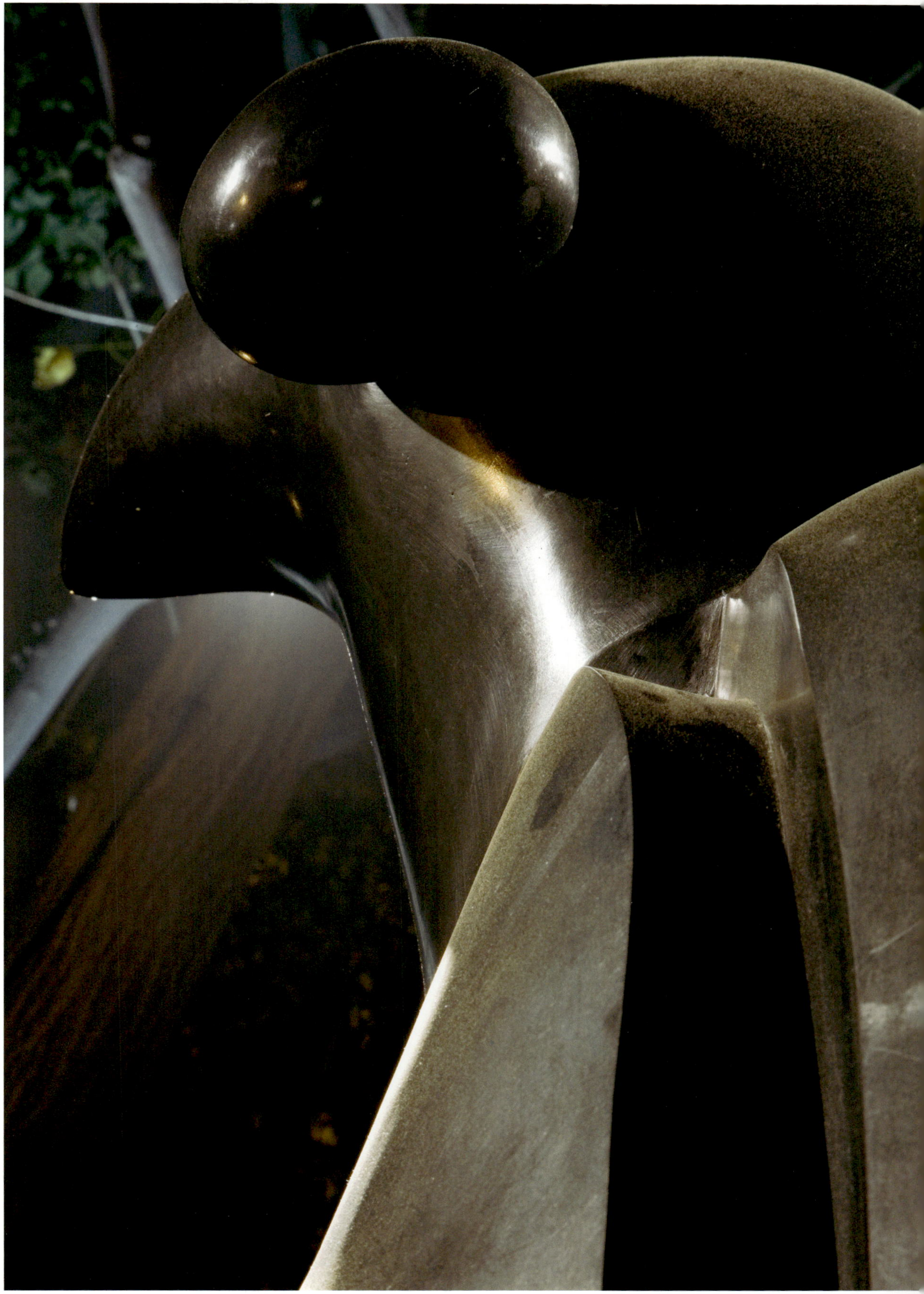

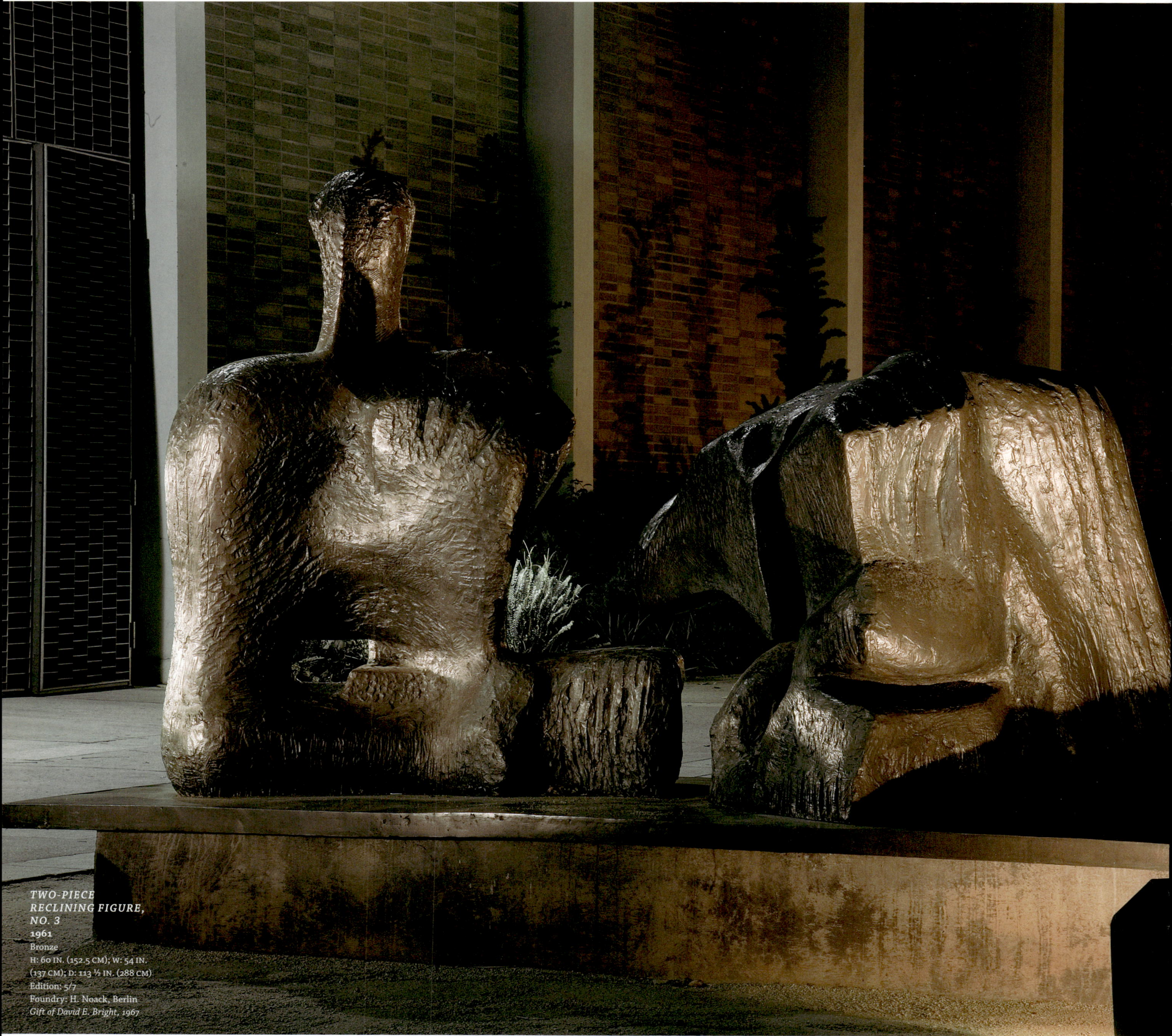

TWO-PIECE RECLINING FIGURE, NO. 3
1961
Bronze
H: 60 IN. (152.5 CM); W: 54 IN. (137 CM); D: 113 ½ IN. (288 CM)
Edition: 5/7
Foundry: H. Noack, Berlin
Gift of David E. Bright, 1967

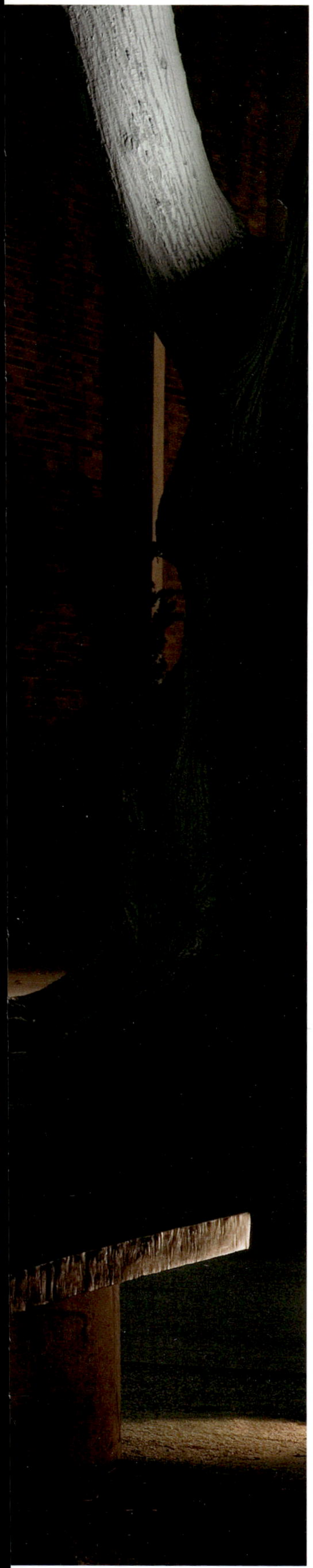

HENRY MOORE

(BRITISH, 1898–1986)

Henry Moore was born in Yorkshire, in northern England, the son of a mining engineer. Following World War I he received an ex-serviceman's grant to continue his education and became the first student of sculpture at Leeds School of Art in 1919. He studied the old masters firsthand on a six-month educational trip to Italy in 1924 and pursued his exploration of modeling and carving at London's Royal College of Art. Moore and his wife, Irina, were central figures in the community of avant-garde painters and sculptors in Hampstead, together with his friends Barbara Hepworth and Naum Gabo. He rose to rapid recognition, spearheaded the sculpture department at Chelsea School of Art, and in 1948 won the International Sculpture Prize at the Venice Biennale. He secured a string of exhibitions worldwide, including a retrospective at New York's Museum of Modern Art in 1946, and by the 1970s there were some forty shows a year featuring his work. Today he is considered one of Britain's most important and influential artists. Some of his most famous works were conceived at his farmhouse in Hertfordshire, where the Moores spent the longest and happiest period of their lives.

Moore is the ultimate master of the reclining figure. With his abstract sculptures, which seem neither male nor female, the classical and historical theme of the reclining nude is carried through to the modern era. It was through his appreciation of Greek marbles and pre-Columbian art at the British Museum that he "came to realise how very much a reclining figure can contain."[1] *Two-Piece Reclining Figure, No. 3* belongs to a series he began in 1959 in which the bodies are separated at the waist, a culminating moment in his development of the reclining figure theme. By dividing the body into two parts, Moore played with multiple viewpoints and malleable spaces. He donated the plaster maquette for this work to the Art Gallery of Ontario in Toronto.[2] Cast in bronze, the finished piece is a harmonious conflagration of protruding limbs and twisting forms. The skeletal structure is reminiscent of the distant past, yet its androgynous and abstract features belong simultaneously to the future. **A.P.**

Notes

1 *Henry Moore, quoted in Henry J. Seldis,* Henry Moore in America *(London: Phaidon, 1973),* 23.

2 *Cynthia Burlingham and Elizabeth Shepherd, eds.,* In the Sculptor's Landscape: Celebrating Twenty-five Years of the Franklin D. Murphy Sculpture Garden *(Los Angeles: Wight Art Gallery and Grunwald Center for the Graphic Arts, University of California, 1993), 87, fig. 80.*

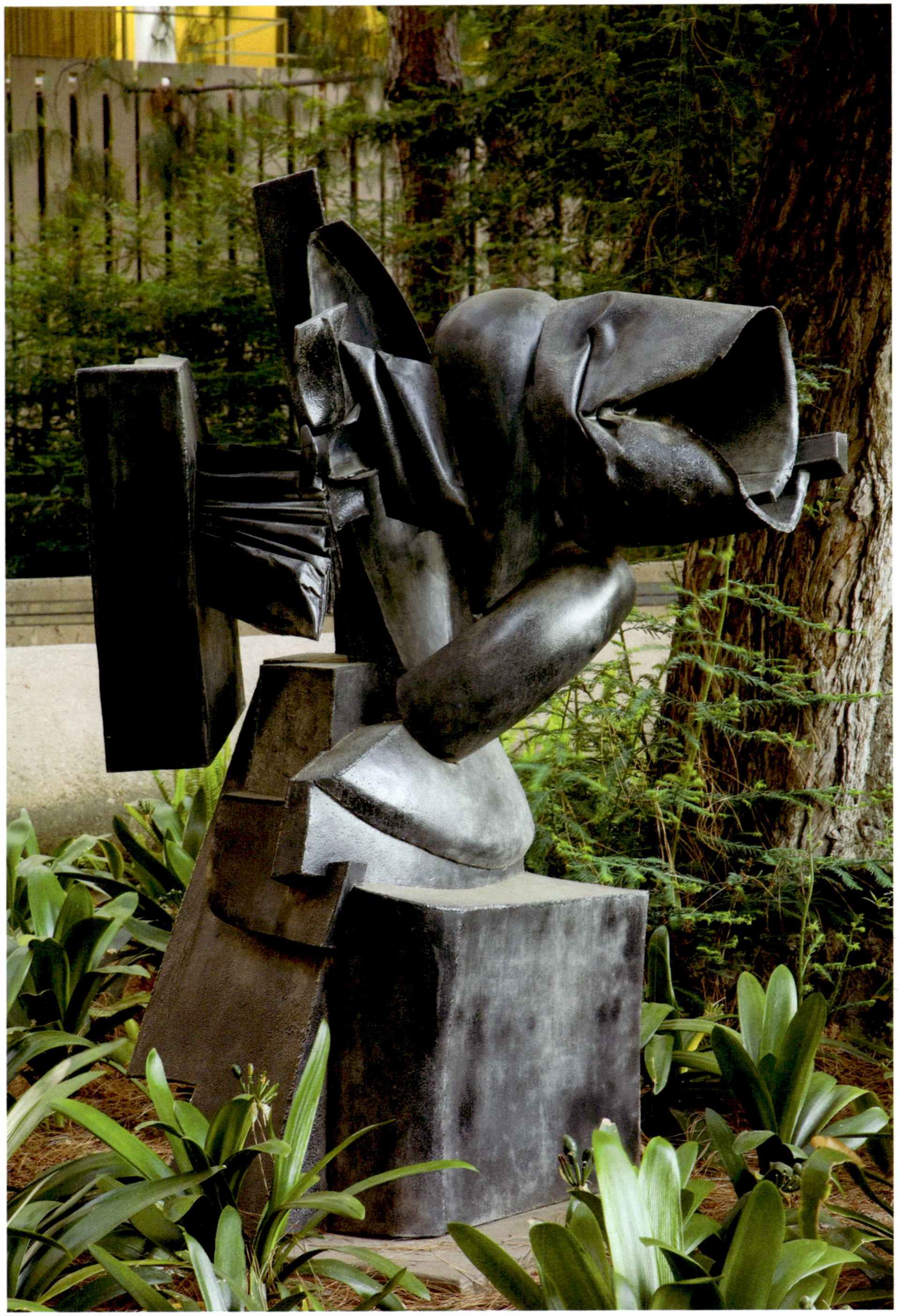

AUTEL / ALTAR
1962–64
Painted iron
H: 74 IN. (188 CM); W: 47 IN. (119.4 CM); D: 37 IN. (94 CM)
Gift of David E. Bright, 1967

Robert Müller studied sculpture with Germaine Richier and Charles-Otto Bänninger in his native Zurich from 1939 to 1944. In 1949 he settled in Paris and began to sculpt in iron, learning the blacksmithing process. His first solo exhibition was held at Galerie Craven in Paris in 1954. In 1961 he moved to Villiers-le-Bel, a suburb outside Paris. As a sculptor Müller worked mainly in the medium of welded metal, creating unique assemblages of different pieces of found and crafted metal in which the individual function of each element of the composition disappears. Müller exhibited widely throughout Europe and North and South America. From 1977 until his death in 2003 he spent periods of each year on the Greek island of Crete and for the most part abandoned his sculptural pursuits, working instead on drawings and woodcuts.

An assemblage of forged, molded, and found iron elements, *Altar* was first exhibited at the Stedelijk Museum in Amsterdam in 1964. *Altar* is similar to Müller's other constructed assemblages of the early 1960s. Welding found objects together with pieces that he had constructed, Müller painted all the metal surfaces of the sculpture in opaque black. The crumpled and folded components imbue the abstract iron piece with an organic quality despite its overall machinelike form, suggestive at first glance of a damaged engine component. According to specifications provided by the artist, *Altar* was intended as a "two-dimensional" sculpture, to be set against a background wall or shrub, and not to be viewed from every angle in the round.[1] C.D.

Notes
1 *See Myriam Prevot's catalogue description in Pierre Descargues,* Robert Müller *(Brussels: La Connaissance, 1971).*

ROBERT MÜLLER

(SWISS, 1920–2003)

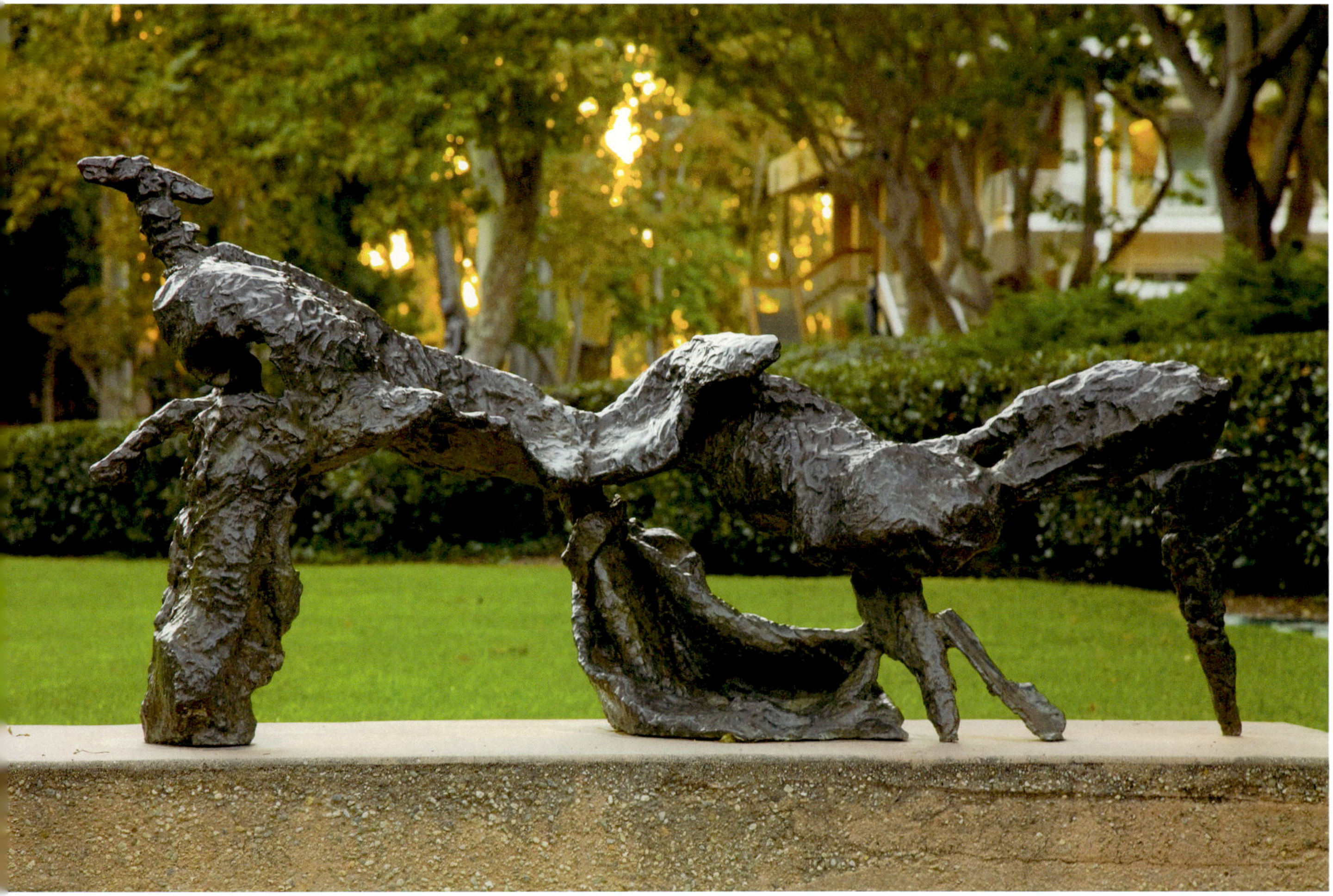

LA CHAMBRE À COUCHER DE L'EMPEREUR
1954
Bronze
H: 37 IN. (94 CM); W: 70 IN. (178 CM); D: 23 IN. (58.4 CM)
Edition: 2/3
Foundry: Modern Art Foundry, New York
Gift of Marcia and Frederick Weisman, in honor of Franklin D. Murphy, 1977

REUBEN NAKIAN

(AMERICAN, 1897–1986)

Following his apprenticeship with Paul Manship in New York, Reuben Nakian established a studio with Manship's assistant Gaston Lachaise from 1920 to 1922. Awarded a monthly stipend and studio expenses by Gertrude Vanderbilt Whitney in 1922, Nakian established his own studio in Weehawken, New Jersey, and in 1928, when the stipend ended, he moved back to New York. During this period his works were mainly series of animal drawings and sculptures. In the early 1930s he started to create small bronze, marble, and wood animal figures, and in 1932 he created his first series of portrait busts, including one of Franklin D. Roosevelt. In 1946 Nakian settled in Connecticut, where he lived for the next forty years. From 1946 to 1951 he was an instructor at the Newark School of Fine and Industrial Arts in New Jersey, and during this time he also refined his firing of large terra-cotta pieces and began his series of terra-cotta sculptures and drawings based on mythological themes.

In the mid-1950s Nakian invented a method of constructing sculptures by applying thin coats of plaster over sturdy cloth such as burlap and attaching this to an armature of steel pipes or wire mesh, creating an open-form sculpture. First conceived in plaster before being cast in bronze, *La chambre à coucher de l'empereur* was Nakian's first monumental sculpture to employ this new method of construction. The sculpture is formed of various bronze pieces that suggest body parts, bedsheets, and drapery, albeit in a surrealist sense. As Robert P. Metzger has noted: "[The] work is a metaphor for Napoleon, Josephine and their bedchamber. Bodies are merely suggested, entwined in the drapery which wraps and contorts their anatomical features....Their haunting love story is presented horizontally as they rapturously recline in an unbuttressed bed that displays them ecstatically twisting in space."[1] C.D.

Notes
1 *Robert P. Metzger,* Reuben Nakian: Centennial Retrospective, 1897–1986 *(Reading, Pa.: Reading Public Museum, 1990), 12–13.*

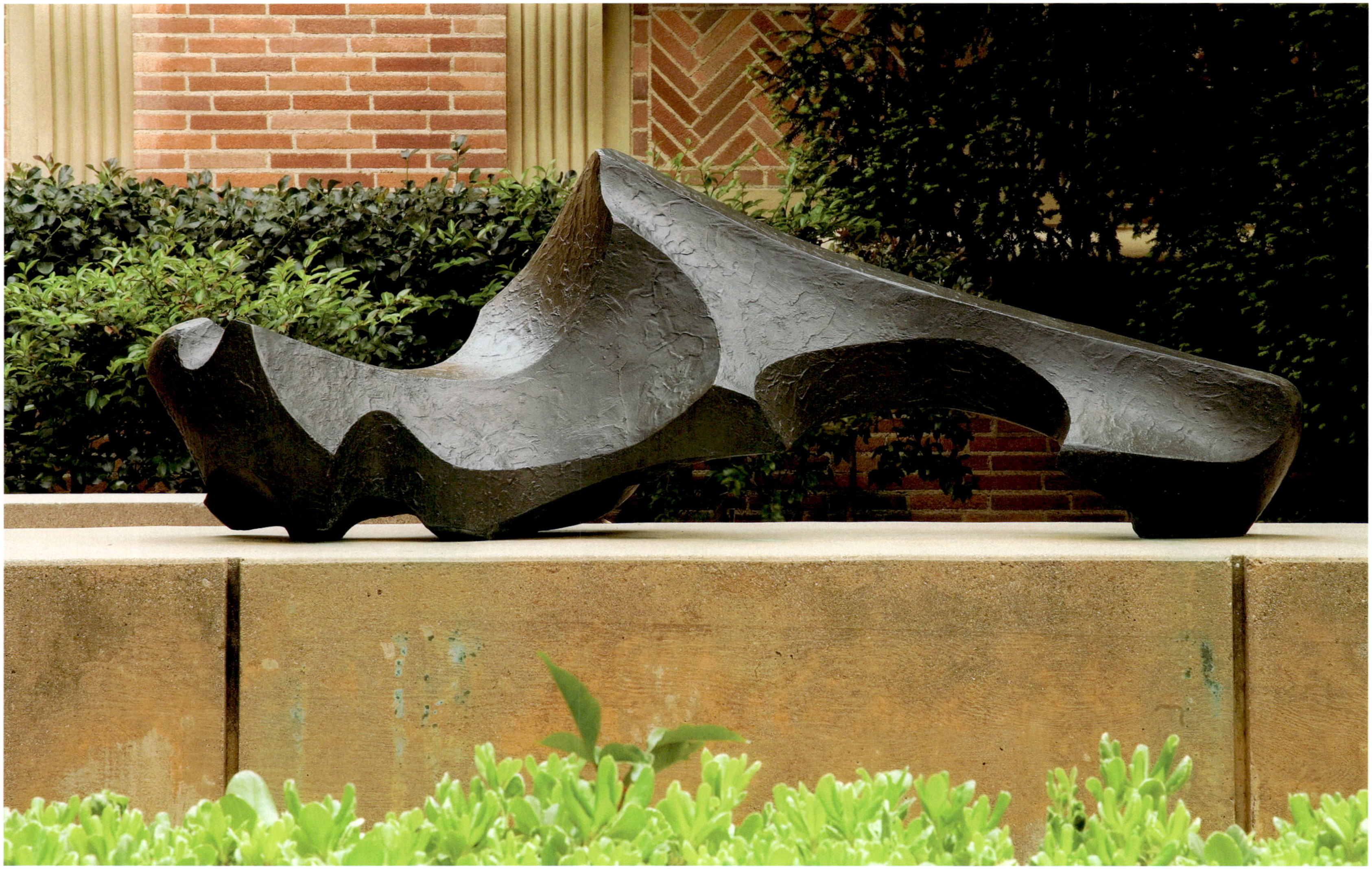

HORIZONTAL FORM
1970
Bronze
H: 21 IN. (53 CM); W: 61 IN. (153 CM); D: 17 IN. (43 CM)
Edition: 1/6
Gift of Elisabeth Roblee Augerson in memory of Florence Allen Roblee, 1970

Gordon Newell attended Occidental College and the University of California, Berkeley. In the early 1930s he worked as an apprentice to the sculptor Ralph Stackpole on the sculptural decoration for the San Francisco Stock Exchange Building. Newell shared Stackpole's admiration for the monumental forms and designs of Aztec architecture and hand-cut stone carving, and his participation in this project harked back to the processes of the ancient Mexican culture, including mold making and casting of small models as well as the final carving of the granite. After settling in Carmel, California, in the late 1930s, Newell joined a group of artists and writers—including Edward Weston, Henrietta Shore, and Robinson Jeffers—who had a profound influence on the development of his art. A few decades later, Newell was a founding member of the Monterey Sculpture Center, a small artists' cooperative begun in the late 1960s. Although much of his late work was in bronze, he continued to work extensively in stone, a material that fascinated him because of the important part it has played in the development of human civilization.

Horizontal Form, according to the artist, represents a reclining figure. It was executed while he was working at the Sculpture Center in Monterey. Its most salient quality is its starkness, or, to quote Newell, "its reduction to positive and negative precision."[1] Other pieces that exhibit a similar play between positive and negative form include *Moth* (black granite, ca. 1965) and *Swallow* (black granite, ca. 1967). C.D.

Notes
1 *Gordon Newell, telephone interview with Robyn Roslak, April 17, 1984, notes in Murphy Sculpture Garden Archives, Hammer Museum.*

GORDON NEWELL
(AMERICAN, 1905–1988)

GARDEN ELEMENTS
1962
Bronze (set in aggregate concrete)
H: 10¾ IN. (27.3 CM); W: 96 IN. (243.8 CM); D: 120 IN. (304.8 CM)
Edition: 1/6
Gift of the UCLA Graduating Class of 1967

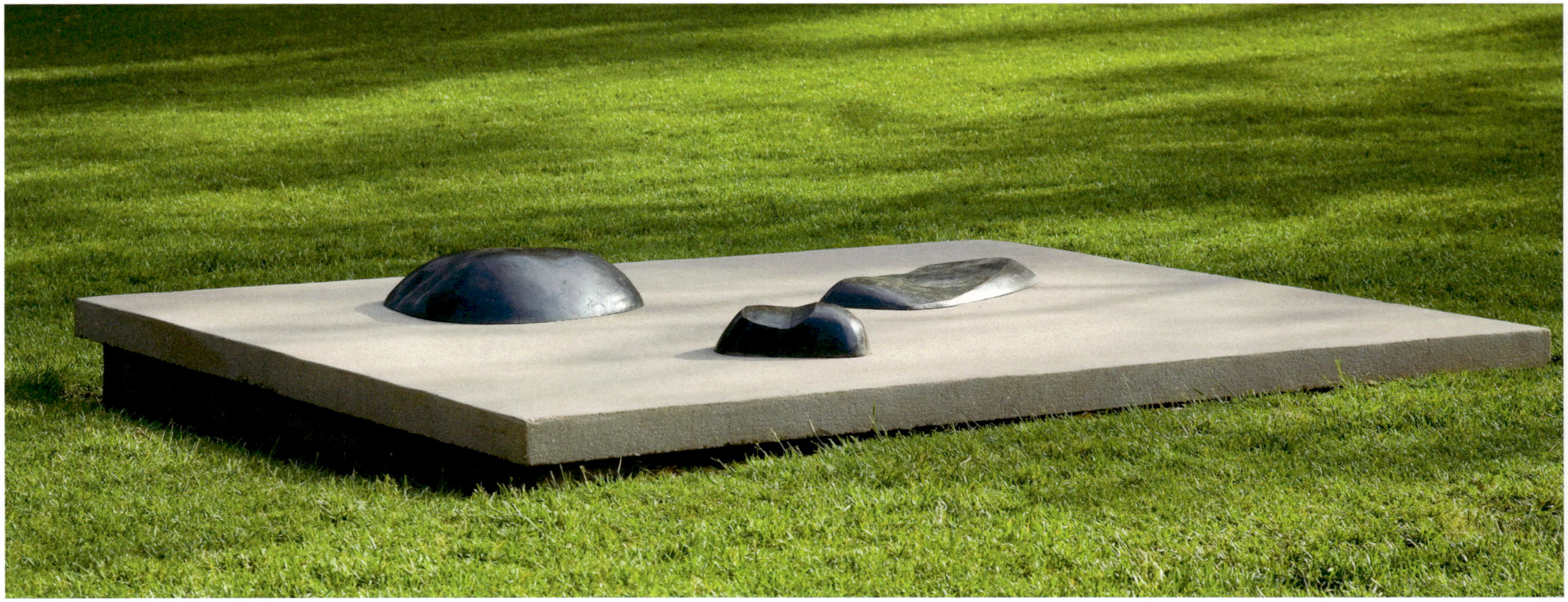

ISAMU NOGUCHI

(AMERICAN, 1904–1988)

Born in Los Angeles to an American mother and Japanese father, Isamu Noguchi lived in Japan from 1906 to 1918. He returned to the United States and studied sculpture at the Leonardo da Vinci Art School in New York from 1924 to 1925. In 1927 he went to Paris on a Guggenheim Fellowship and worked as an assistant in the studio of Constantin Brancusi. In 1930 Noguchi returned to Asia, where, for the next two years, he studied traditional ink painting and ceramics in Kyoto, Tokyo, and Beijing. Renowned for his monumental public sculptures throughout the world, Noguchi found inspiration for his art in his study of other cultures and artistic media. He also designed furniture in the 1940s and developed the Akari Light Sculptures, a line of paper lamps, in 1951. Between 1981 and 1982 the artist established and designed his own museum on the land adjacent to his Long Island City, New York, studio, and the Isamu Noguchi Museum and Garden opened to the public in May 1985.

Garden Elements is a bronze floor sculpture that belongs to a series of such works executed between 1960 and 1962. Composed of three pieces, this work, like others in the series, consists of elements arranged in a manner that is evocative of the classical Japanese garden, most specifically the famous temple garden of Ryoanji in Kyoto. As Valerie Fletcher notes: "[Noguchi's] three-element, odd number of islands or mountain forms are a free-form composition that can be configured in any arrangement. The dominant or 'master rock' is consistently surrounded by the 'attendant' stones or smaller islands. The mountain form, fundamental to Zen garden design, is meant to be perceived with awe and reverence, as a sacred element rising from the earth."[1] Installed directly on the ground, as Noguchi intended it to be, *Garden Elements* becomes part of the fabric of the landscape, showcasing the artist's ability to synthesize nature with artifice. C.D.

Notes
1 *Valerie J. Fletcher,* Isamu Noguchi: Master Sculptor *(Washington, D.C.: Smithsonian Institution; New York: Whitney Museum of American Art, 2004), 206.*

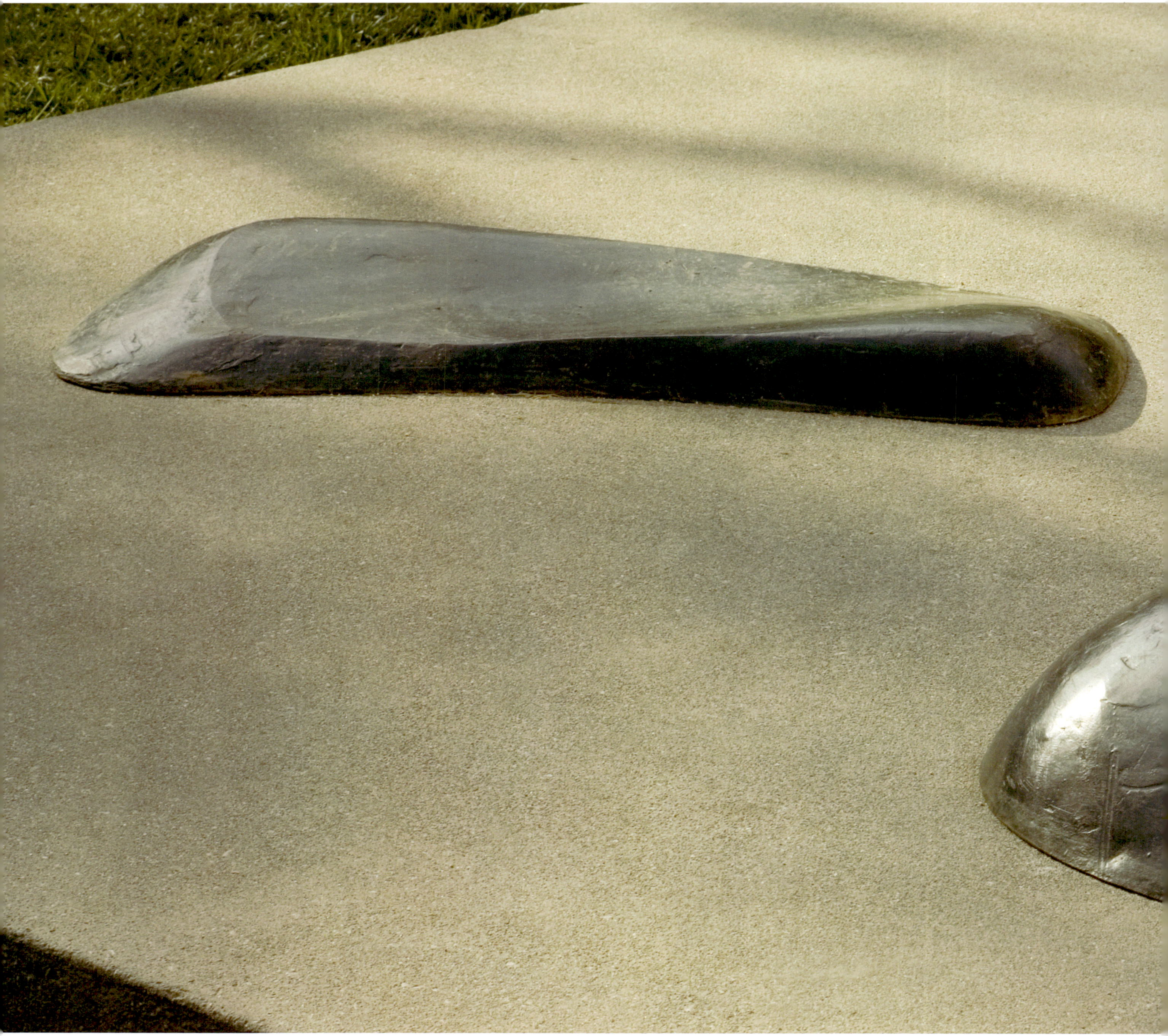

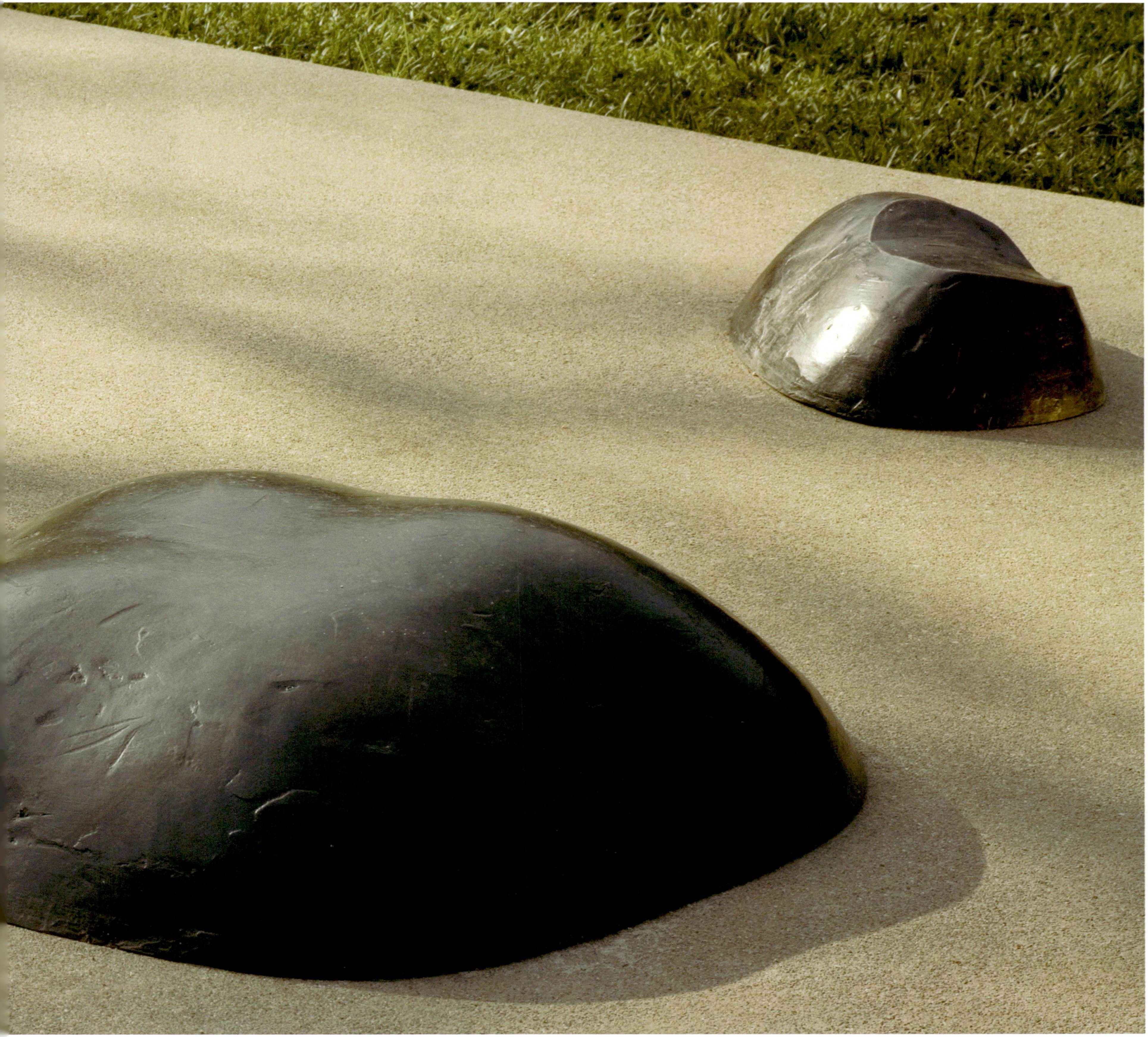

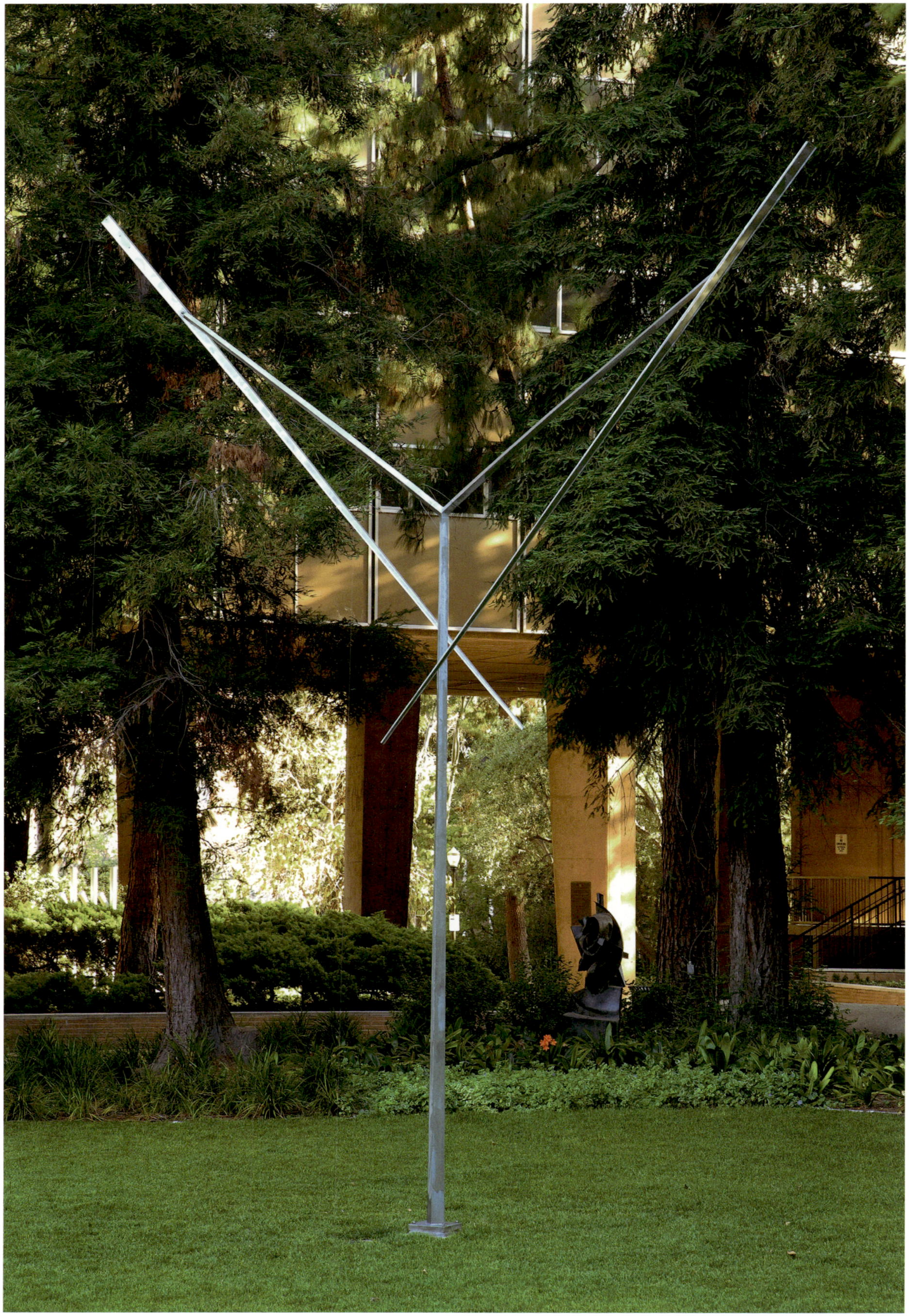

TWO LINES OBLIQUE DOWN (VARIATION III)
1970–74
Stainless steel
H: 252 IN. (640 CM); W: 180 IN. (465 CM)
Edition: 4/8
Gift of the UCLA Art Council, 1971

Notes
1 *Quoted in* George Rickey: Skulpturen, Material, Technik *(Berlin: America House, 1979), 23.*
2 *Quoted in* George Rickey: Retrospective Exhibition *(Los Angeles: UCLA Art Galleries, 1971), 16, 35.*

George Rickey was the son of an engineer at the Singer Sewing Machine Company and the grandson of a clock maker. He was born in South Bend, Indiana, but his father transferred the family to Scotland in 1913, when George was six. He remembers: "I loved to visit my father's factory and watch the casting of iron, the turning of the lathes, the electric generators, and also the decals with which the sewing machines were decorated."[1] An artistic career seemed unlikely to him when he chose to read history at Oxford's Balliol College, although he secretly attended courses at the Ruskin School of Drawing nearby. He thereafter opted to paint professionally, first in Paris and then in the United States, to which he returned in 1930. He discovered his aptitude for mechanics and engineering while in the U.S. Army Air Corps in 1942. This skill, combined with his deep interest in the history of art and a determination to evolve his own style, prompted Rickey to start making sculpture in 1949,at age forty-two. In 1950 he found scraps of stainless steel at the university dump in Bloomington, Indiana, and decided to make it his material. He learned to weld with the help of David Smith, visited the master of kinetics Alexander Calder in 1951, and rapidly evolved his own distinct style of moving sculptures. He held his first exhibition in a gallery in New York in 1955, and his works, often monumental constructions conceived for the outdoors and triggered by air currents, were immediately sought after.

Two Lines Oblique Down (Variation III) is based on the principle of the pendulum, which Rickey adopted in 1961, in which weight is distributed slightly unevenly on either side of a fulcrum. Two fifteen-foot-long blades are mounted on a Y-shaped chassis. They sway with the wind and slowly delineate the surrounding space with mutating symmetry. Their meditative motion is like a reminder to passersby to reduce their pace, to reflect. "From the start I had the idea I would compose with movement," Rickey said. "My analogy... is choreography, which is also a time art, a time-space art. I like to go to the ballet, and I enjoy very much seeing how thoroughly controlled... good dancing is."[2] **A.P.**

GEORGE RICKEY

(AMERICAN, 1907–2002)

Giorgio Amelio Roccamonte was born in Buenos Aires, Argentina, and studied at the Academia de Altamira, the art school established by Lucio Fontana in 1946, during his extended sojourn in the city. That year Roccamonte was one of the ten signers of the *Manifesto blanco*, a revolutionary declaration inspired by Fontana's vision of a new, nonfigurative art that would incorporate color, sound, movement, time, and space, as well as engaging science and technology. In 1947 Roccamonte moved to Italy and attended the Accademia di Brera in Milan. Thereafter he chose Italy as his home and pursued a teaching career in Rome. His first solo exhibition was held at the Galleria dello Zodiaco in Rome in 1951, and in 1973 he was one of eleven sculptors selected for a permanent installation in Milan's Parco Sempione. His sculptures are little known outside Italy.

Abstraction is a unique bronze cast. It incorporates the tensions of conflicting forms and textures. Polished planes amalgamate with rougher, meteorite-like surfaces. Straight edges are interrupted by curves and intersect with earthier, volcanic forms. The punctured areas and explosive effect are particularly reminiscent of sculptures by Fontana made a few years earlier, in 1959 and 1960.[1] A.P.

Notes
1 *Enrico Crispolti, ed.,* Fontana *(Milan: Charta, 1999), 194–95, 290, nos 201–4.*

GIORGIO AMELIO ROCCAMONTE

(ARGENTINEAN, 1927–1980)

ABSTRACTION
1963
Bronze
H: 38 IN. (96.5 CM); W: 32 IN.
(81.3 CM); D: 18 IN. (45.7 CM)
Foundry: Fontana, Milan
Gift of Mrs. David E. Bright, 1969

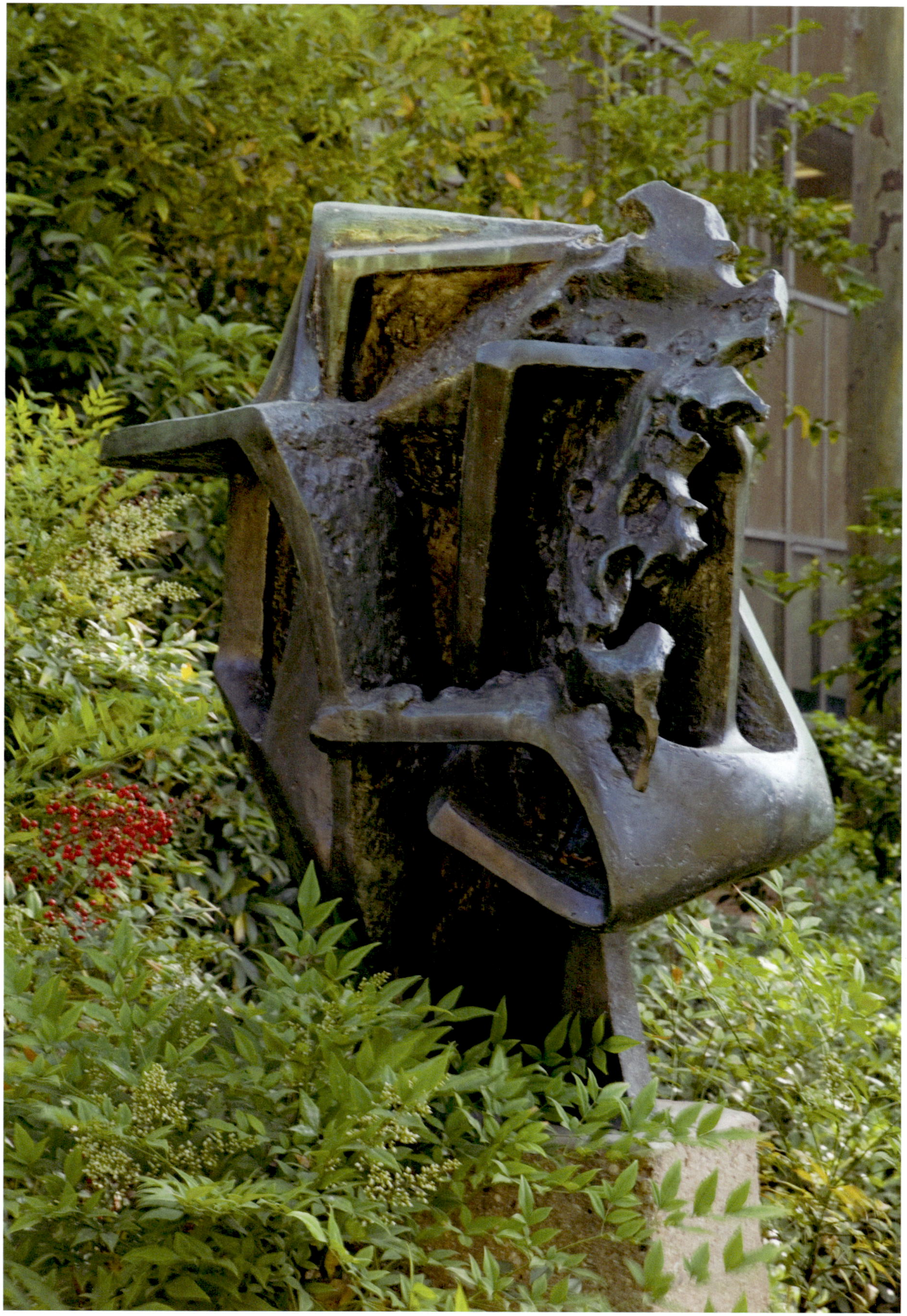

Notes

1 *Albert Elsen,* Rodin and His Studio *(Ithaca, N.Y.: Cornell University Press, 1980), 187.*

2 *Albert Elsen,* Rodin *(New York: Museum of Modern Art, 1963), 32.*

3 *John L. Tancock,* The Sculpture of Auguste Rodin: The Collection of the Rodin Museum, Philadelphia *(Philadelphia: Philadelphia Museum of Art, 1976), 363, and Albert Elsen, in collaboration with Henry Moore, "*Rodin's Walking Man *as Seen by Henry Moore,"* Studio International *(New York), no. 174 (July–August 1967): 26–31.*

Auguste Rodin studied first with Antoine-Louis Barye and later with Albert-Ernest Carrier-Belleuse in Paris before attending the École de Dessin from 1854 to 1857. Refused admission to the École des Beaux-Arts three times, Rodin first supported himself as a decorative artist. He made his public debut at the Paris Spring Salon in 1877 with the sculpture *The Age of Bronze*. Once he became an established artist, he received many major public commissions, including *The Gates of Hell* (1880–1900) and *The Burghers of Calais* (1884–95). By the 1890s he employed almost fifty assistants, and throughout his career he engaged as many as twenty-eight foundries in order to meet demand for his bronzes. In 1916 he willed all his art and the reproduction rights to his work to the French government, which has continued to cast editions of his sculpture after his death.

The complicated history of *The Walking Man* begins with a torso executed around 1877–78, possibly as a study for *Saint John the Baptist Preaching* (1878). According to Albert Elsen, this torso was later reworked into an armless half-life-size plaster of the same subject, discovered by Elsen in 1977 in the Meudon Reserve.[1] Around 1900 a new clay cast of the original and the legs of the half-size study were presumably joined, with the trailing leg elongated to give the impression of greater movement, creating what we now know as *The Walking Man*. Rodin exhibited this half-size sculpture in plaster at his 1900 retrospective. In 1905 the work was enlarged to over life size. In this enlarged version, exhibited in plaster at the Salon of 1907, the right shoulder is slightly bent, increasing the figure's forward momentum.[2] In 1916 the first bronze cast of this enlarged version was sent to Rome for exhibition at the Farnese Palace.

It has been suggested that both *Saint John* and *The Walking Man* had as their source an untrained model named César Pignatelli, who would later model for Henri Matisse's sculpture *The Serf* (1900–1903) under the name Bevilacqua.[3] The difference between the smooth surface of the earlier *Saint John* and the extreme roughness of surface of the later *Walking Man* illuminates the radical change that took place in Rodin's conception of the freestanding figure. In this headless, armless figure, portraying no recognizable personage, harmony and consistency of form were secondary to the pursuit of movement. C.B.

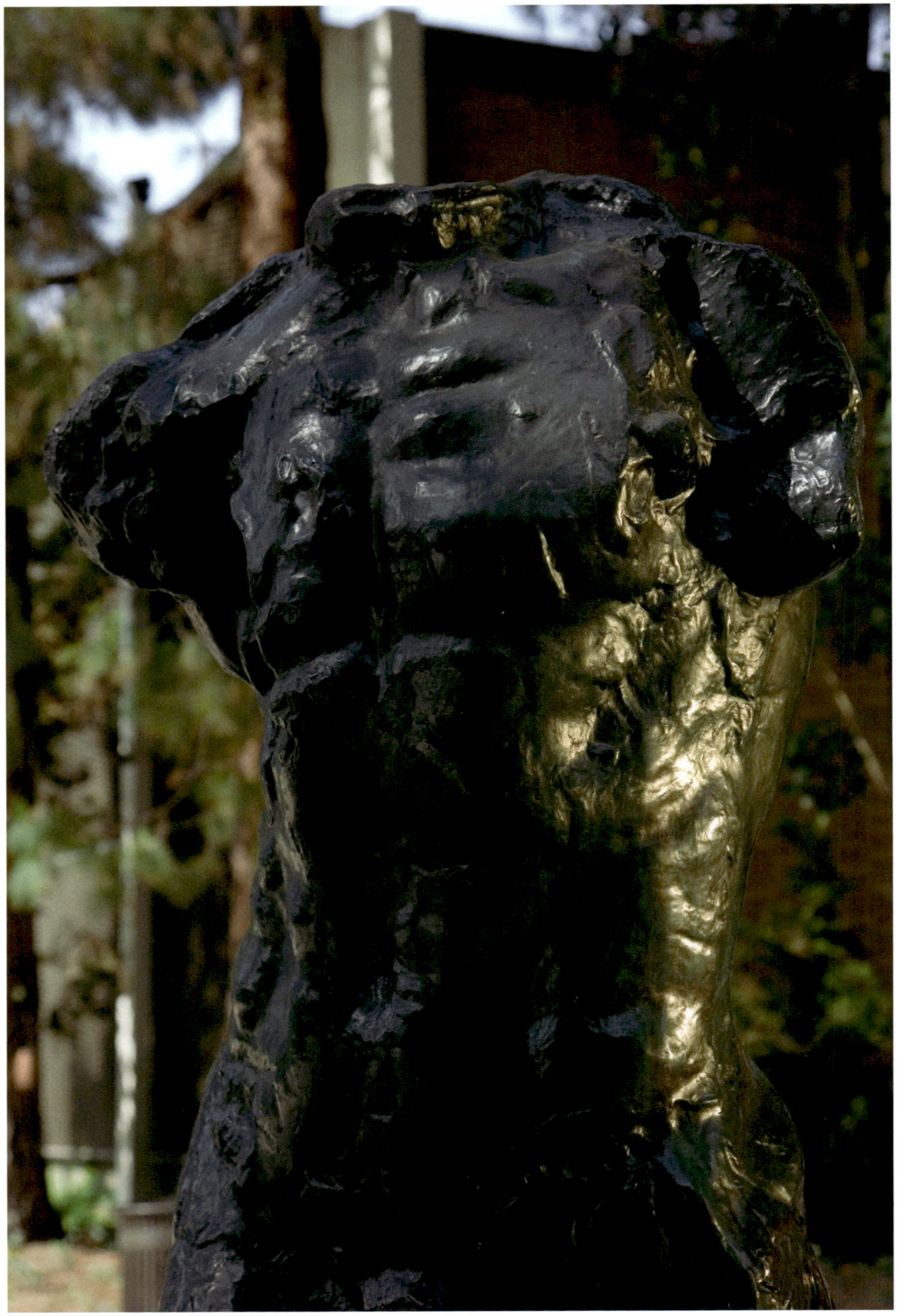

AUGUSTE RODIN

(FRENCH, 1840–1917)

L'HOMME QUI MARCHE / THE WALKING MAN
1878 and 1899–1900, enlarged 1905–7
Bronze
H: 83⅞ IN. (213 CM);
W: 35 IN. (88.9 CM);
D: 17 IN. (43.2 CM)
Edition: 11/12 (cast 1966)
Foundry: Georges Rudier, Paris, 1966
Gift of the UCLA Alumni Association and an anonymous donor as a tribute to Franklin D. Murphy, 1966

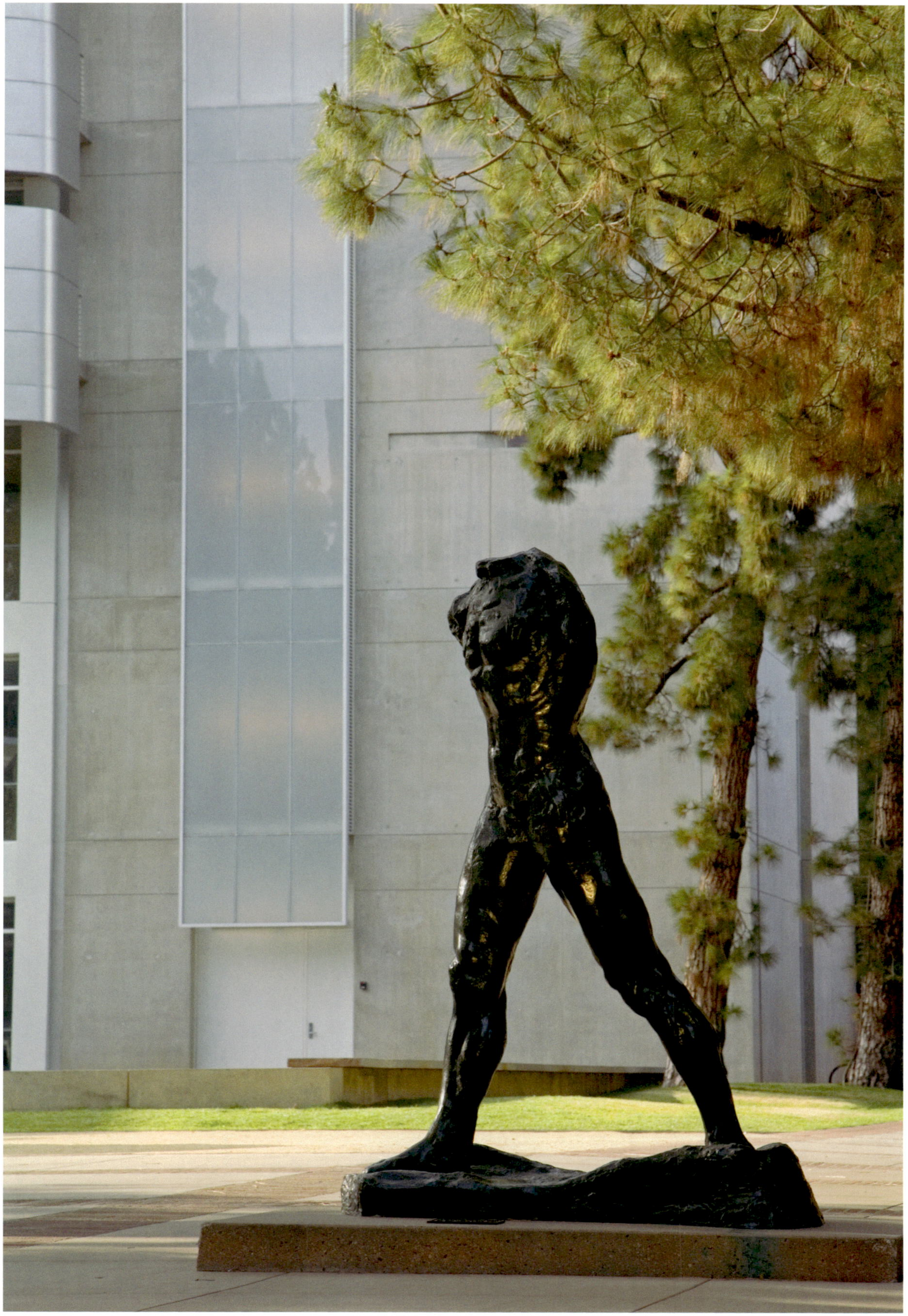

ABSTRACT PLAQUE
1964
Welded sheet bronze
H: 62 IN. (157.5 CM); W: 112 IN. (284.5 CM); D: 16 ¼ IN. (41.3 CM)
Gift of David E. Bright, 1967

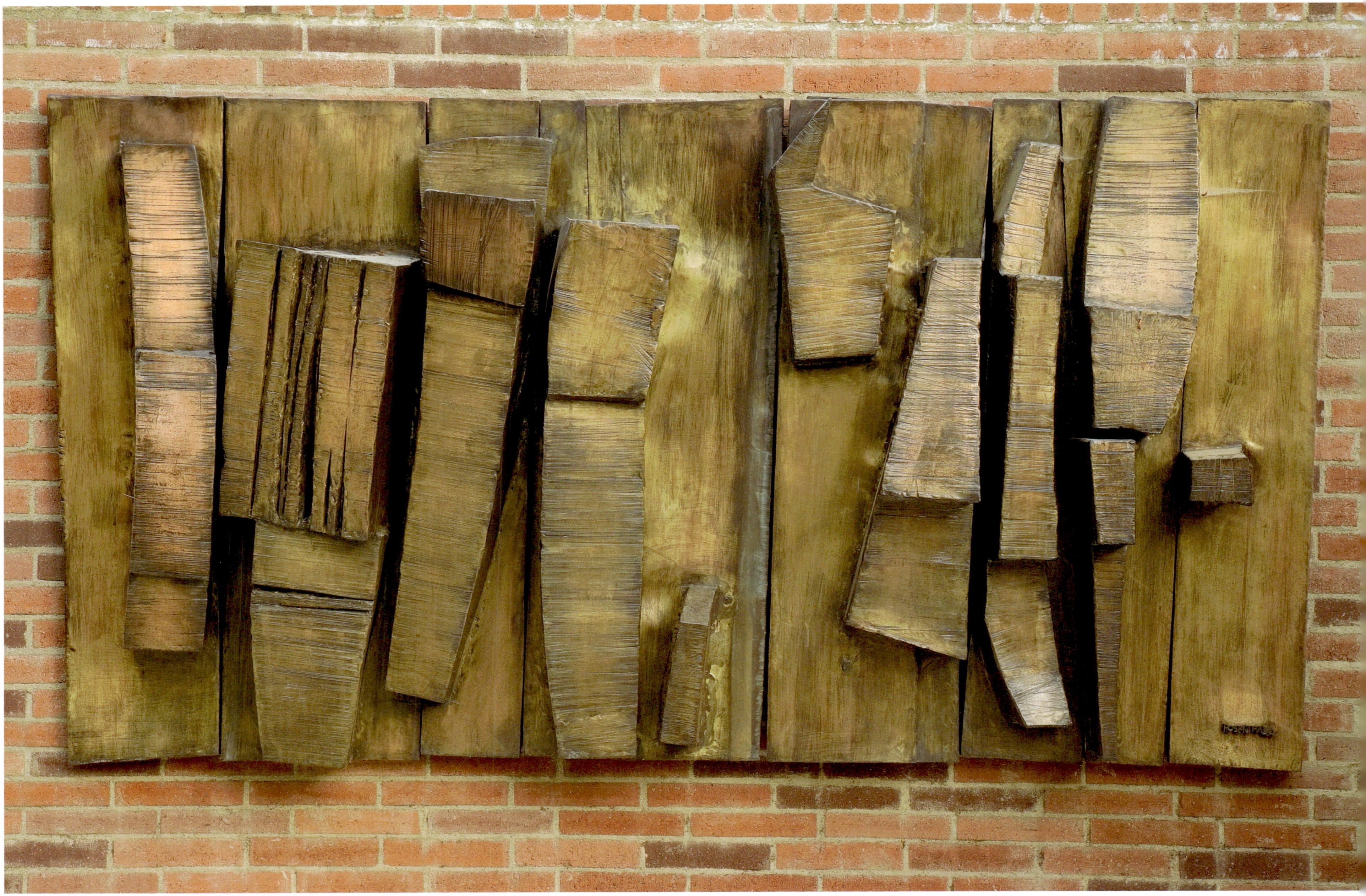

Tony (Bernard) Rosenthal decided to become a sculptor while attending the University of Michigan, Ann Arbor, between 1932 and 1936. In 1939 he enrolled at Cranbrook Academy of Art in Bloomfield Hills, Michigan, where he studied under sculptor-in-residence Carl Milles. During World War II Rosenthal was stationed in Europe, where he produced topographical models of French, Italian, and German terrain for use by the U.S. Army and Air Force. After the war he moved to Southern California at the suggestion of the designer Charles Eames, a colleague from Cranbrook. While living in Los Angeles from 1946 to 1959, Rosenthal participated in many exhibitions and received numerous public commissions; in 1952 he was hired as the first instructor of sculpture at UCLA. In 1960 the artist moved to New York, where he still lives.

Consisting of five panels of sheet bronze, *Abstract Plaque* is a unique work. Using an electric band saw, Rosenthal cut geometric shapes from a thick sheet of metal, allowing the irregular marks of the saw teeth to leave a ragged texture on the surface of the bronze. As Sam Hunter has noted, when looking at Rosenthal's metal sculptures, "one grows aware of the importance of touch, incised line, relief projection and shallow recession as a counterforce to the uniformities of the core shapes. The dazzle of high surface polish also has a noticeable dynamic of its own; forms gleam like severe, efficient hardware, but they also look like consciously well-made objects....The interplay of a subtly nuanced individual craftsmanship against an impersonal canon of style creates a sense of tension, and vibrancy."[1] C. D.

Notes
1 *Sam Hunter,* Rosenthal: Sculptures *(New York: M. Knoedler & Co., 1968), 9, 12.*

TONY (BERNARD) ROSENTHAL

(AMERICAN, B. 1914)

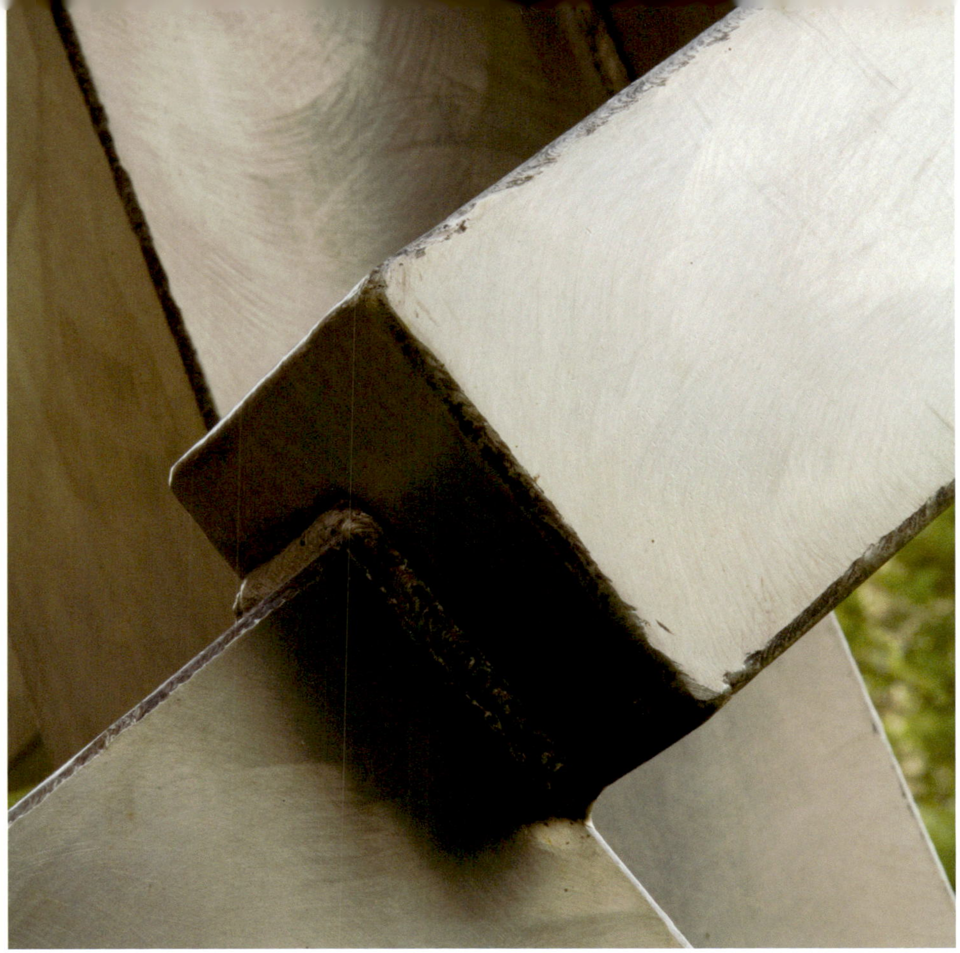

From 1926 to 1932 David Smith attended the Art Students League of New York, where he studied painting under John Sloan and Jan Matulka. In 1929 Smith and his first wife, artist Dorothy Dehner, bought a twenty-six-acre property in Bolton Landing, in upstate New York, and he soon began to install his sculptures in the fields surrounding his house and studio. Smith made his first welded sculptures in 1933, inspired in part by magazine reproductions of the welded-metal constructions of Pablo Picasso and Julio González. In that year the artist rented studio space in the Terminal Iron Works building in Brooklyn, where he practiced his technical skills with professional welders and machinists. He returned permanently to Bolton Landing in 1940, building a studio named after his Brooklyn studio. Smith received increasing recognition by the early 1950s, showing regularly in solo and group exhibitions as well as teaching and lecturing throughout the country. In 1952 the first major retrospective of his work was shown at the Museum of Modern Art, New York.

Smith began working on his last series, the Cubis, in 1961 and would continue working on it until his death in 1965. As with his other serial work, the Cubis are numbered in order of conceptualization rather than completion. The series comprises twenty-eight large stainless-steel sculptures composed of prefabricated cylindrical or rectangular parts welded together, their reflective surfaces burnished with calligraphic patterns. The artist worked on several sculptures in the series simultaneously. *Cubi XX* is part of a group—along with *Cubi XVII* (Dallas Museum of Art), *Cubi XVIII* (Museum of Fine Arts, Boston), and *Cubi XIX* (Tate, London)—that the artist worked on from December 1963 through February 1964. In this group of works, forms are balanced on a crossbeam elevated by a square or cylindrical vertical beam. This vertical beam in *Cubi XX* is shorter than that of the other three sculptures, terminating in a larger box shape rather than a low platform. *Cubi XX* was completed on February 29, 1964, nine days after *Cubi XIX*, and was shown at the Marlborough-Gerson Gallery in 1964. In an interview published in the catalogue of that exhibition, Smith noted, "I made them and polished them in such a way that on a dull day, they take on the dull blue, or the color of the sky in the late afternoon sun, the glow, golden like the rays, the colors of nature."[1] C.B.

Notes

1 *David Smith, quoted in Thomas B. Hess, "The Secret Letter," in* David Smith *(New York: Marlborough-Gerson Gallery, 1964), unpaged. For a discussion of the importance of landscape and the outdoor siting of his work, see Michael Brenson, "The Fields," in* David Smith: A Centennial, *curated by Carmen Giménez (New York: Guggenheim Museum, 2006), 39ff.*

DAVID SMITH

(AMERICAN, 1906–1965)

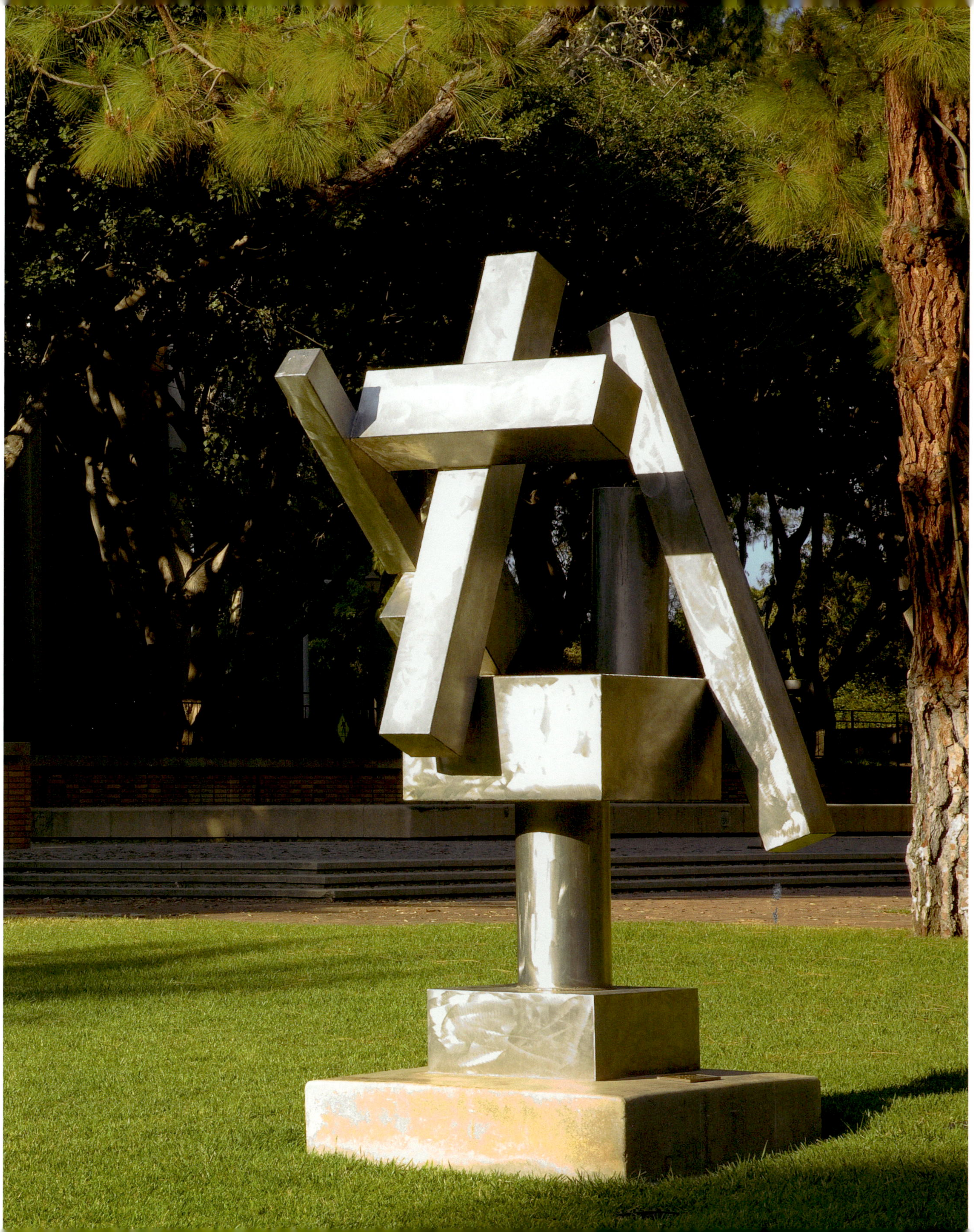

CUBI XX
1964
Welded stainless steel
H: 111 IN. (282 CM); W: 55 IN. (139.7 CM); D: 56 ½ IN. (143.5 CM)
Gift of David E. Bright, 1967

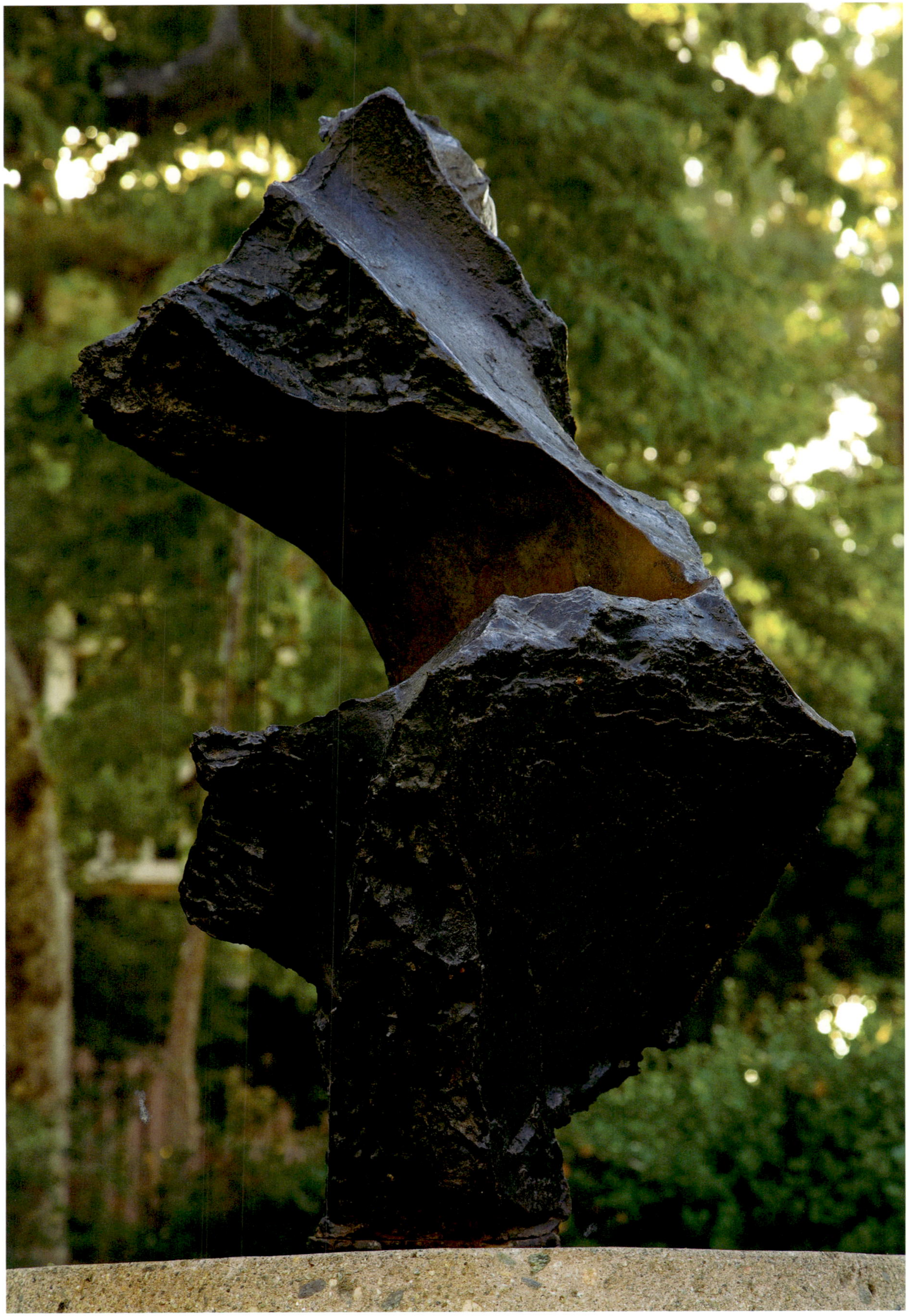

VERTICALE-ASSALONNE / VERTICAL-ABSALOM
1959
Iron
H: 35 IN. (89 CM); W: 26¼ IN. (66.7 CM); D: 21¾ IN. (55.2 CM)
Gift of Mrs. David E. Bright, 1969

Francesco Somaini was born near Como, in northern Italy, and trained at the Accademia di Brera in nearby Milan during the 1940s. He also received a degree in law in 1950 but chose to pursue an artistic career thereafter. He conceived a technique that involved processing his wax or gesso models with jets of compressed air and sand, thus endowing his sculptures with a unique organic vitality and immediacy. His forms are reminiscent of people in moments either of intense tragedy—of martyrdom, for instance—or of exaltation and triumph. In 1959 he won the international first prize in sculpture at the Fifth São Paulo Bienal, and he has had solo exhibitions throughout Europe, including one at the Venice Biennale in 1960 and one at the Museum of the Twentieth Century in Vienna in 1976. *Monument to the Sailors of Italy* of 1965–67 on the Corso XXII Marzo in Milan, with its surrounding garden, is among his most renowned public pieces. Somaini also designed *Anthropomorphic Garden* for the Parc de la Villette in Paris in 1982. More recently, in 2001, he was commissioned to produce a set of four monumental mosaics for the city of Genoa.

The biblical figure Absalom was the third son of King David. He was caught by his hair in the boughs of an oak tree during a battle fought against his father in the wood of Ephraim. Joab, David's nephew and commander of his army, thrust three spears through his heart. The spiraling form in Somaini's sculpture is easily interpreted as an abstracted body in motion and thus as Absalom's struggle in the branches. Somaini experimented with a range of media and chose to cast *Vertical-Absalom* in iron, as in the present example, as well as in bronze.[1] Large cylinders were used for the polished circular planes that appear to cut through the rougher surface of the sculpture. Here, as in much of Somaini's work, there is an underlying conflict between the forces of nature and human intervention. A.P.

Notes

1 *See* Francesco Somaini: Sculture, 1958–1972 *(Gubbio: Palazzo dei Consoli, 1973), 8, ill. 20–23, and Fred Licht and Luisa Somaini, eds.,* Somaini: Sculture dipinti e disegni, 1950–2001 *(Milan: Electa, 2001), 71, no. 18.*

FRANCESCO SOMAINI

(ITALIAN, 1926–2005)

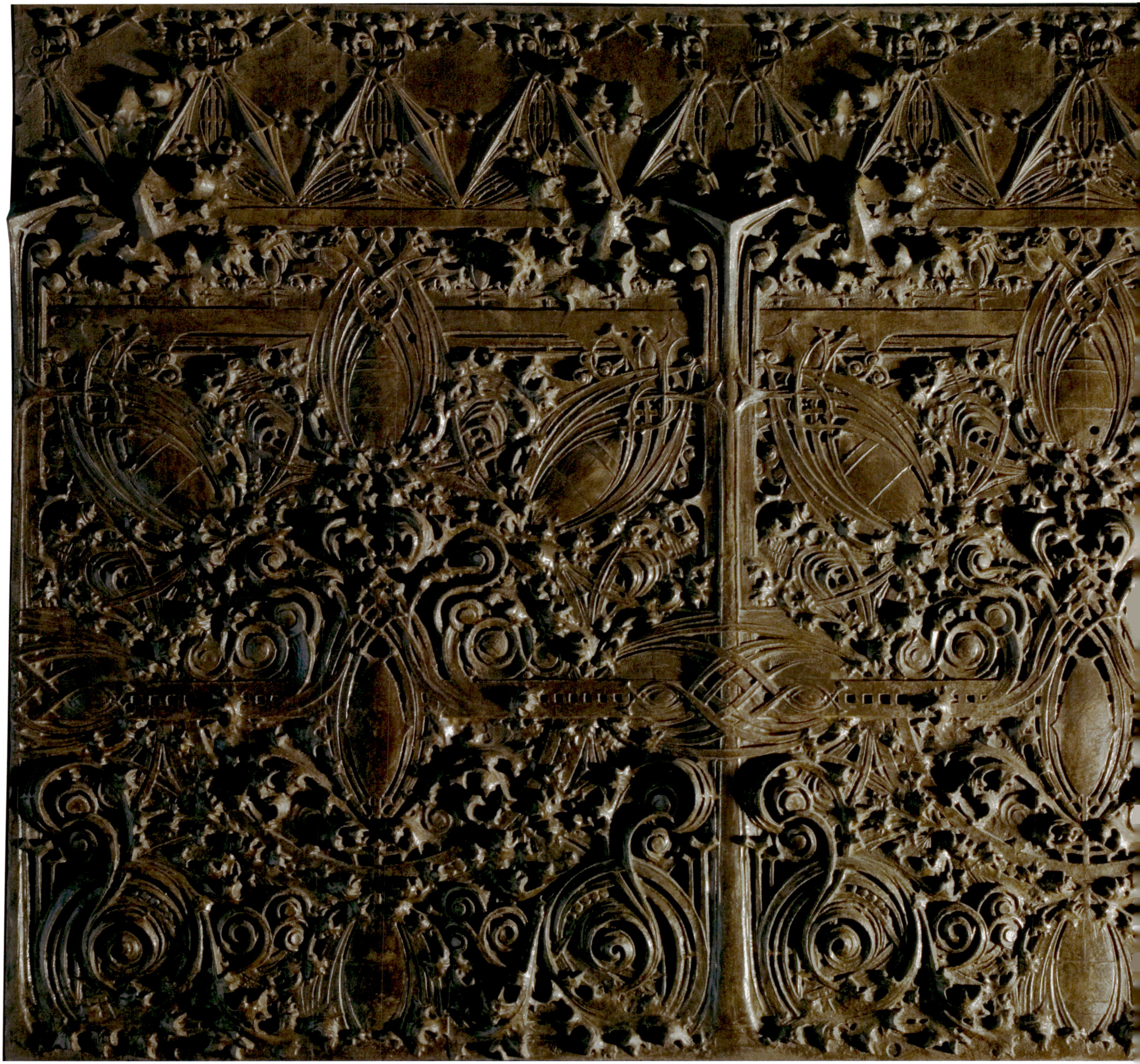

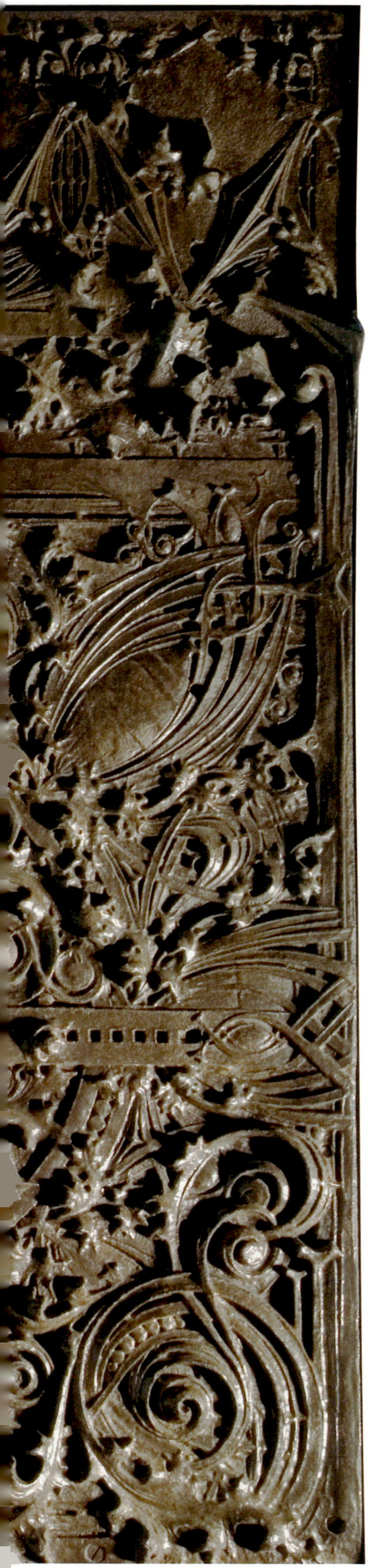

DECORATIVE PANEL FROM THE GAGE BUILDING, CHICAGO
1898–99
Cast iron (treated)
H: 51 IN. (129.5 CM); W: 69 IN. (175.3 CM); D: 1½ IN. (3.8 CM)
Gift of Vicci Sperry, 1966

LOUIS H. SULLIVAN

(AMERICAN, 1856–1924)

One of the most important American architects, Louis H. Sullivan first worked in Chicago as a draftsman for a number of firms before becoming a full partner in Dankmar Adler's firm in 1881. As the chief building designer at the firm that became known as Adler and Sullivan, Sullivan was responsible for more than one hundred buildings during his twelve-year tenure and is now considered the most influential designer of early skyscrapers in the Chicago school. During this time Frank Lloyd Wright worked as Sullivan's apprentice.

In addition to his prominence as an architect, Sullivan was also regarded as a master ornamentalist. The flowing lines and shapes that were characteristic of the art nouveau movement, which he had studied at the École des Beaux-Arts in Paris, were also inherent in the architect's own study of nature and interest in organic evolution. The panel in the Murphy Sculpture Garden was originally installed on Chicago's Gage Building, which was situated on the city's most magnificent thoroughfare, Michigan Avenue. The Gage Building—designed by the architectural firm of Holabird and Roche, where Sullivan was also an associate—was a three-unit structure, and he was commissioned to design the facade of the northernmost unit. The other two units had red-brick facades, so Sullivan decided instead to specify ornamental iron at the base and brown terra-cotta for the upper areas of the unit he was assigned. In the 1950s the Gage Building was renovated, and the decorative elements were removed, preserved, and ultimately acquired by several museums and collections, including the Art Institute of Chicago, the Museum of Modern Art in New York, and the Franklin D. Murphy Sculpture Garden at UCLA. Although this panel is part of the Murphy Sculpture Garden collection, for conservation reasons it is now installed on an interior wall in the UCLA architecture building, Perloff Hall. C.D.

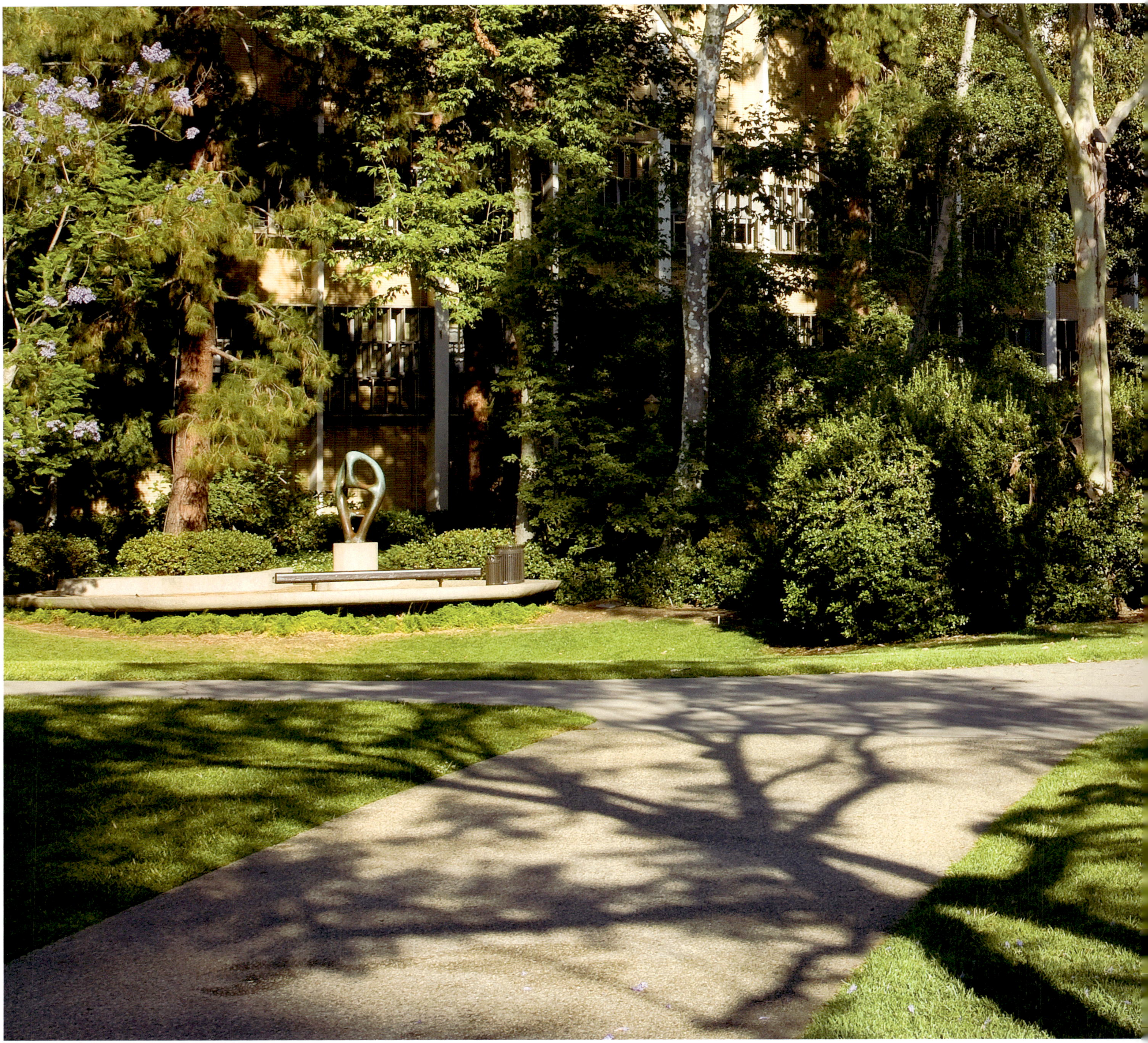

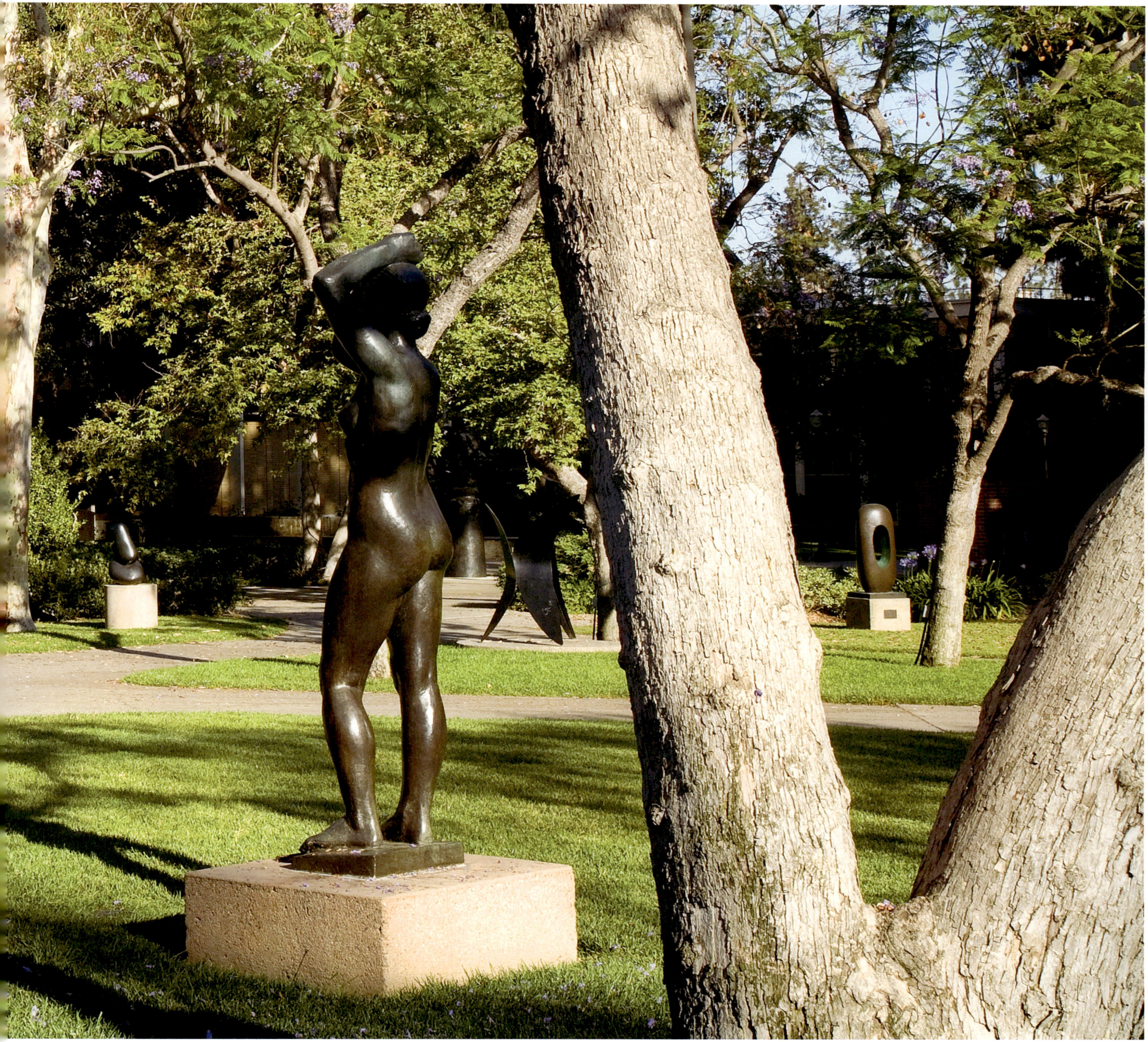

During World War II Kansas-born Elden Tefft served as an artist with the U.S. Army Air Corps in the South Pacific. In the late 1940s and early 1950s he studied art at the University of Kansas in Lawrence and at Cranbrook Academy of Art in Bloomfield Hills, Michigan. He was instrumental in developing the sculpture program at the University of Kansas, where he served as professor of art and sculpture for forty years, until his retirement in 1990. In 1960 he founded the world's largest association of sculptors, the International Sculpture Conferences and Center. Drawing inspiration for his art from travels throughout the world, he is the author of several publications about the lost-wax casting process. Tefft continues to produce bronze and stone sculptures at his foundry and studio in Lawrence, Tefft Terra Studios, which was established by the artist and his son Kim Tefft.

Working primarily in bronze and stone, Tefft has also created sculptures in wood and ceramic. His projects include portrait busts such as UCLA's *Franklin D. Murphy*, as well as architectural installations, commemorative plaques, and medallions. He obtained important commissions from his alma mater, including the design for the official seal of the University of Kansas. In addition, Tefft created portrait busts for four chancellors at the University of Kansas, including Franklin D. Murphy, whose tenure there lasted from 1951 to 1960. The first cast of this portrait bust of Murphy is installed at Murphy Hall on the Lawrence campus; UCLA's cast dates from later in the edition. In 1960 Dr. Murphy moved to Los Angeles to become chancellor at UCLA, where his influence and legacy are honored in the Franklin D. Murphy Sculpture Garden. C.D.

ELDEN TEFFT

(AMERICAN, B. 1919)

George Tsutakawa's earliest years were spent in Seattle, where he was born. At the age of seven he was sent to Japan to live with his grandparents, with whom he explored local artistic and cultural traditions, including calligraphy, pottery making, tea ceremonies, lessons with a Zen master, and attending traditional theater performances. Japan's artistic heritage and the country's landscapes would remain enduring influences on his own creations later in life. Tsutakawa was sent back to Seattle in 1927 to work in the family business and complete his high school education. He studied art at the University of Washington with sculptors Dudley Pratt and Alexander Archipenko. After completing his undergraduate studies in 1937, he managed a retail outlet for his father's import-export company in Seattle, while also becoming immersed in the downtown arts scene along with up-and-coming painters Mark Tobey and Morris Graves.

Tsutakawa's career was interrupted for four years during World War II; ironically, while he was serving as a soldier abroad, his family's business was confiscated under the U.S. government's program to restrict the activities of people of Japanese ancestry. On his return in 1946 he resumed his artistic pursuits and a year later joined the faculty of the School of Art at the University of Washington. Tsutakawa was a core figure at that institution for more than thirty years. In 1959 he received a fountain commission for the Seattle Public Library. This was the first of more than sixty public fountains he produced in the United States and Japan. Retrospectives of his work were held at the Japan American Sculpture Center in Sendai, Japan, in 1981 and at the Bellevue Art Museum in Bellevue, Washington, in 1990.

Tsutakawa's Obos series was inspired by the Tibetan practice of piling rocks along a travel route as an expression of gratitude to the gods for safe passage. He was compelled by these anonymous forms and by their public role in a natural setting. They became the basis of his fountains, combined with the symbolic cycle of water and its perpetual flow in human beings and their universe. In his fountains Tsutakawa attempts to unify water, and its continuous cycle, with an immutable metal form. Water is indeed integral to the bronze elements of *Obos 69*. The movement varies from calm flushes at the summit to rapid shafts below the base, where the water melds into the surrounding pool. A.P.

GEORGE TSUTAKAWA

(AMERICAN, 1910–1997)

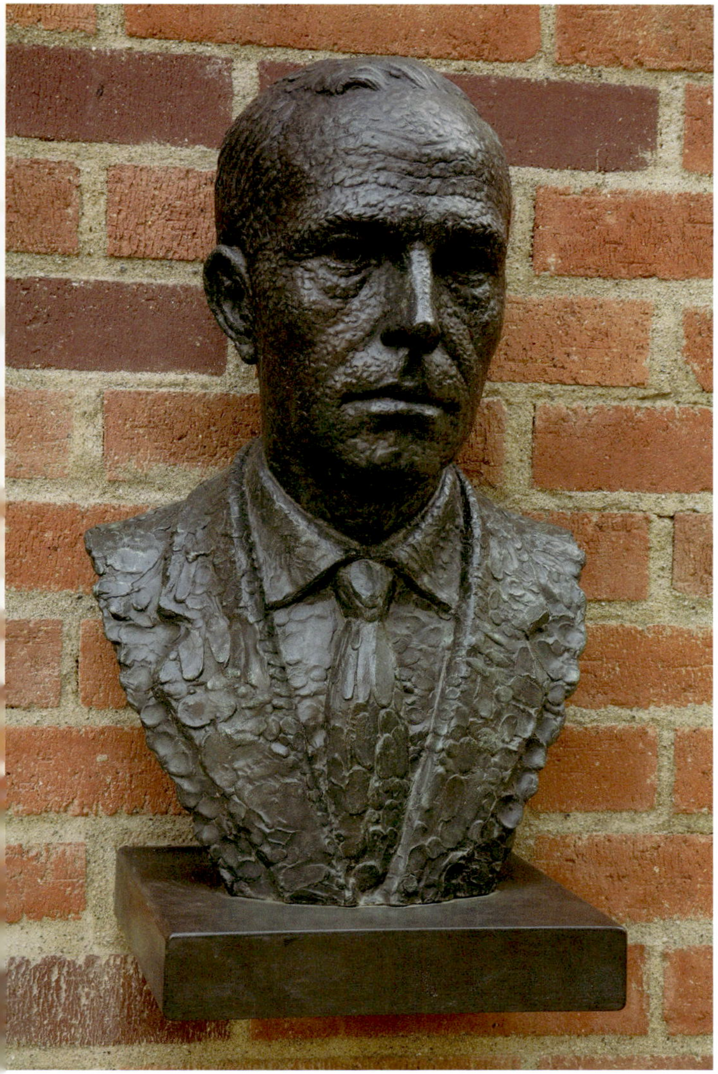

FRANKLIN D. MURPHY
1960
Bronze
H: 20¼ IN. (51.4 CM);
W: 13¾ IN. (34.9 CM);
D: 10½ IN. (26.7 CM)
Gift of Judith H. Murphy, 1969

OBOS 69
1969
Silicon bronze
H: 84 IN. (213.5 CM);
W: 45 IN. (114.3 CM);
D: 48¾ IN. (123.8 CM)
Acquired through the Michael J. Connell Memorial Fund, 1969

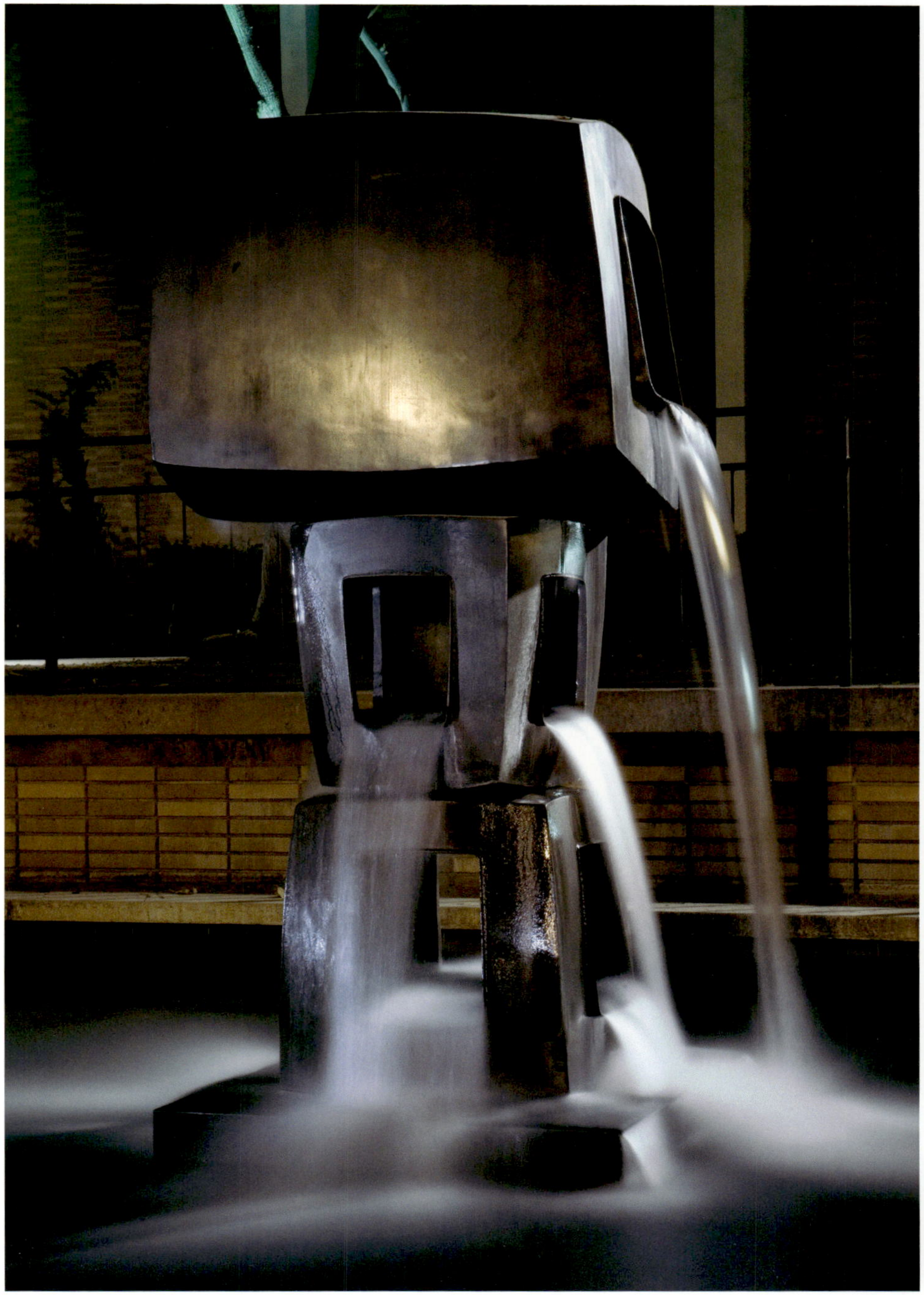

WILLIAM TUCKER

(AMERICAN, B. 1935)

William Tucker was born to English parents in Cairo, Egypt. His family returned to England in 1937, and he studied history at Oxford University between 1955 and 1958. In 1959 he began studying sculpture in London, at the Central School of Art and Design and at St. Martin's School of Art, where Anthony Caro was one of his teachers. Like Caro, Tucker chose to dispose of the pedestal and to use the ground as a reference point for his sculptures. At this time he worked with tractable industrial materials such as fiberglass and plastic, usually uniformly colored, and characteristically precise and constructivist. He soon established himself as a leading British sculptor and was chosen to represent Britain at the 1972 Venice Biennale. He wrote *The Language of Sculpture* in 1974 and the following year was invited to curate the exhibition *The Condition of Sculpture* at the Hayward Gallery in London. The book and the show are landmarks in the history of modernist sculpture in Britain.

Tucker immigrated to New York in 1978 and taught at Columbia University and the New York Studio School. Here his strictly linear, abstracted forms mutated to more earthly, semifigurative creations, reminiscent of the work of Italian sculptor Medardo Rosso. Tucker received the Guggenheim Fellowship for Sculpture in 1981 and the National Endowment for the Arts Fellowship in 1986, the year he became an American citizen. His retrospective at the Storm King Art Center in 1988 further consolidated his reputation in America. He was appointed cochairman of the art department at Bard College in Annandale-on-Hudson, New York, in 1993.

The grid of intersecting steel poles in his untitled sculpture of 1967 boldly marks the landscape that surrounds it. Geometry reigns in this work in which nine poles, painted white, are divided into groups of three, which connect to one another as well as to the ground. In 1968 it was included in *New British Painting and Sculpture*, an exhibition organized by the Whitechapel Gallery in London for the UCLA Art Galleries, and was acquired shortly thereafter. A.P.

UNTITLED
1967
Painted steel
H: 80 IN. (203 CM); W: 93¼ IN. (236.9 CM); D: 76½ IN. (194.3 CM)
Acquired through the Michael J. Connell Memorial Fund, 1969

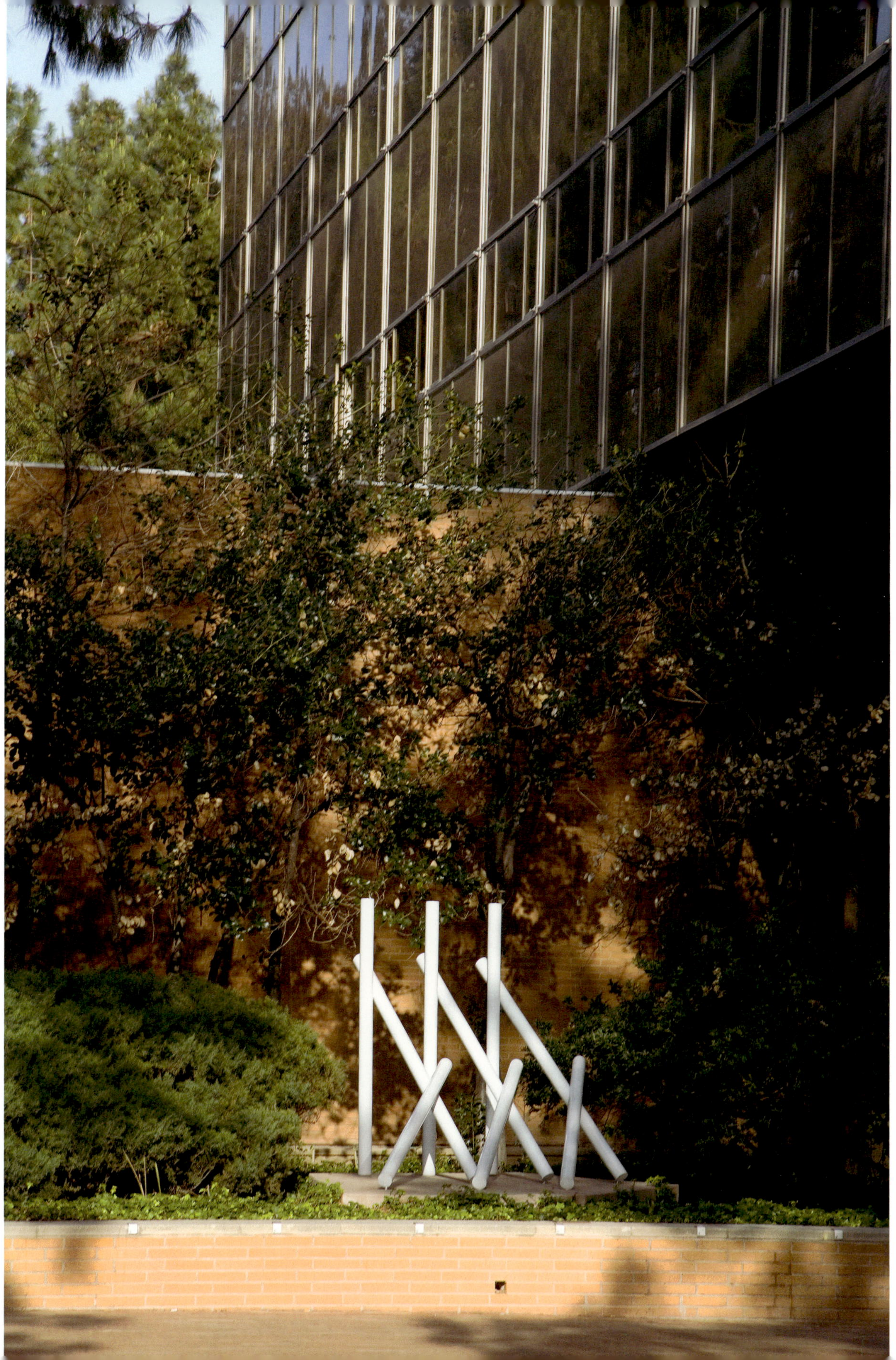

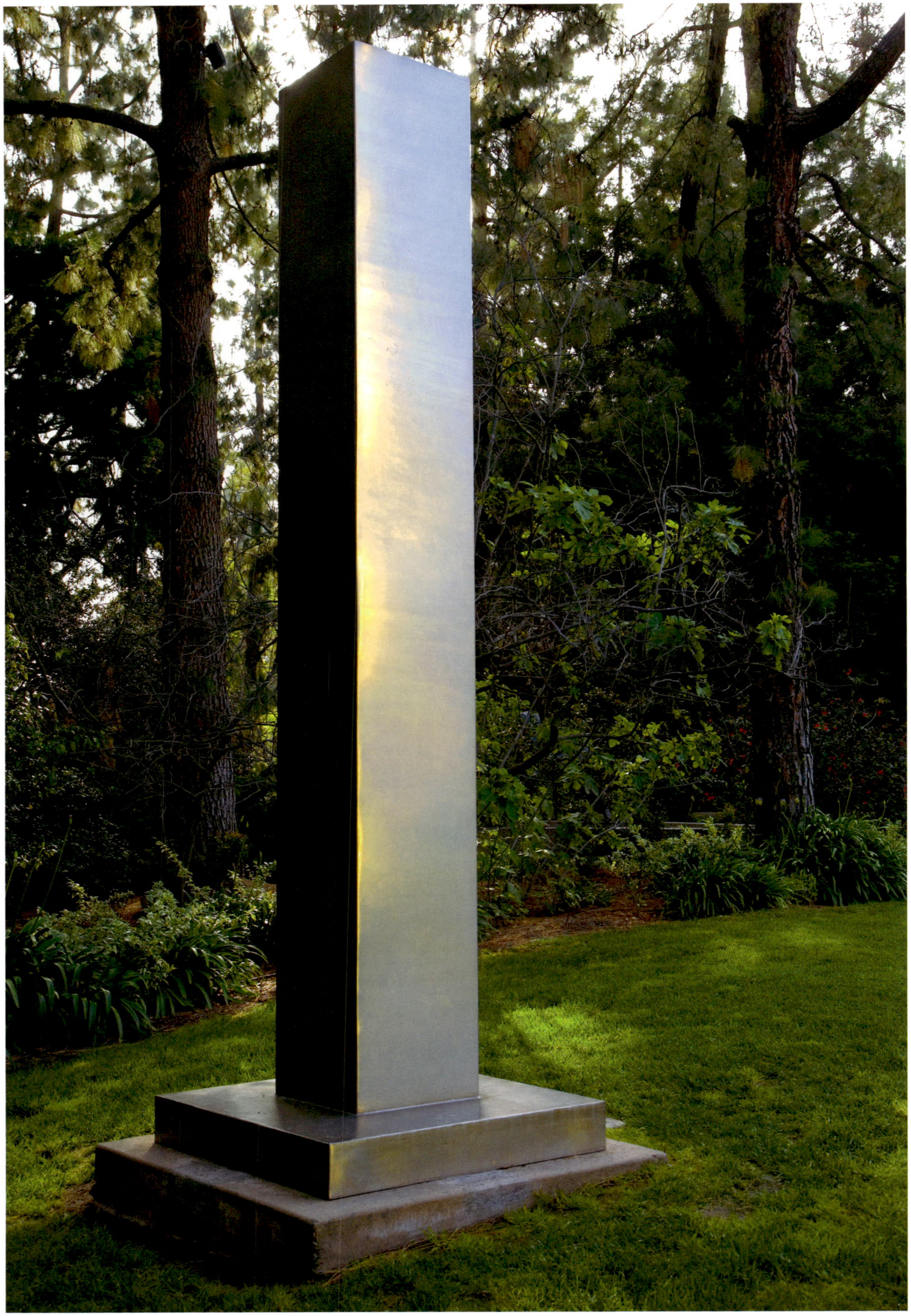

COLUMN
1970
Stainless steel
H: 144 IN. (365.8 CM); W: 20 IN. (50.8 CM); D: 20 IN. (50.8 CM)
Gift of Frederick Weisman Company in honor of Nancy M. Berger, President of the UCLA Art Council (1979–1980), 1980

William Turnbull is a sculptor, painter, and printmaker. Born in Dundee, Scotland, he left school at fifteen and worked as an illustrator of detective and romance stories for a local publishing house, D. C. Thompson, while taking evening classes in art. After serving as a Royal Air Force pilot in World War II, he studied at the Slade School of Art in London and lived in Paris from 1948 to 1950. His early sculptures were influenced by surrealism and tribal art. Frequently made of bronze, they had worn, crusty surfaces. Two exhibitions at the Tate Gallery in London, *Modern Art in the United States* (1956) and *New American Painting* (1959), had a decisive impact on Turnbull's painting and sculpture. After his first visit to the United States, in 1957, he moved toward a purer form of abstraction. His bronzes of the mid- to late 1950s were tall and monolithic in structure. In the early 1960s he began to work with steel, which appealed to him because its strength allowed him to create more open forms and it could also be painted. Turnbull represented Britain in a group exhibition at the Venice Biennale in 1952 and has participated in many solo and group exhibitions both in Britain and abroad. In 1995 a retrospective of his work was presented at the Serpentine Gallery in London, and he had a major solo exhibition at the Yorkshire Sculpture Park in 2005.

Column was commissioned by Frederick Weisman in 1970. It belongs to Turnbull's tradition of totems and attests to his desire to transform light and reflection into three-dimensional volume. Here the modulated surface of stainless steel flickers, yet the clear-cut vertical form has the poise and stillness of an ancient column. *Column* reflects Turnbull's aim to dominate space in an immediate way: "The work must be perceived instantly, not read in time."[1] A.P.

WILLIAM TURNBULL

(SCOTTISH, B. 1922)

Notes

1 William Turnbull: Sculpture and Paintings *(London: Merrell Holberton in association with Serpentine Gallery, 1995), 34.*

VLADAS VILDŽIŪNAS

(LITHUANIAN, B. 1932)

One of the most important contemporary sculptors in Lithuania, Vladas Vildžiūnas studied at the Art Institute of Vilnius in 1958 and began his career as a professor there in 1975. According to the late Marija Gimbutas, his works are inspired by the anonymous sculptors of divine images in Lithuania, who were extremely forward-thinking in their adoption of abstract forms.[1] Although he did not travel extensively during his early career, except for one trip to the United States in 1977, Vildžiūnas studied Western sculpture in Lithuania and began a correspondence with a number of European artists in the 1960s, including fellow Lithuanian-born sculptor Jacques Lipchitz, who became an advocate for his work. The most important sculpture commissions he has received are all in Lithuania: *The Three Kings* in Kaunas (welded copper), *Lithuanian Ballad* in Vilnius (dolomite), and *Čiurlionis* in Druskieniki (bronze). The latter work is a statue of painter and composer Mikalojus Konstantinas Čiurlionis (1875–1911), who was well known in Vildžiūnas's native country.

During his visit to America in 1977 Vildžinas brought some models of works made in Lithuania that he was able to cast in bronze in workshops in New York and Los Angeles. One original work he conceived and executed during this trip was *The Bird Goddess*, an abstract bronze work that represents a prehistoric goddess who nourished and protected humanity while offering security and protection from evil. This goddess was dominant in European folklore for some twenty thousand years, dating to the Upper Paleolithic era and reemerging as the goddess Athena in ancient Greece.[2] The Lithuanian community at UCLA—including its alumni, faculty, and friends support group—generously provided the funds to acquire *The Bird Goddess* for the collection of the Murphy Sculpture Garden in 1977. C.D.

Notes

1 *Lithuanian-born Marija Gimbutas was on the faculty of the department of archaeology at UCLA in 1977 and was instrumental in obtaining* The Bird Goddess *for the Murphy Sculpture Garden collection. An authority in the field of European folk cultures, Gimbutas was widely published. On the history of Lithuanian folk sculpture, see also Alė Počiulpaitė, "Gnarled Branches: Lithuanian Folk Sculpture," in* Sacred Wood: The Contemporary Lithuanian Woodcarving Revival, *ed. Ruta T. Saliklis, trans. Edmond Saliklis (Madison: Elvehjem Museum of Art, University of Wisconsin, 1998), 19–22.*

2 *Marija Gimbutas,* The Goddesses and Gods of Old Europe: Myths and Cult Images *(London: Thames & Hudson, 1982), 112–51.*

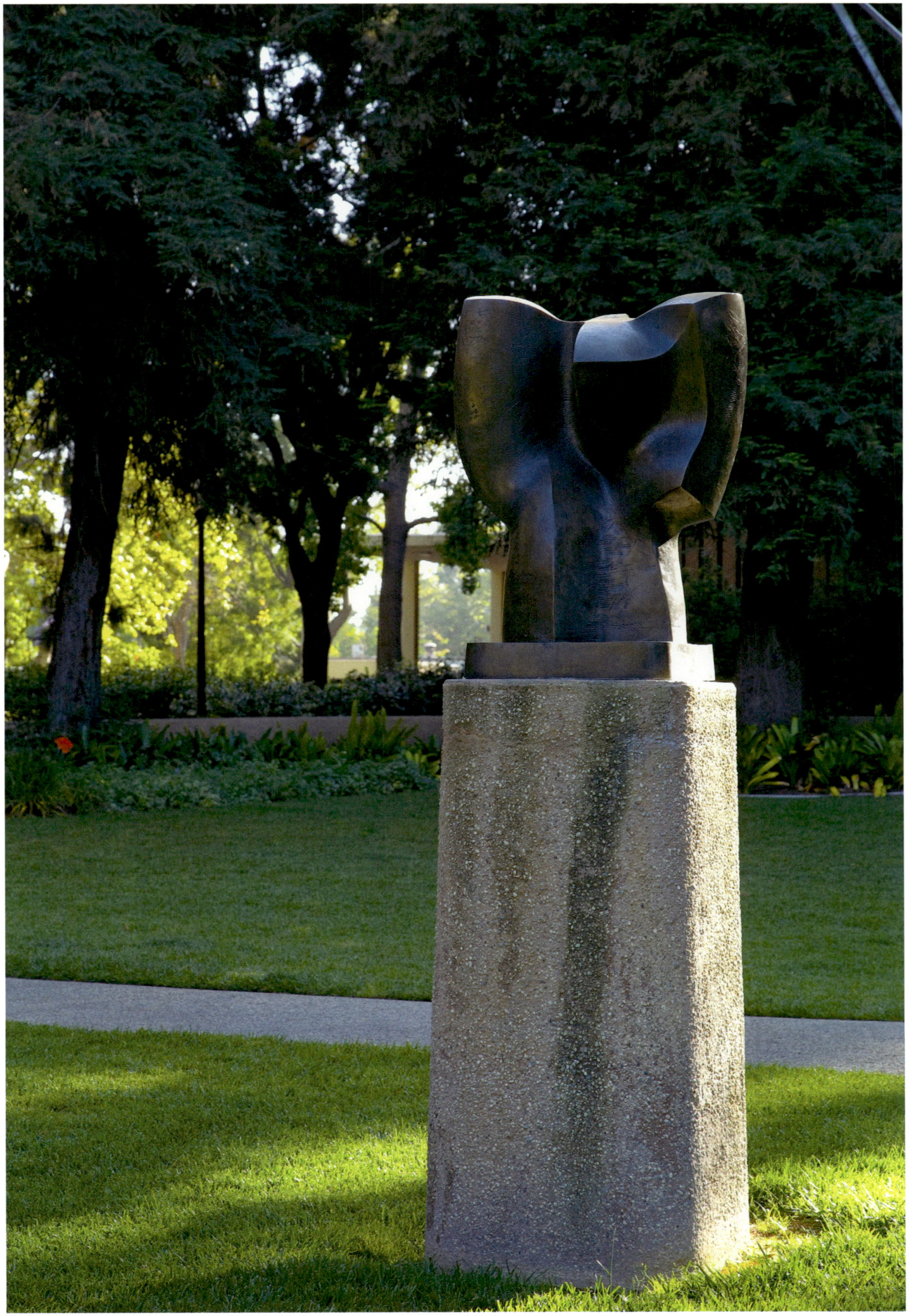

THE BIRD GODDESS
1977
Bronze
H: 35 IN. (89 CM); W: 25½ IN. (64.8 CM); D: 21⅛ IN. (53.7 CM)
Edition: artist's proof
Foundry: Tallix, Peekskill, New York
Gift of the Lithuanian Alumni, Faculty, and Friends of UCLA, 1977

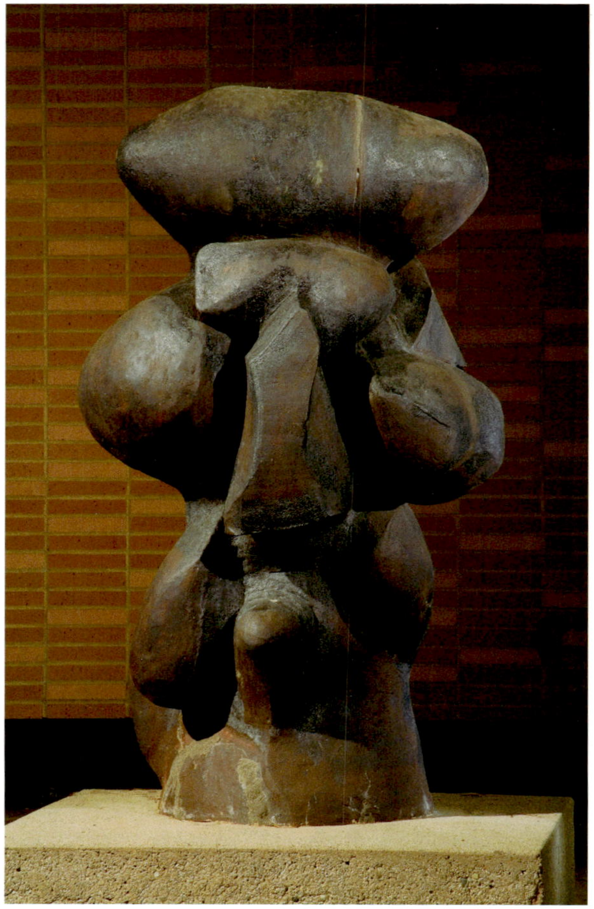

SOLEARES
CA. 1959
Stoneware with slip, gas-fired
H: 63 IN. (160 CM); W: 38 IN. (96.5 CM); D: 30¾ IN. (78.1 CM)
Gift of Mr. and Mrs. John Rex, 1972

Born in Bozeman, Montana, Peter Voulkos graduated from Montana State University in 1951 and received his MFA from the California College of Arts and Crafts, Oakland, in 1952. He served as professor and chairman of the ceramics department at the Otis Art Institute, Los Angeles, from 1954 to 1958. Working primarily as a painter and ceramist, he began to make large-scale ceramic sculptures in 1958, using epoxy resins. From 1959 to 1985 he served as a professor of ceramics at the University of California, Berkeley. Around 1960 he began to work on bronze sculpture, though he continued to produce work in the ceramic medium throughout his career. His work has been the subject of numerous solo exhibitions, including one at the Museum of Modern Art, New York, in 1960, curated by Peter Selz. Major international touring exhibitions include those organized by the American Crafts Council and the Museum of Contemporary Crafts in 1978; Art Center Hall, Tokyo, in 1983; and the Sezon Museum of Art, Tokyo, and the Oakland Museum of Art, both in 1995.

Soleares was the first large-scale clay piece made at the new kiln at the artist's Glendale, California, studio, built to accommodate works up to six feet in height. It is typical of Voulkos's work of the late 1950s in that he used the wheel to make the desired shapes and then combined them in a complex construction. The seven-foot-high *Gallas Rock* is of the same period and was commissioned by Digby Gallas of Los Angeles, whose wife gave it to the Murphy Sculpture Garden in 1973. It is the largest and most elaborate of a series of seventeen works initiated in 1958 and 1959. The artist completed the work in 1960, commuting from his teaching position at Berkeley to his studio in Glendale. The work is clay stoneware, finished with a light iron oxide solution for the enhancement of the natural clay color. Voulkos described *Gallas Rock* as follows: "The basis of the sculpture, and the smaller ones that preceded it, is the core cylinder inside, with other cylinders going in different directions to take the weight of the slabs. There is a lot of construction inside—stacked cylinders to support a lot of weight—sometimes several cylinders at the bottom. Outside and inside grew together, building on themselves and each other. I was working in such a way that I had to relate to everything at the same time and keep the spontaneity."[1] C.B.

Notes
1 *Quoted in Rose Slivka, "The Artist and His Work: Risk and Revelation," in* The Art of Peter Voulkos, *by Rose Slivka and Karen Tsujimoto (New York: Kodansha International in collaboration with the Oakland Museum, 1995), 50.*

PETER VOULKOS

(AMERICAN, 1924–2002)

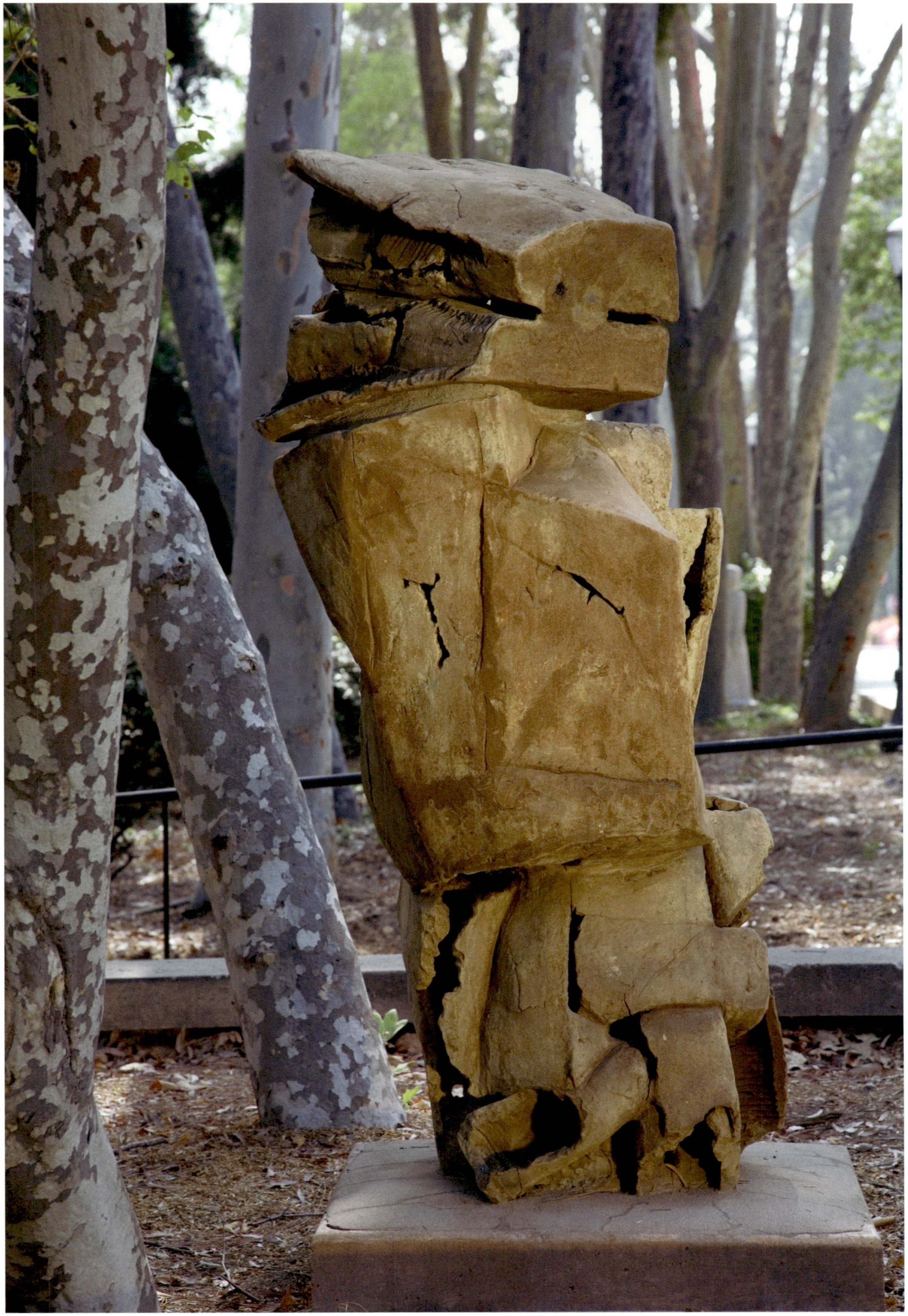

GALLAS ROCK
1960
Stoneware with slip and glaze, gas-fired
H: 84 IN. (213.4 CM); W: 37 IN. (93.9 CM); D: 26 ¾ IN. (67.9 CM)
Gift of Julianne Kemper, 1973

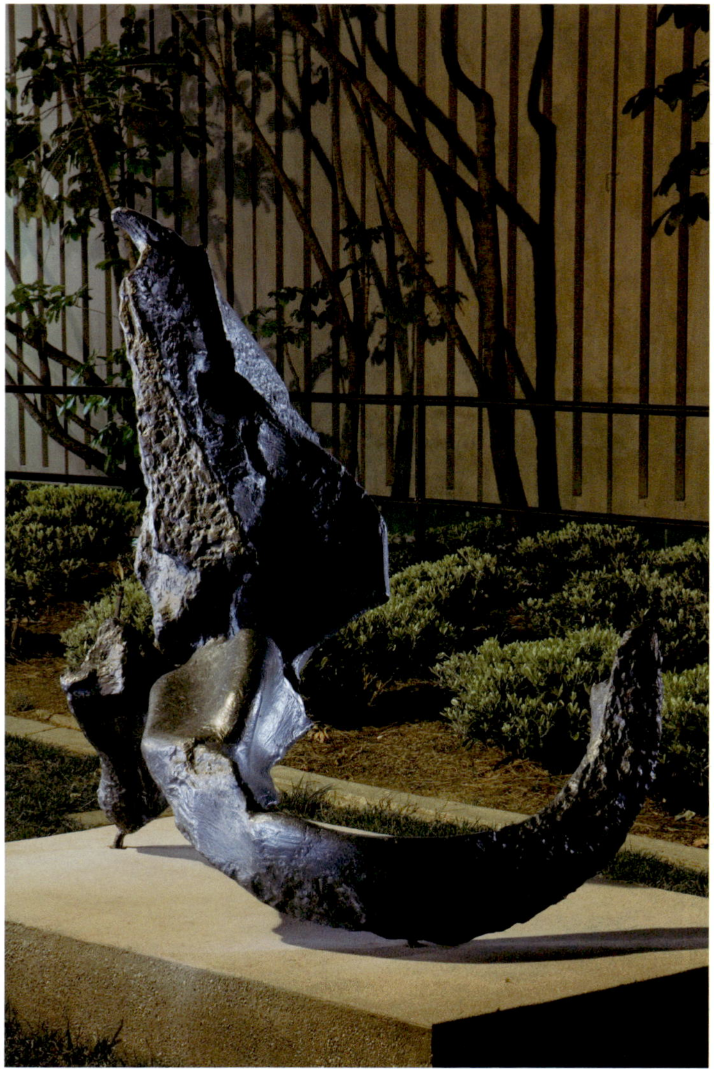

RAM HEAD WITH BROKEN HORN, VI
1963
Bronze
H: 57 ⅜ IN. (146 CM); W: 58 ½ IN. (148.6 CM); D: 34 ¼ IN. (87 CM)
Gift of the UCLA Art Council in Memory of David E. Bright, 1967

JACK ZAJAC

(AMERICAN, B. 1929)

Born in Youngstown, Ohio, Jack Zajac came to California as a teenager with his family and studied art at Scripps College in Claremont from 1949 to 1953. Through the assistance of various Rome Prize Fellowships in the mid-1950s, he continued his formal studies at the American Academy in Rome, where his primary interest shifted from painting to sculpture. Subsequent honors have included various travel grants, many solo and group exhibitions in the United States and Europe, and representation in numerous public collections, including the Hirshhorn Museum and Sculpture Garden in Washington, D.C., and the Museum of Modern Art in New York. Zajac works primarily in bronze and marble and has taught at Dartmouth College and the University of California, Santa Cruz.

Beginning in the 1950s Zajac explored his own concerns with spirituality and the human condition, as symbolized in his Goats and Metamorphoses series. The sculptures of sacrificial goats were inspired by a trip he took in 1956 to Greece, where he attended a Greek Orthodox Easter pageant in which a goat or lamb was the paschal sacrifice and the object of the feast. Although not religious in a conventional sense, these sculptures depict animals under restraint, sometimes pierced by sacrificial stakes—symbols of the crucified Christ, according to the artist.[1] *Bound Goat, Wednesday* in the Murphy Sculpture Garden collection is from a series from the early 1970s, when Zajac returned to the subject he had concentrated on more than ten years earlier, and is a companion to *Bound Goat, Thursday*, recently donated by the artist to Pasadena City College's Boone Sculpture Garden. In contrast, Zajac's "skull" pieces, such as UCLA's *Ram Head with Broken Horn, VI*, suggest a prehistoric discovery, an unearthed archaeological remnant, reminiscent of a geologic artifact rather than a Christian relic. C.D.

Notes
1 *David S. Stevens Schaff, "An Interview with Jack Zajac,"* Art International *19 (October 15, 1975): 35.*

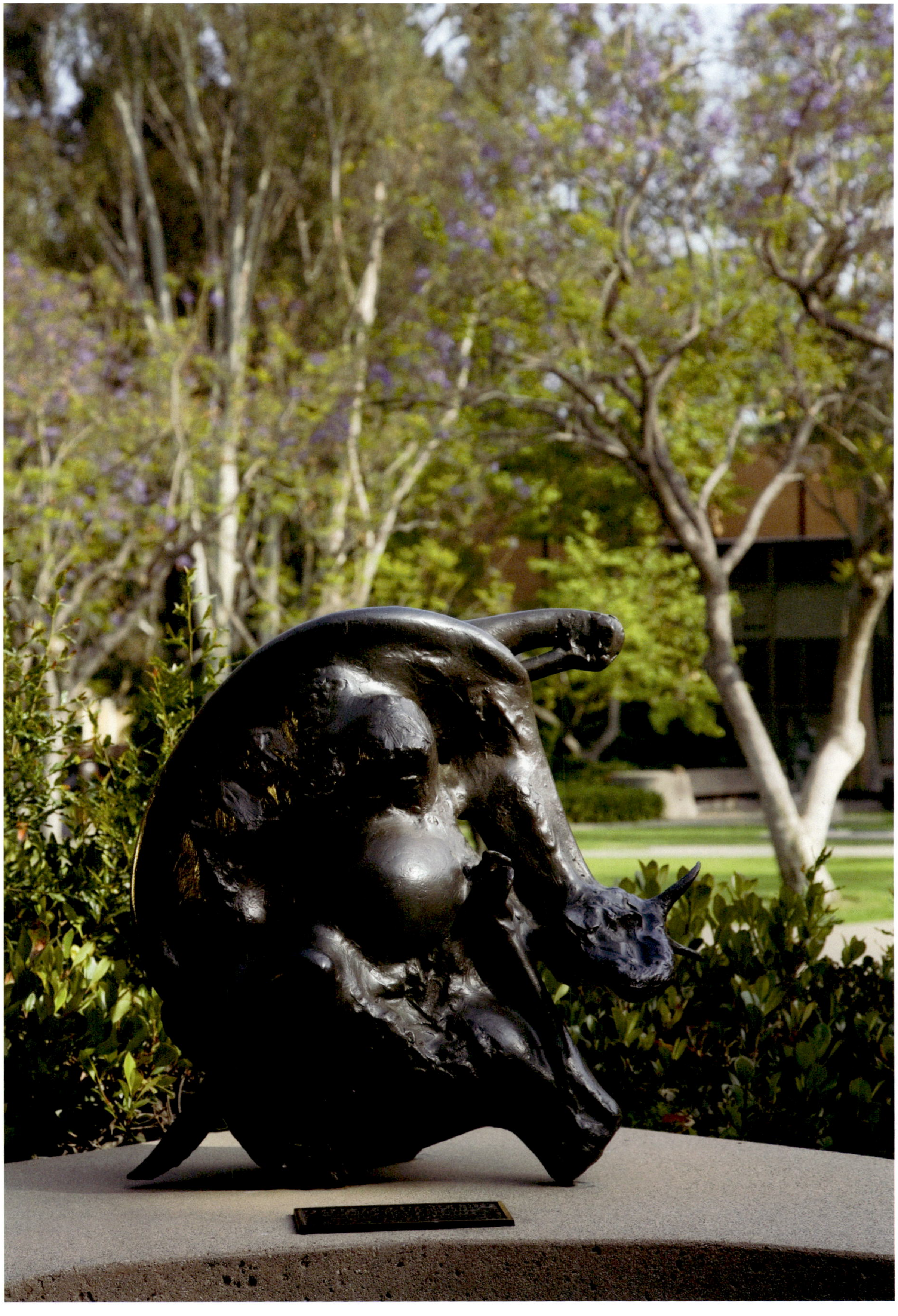

BOUND GOAT, WEDNESDAY
1973
Bronze
H: 29 IN. (73.5 CM); W: 28 IN. (71 CM); D: 19 ¼ IN. (48.9 CM)
Edition: 3/6
In memory of Gabriel Mekler (1942–1977), donated by Adam and Joan Mekler, Oscar and Judith Mekler, Tim and Mani Van Kluyve, Alett Mekler, and Nancy Bacal, 1977

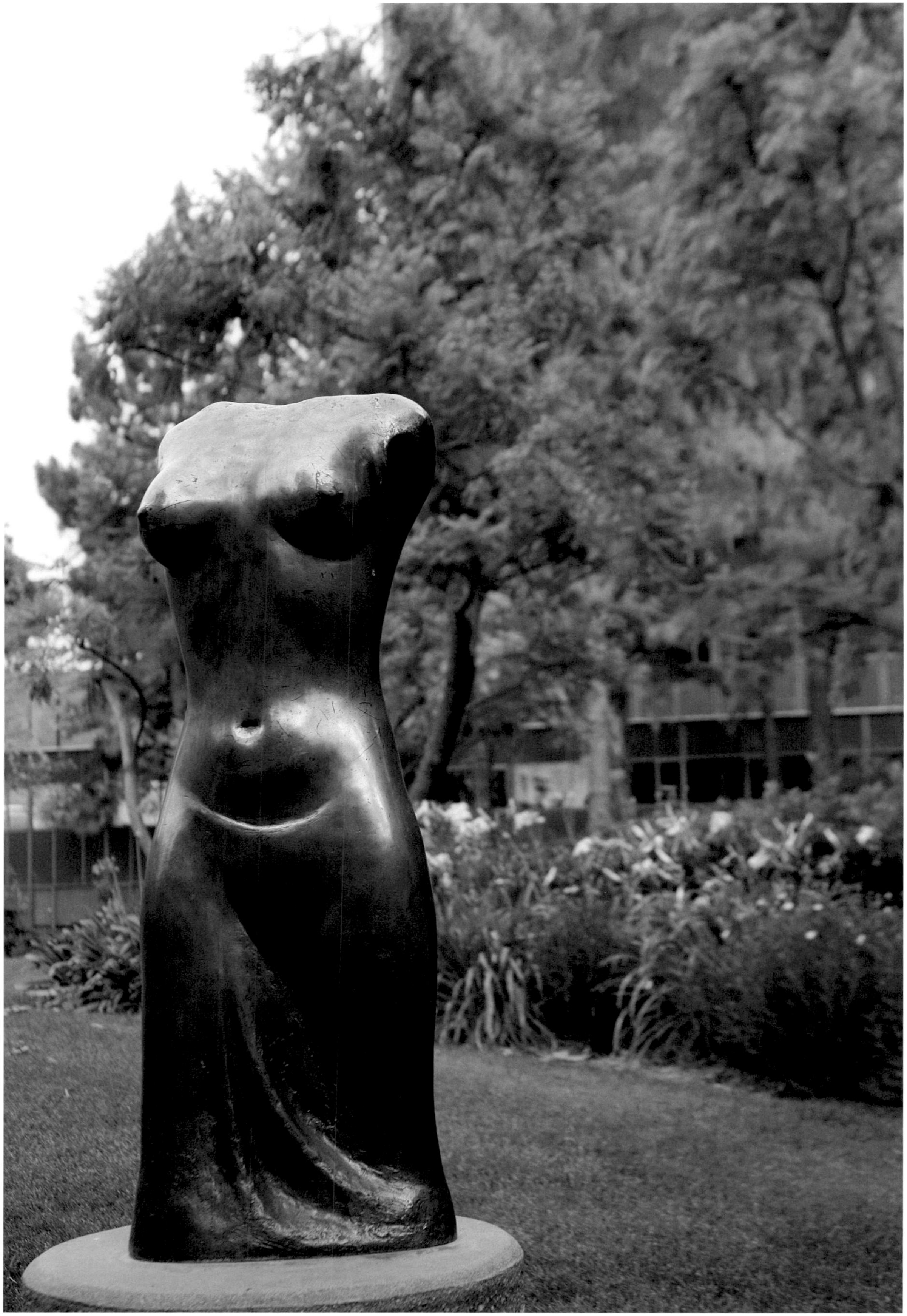

VICTORY
1950
Bronze
H: 41 IN. (104 CM); W: 18 IN. (40.6 CM); D: 11 IN. (27.9 CM)
Edition: /6
Foundry: artist's studio
Acquired through the Michael J. Connell Memorial Fund, 1965

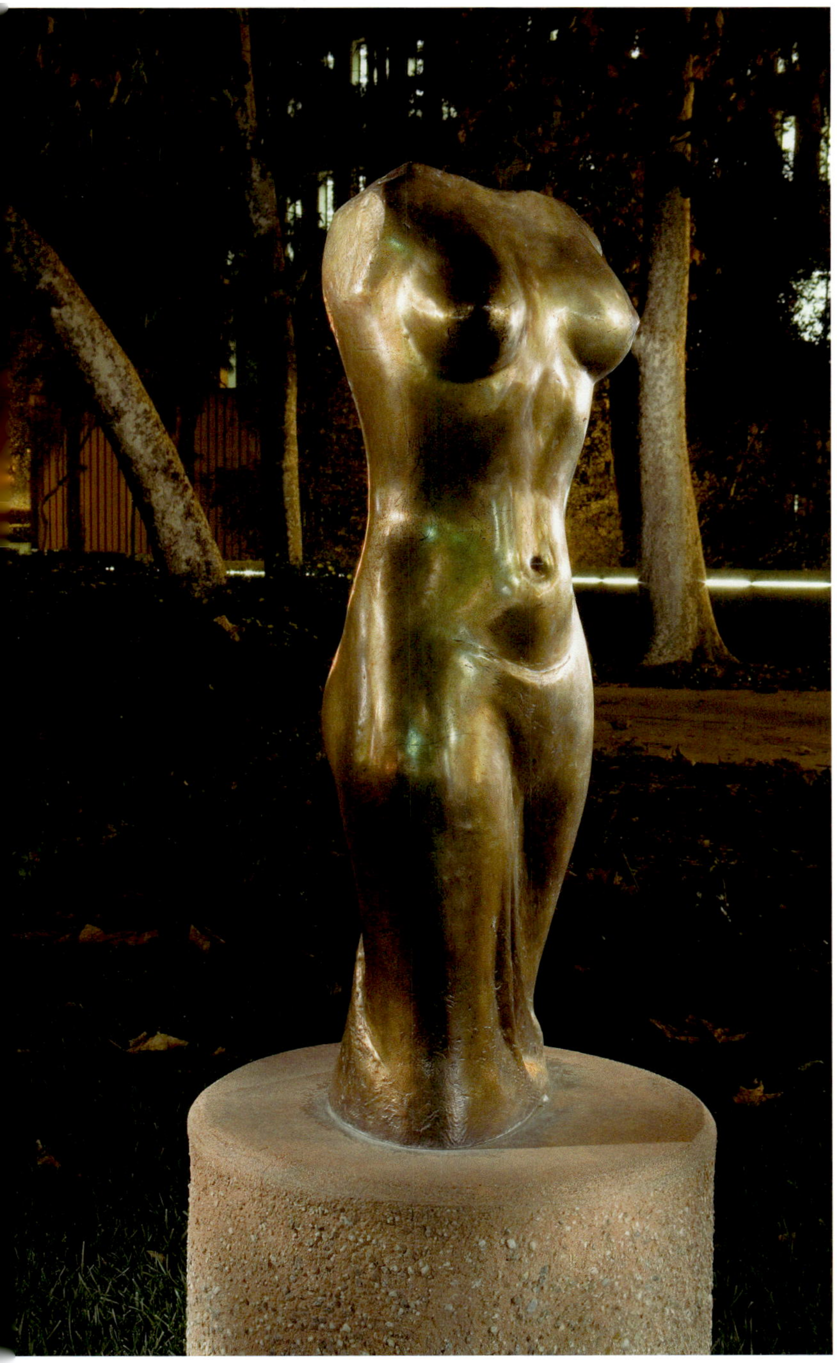

William Zorach was born in Lithuania and immigrated to America with his family in 1891. He worked as an apprentice at the Morgan Lithograph Company in Cleveland while attending the Cleveland School of Art between 1902 and 1905. A few years later he moved to New York to study drawing and painting at the National Academy of Design. He spent several years in Paris, where four of his paintings were selected for the Salon d'Automne in 1912. There he also met his future wife, the American artist Marguerite Thompson. On his return to New York in 1914 Zorach worked as a commercial lithographer while pursuing painting on the side. Initially he was influenced by Matisse's Fauve paintings, and in 1917 he turned his attention to tribal art and cubism, but he finally settled on traditional nudes and figurative subject matter. His experimentation with wood carving led to a preference for sculpture, and he soon became a leader in the revival of direct carving. His three-dimensional works retain a sense of the original material and its texture, with characteristically monumental and simplified forms.

Zorach's *Victory* instantly recalls the famed Greek marble *Winged Victory of Samothrace* in the Musée du Louvre, Paris. Like her ancient counterpart, Zorach's figure has a frontal, confident stance, with her chest thrust forward and her right leg placed before her left. The faint hint of clinging drapery across her front thigh is also reminiscent of Greek and Roman goddesses, and Zorach further accentuated the connection to fragments of ancient statuary by excluding her head and arms. Nonetheless, his *Victory*'s abstracted form and its polished bronze surface, which appears almost gilded, belong unmistakably to the twentieth century. An earlier work in French marble is now in the Smithsonian American Art Museum, Washington, D.C.[1] A.P.

Notes

1 *John I. H. Bauer,* William Zorach *(New York: Praeger for Whitney Museum of American Art, 1959): 38–39, fig. 63.*

WILLIAM ZORACH

(AMERICAN, 1887–1966)

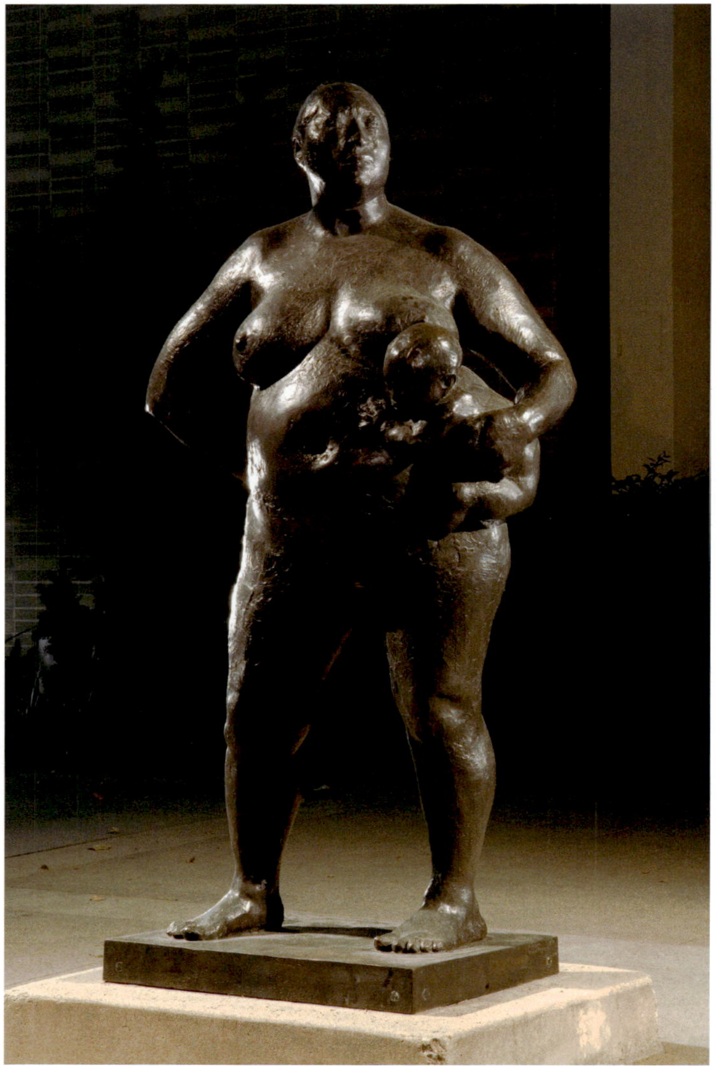

MADRE CON NIÑO EN LA CADERA / MOTHER WITH CHILD AT HER HIP
1979
Bronze
H: 74 ¾ IN. (190 CM); W: 30 IN. (76 CM); D: 22 IN. (55.5 CM)
Edition: 2/4
Foundry: Carlos Rojas, Mexico
Gift of Lisa and Ernest Auerbach, 1980

FRANCISCO ZÚÑIGA

(MEXICAN, 1912–1998)

Francisco Zúñiga's career as a sculptor began in Costa Rica in the workshop of his father, a carver of religious figures, altars, and altarpieces. With the funds won in a competition, he moved to Mexico City in 1936 and pursued his studies at the School of Direct Carving (now the School of Painting and Sculpture). He began teaching sculpture and art theory there in 1938 and continued for more than thirty years. Under the direction of Guillermo Ruiz, who taught him how to cast in bronze, and the painters Oliviero Martinez and Manuel Rodríguez Lozano, Zúñiga developed his own concept of monumental form. He was first recognized as an independent artist in the 1940s, participating in exhibitions in Mexico and North America. In 1942 the Museum of Modern Art in New York acquired a carved head by Zúñiga, and in 1946 the Metropolitan Museum of Art secured some of his drawings.[1] He received his first independent commission in 1946 for *Monument Valsequillo*, in Puebla.[2] Although he did not travel to Europe until he was fifty-five, he was aware of artistic movements there and was drawn to the works of Aristide Maillol, Henry Moore, and Auguste Rodin. Their impact was combined with inspiration closer to home, especially pre-Columbian and colonial art. He produced public works, such as the stone reliefs *Allegory of the Earth and Communications* at the Secretaría de Comunicaciones in Mexico City (1953–54), but also conceived sculptures for more intimate settings, such as *Seated Yucatan Woman,* now in the Hirshhorn Museum and Sculpture Garden, Washington, D.C. (1974). Zúñiga is associated in particular with his emphatic renderings of the female figure. Although he experimented with clay, plaster, and marble, his preferred medium was cast bronze.

Zúñiga chose a difficult pose for his female model in *Reclining Nude*. She squats on the ground and rests her body on her elbows, with her head turned casually to the side. Although she nestles below the viewer, her bold, muscular features do not go unnoticed. Zúñiga's fascination with reclining figures is expressed in his drawings, many of which served as starting points for the sculptures. The crouching posture seen here appears in pencil studies of 1963, seven years before *Reclining Nude* was made, while other related drawings postdate it.[3] These sheets, which were presumably scattered around his studio, served as integral parts of his working method.

When standing upright, Zúñiga's women often tower above the viewer, as does *Mother with Child at Her Hip* of 1979. With her wide, protruding belly, her large breasts, and a child clinging to her waist, this woman recalls the traditional personification of Charity. She also has the unfaltering stance and assertiveness historically associated with male figures and heroic monuments. Zúñiga's most direct inspirations, however, were native Mexican women and the ancient fertility goddesses of Aztec and other pre-Columbian cultures: "You can see in archaic art certain forms that I have adopted, not literally but interpretatively.... My concern is to integrate, to understand the essence of this sculpture, relating it to its own people and its origins."[4] **A.P.**

Notes
1 Francisco Zúñiga: Homenaje nacional *(Mexico City: Consejo Nacional para la Cultura y las Artes, 1994), 196.*
2 *Ibid.*
3 *Cynthia Burlingham and Elizabeth Shepherd, eds.,* In the Sculptor's Landscape: Celebrating Twenty-five Years of the Franklin D. Murphy Sculpture Garden *(Los Angeles: Wight Art Gallery and Grunwald Center for the Graphic Arts, University of California, 1993), 104–5, figs. 97–99.*
4 *Sheldon Reich,* Francisco Zúñiga, Sculptor: Conversations and Interpretations *(Tucson: University of Arizona Press, 1980), 53.*

DESNUDO RECLINADO / RECLINING NUDE
1970
Bronze
H: 22½ IN. (57 CM); W: 37½ IN. (95.5 CM); D: 28¾ IN. (73 CM)
Edition: 3/4
Foundry: Moisés del Aguila, Mexico
Gift of Elsie Browning Ballantyne in memory of her mother, Rachel Teresa Browning, 1975

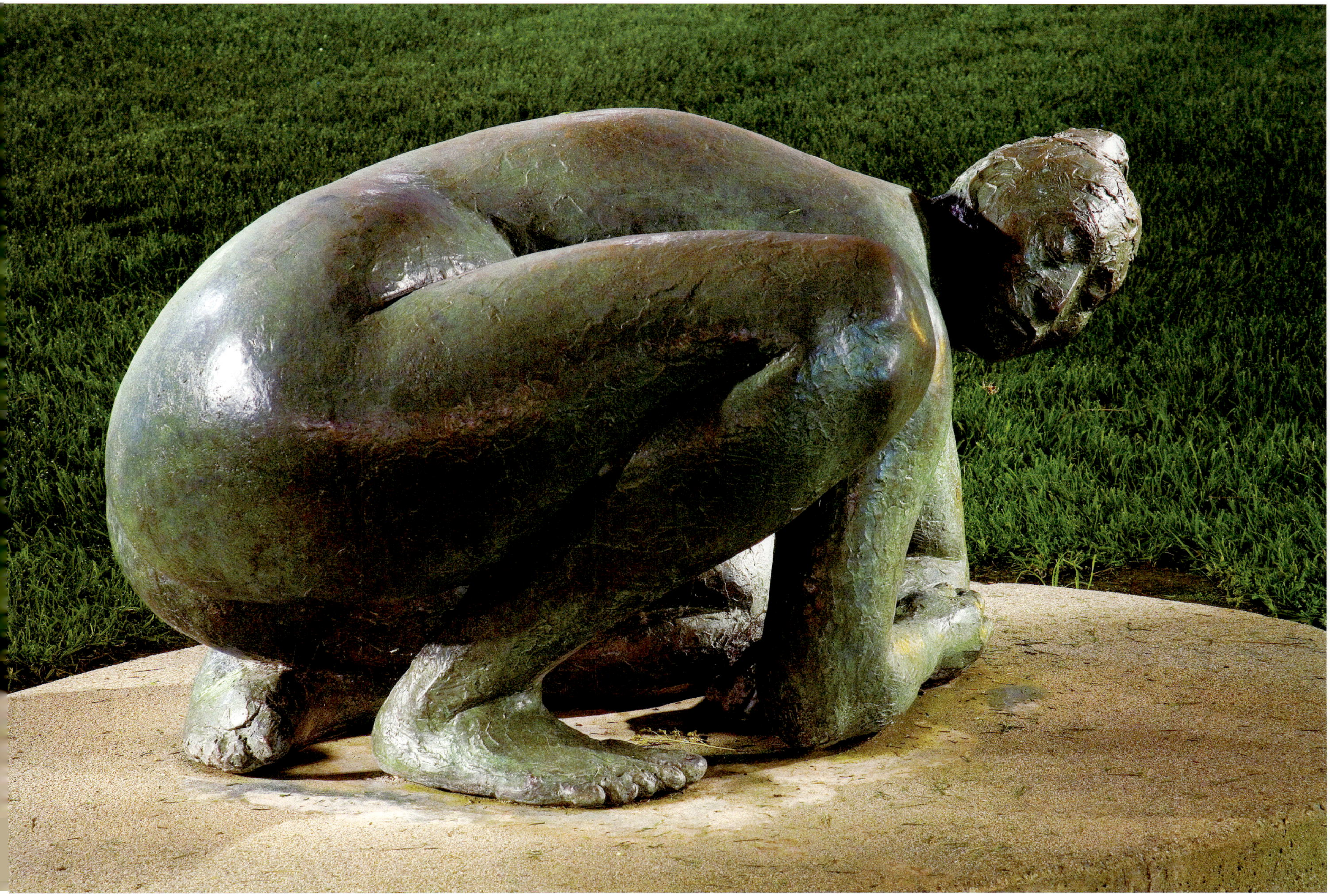

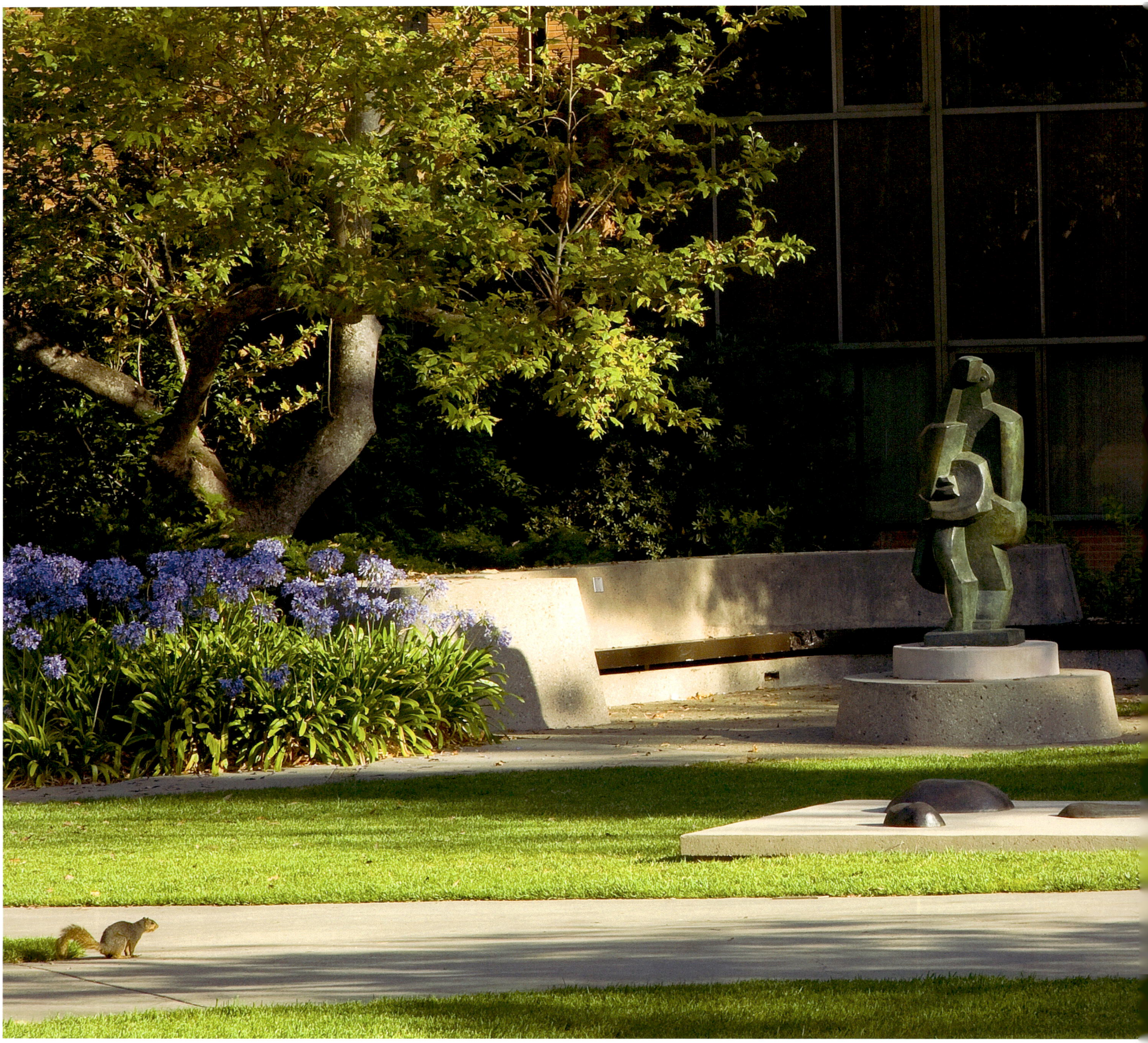

1

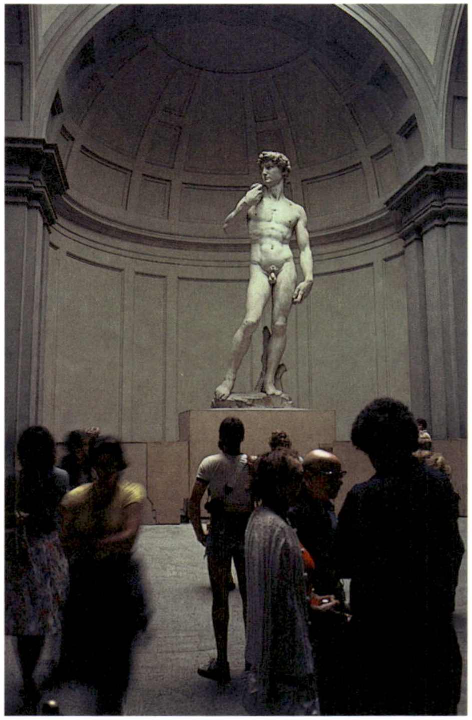

2

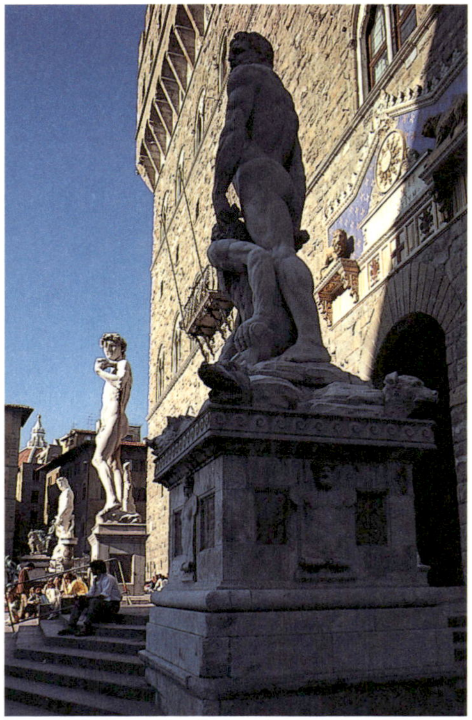

3

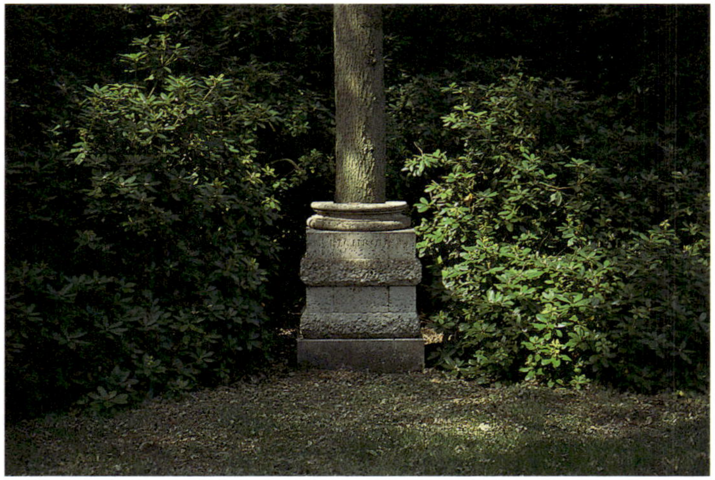

4

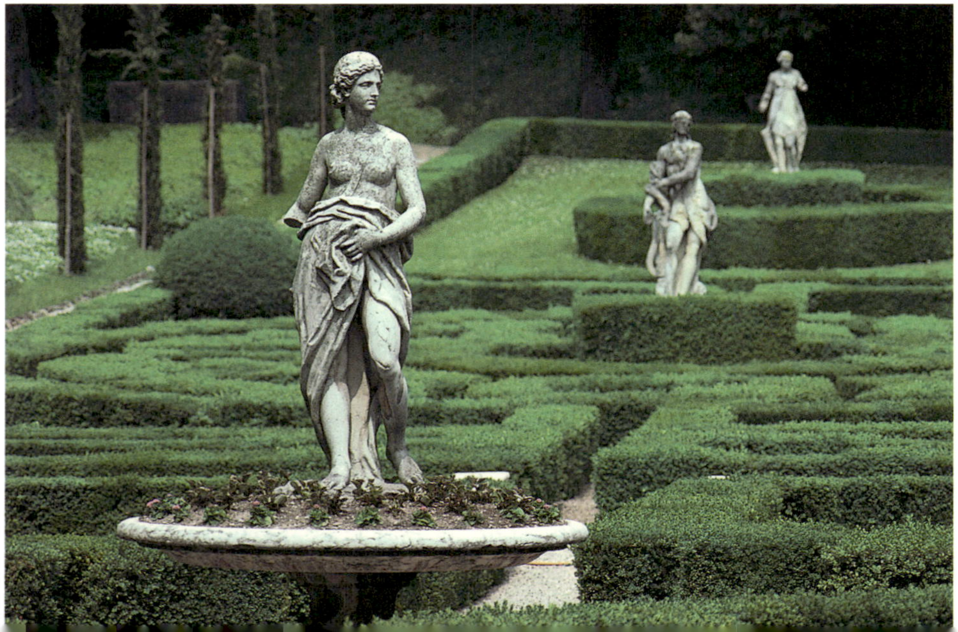

5

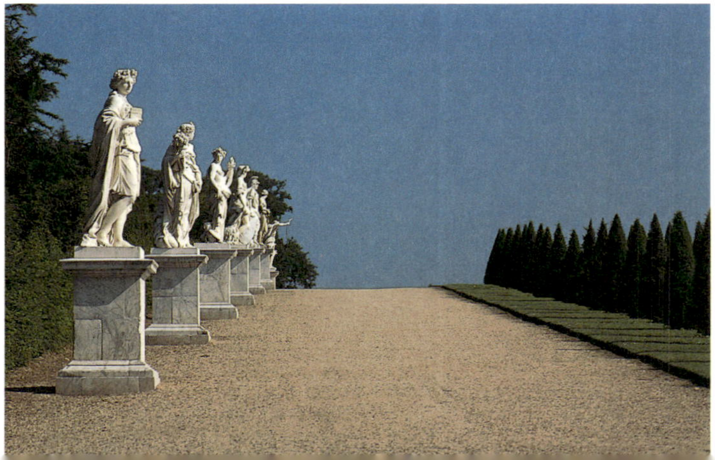

Indoors / Outdoors

Today one encounters the *David* within the sheltering confines of the Accademia, protected from the natural elements though still exposed to the onslaught of tourist hordes (FIG. 1). The light is soft and relatively constant within the gallery, and the statue stands free, like an obelisk in a piazza. Historically, however, the *David* served a far different audience in a far different setting (FIG. 2). Created to symbolize triumph against superior forces, Michelangelo's great work was purposely realized at almost three times life size and set before the walls of the Palazzo della Signoria, the seat of civic government and the symbol of Florentine authority. It stood outdoors, exposed to the elements and public scrutiny from near and far. The light upon it was never constant, neither in direction or intensity, nor in degree of acuity. On cloudy days the diffused light flattened the relief of its details, and the sense of surface prevailed over the reading of individual features. On sunny days the depth of the modeling advanced, heightening the presence of the toes, the fingers, and the eyes. In rain the marble surfaces cried with precipitation, and descending lines of water traced the contour of the heroic body.

Exterior display welcomes change; interior display maintains conditions nearly constant through time.

Change is one of the prime factors that instigate and sustain the making of sculpture gardens: sculpture set outdoors enjoys a broad range of viewing conditions that stimulate a plethora of readings. These, in turn, encourage our engagement, foster understanding, and stimulate aesthetic appreciation (FIG. 3). Change is but one factor in the equation, however, for if the setting provides the environmental and perceptual contexts for viewing sculpture, the number and characteristics of the works on view affect the reading of the context itself.

Consider the role of sculpture in Italian Renaissance or French formal gardens. In the former, the landscape designer might have been called upon to position recently unearthed statuary from classical antiquity or works newly created. Because the garden stood before the arrival of the sculpture, the designer needed to position the fragment or statue in a way sympathetic to both (FIG. 4). A century or so later, with gardens inflated to enormous dimensions in the Île de France, statuary became spatial markers that punctuated and articulated the landscape, rhythmically tracing the course of an axis or providing a focal point for a bosquet set at some remove from a château (FIG. 5). A century later sculpture and pavilions played a related role in the English landscape garden, as visual attractions within a naturalistically conceived landscape (FIG. 6). These three examples—admittedly caricatured in this brief description—all shared one common property, what might be termed an interactive symbiosis. The landscape supported the artwork while the artwork supported the landscape.

Today many art museums—and universities—possess sculpture collections, sculpture gardens, or sculpture courtyards.[1] These may be singular pieces, like Claes Oldenburg's giant button at the University of Pennsylvania in Philadelphia, or numbers of sculptural reliefs and objects, like the works by Carl Milles and Constantino Nivola that enrich the grounds of the Cranbrook Academy of Art and Yale University's Ezra Stiles and Morse Colleges, respectively (FIGS. 7–9). In other institutional settings the sculpture garden complements the galleries of the museum; today outdoor display spaces are often linked to the museum's café or restaurant. The Museum of Modern Art in New York is the classic representative of this type, positioning its sculptures outdoors within a fluid modernist space defined primarily by its boundary walls and clusters of trees (FIG. 10).[2]

Scale is one issue behind the creation of these landscapes. The exterior court or garden's more abundant area and volume permit the display of more and/or larger works that also benefit from the qualities of an outdoor setting described above. Expanding the scale further still yields the sculpture park, a landscape that in many ways appropriates the lessons and forms of the eighteenth-century English landscape garden but substitutes large-scale sculpture for the architectural folly. The Kendall Sculpture Gardens at PepsiCo World Headquarters and the Storm King Art Center in lower New York state are prime examples of this type (FIG. 11). For the Kendall Sculpture Gardens, landscape architects Edward D. Stone Jr. and Russell Page designed a series of sites for artworks that vary in manner from the architectural to the naturalistic. These varied spaces include broad lawns displaying works by Claes Oldenburg, George Segal, Alexander Calder, and Arnoldo Pomidoro; groves of conifers and deciduous trees; and more intimate settings defined by flowers and shrubs, featuring sculptures by Isamu Noguchi and David Smith. At Storm King, the landscape architect William A. Rutherford

1
Michelangelo; David, *1504; marble; height: 204 1⅛ in. (522 cm); Accademia, Florence*

2
Michelangelo; David, *1504; Piazza della Signoria, Florence*

3
Ian Hamilton Finlay; Five Columns for the Kröller-Müller *(detail), 1982; limestone; Otterlo, the Netherlands*

4
Giardino Giusti, Verona, Italy, late fifteenth century with subsequent modifications

5
André Le Nôtre, gardens at Versailles, 1661+

A COMMUNITY OF SCULPTURE

Marc Treib

6

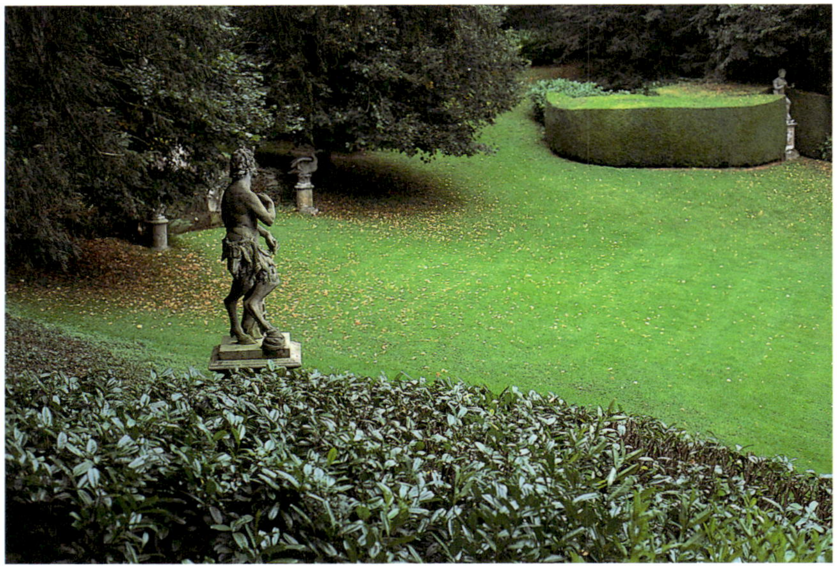

7

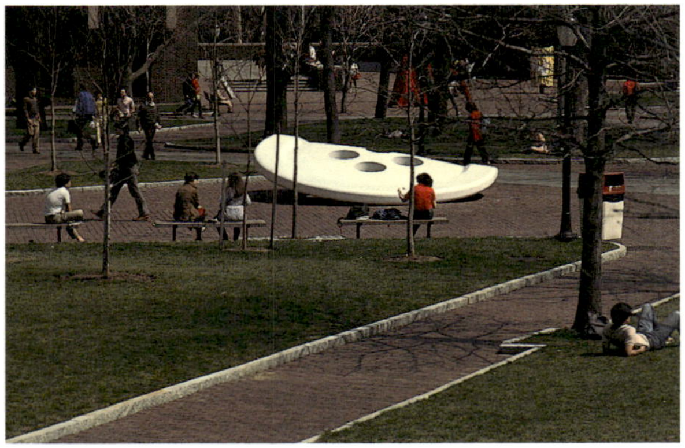

6
William Kent, Venus Vale, Rousham Park, 1738+, Oxfordshire, England

7
Claes Oldenburg and Coosje van Bruggen, Split Button, *1981; aluminum painted with polyurethane enamel; diameter: 192 in. (487.7 cm), depth: 10 in. (25.4 cm), height from ground: 59 in. (149.9 cm); Levy Park, University of Pennsylvania, Philadelphia*

8
Carl Milles, Orpheus Fountain, *1934–36; bronze; height: 108 in. (274.3 cm); Cranbrook Academy of Art, Bloomfield Hills, Michigan*

9
Constantino Nivola, sculpture for Ezra Stiles and Morse Colleges, Yale University, New Haven, Connecticut, 1962

10
Philip Johnson and James Fanning, Museum of Modern Art Sculpture Garden, New York City, 1951

8

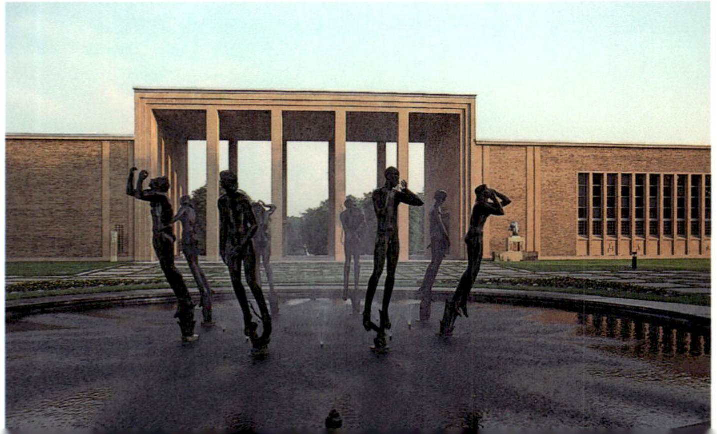

9

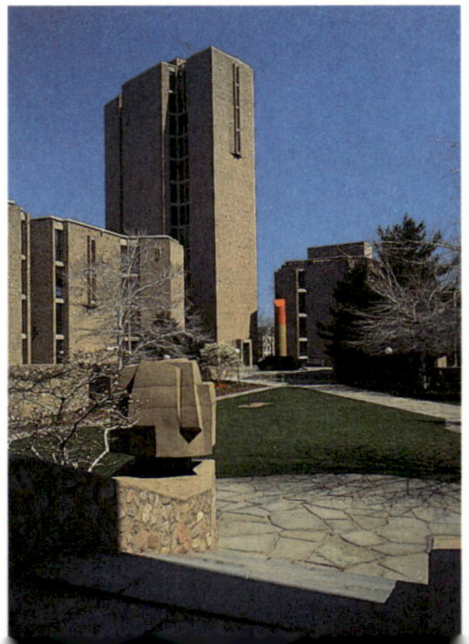

10

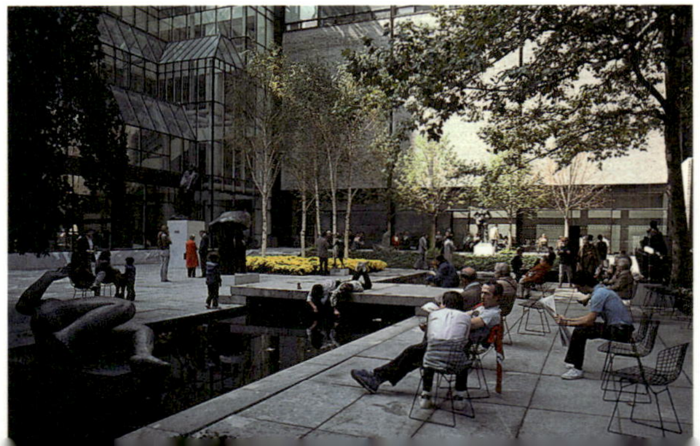

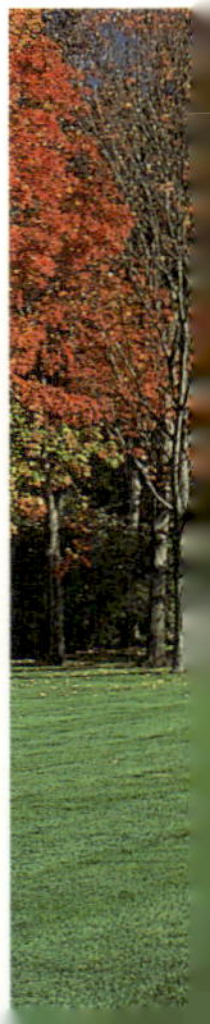

recast the grounds of an old estate as an outdoor gallery, playing open areas of lawn against enclosures of woodlands or fields planted to sorghum.[3] The extensive collection, which features several monumental works by Mark di Suvero, draws upon the space of the setting for its aesthetic power. But these remain works created in the studio and sited only thereafter.[4] In recent years some pieces, including sculptures by Richard Serra and Andy Goldsworthy, have been commissioned as site-specific works that engage the landscape more directly—or are even derived from the specific conditions of the site—raising the question: Which came first, the artwork or the landscape?

Community

UCLA's Murphy Sculpture Garden is, of course, a far smaller enterprise and only one part of a vibrant university campus rather than an exurban art center (FIG. 12). As such it serves a far different purpose, attracting a more quotidian audience, for whom art occupies only a fragment of the program, rather than visitors who travel to experience art in the landscape. In this sense the UCLA audience is a sculptural community within an academic community. *Community* is a key word here, and it suggests at least two sets of relationships: those between the viewer and the artwork, and those among the sculptures themselves. For the readings—and ultimately the range of possible interpretations—hinge not only on the association of the sculpture with its landscape setting (landscape taken here more inclusively to include architecture as well as vegetal elements) but also on the relation of one sculpture to another. Through the curator's positioning of the work, sculptures engage one another or turn their backs in detached isolation (FIG. 13). What is the relationship of a work by Alexander Calder to one by David Smith or Jacques Lipchitz? Many of the pieces share the common material of bronze; most are of a relatively small, personal scale. Even if they are nonfigurative, a residual anthropomorphic dimension is derived from the dimensions of the piece measured against those of the human body. The collection as a whole, whether intentionally or not, coheres as a community started by the work of the curator but completed by the viewer.

When the idea for the sculpture garden was raised by Franklin Murphy, the collection was still in its infancy. Ralph Cornell of Cornell, Bridges and Troller designed the garden with sufficient formal interest to succeed without the addition of sculpture—yet in sufficiently subdued manner to allow, or even foster, its inclusion. One sees in the garden's plan the play of the orthogonal superstructure addressing the surrounding buildings against the modeled forms favored by midcentury modernist landscape architects. Thomas Church's Donnell garden in Sonoma County (1947), particularly its swimming pool and central sculpture by Adaline Kent, announced the arrival of a vocabulary that rejected both the naturalism of the English tradition and the formal outlines of the French and Italian landscapes (FIG. 14). Referencing modern painting and sculpture, Church's biomorphism echoed in abstraction the contours of the land—in this case the meanders of the rivers draining into the northern limits of San Francisco Bay. Closer to UCLA, Garrett Eckbo's 1968 plaza design for Union Bank in downtown Los Angeles employed a vocabulary of curvilinear forms that shared much in common

11
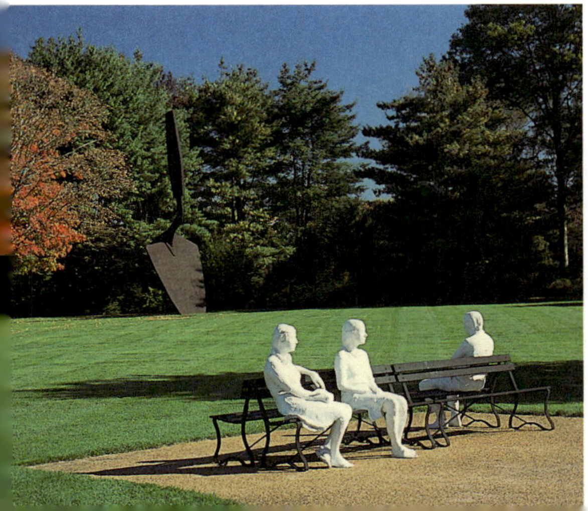

11
Edward D. Stone Jr. and Russell Page, Donald M. Kendall Sculpture Gardens, PepsiCo World Headquarters, Purchase, New York, 1980+, with George Segal's Three People on Four Benches *(1979) and Claes Oldenburg and Coosje van Bruggen's* Trowel II *(1976)*

12
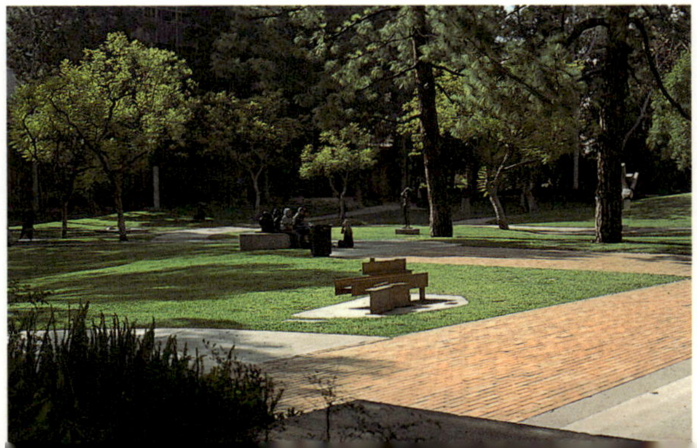

12
Ralph Cornell, Franklin D. Murphy Sculpture Garden, UCLA, 1969: view looking southwest toward the jacarandas and pines with Anthony Caro's Halfway *(1971)*

13
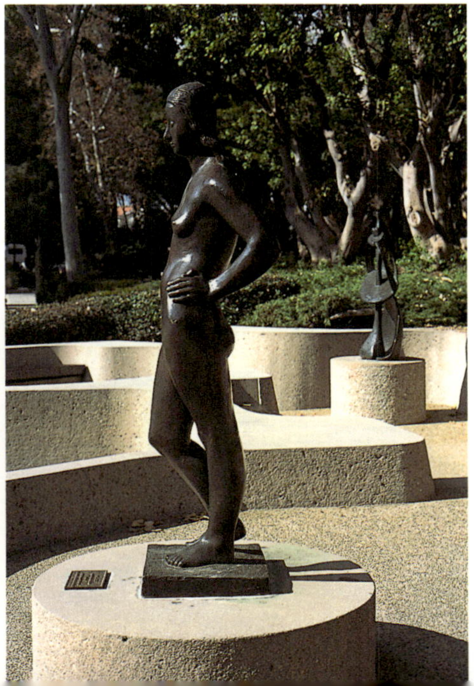

13
Ralph Cornell, Franklin D. Murphy Sculpture Garden, UCLA, 1969: biocubic seating areas as supports for sculpture, with Gerhard Marcks's Freya *(1950) and Alexander Archipenko's* Queen of Sheba *(1961)*

with Cornell's matrix for the sculpture collection in its bulky concrete railings, its use of the bridge, and its curvilinear surfaces (FIG. 15).

At the time of design Cornell did not know which pieces would occupy the garden, much less where they would be positioned. But he and Chancellor Murphy agreed that each work should look as if it had always existed in that place.[5] This lacuna is endemic to sculpture garden design. For example, the pieces to be displayed in the sculpture garden at the Museum of Fine Arts, Houston, were not known to its designer, Isamu Noguchi, although he could anticipate their scale and the probable inclusion of freestanding works, reliefs, and other pieces supported by walls.[6] In Jerusalem, Noguchi designed for a specific collection donated by the showman Billy Rose, but he knew—and hoped—that there would be more and better pieces acquired in future years.[7] In no way, however, could Noguchi foresee that one of James Turrell's Skyspaces would be installed within one of the earthen cusps he had shaped to create more flat land for display (FIG. 16). Even in a recent project such as the 2003 Nasher Sculpture Center Garden in Dallas, designed by Peter Walker Partners, the core collection was certain to grow in coming years (FIG. 17). And today, given the scale of much contemporary sculpture, accommodating future acquisitions becomes more problematic.[8] It must be kept in mind that, unless a collection is fixed at the time of design, the ultimate reading of the artwork will always be in flux—especially if the collection and curators change and the landscape matures.

Because so much rests on the curator's use of the landscape matrix, it is no exaggeration to say that he or she becomes the landscape's codesigner. One might even argue that the installation of the collection is of greater consequence than the design of the landscape itself. The landscape is the frame, but the setting and counterpoising of the sculptures constitute the picture—together with the vegetation and walls, of course. As with a voice in a choir, however, the collective effect may override the individual effort. Viewing a sculpture garden is unlike listening to a choir, however, in that it gives us the opportunity to engage a single piece, a group, or the whole—on a single visit or on a daily basis over many years.

Sculpture on Campus

Since classical antiquity, sculpture has served two principal uses. The first use integrated figurative or ornamental patterns with architectural forms, enlivening the friezes of temples and civic buildings and gracing them with pictorial content. The second use imbued the object-sculpture with the status of effigy, a freestanding statue of a deity or ancestor perhaps, carefully positioned within the home, civic building, or forum. In medieval times sculpture embellished the great portals of the French cathedrals with elaborate iconographic programs that recast the doors to the church as an entrance to the divine realm (FIG. 18). In this application art served both syntactic and semantic purposes. Syntactically it articulated the flow of structural ribs and surfaces by which the nave was spanned; semantically it wedded a narrative program to the building's fabric. Those two applications, the engaged and the freestanding, continued well into

14
Thomas Church, Donnell garden, Sonoma County, California, 1947

15
Garrett Eckbo, Union Bank Plaza, Los Angeles, 1968

16
Isamu Noguchi, Billy Rose Sculpture Garden, Israel Museum, Jerusalem, 1965

17
Peter Walker Partners, Nasher Sculpture Center Garden, Dallas, Texas, 2003, with Barbara Hepworth's Squares with Two Circles *(1963)*

18
West portal, Bourges Cathedral, France, thirteenth century

19
Henry Hobson Richardson, Trinity Church, Boston, 1896

14

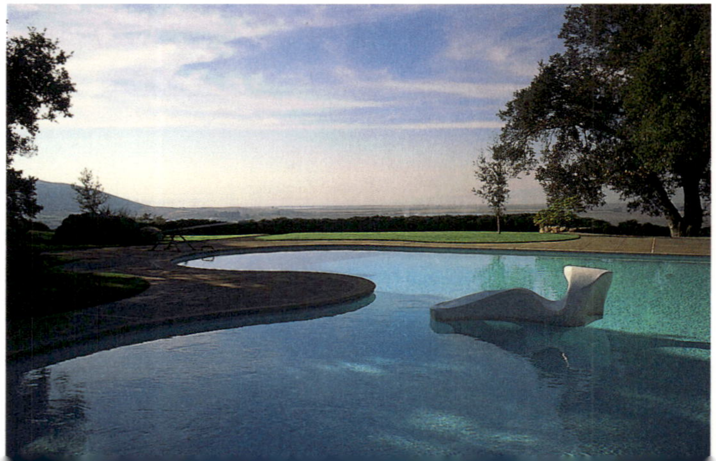

15

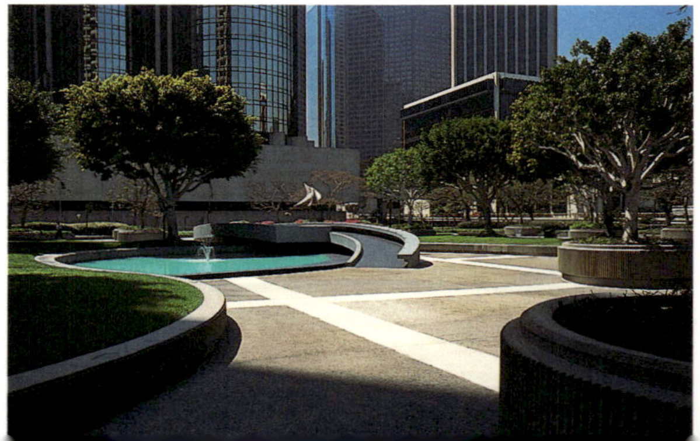

1

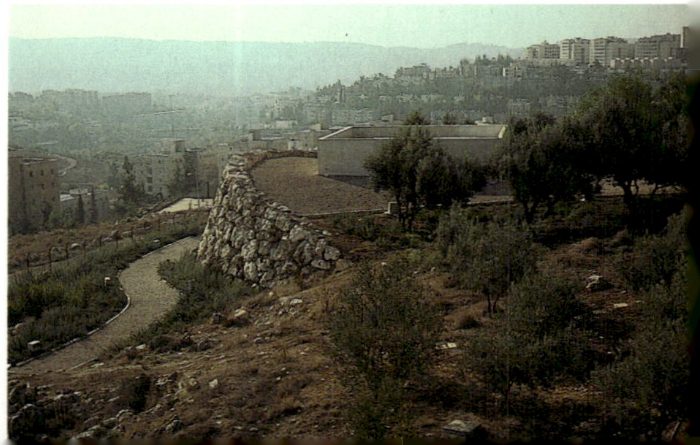

the twentieth century. But architectural modernism—with its concomitant rejection of ornamentation, especially figurative or vegetal ornamentation—dealt a deathblow to the firm integration of sculpture and architecture.

As early as 1908 the Viennese architect Adolf Loos had asserted that ornament is crime. "The evolution of culture," Loos proclaimed in a celebrated essay, "is synonymous with the removal of ornament from objects of daily use."[9] There were counterarguments to be sure, and Loos's call was left largely unheeded. The American architect Louis Sullivan, some decades before Loos, had himself assured his readers that ornament was acceptable and even necessary to the making of great architecture. But, Sullivan asserted, rather than being applied after the building's design had been determined, like icing on a cake, ornament needed to be "integral" to the idea and form of the building.[10] He remains one of the great nineteenth-century designers of ornament, and although the decorative elements of his buildings assume a life of their own independently of their architectural setting, they achieve greater vibrancy when viewed in situ.[11]

Given its embrace of Renaissance values, Beaux-Arts classicism at the turn of the twentieth century treated sculpture as an important feature of its architecture, as did the Romanesque Revival. The modeling on H. H. Richardson's Trinity Church in Boston, for example—like that on McKim, Mead, and White's neoclassical Boston Public Library, which faces it across Copley Square—enriched its surfaces while conveying to the celebrant the architect's message of history and belief (FIG. 19).[12] Richardson favored John La Farge as his artistic collaborator; Charles McKim, Augustus Saint-Gaudens. But in these architectural styles, these returns to architectures and practices past, one glimpses a last gasp soon extinguished by the planar architecture of modernism, with its severe surfaces of steel, aluminum, and glass.

In conjunction with this shifting of architectural form, sculpture became even more detached and independent, both within and without the building. A mural or other artwork might enliven the reductive modernist surfaces, which the public generally found cold and untoward. Over time it became common, almost the norm, to pair a building set back from the street with a plaza set before it. In response, sculpture moved outdoors as a symbol, a marker, a sign of completion and good taste—and at times as the last vestige of nonorthogonal form and color. One thinks here of Alexander Calder's brilliant orange *Flamingo* (FIG. 20), which occupies Chicago's Federal Center Plaza, a space defined by Ludwig Mies van der Rohe's dour buildings of black steel and glass—or perhaps Isamu Noguchi's red cube, tilted on one point, commanding a plaza within the architectural caverns of lower Manhattan. These sculptures tended to take form as singular pieces set in space; in some instances they injected a single spark of energy into an otherwise lifeless plaza or street. More often, however, they contributed little to making their settings more visually stimulating, or more enjoyable as a physical experience.

17
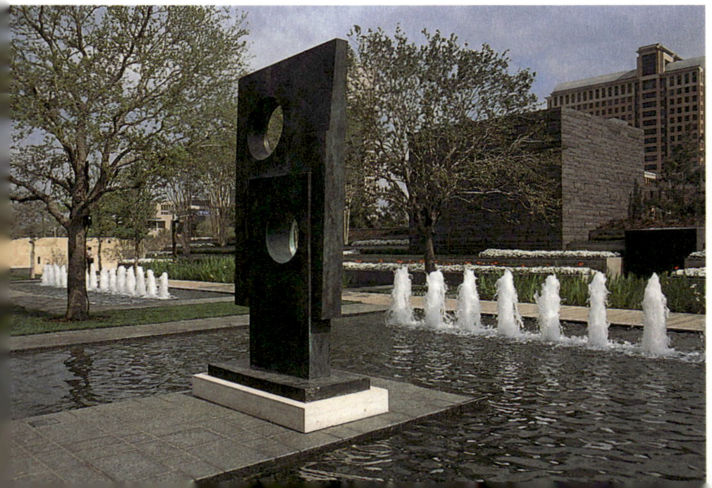

18
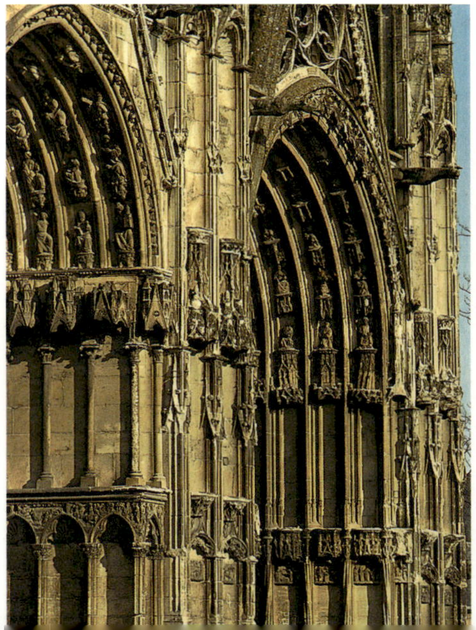

19
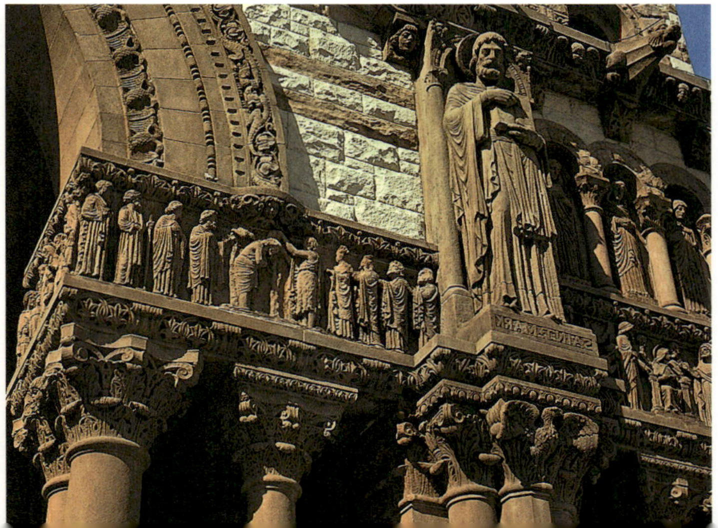

University campuses in the postwar era evolved within this architectural climate. Historically campus sculpture comprised statues commemorating a person or an event—often the "Gift of the Class of '09." But campaigns to increase the presence of the arts on campus, particularly as a countermeasure to the rise of the sciences after the launch of *Sputnik*, introduced considerable numbers of sculptures to the university environment. Many of these pieces remained as individual works set within a sylvan or plaza setting. But some campuses developed collections impressive enough in size and quality to constitute museums in and of themselves. The UCLA collection is one case in point, although the works are concentrated in a single area.

Ambitious programs to distribute artworks throughout academic surroundings are represented by the Stuart Collection at the University of California, San Diego, and the Manilow Sculpture Park at Governors State University in University Park, south of Chicago. The Governors State collection developed from an exhibition organized in 1976 by the university's departing president, William Engbretson.[13] The exhibition, *The Sculptor, the Campus, and the Prairie*, brought a number of monumental works to the campus for the first time; donations and endowments allowed the university to retain these pieces to form the core of the new collection. Over the next decades additional sculptures, many of them conceived as site-specific works, augmented these modest beginnings. Among them Mary Miss's *Field Rotation* (1982) and Bruce Nauman's *House Divided* (1983) stand out as particularly impressive examples. *Field Rotation* is a centrifugal work that draws in the surrounding landscape with its pinwheeling constructions of pits, planes, and towers (FIG. 21). *House Divided*, in contrast, is more centripetal, luring the visitor into its meager interior space through the contrast of solid and void (FIG. 22). Both pieces, each of architectural scale, operate as markers within the landscape, creating a network of visual destinations that guide us, through dead reckoning, as we negotiate the campus.

The Stuart Collection at the University of California, San Diego, was the product of an initiative begun in 1983 that drew upon funding from a variety of sources, among them the Stuart Foundation, the university itself, and other agencies.[14] Most of the works are specific to the campus; many are specific to the site. The collection is impressive in its diversity, ranging from relatively singular artworks such as Terry Allen's lead-covered talking *Trees* (1986) to Alexis Smith's *Snake Path* (1992), which conflates a hillside walkway with a mosaic snake, and Robert Irwin's *Two Running Violet V Forms* (1983), in which planes of chain-link fencing (which was originally magenta but is now light blue) mark the passage of the university community on walkways traversing a eucalyptus grove (FIG. 23). Depending on the direction and intensity of the sunlight, the blue fencing either stands in strong contrast to the trees or disappears completely among them. Its identity and effect truly depend upon the conditions of being outdoors. The Murphy Sculpture Garden, in contrast to these other examples, features a collection that was more or less defined in its early years and enjoys a landscape designed with a regard for its size and materials.

20
Alexander Calder, Flamingo, *1974; painted steel; height: 53 ft. (16.15 m); Federal Center Plaza, Chicago*

21
Mary Miss, Field Rotation, *1981; wood, steel, gravel, earth; 60 x 60 x 7 ft. (18.3 x 18.3 x 2.1 m) on a five-acre site; Manilow Sculpture Park, Governors State University, University Park, Illinois*

20

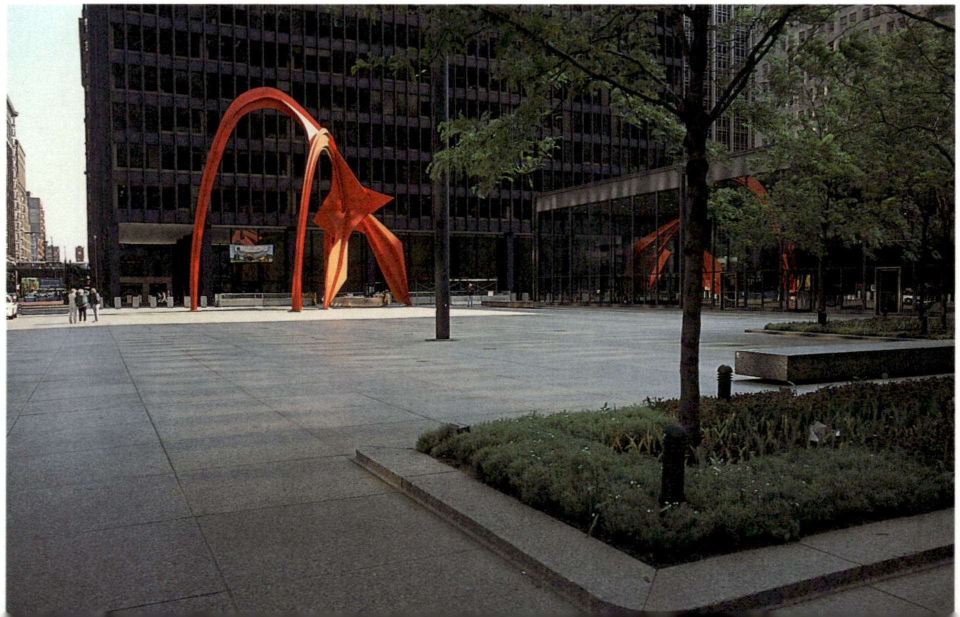

21

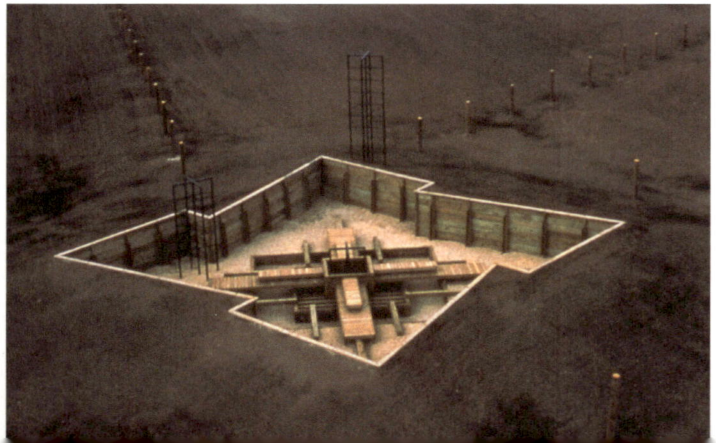

Making the Murphy

Ralph Cornell (1890–1970) had served as UCLA's supervising landscape architect for more than thirty years before he received the commission to design the Franklin D. Murphy Sculpture Garden.[15] As a key parcel of the north campus development, conceived and executed to a consequent level of detail, it was in many ways Cornell's most complex, sophisticated, and identifiable work on the campus. In 1937, when he was appointed supervising landscape architect, the university's fabric was concentrated in a small group of buildings clustered around Royce Hall, near the southern edge of the campus. A sizable arroyo, running roughly north-south, divided the campus. In correspondence and his reminiscences recorded in 1970, Cornell recounted the opportunities for campus expansion thwarted by this topographic divide.[16] Today we would probably regard the arroyo as a natural system meriting preservation, but at that time the depression was regarded as a hindrance to big ideas and grand schemes—especially if those schemes were predicated on a formal idiom.

In 1944 Cornell—working in collaboration with the campus supervising architect, David Allison—prepared a master plan for expanding the UCLA campus. They presented two versions—labeled the A and B schemes—but both required filling the arroyo to provide sufficient serviceable land for new construction.[17] A central quadrangle formed the core of the B plan; academic structures defined a semicircular road, much like the apse of a church writ large, that terminated each of the crossed axes structuring the scheme. Nothing much happened with either version during the war years, but with the return of peace in 1945, universities suffered increased pressures to accommodate returning servicemen and servicewomen under the GI Bill. In 1946 the state legislature appropriated more than $8 million for the development of the UCLA campus, and approved the task of filling the troublesome ravine.[18] The soil would be acquired by scraping the top of a hill north of Royce Hall, a process that landscape professionals call "cut and fill."[19] The Murphy Sculpture Garden today occupies a site that once lay near the northern head of the arroyo, a direct by-product of that eradication of the canyon. By the time the postwar boom occasioned new construction, the tenets of neoclassicism had relaxed their hold on the campus planners. In response the wartime schemes were jettisoned, and the more freely flowing spaces that characterized modernism came to be the norm.

Ralph Cornell received his bachelor's degree from Pomona College, outside Los Angeles. A course in botany with Charles Fuller Baker had sparked the student's interest in plant collecting and categorizing, and ultimately in landscape architecture.[20] He had partnered with a fellow student to sell avocado seeds—the fruit had not yet become popular north of the Mexican border—and the sale of this business netted sufficient funds to support his graduate study. He headed to Harvard University to earn his master's degree in landscape architecture, which he received in 1917. At that time, and for a decade thereafter, landscape architecture studies at Harvard were dominated by the more formal predilections of the Beaux-Arts method, but two prominent professors steered the curriculum with rigor: Sturgis Pray, who chaired the program, and Henry Vincent Hubbard, a

22
Bruce Nauman, House Divided, *1983; concrete; 360 x 240 x 186 in. (914.4 x 609.6 x 472.4 cm); Manilow Sculpture Park, Governors State University, University Park, Illinois*

23
Robert Irwin, Two Running Violet V Forms, *1983; plastic-coated fencing, stainless-steel poles, ice plant; height: 28 ft. (8.5 m), length: 196 ft. (59.7 m), poles 5 in. (12.7 cm) diameter on a 3000-square-foot (278.7-square-meter) site; Stuart Collection, University of California, San Diego*

22

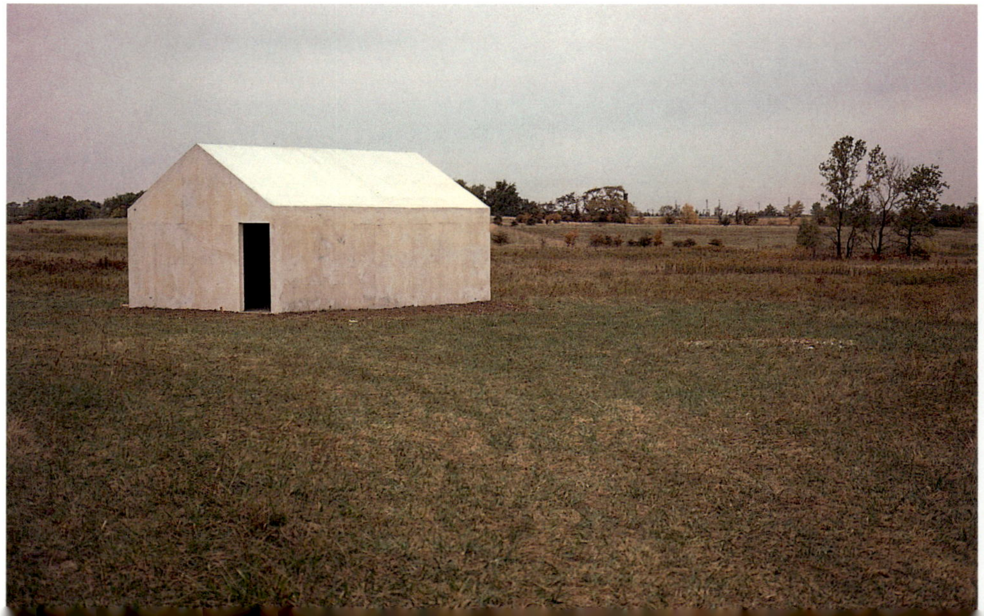

23

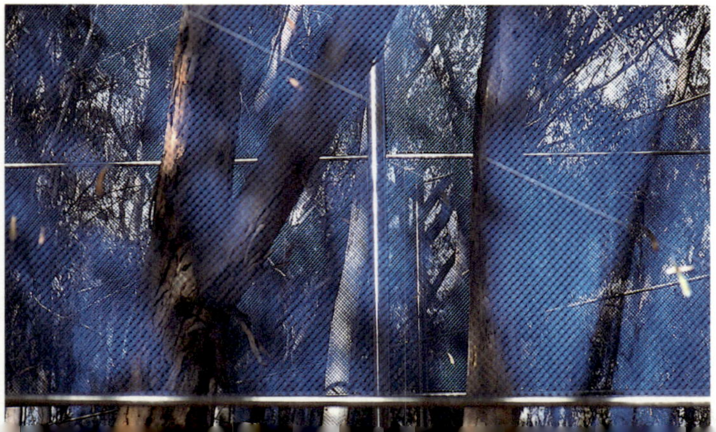

principal in the Olmsted firm. Hubbard, a prolific author, was coauthor with Theodora Kimball of what would become the key text on landscape design for decades to come: *An Introduction to the Study of Landscape Design*, first published in 1917.[21]

After a short tenure working in an office in Toronto, Cornell enlisted for military service and served in the combat infantry in France and Belgium during World War I. With demobilization he returned to Los Angeles and opened his own practice in 1919, reported to be the first in the city to be run by an academically trained landscape architect.[22] As he had spent the better part of four years in Pomona during his college studies, he was intimately familiar with the natural and physical environment of the area. In 1919, with virtually no professional experience to his credit, Cornell was solicited to serve as consulting landscape architect for the Pomona College campus and its surroundings, a position he would hold, remarkably, until 1969. It was this work on the Pomona campus, Cornell believed, that led to his appointment as supervising landscape architect for UCLA.[23]

In general, Cornell's designs were thoughtful, respectful, and representative of a highly qualified and experienced practitioner. Campus work is rarely spectacular; it is more about thinking of the whole while executing the piece, as the landscape is the matrix that binds the disparate architecture of the campus together. Architecture is of its time; landscape architecture shares that characteristic to a lesser degree. The inherent timeless quality of the tree, the shrub, and the flower makes it easier to achieve a sense of unity with vegetation than with buildings—unless the architects are in accord or unreasonably stringent demands are placed upon them to conform to the shapes, forms, and materials of architectures past.

24

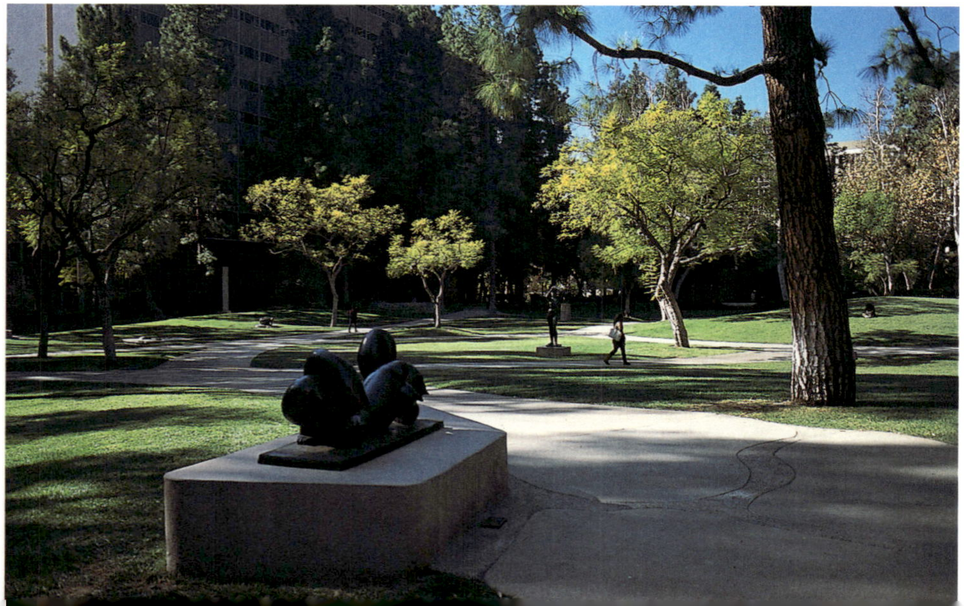

In the 1960s, before the project began, the land now occupied by the Murphy Sculpture Garden was a dusty parking lot. The buildings that surround it today were already built or under construction at the time. It would seem logical that the display of outdoor sculpture would be a welcome complement to the plaza fronting what was then Dickson Art Center.[24] But this path was not taken. In discussions with Murphy, and presumably the campus architect, it was determined that the sculpture garden would be located south of the Dickson center. It would be the signature feature of the North Campus Plan, as the project was known.

The buildings bounding the garden's site did not offer Cornell an easy solution. The principal mass of the Dickson Art Center was tall but set back from what was to become the sculpture garden, relieving to some degree the effects of its mass. To the south, however, the glassy bulk of Bunche Hall threw the balance of the space out of whack, although, being raised on columns, the building did create an almost monumental gateway into the proposed sculpture garden. The building's height also guaranteed that it would cast a prominent shadow on much of the garden much of the day, however. To the east, the Graduate School of Management was softer in aspect and a bit removed from the other structures of the cluster and thus presented less of a problem.[25] To the west, the four stories of the Research Library and the run of Macgowan Hall—the performing arts wing of the arts center to the north—offered a scale more sympathetic to the open space destined to become the Murphy project.

Cornell believed that his task centered on the making of space rather than form. In an undated introduction to an exhibition of his work, he stated: "Being a fine art, landscape architecture seeks the unities of good design. It strives for beauty through the unity of design, seeking rhythm, repetition, balance, sequence, harmony, accent, and above all proper space composition. Being a fine art its vocabulary is the same as sculpture, architecture, painting, and music."[26] Creating a landscape that would be a work of art in itself was his goal when designing the Murphy Sculpture Garden. Murphy, too, had his own idea for the garden, primarily that it should embody "a balance between the creativity of nature and the creativity of man."[27]

24
Ralph Cornell, Franklin D. Murphy Sculpture Garden, UCLA, 1969: central area with hillock, with Henri Laurens's Autumn *(1948)*

25
Ralph Cornell, Franklin D. Murphy Sculpture Garden, UCLA, 1969: northeast entrance terrace

At the start of the garden's design the collection itself was nascent, although Murphy's vision for it was strongly focused. Most of the works were and would be about the size of the human body, and thus a certain intimacy would be required to engage the visitor. The material for most of the artworks was bronze, dark and somewhat mute, whose aesthetic effect benefited from the presence of sunlight. There were also pieces in granite and stainless steel, however, and these demanded their own particular considerations. As the site occupied the epicenter of the north campus, pedestrian circulation was an important consideration; students would traverse the site in all directions as they marched from building to building and entered or left the campus proper (FIG. 24). Circulation through Bunche Hall acknowledged the north-south pathway that skirted the west side of the former arroyo—a strong path but perhaps not a true axis—ending some few steps up in the plaza fronting Dickson Art Center. In Cornell's scheme a straight, bridgelike walk directs the through circulation from the central campus to the steps of Dickson Art Center. Paired with the elevated promenade along the flank of Macgowan Hall, it became the most heavily trafficked route, allowing the sculpture garden's green areas to be more removed and conducive to introspection and the individual. These were the programmatic and site considerations that Cornell acknowledged in his design for a landscape for art.

Viewed as a planning strategy, the sculpture garden is typical for its time. Seen as a total design, however, it is a unique work. In plan the shape of the space was basically rectangular, and in each of its corners Cornell used shapes that were essentially rectangles to effect a transition between the orthogonal geometry of the architecture and the naturalism or biocubic vocabulary of the central garden (FIG. 25). The rectangular concrete slabs serve as a kind of launch or arrival pad, the stepping-off points for the subsidiary circulation. The walks that appear so free and curvilinear are basically diagonals crossing the garden: one path runs northeast to southwest; two more support movement from northwest to southeast, trapping between them the highest hillock within the garden.

"I wanted something expansive," recalled Murphy, "so Ralph conceived a garden that caught a sense of movement in the terrain as it moved over the hillocks."[28] Cornell modeled the earth and used these elevations purposefully to energize the topography and heighten the experience within the garden—to create long views that would play against shorter regards directed toward the sculpture. In addition, the mounds diminish the visual prominence of the retaining walls that support the terrace and promenade along the south side of Macgowan Hall—a good eight feet above garden level. In all, the shaping of the land—the filled land that had been flat and characterless before the start of construction—became the foundation for the landscape's design.

Then came the primary vegetation. The garden's predominant surface material is grass, long regarded as the most attractive and welcoming of ground covers. Cornell possessed an expert knowledge of plants and had even begun his academic studies and early employment with courses and work assignments in botany.[29] His botanical experiences had spanned nearly fifty years, and he had written scores of articles and even a book about them.[30] In his youth he had worked in the desert east of Palm Springs, at one point helping to develop a citrus crop, at another time sowing the seeds of what would become the extensive date farms in the area. As campus landscape architect at Pomona College and UCLA, Cornell used trees and vegetation as vehicles for cohering campus buildings heterogeneous in period and style. He believed that architectural style and construction manner must necessarily change with the years, but this heterogeneity in vocabulary normally produced an environment unwelcome in its disjunctive spaces and vocabularies. In these situations

25

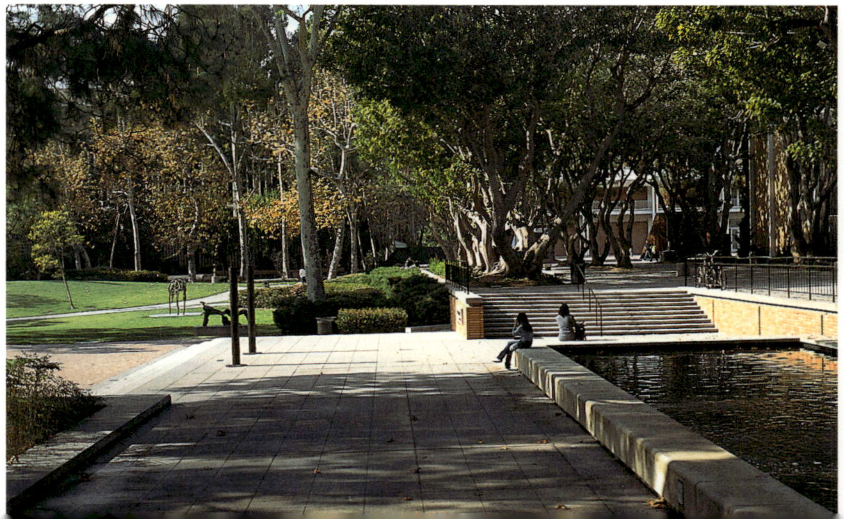

judicious planting could mitigate any disparities in mass, materials, and manner:

> *Your planting is not just putting in flowers or interesting things. But it is trying to set off the architecture, augment it, help it where it needs it and supplement the form and accent which it attempts or achieves... in regard to the north campus here, five architects, five buildings, then you keep saying that the landscape will pull it together. Well, it may do so.... I think it does because it forms a cohesive treatment which creates views and vistas and screens out defects and gives spaciousness. And so your landscape design is just as functional, is just as important as anything else.*[31]

Bunche Hall continued to trouble Cornell. Built in 1964 to designs by Maynard Lyndon, the eleven-story building, with its substantial mass, shaded much of the garden from midmorning through the afternoon. Nothing in the garden's design could dispel the problem of the shadows. But to reduce the effect of the building's tall brown-glass facade, Cornell planted a stand of Canary Island pines (*Pinus canariensis*), whose height and evergreen mass also afforded a transition to the shorter shrubbery and ultimately to the lawn areas below. A corresponding pine grove screened the west facade of the Graduate School of Management, set diagonally across the garden. In their strength and height the pines assumed the role of an armature for the scheme, firmly anchoring two of its corners. The second anchor took the form of a linear arrangement rather than a clump, a handsome allée of coral trees (*Erythrina caffra*) paralleling the south facade of Macgowan Hall. In summer, the dense canopies of the trees, which bloom an intense lipstick red, buffered the brick and concrete facade; in leaf they formed a colonnade that directed pedestrian movement along the northern edge of the site. In winter their highly sculptural trunks sketched a visual labyrinth of shadow patterns that fell equally upon walls and walks. In a deft move, Cornell set off two bays of the coral tree allée as an independent grove that simultaneously continued the rhythm and mass of the promenade while partially enclosing the plaza fronting Dickson Art Center. Like an iceberg floating adrift from its parent glacier, this group of four trees was at once a pivot between the two axes set perpendicularly, and the pivot between the plaza and the sculpture garden.

Cornell planted the garden with a number of species, including the jacaranda (*Jacaranda acutifolia*), which offers a soft violet flower in late spring, and concentrations of California sycamore (*Platanus racemosa*), mixed with redwoods (*Sequoia sempervirens*) and eucalyptus (*Eucalyptus maculata*). After blooming, the jacaranda's multipartite leaves, a soft yellow-green in color, sport a delicately textured canopy that graces a handful of the trees set informally around the garden's curving paths. Larger and more massive is the Californian variety of the American sycamore, whose selection was deliberate: "California sycamore is rather prone to picturesque growth. If we had used the oriental plane instead of this we would have had a much tighter, more cylindrical, compact mass. We used the California sycamore because of that informal tendency.... But I also feel that the informality of the California sycamore adds to the appearance and helps it."[32] The qualities Cornell sought are especially apparent during the winter months, when the structure of the trunks

26
George Tsutakawa; Obos 69, *1969; silicon bronze; height: 84 in. (51.5 cm); Franklin D. Murphy Sculpture Garden, UCLA*

27
Ralph Cornell, Franklin D. Murphy Sculpture Garden, UCLA, 1969: sheltered seating area

26

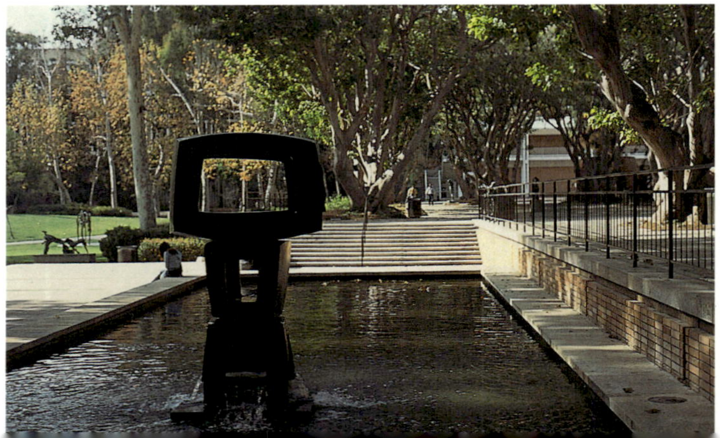

27

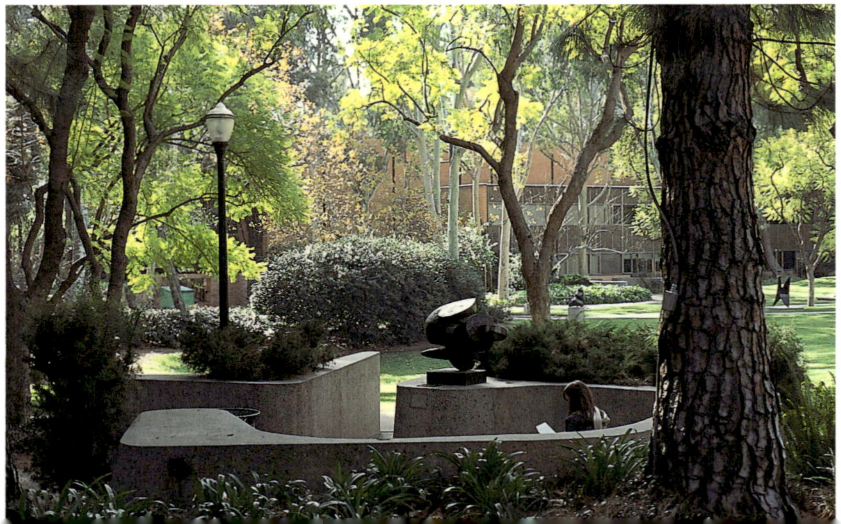

29

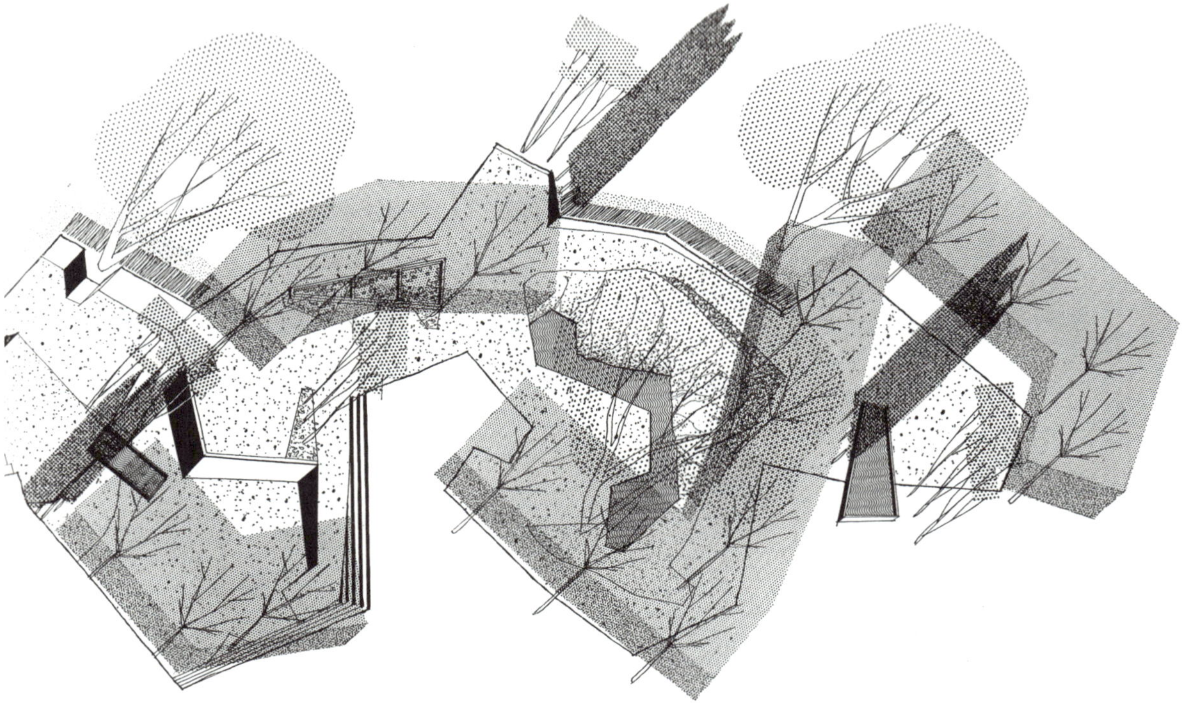

28
Robert Royston, wading pool, Mitchell Park, Palo Alto, California, 1957
29
James Rose, "Free Form," 1958
30
Ralph Cornell, Franklin D. Murphy Sculpture Garden, UCLA, 1969: concrete seating forms with sloping bush-hammered sides and smooth, trowel-finished tops

28

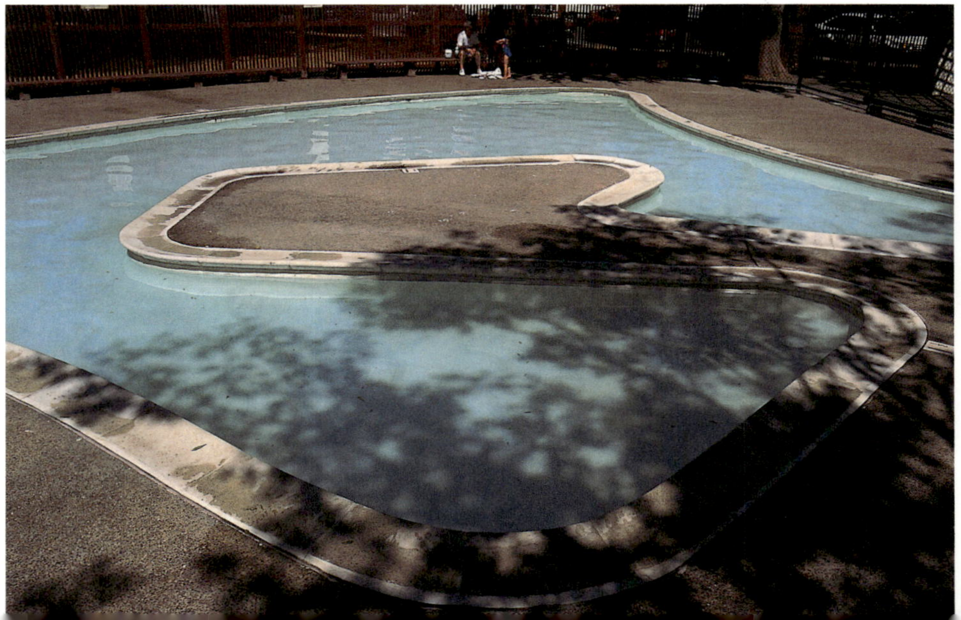

30

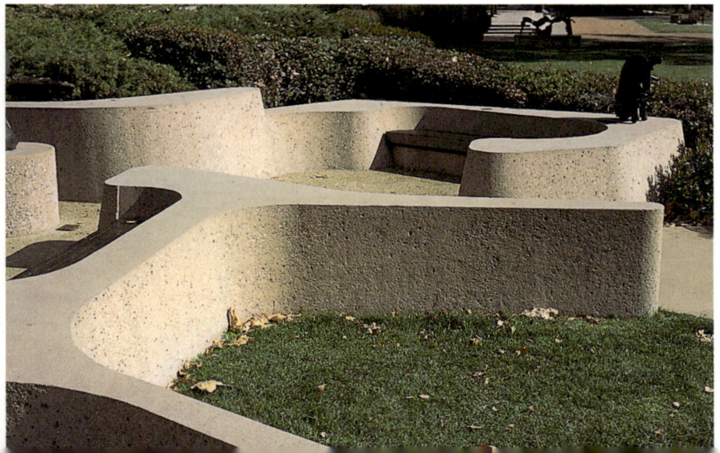

and branches is more evident due to the loss of leaves, a texture further enriched by the mottled colors of the tree's bark. A variety of shrubs complete the palette and complement the trees that provide the garden's primary arboreal structure.

The shallow pool, an architectonic anchor at the garden's northeast corner, is removed from the central green (FIG. 26). Set beneath the dense canopies of coral trees and pines, its surface remains shaded most of the day; its fountain—designed by the artist George Tsutakawa—is an unadorned affair of stacked cubic volumes of bronze with two sides of each left open. From these water spills in sheets into the pool below, a source at once of sound and animation.

Cornell first delineated each of the corners with brick terrace areas that gave way to the softer shapes of the garden (SEE FIG. 12). In addition to the curving pathways and the softly rolling earth forms, he proposed sculptured constructions as foils for the prismatic forms of the surrounding architecture. On the perimeter of the garden he positioned six sets of concrete enclosures with wooden benches that do double duty as seating areas and bases for smaller artworks (FIG. 27). The vocabulary is "biocubic," a cross between the pure biomorphism so characteristic of the landscape architecture of the 1940s and 1950s and the segmented forms of synthetic cubism. It too was an idiom that pervaded modernist landscape architecture, although its use tended to follow the biomorphic years, becoming popular in the late 1950s and 1960s. Robert Royston's design for Mitchell Park in Palo Alto, completed in 1957, featured a playground, several of whose features were executed in this manner—particularly the wading pool, with its segmented yet flowing perimeter (FIG. 28). The contemporaneous work of the landscape architect James Rose also relied to a great degree on the biocubic manner, a fondness evident in both his drawings and his built work (FIG. 29). Rose, in fact, would retain his attachment to the vocabulary through much of his life, at least well into the 1980s.[33]

In Cornell's hands biocubism found a sophisticated expression. Five of the seating areas take the form of a single or double horseshoe, each configured with its back to the boundary of the garden and opening to the central green (FIG. 30). The material is concrete throughout, but concrete used in a highly refined way. For one, an integral color warms the tone of the material and denies associations with the cold gray normally associated with it.[34] The sides of the enclosures have been battered at a slight angle to soften their effect, and the concrete has been bush-hammered to reveal the aggregate and texture of the vertical planes. In contrast, the top surfaces have been given a "trowel coat" to be smooth to the eye and the finger.

31
Ralph Cornell, Franklin D. Murphy Sculpture Garden, UCLA, 1969: biomorphic concrete paving slabs

32
Ralph Cornell, Franklin D. Murphy Sculpture Garden, UCLA, 1969: David Smith's Cubi XX *(1964) and Deborah Butterfield's* Pensive *(1996)*

31

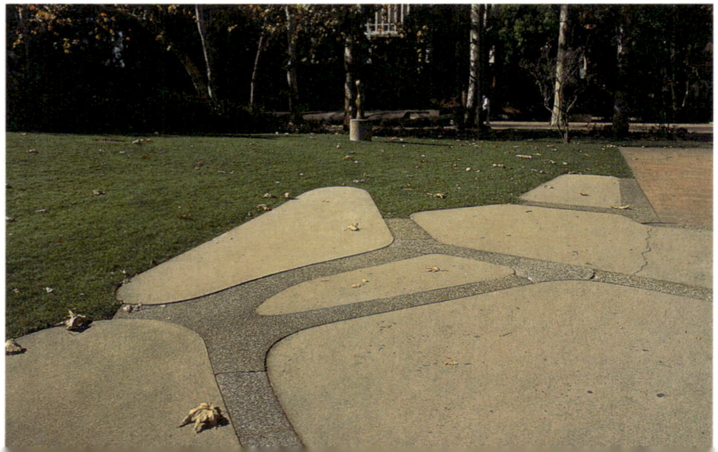

32

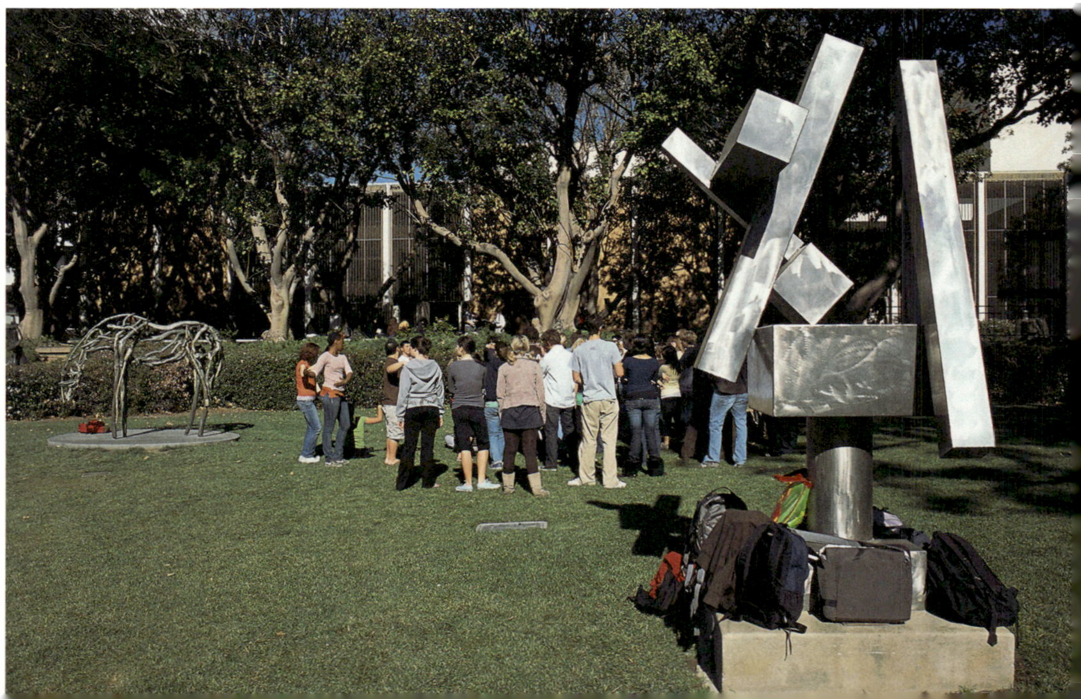

The paving within the garden is uniformly of concrete but also treated in a variety of finishes. The paths, the minor "terraces," and the bases for the sculpture all share the same shapes and warm tint. The terraces are in essence merely the widening of the circulation paths, but articulated in a biomorphic vocabulary that resembles a compression of water lily pads or cellular structure (FIG. 31). The linear areas between the pads use an exposed aggregate to distinguish the two types of surfaces.

One of the distinctive characteristics of the Murphy Sculpture Garden is that it is open throughout the day and night, and throughout the year. Nighttime lighting was a consideration, and on this subject Murphy seems to have had the final word: "'Ralph, from now on'—this is when we were working on the north campus court—'I want everything to be overplanted, overseated, and underlighted.'"[35] At night, the garden lives up to Murphy's wish, and only the principal paths are lit. The remainder of the garden and its art remain mute and nearly invisible, which is to some degree unfortunate.

From the very inception of the project, Murphy believed that the sculpture garden should remain accessible at all times. "When I was trying to sell the idea of a sculpture garden to the regents of the university...I kept saying I wanted it to be used the way Europeans use their public spaces. You go to the Piazza di Spagna in Rome, you know, and there are kids playing in the fountain by Bernini. 'I want it to be used and I want it to be loved,' I kept saying."[36] On the one hand, a sculpture garden on a university campus is hardly an urban plaza, and to compare the two is somewhat fatuous. On the other hand, the location of the garden within a confluence of pedestrian circulation routes and well-populated buildings does guarantee a continuous flow of people throughout a good part of the day and into the evening. If not a true urban plaza, it is without question a campus nexus.

Unrestricted admittance creates potential problems of graffiti and vandalism, especially in times of student unrest. During the turmoil of the 1960s there was considerable pressure to fence off the garden to protect the works of art from attack. But Murphy was adamant that the garden should remain welcoming at all times. Should it be fenced off, he reasoned, the students would regard the garden as the province of the Establishment, creating greater provocation for assault. It remained unfenced; it remained open, twenty-four hours a day, every day. Although the campus buildings around it were marred by abundant graffiti, the sculpture garden was left unmolested, proving Murphy's contention.

Two men played the principal roles in creating the Franklin D. Murphy Sculpture Garden: the landscape architect Ralph Cornell and the chancellor Franklin D. Murphy, for whom the garden would be named. But from its inception the garden has been the province of the academic community and the community of those who visit each year. And there is that third community, the community established by the interrelation, in a most handsome way, among art, landscape architecture, and building (FIG. 32). Cornell was awarded an honorary doctorate in 1972, some months after his death. Part of the citation reads: "You have almost magically transformed these once-barren hills into a camelot of beauty." He also managed to transform a dusty parking lot into a moving and significant landscape.

Notes

1 *I have explored this topic in greater detail in "A Sculpture for Sculpture," in* Isamu Noguchi: A Sculpture for Sculpture: The Lillie and Hugh Roy Cullen Sculpture Garden, *ed. Alison de Lima Greene (Houston: Museum of Fine Arts, 2006), 109–23.*

2 *For a comprehensive telling of the story of the Museum of Modern Art garden, see Mirka Beneš, "A Modern Classic: The Abby Aldrich Rockefeller Sculpture Garden," in* Philip Johnson and the Museum of Modern Art, *Studies in Modern Art, no. 6 (New York: Museum of Modern Art, 1998), 104–51.*

3 *John Beardsley,* A Landscape for Modern Sculpture: Storm King Art Center *(New York: Abbeville Press, 1985).*

4 *See Robert Irwin,* Being and Circumstance: Notes toward a Conditional Art *(Larkspur, Calif.: Lapis Press, 1985).*

5 *Murphy: "Cornell and I agreed that the sculpture should look as if it belonged on that particular spot, as if it had been there forever" (Paul Gardner, "Murphy's Secret Garden,"* Art News *84 [January 1985]: 14).*

6 *See Treib, "A Sculpture for Sculpture."*

7 *On the Rose Sculpture Garden, see Isamu Noguchi,* The Isamu Noguchi Garden Museum *(New York: Harry N. Abrams, 1987), 170–71; Isamu Noguchi,* A Sculptor's World *(New York: Harper & Row, 1968), 172–74, figs. 234–38; and Ana Maria Torres,* Isamu Noguchi: A Study in Space *(New York: Monacelli Press, 2000), 128–35.*

8 *Consider only, for example, the works of Richard Serra—which are large, heavy, and ponderous—and those of James Turrell—which are immovable and site-specific, instruments for seeing light and perceiving perception. For some of the problems inherent to making a sculpture garden today, see Jane Amidon, ed.,* Peter Walker and Partners: Nasher Sculpture Center Garden *(New York: Princeton Architectural Press, 2006).*

9 *Adolf Loos, "Ornament and Crime" (1908), reprinted in Yehuda Safran and Wilfried Wang, eds.,* The Architecture of Adolf Loos *(London: Arts Council of Great Britain, 1985), 100.*

10 *"I take it as self-evident that a building, quite devoid of ornament, may convey a noble and dignified sentiment by virtue of mass and proportion," Sullivan admitted in an essay on the subject published in 1892. To achieve "an organic system of ornamentation," however, "it should appear, when completed, as though by the outworking of some beneficent agency it had come forth from the very substance of the material and was there by the same right that a flower appears amid the leaves of its parent plant" ("Ornament in Architecture,"* Engineering Magazine, *August 1892; reprinted in Isabella Athey, ed.,* Louis H. Sullivan: Kindergarten Chats and Other Writings *(New York: George Wittenborn, 1947), 187, 189.*

11 *The Murphy collection contains an ornamental panel from Sullivan's Gage Building (Chicago, 1899, destroyed), but it is not displayed in the sculpture garden.*

12 *Trinity Church is regarded as Henry Hobson Richardson's masterpiece, the prime example of the Romanesque Revival, or what has also been termed Richardsonian Romanesque. Richardson himself tells the story of its design, construction, and decoration in a small pamphlet, "A Description of Trinity Church," presumably published at the time the construction was well under way. The architect died in 1886, and his successor firm continued to oversee the construction for another decade. See Theodore Stubbins Jr., "Richardson and Trinity Church: The Evolution of a Building,"* Journal of the Society of Architectural Historians *27 (December 1968) (reprint, unpaged).*

13 *"History of the Park," Nathan Manilow Sculpture Park at Governors State University, http://webserve.govst.edu/sculpture/history.html.*

14 *"About the Stuart Collection," Stuart Collection, University of California, San Diego, http://stuartcollection.ucsd.edu/StuartCollection/About%20Us.htm.*

15 *The primary sources for information on Cornell's life and career are Ralph D. Cornell, "Half a Century as a Southern California Landscape Architect," oral history transcript, interviewed by James V. Mink, Enid H. Douglass, and Richard K. Nystrom, 1967 (Los Angeles: Oral History Program, University of California, 1970), and the entire issue of* California Horticultural Journal *33 (October 1972), which was dedicated to Cornell's memory. His wife, Vera, contributed a personal biography of the landscape architect.*

16 *See Cornell, "Half a Century," 103–9.*

17 *The perspective drawings are dated September 7, 1944 (Cornell Papers, University of California, Los Angeles, Special Collections; hereafter CP/UCLA).*

18 *On August 15, 1944, Cornell wrote a confidential letter to J. W. Gregg, professor of landscape architecture at the University of California, Berkeley, and de facto state landscape architect. In this document Cornell establishes the importance of filling eight to ten acres of the ravine, and he values the land at $200,000: "The U.C.L.A. campus is split at its heart by a deep ravine over which a bridge was built to connect the bivalve halves of its area" (CP/UCLA). Gregg replied to Cornell on August 28, 1944, concurring but questioning the structural properties of the soils to be used for fill (CP/UCLA).*

19 *The source of the fill was established in an unsigned letter [from David C. Allison?], supervising architect, Los Angeles campus, to James H. Corley, comptroller, University of California, August 7, 1944: "This plan contemplates the removal of soil from the low hills north of Royce Hall and north of the Administration building, and the redistribution of this material in the canyon on each side of the bridge" (CP/UCLA).*

20 *Cornell regarded this encounter as formative ("Half a Century," 7–10).*

21 *Henry Vincent Hubbard and Theodora Kimball,* An Introduction to the Study of Landscape Design *(New York: Macmillan, 1917).*

22 *In a letter to William Wilson of the* Los Angeles Times, *dated June 23, 1975, Mrs. Ralph D. [Vera] Cornell wrote that Cornell was the "first professional landscape architect to open an office in the city of Los Angeles" (CP/UCLA).*

23 *Late in life Cornell told an interviewer that he probably became the campus landscape architect for UCLA because of what he had accomplished at Pomona, "which Dr. Sproul had liked and thought fine, or satisfactory from his viewpoint" ("Half a Century," 103).*

24 *Recently renovated, it is known today as the Broad Art Center.*

25 *Now the School of Public Policy.*

26 *"Landscape Architecture as a Fine Art," undated text board from exhibition (CP/UCLA).*

27 *Franklin Murphy, quoted in Gardner, "Murphy's Secret Garden," 13.*

28 *Quoted in Gardner, "Murphy's Secret Garden," 14.*

29 *In light of his early college education and professional experience, Cornell's belief that "he who enters the profession through the horticultural channel enters through the back door" is quite curious (minutes of meeting of American Society of Landscape Architects, Pacific Coast Chapter, San Francisco, April 2, 1934, San Francisco, H. W. Shepherd, secretary, 3; CP/UCLA).*

30 *See Ralph D. Cornell,* Conspicuous California Plants, with Notes on Their Garden Uses *(Pasadena, Calif.: San Pasqual Press, 1938); Cornell was also coauthor, with George Wharton James and Paul B. Popenoe, of* Date Culture in Southern California *(Los Angeles: Out West, [1917?]).*

31 *Cornell, "Half a Century," 225.*

32 *Ibid, 278–79.*

33 *On James Rose, see James Rose,* Creative Gardens *(New York: Reinhold, 1958), and Marc Snow,* Modern American Gardens—Designed by James Rose *(New York: Reinhold, 1967).*

34 *Cornell called the color, the product of a mineral pigment, "Uclan" buff ("Half a Century," 256).*

35 *Ibid.*

36 *Franklin Murphy, quoted in Diana Rico, "Garden Sprouts Sculptural Delights,"* Los Angeles Daily News, *L.A. Life section, August 26, 1984.*

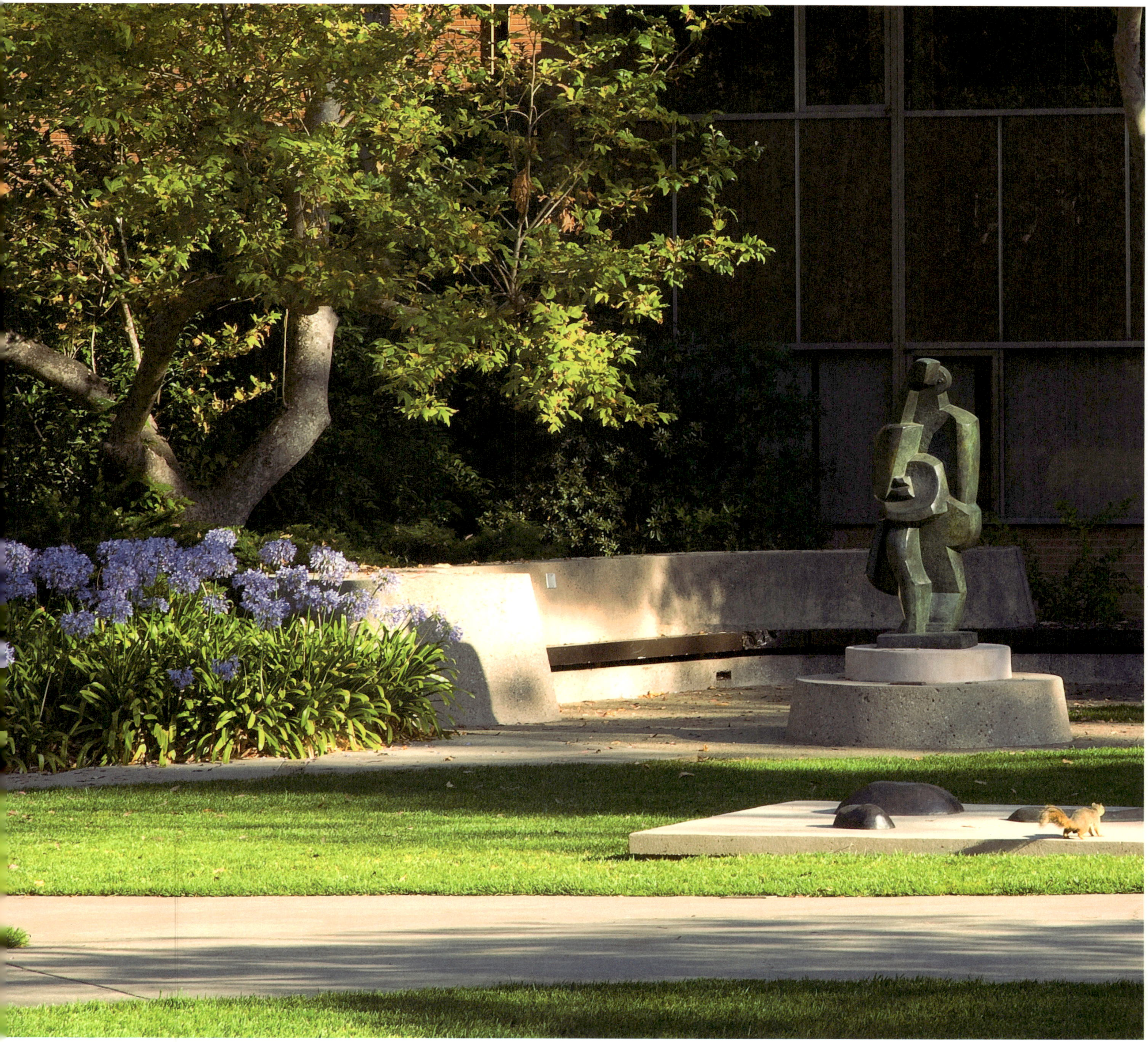

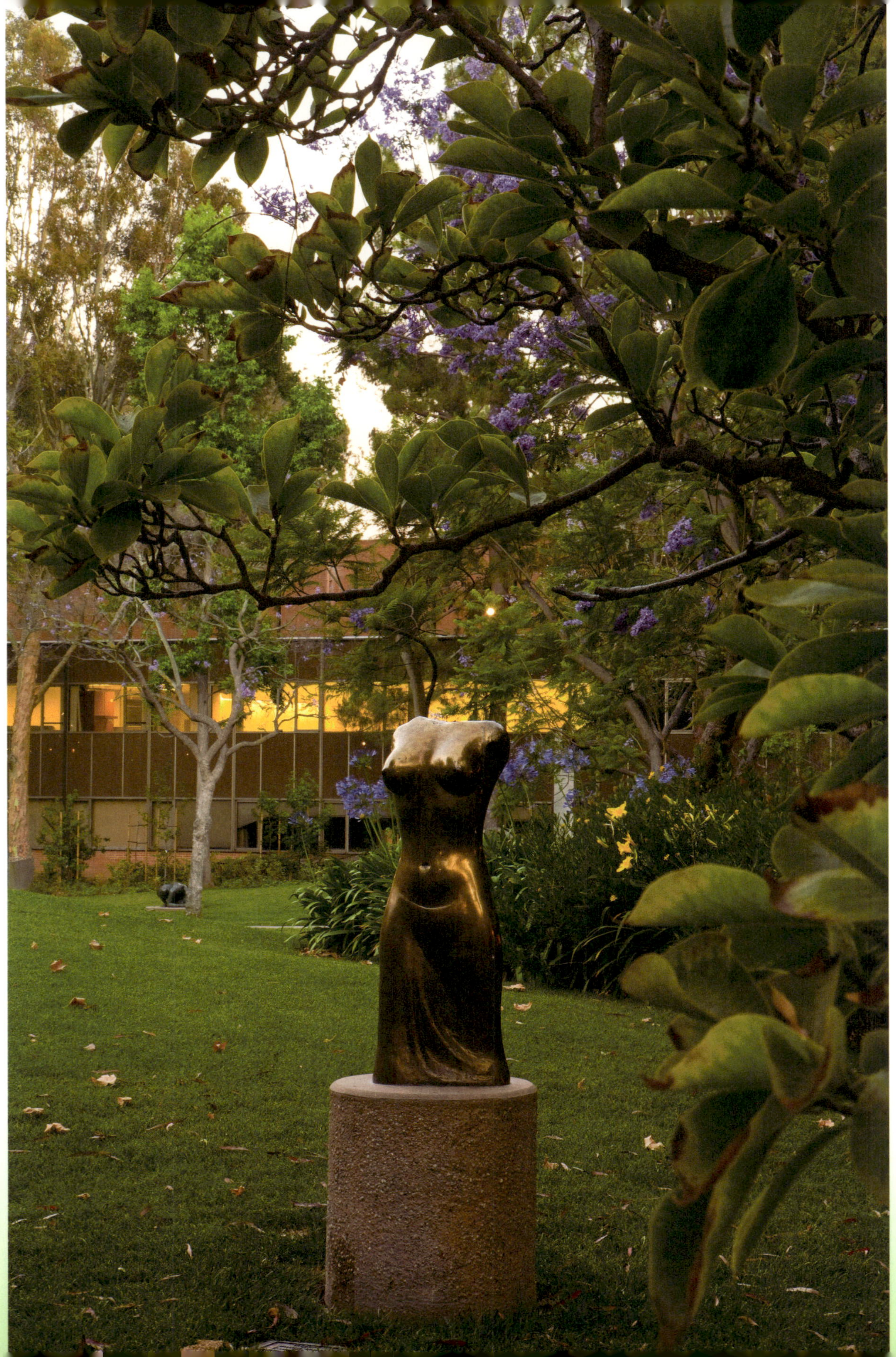

DONORS TO THE FRANKLIN D. MURPHY SCULPTURE GARDEN

The Ahmanson Foundation, Los Angeles
Anna Bing Arnold
Madame Marguerite Arp
Lisa and Ernest Auerbach
Elisabeth Roblee Augerson
Nancy Bacal
Elsie Browning Ballantyne
Ted and Jarma Bensinger
David E. Bright
Mrs. David E. Bright
Mr. and Mrs. Sidney F. Brody
Alberto Burri
Deborah Butterfield
B. Gerald Cantor
B. G. Cantor Art Foundation
Mr. and Mrs. Arthur L. Caplan
Leo Cherne
Michael J. Connell Memorial Fund
Carol and Roy Doumani
Mrs. Charles E. Ducommun
Henry Ford II
Thomas A. Freiberg Family
Mrs. Robert E. Gross
Michael Hall, Esq.
Donald H. Karshan
Julianne Kemper
Lithuanian Alumni, Faculty, and Friends of UCLA
Mr. and Mrs. Walter McC. Maitland
Adam and Joan Mekler
Alett Mekler
Oscar and Judith Mekler
Judith H. Murphy
Evelyn A. Nerlove
The Nathaniel and Margaret Wentworth Owings Foundation
Mr. and Mrs. John Rex
Robert W. Sarnoff
Mr. and Mrs. Norton Simon
Vicci Sperry
Mr. and Mrs. Arthur Spitzer
Jean and Irving Stone
UCLA Alumni Association
UCLA Art Council
UCLA Graduating Class of 1967
Tim and Mani Van Kluyve
Hal Wallis Family
Mr. and Mrs. Jack Warner
Frederick Weisman Company
Frederick Weisman, Inc.
Marcia and Frederick Weisman
The Marcia Simon Weisman Foundation
Mr. and Mrs. Donald Winston
Several anonymous donors

SELECTED BIBLIOGRAPHY

General

Ashton, Dore. Modern American Sculpture. *New York: Harry N. Abrams, 1968.*

Beebe, Mary Livingstone, James Stuart DeSilva, and Robert Storr. Landmarks: Sculpture Commissions for the Stuart Collection at the University of California, San Diego. *New York: Rizzoli, 2001.*

Burlingham, Cynthia, and Elizabeth Shepherd, eds. In the Sculptor's Landscape: Celebrating Twenty-five Years of the Franklin D. Murphy Sculpture Garden. *Los Angeles: Wight Art Gallery and Grunwald Center for the Graphic Arts, University of California, 1993.*

Cornell, Ralph D. "Half a Century as a Southern California Landscape Architect." Oral history transcript, interviewed by James V. Mink, Enid H. Douglass, and Richard K. Nystrom, 1967. Los Angeles: Oral History Program, University of California, 1970.

Franklin D. Murphy Sculpture Garden, University of California, Los Angeles: An Annotated Catalog of the Collection. *Los Angeles: University of California, Los Angeles, 1978. Rev. ed., 1984.*

Hamilton, Andrew, and John B. Jackson. UCLA on the Move during Fifty Golden Years, 1919–1969. *[Los Angeles]: Ward Ritchie Press, [1969].*

McCarthy, Jane, and Laurily K. Epstein. A Guide to the Sculpture Parks and Gardens of America. *New York: Michael Kesend Publishing, 1996.*

Murphy, Franklin D. "My UCLA Chancellorship: An Utterly Candid View." Oral history transcript, interviewed by James V. Mink. Los Angeles: Oral History Program, University of California, 1976.

New British Painting and Sculpture. *Los Angeles: UCLA Art Galleries, 1968.*

Ritchie, Andrew C. Sculpture of the Twentieth Century. *New York: Museum of Modern Art, 1952.*

Wechsler, Jeffrey. Vanguard American Sculpture. *New Brunswick, N.J.: Rutgers University Art Gallery, 1979.*

Wight, Frederick Stallknecht. "Of Art and Exhibitions." Oral history transcript, interviewed by Bernard Galm. Los Angeles: Oral History Program, University of California, 1982.

X: A Decade of Collecting, 1965–1975. *Los Angeles: Los Angeles County Museum of Art, 1975.*

Oliver Andrews

Andrews, Oliver. Living Materials: A Sculptor's Handbook. *Berkeley: University of California Press, 1983.*

"Oliver Andrews." Oral history transcript, interviewed by George M. Goodwin, 1976–77. Los Angeles: Oral History Program, University of California, 1977.

Alexander Archipenko

Alexander Archipenko. *[Los Angeles]: Ward Ritchie Press, 1967.*

Jánszky, Katherine, and Nehama Guralnik. Alexander Archipenko: A Centennial Tribute. *Washington, D.C.: National Gallery of Art; Tel Aviv: Tel Aviv Museum, 1986.*

Karshan, Donald H. Archipenko: Content and Continuity, 1908–63. *Chicago: Kovler Gallery, 1968.*

Jean Arp

Giedion-Welcker, Carola. Jean Arp. *London: Thames & Hudson, 1957.*

Lejwa, Madeline. Jean Arp. *New York: Chalette International, 1975.*

Read, Herbert. The Art of Jean Arp. *New York: Harry N. Abrams, 1968.*

Soby, James Thrall. Arp. *New York: Museum of Modern Art, 1958.*

Leonard Baskin

Baskin, Leonard. Sculpture, Drawings, and Prints. *New York: George Braziller, 1970.*

Fern, Alan. Leonard Baskin. *Washington, D.C.: National Collection of Fine Arts, 1970.*

Jaffe, Irma B. The Sculpture of Leonard Baskin. *New York: Viking Press, 1980.*

Fletcher Benton

Neubert, George, et al. The New Constructivism of Fletcher Benton. *Lausanne: Acatos, 2001.*

Émile-Antoine Bourdelle

Émile-Antoine Bourdelle (1861–1929): Sculptures. *Montauban: Musée Ingres, 2000.*

Jianou, Tonel, and Michel Dufet. Bourdelle. *Paris: Editions d'Art, 1975.*

Alberto Burri

Nordland, Gerald. Alberto Burri Retrospective Exhibition. *Los Angeles: University of California, 1977.*

Deborah Butterfield

Gordon, Robert. Deborah Butterfield. *New York: Harry N. Abrams, 2003.*

Horses: The Art of Deborah Butterfield. *Coral Gables, Fla.: Lowe Art Museum, University of Miami; San Francisco: Chronicle Books, 1992.*

Alexander Calder

Calder. *Introduction by H. H. Arnason. New York: Viking Press, 1971.*

Lipman, Jean. Calder's Universe. *New York: Viking Press, 1976.*

Prather, Marla. Alexander Calder, 1898–1976. *Washington, D.C.: National Gallery of Art, 1998.*

Rower, A. S. C. Calder Sculpture. *Washington, D.C.: National Gallery of Art; New York: Universe, 1998.*

Anthony Caro

Anthony Caro: Drawing in Space: Sculptures from 1963 to 1988: The Last Judgement, 1995–1999. *Barcelona: Fundació Caixa Catalunya, 2002.*

Moorhouse, Paul, ed. Anthony Caro. *London: Tate Publishing, 2005.*

Rubin, William. Anthony Caro. *New York: Museum of Modern Art, [1975].*

Aldo Casanova

Aldo Casanova: A Retrospective. *Essay by Suzanne Muchnic. Claremont, Calif.: Ruth Chandler Williamson Gallery, Scripps College, 2002.*

Leo Cherne

Cherne, Leo. The Rest of Your Life. *New York: Doubleday, Doran & Co., n.d.*

Sorel Etrog

Restany, Pierre. Sorel Etrog. *Munich: Prestel, 2001.*

Claire Falkenstein

Claire Falkenstein: Structure and Flow: Works from 1950–1980. *West Hollywood, Calif.: Louis Stern Fine Arts, 2006.*

Eric Gill

Gill, Eric. Autobiography. *London: J. Cape, 1940.*

Robert Graham

Beal, Graham W. J., and George W. Neubert. Robert Graham: Statues. *Minneapolis: Walker Art Center, 1981.*

Robert Graham: The Duke Ellington Memorial in Progress. *Los Angeles: Los Angeles County Museum of Art, 1988.*

Dimitri Hadzi

Dimitri Hadzi: Recent Sculpture. *Introduction by Albert E. Elsen. New York: Gruenebaum Gallery, 1978.*

Richard Hunt

Liebermann, William S. Sculpture of Richard Hunt. *New York: Museum of Modern Art, 1971.*

Fritz Koenig

Fritz Koenig: Recent Sculptures. *Introduction by George W. Staempfli. New York: Staempfli, 1972.*

Gaston Lachaise

Kirstein, Lincoln. Gaston Lachaise: Retrospective Exhibition. *New York: Museum of Modern Art, 1935.*

Kramer, Hilton. The Sculpture of Gaston Lachaise. *New York: Eakins Press, 1967.*

Nordland, Gerald. Gaston Lachaise: The Man and His Work. *New York: George Braziller, 1974.*

———. Gaston Lachaise: Sculpture and Drawings. *Los Angeles: Los Angeles County Museum of Art, 1963.*

Henri Laurens

Henri Laurens. *Paris: Galerie Claude Bernard, 1960.*

Hofmann, Werner. The Sculpture of Henri Laurens. *New York: Harry N. Abrams, 1970.*

Laurens, Marthe. Henri Laurens: Sculpteur. *Paris: Pierre Beres, 1955.*

Wilhelm Lehmbruck

Heller, Reinhold. The Art of Wilhelm Lehmbruck. *Washington, D.C.: National Gallery of Art, 1972.*

Jacques Lipchitz

Hope, Henry R. The Sculpture of Jacques Lipchitz. *New York: Museum of Modern Art, 1954.*

Jacques Lipchitz: A Retrospective Selected by the Artist. *Los Angeles: UCLA Art Council, 1963.*

Lipchitz, Jacques. My Life in Sculpture. *New York: Viking Press, 1972.*

Pütz, Catherine. Jacques Lipchitz: The First Cubist Sculptor. *London: Paul Holberton Publishing in association with Lund Humphries, 2002.*

Anna Mahler

Anna Mahler. *Vienna: Paul Zsolnay, 1950.*

Gombrich, Ernst. Anna Mahler: Her Work. *Stuttgart: Belser, 1975.*

Aristide Maillol

Rewald, John. Maillol. *London: Hyperion Press, 1939.*

Waldemar, George. Maillol. *Greenwich, Conn.: New York Graphic Society, 1965.*

Gerhard Marcks

Gerhard Marcks. *Los Angeles: UCLA Art Galleries, 1969.*

Henri Matisse

Henri Matisse. *Texts by Herbert Read, Jean Leymarie, and William S. Lieberman. Berkeley: University of California Press, 1966. Catalogue of a retrospective exhibition organized by the UCLA Art Council and the UCLA Art Galleries.*

Kosinski, Dorothy, Jay McKean Fisher, and Steven Nash. Matisse: Painter as Sculptor. *Baltimore: Baltimore Museum of Art; Dallas: Dallas Museum of Art and Nasher Sculpture Center; New Haven: Yale University Press, 2007.*

Henry Moore

Russell, John. Henry Moore. *New York: Putnam, 1968.*

Seldis, Henry J. Henry Moore in America. *New York: Praeger; Los Angeles: Los Angeles County Museum of Art, 1973.*

Robert Müller

Descargues, Pierre, and Myriam Prevot. Robert Müller. *Brussels: La Connaissance, 1971.*

Kunz, Stephan. Robert Müller: Skulpturen und Zeichnungen. *Gemsberg, Switzerland: Galerie Carzaniga, 2005.*

Reuben Nakian

Metzgar, Robert P. Reuben Nakian: Centennial Retrospective, 1897–1986. *Reading, Pa.: Reading Public Museum, 1990.*

O'Hara, Frank. Reuben Nakian. *New York: Museum of Modern Art, 1966.*

Reuben Nakian. *Los Angeles County Museum of Art, 1961.*

Isamu Noguchi

Fletcher, Valerie J. Isamu Noguchi: Master Sculptor. *Washington, D.C.: Smithsonian Institution; New York: Whitney Museum of American Art, 2004.*

Hunter, Sam. Isamu Noguchi. *New York: Abbeville Press, 1978.*

George Rickey

George Rickey: Retrospective Exhibition, 1951–71. *Los Angeles: UCLA Art Council and UCLA Art Galleries, 1971.*

Rickey, George. Constructivism: Origins and Evolution. *New York: George Braziller, 1967.*

Auguste Rodin

De Caso, Jacques, and Patricia B. Sanders. Rodin's Sculpture: A Critical Study of the Spreckels Collection, California Palace of the Legion of Honor. *San Francisco: Fine Arts Museums of San Francisco, 1977.*

Elsen, Albert. Rodin and His Studio. *Ithaca, N.Y.: Cornell University Press, 1980.*

———. Rodin's Art: The Rodin Collection of the Iris and B. Gerald Cantor Center for Visual Arts at Stanford University. *New York: Oxford University Press, 2003.*

Tancock, John L. Sculpture of Auguste Rodin: The Collection of the Rodin Museum, Philadelphia. *Philadelphia: Philadelphia Museum of Art, 1976.*

Tony Rosenthal

Albee, Edward, and Sam Hunter. Tony Rosenthal. *New York: Rizzoli, 2000.*

Hunter, Sam. Rosenthal: Sculptures. *New York: M. Knoedler & Co., 1968.*

Wight, Frederick S. Bernard Rosenthal. *New York: Catherine Viviano, 1958.*

David Smith

Cone, Jan Harrison. David Smith, 1906–1965: A Retrospective Exhibition. *Cambridge: Fogg Art Museum, Harvard University, 1966.*

David Smith: A Centennial. *Curated by Carmen Giménez. New York: Guggenheim Museum, 2006.*

David Smith, 1906–1965. *New York: Museum of Modern Art, 1966.*

Gray, Clive, ed. David Smith by David Smith: Sculptures and Writings. *London: Thames & Hudson, 1968.*

Francesco Somaini

Francesco Somaini: Sculpture, 1958–72. *Introduction by Vittorio Fagone. Gubbio, Italy: Palazzo dei Consoli, Salone dell'Aregno, 1973.*

Louis Sullivan

Twombly, Robert C., and Narciso G. Menocal. Louis Sullivan: The Poetry of Architecture. *New York: W. W. Norton & Co., 2000.*

Van Zanten, David. Sullivan's City: The Meaning of Ornament for Louis Sullivan. *New York: W. W. Norton & Co., 2000.*

Elden Tefft

Tefft, Elden. Lost Wax Sculpture Foundry Equipment: Recommendations and Sources. *Lawrence: International Sculpture Centre, University of Kansas, 1977.*

Vladas Vildžiūnas

Gimbutas, Marija. The Goddesses and Gods of Old Europe: Myths and Cult Images. *London: Thames & Hudson, 1982.*

Peter Voulkos

Slivka, Rose. Peter Voulkos: A Dialogue with Clay. *New York: New York Graphic Society, 1978.*

Slivka, Rose, and Karen Tsujimoto. The Art of Peter Voulkos. *Tokyo: Kodansha International in collaboration with the Oakland Museum, 1995.*

Jack Zajac

Seldis, Henry. Jack Zajac Retrospective Exhibition. *San Diego: Fine Arts Gallery of San Diego, 1974.*

Seldis, Henry J., and Ulfert Wilke. The Sculpture of Jack Zajac. *Los Angeles: Galland Press, 1960.*

William Zorach

Baur, John I. H. William Zorach. *New York: Praeger for Whitney Museum of American Art, 1959.*

Francisco Zúñiga

Francisco Zúñiga: Homenaje nacional. *Mexico City: Consejo Nacional para la Cultura y las Artes, 1994.*

Reich, Sheldon. Francisco Zúñiga, Sculptor: Conversations and Interpretations. *Tucson: University of Arizona Press, 1980.*

Zúñiga, Ariel. Francisco Zúñiga: Catalogue Raisonné. *Vol. 1,* Sculpture, 1923–1993. *Mexico City: Albedrío in association with Fundación Zúñiga Laborder, 1999–[2003].*

INDEX

Italic page numbers indicate illustrations.

REPRODUCTION CREDITS

Most reproductions are courtesy of the creators and rights holders of the material depicted or their representatives. For certain artwork and documentary photographs we have been unable to locate artists or copyright holders. We would appreciate notification of additional credits for acknowledgment in future editions. Numbers refer to the page on which an image appears.

Unless otherwise noted, all color photographs are by Joshua White: © Joshua White

© Estate of Alexander Archipenko / Artists Rights Society (ARS), New York: 69, 173 (right)

© Artists Rights Society (ARS), New York / ADAGP, Paris: 18, 44 (left), 49 (right), 111, 120, 121, 130, 178

© Artists Rights Society (ARS), New York / BUS, Stockholm: 172 (lower left)

© Artists Rights Society (ARS), New York / DACS, London: 156

© Artists Rights Society (ARS), New York / LATGA-A, Vilnius: 81, 159

© Artists Rights Society (ARS), New York / VG Bild-Kunst, Bonn: back cover, 6 (upper left), 35 (left), 70–73, 119, 150, 151

© Barford Sculptures Ltd.: 42 (left), 86–87, 173 (center)

© Estate of Leonard Baskin, courtesy Salander O'Reilly Gallery: 74

© Fletcher Benton / Artists Rights Society (ARS), New York: 76

© Bowness, Hepworth Estate: 4 (lower left), 59 (right), 104–7, 151, 175 (left)

© Calder Foundation, New York / Artists Rights Society (ARS), New York: 2 (lower right), 4 (upper left), 35 (right), 48 (left), 84, 85, 151, 176 (left)

© Aldo Casanova: 88

© Courtesy of the Lynn Chadwick Estate / Bridgeman Art Library: 42 (right), 66, 89

© Archivio Pietro Consagra, Milan: 91

Department of Special Collections, Young Research Library, UCLA, Los Angeles Times Photo Archives: 12, 57, 59 (right), 60

Courtesy Falkenstein Foundation, reproduced by permission: 52 (right), 53 (left), 94, 95

© Fondazione Palazzo Albizzini "Collezione Burri," Città di Castello, Italy: 2 (upper left), 50–51, 78, 79

© Fundación Zúñiga Laborde A.C./México: 123, 166, 167

© Gallery Paule Anglim, San Francisco, and Deborah Butterfield: front cover, 82–83, 182 (right)

© The George and Helen Segal Foundation / Licensed by VAGA, New York, NY: 173 (left)

© Courtesy of the Eric Gill Estate / Bridgeman Art Library: 3 (upper left), 96

© Robert Graham: 98, 99

Judd Gunderson: 12

© Estate of Dimitri Hadzi: 102, 103

Hammer Museum: 10, 22–26, 28, 29, 31, 33–37, 40, 41, 50–54, 59 (left), 61

© The Henry Moore Foundation: 8 (upper right), 32–33, 128–29

© Robert Irwin / Artists Rights Society (ARS), New York: 177 (right)

© The Isamu Noguchi Foundation and Garden Museum, New York / Artists Rights Society (ARS), New York: 5 (upper right), 34, 47 (right), 66, 133–35, 174 (right)

Joe Kennedy: 57

Courtesy of the Lachaise Foundation: 46 (left), 110

© Estate of Jacques Lipchitz, courtesy, Marlborough Gallery, New York: 12, 31, 38, 56, 57, 114, 115, 169, 185

© Estate of Anna Mahler: 53 (middle), 116, 117

© Estate of Gerhard Marcks: front cover, 39, 45, 47 (left), 81, 100, 122, 123, 151, 173 (right)

© Succession H. Matisse, Paris / Artists Rights Society (ARS), New York: 29, 36–37, 60, 124, 125

© Mary Miss. Commissioned by the Nathan Manilow Sculpture Park, Governors State University Foundation with support from the National Endowment for the Arts. Deeded to Governors State University: 176 (right)

© McKee Gallery, New York: 155

© Successió Miró / Artists Rights Society (ARS), New York / ADAGP, Paris: 126, 127

© Estate of Reuben Nakian: 131

© Nasher Sculpture Center, Dallas, Texas; Raymond and Patsy Nasher Collection: 175 (left)

© Bruce Nauman / Artists Rights Society (ARS), New York, NY, and courtesy Donald Young Gallery, Chicago. Commissioned by the Nathan Manilow Sculpture Park, Governors State University Foundation. Deeded to Governors State University: 177 (left)

© Claes Oldenburg and Coosje van Bruggen: 172 (upper right); 173 (left)

Charles O'Rear: 59 (right)

Karen Page: 52 (left)

© Estate of George Rickey / Licensed by VAGA, New York, NY: 43 (right), 136

© Tony Rosenthal / Licensed by VAGA, New York, NY: 142

© Richard Serra / Artists Rights Society (ARS), New York: 63

Elon Schoenholz: 53 (right)

© Estate of David Smith / Licensed by VAGA, New York, NY: front cover, 45, 46 (right), 80, 144, 145, 182 (right)

John Swope: 30, 32, 35 (left), 42–49

Courtesy Mark Swope: 30, 32, 42–49

Marc Treib: 170, 172–82

© Estate of George Tsutakawa: 153 (right), 180 (left)

University Archives, UCLA: 26, 27, 38, 39, 56

© Voulkos & Company Catalogue Project: 6 (lower right), 160, 161

Robert Wedemeyer: 124, 125

© James Welling: 2–8

Leigh Wiener: 31

© Jack Zajac: 7 (lower right), 40, 41, 49 (left), 162, 163

© Estate of William Zorach, courtesy Zabriskie Gallery: 14, 164, 165, 186

CAPTIONS

Page 14: View of the Franklin D. Murphy Sculpture Garden with William Zorach's Victory *(1950).*

Page 18: View of the Franklin D. Murphy Sculpture Garden with Aristide Maillol's Heroic Head *(1923).*

Page 63: View of the Broad Art Center Plaza with Richard Serra's T.E.U.C.L.A. *(2006).*

Page 66: View of the Franklin D. Murphy Sculpture Garden with Isamu Noguchi's Garden Elements *(1962) and Lynn Chadwick's* Encounter VIII *(1957).*

Pages 80–81: View of the Franklin D. Murphy Sculpture Garden with (from left to right) David Smith's Cubi XX *(1964), Gerhard Marcks's* Maja *(1941), and Vladas Vildžiūnas's* Bird Goddess *(1977).*

Pages 100–101: View of the Franklin D. Murphy Sculpture Garden with Gerhard Marcks's Maja *(1941).*

Pages 118–19: View of the Franklin D. Murphy Sculpture Garden with Jean Arp's Ptolemy III *(1961).*

Pages 150–51: View of the Franklin D. Murphy Sculpture Garden with (from left to right) Jean Arp's Ptolemy III *(1961) and* Hybrid Fruit Called Pagoda *(1934), Gerhard Marcks's* Maja *(1941), Alexander Calder's* Button Flower *(1959), and Barbara Hepworth's* Elegy III (Hollow Form with Color) *(1966).*

Pages 168–69: View of the Franklin D. Murphy Sculpture Garden with Jacques Lipchitz's Bather *(1923–25).*

Page 185: View of the Franklin D. Murphy Sculpture Garden with Jacques Lipchitz's Bather *(1923–25).*

Page 186: View of the Franklin D. Murphy Sculpture Garden with William Zorach's Victory *(1950).*